Exile and Execution in Medieval and Early Modern Society

Explorations in Medieval Culture

VOLUME 29

The titles published in this series are listed at *brill.com/emc*

Exile and Execution in Medieval and Early Modern Society

Edited by

Gila Aloni
Larissa Tracy

BRILL

LEIDEN | BOSTON

Cover illustration: Pierpont Morgan Library, Manuscript M.638, fol. 10v. Paris, France, ca. 1244–1254. Purchased by J.P. Morgan (1867–1943) in 1916. © The Morgan Library & Museum. MS M.638, fol. 10v.

The Library of Congress Cataloging-in-Publication Data is available online at https://catalog.loc.gov
LC record available at https://lccn.loc.gov/2025036359

Typeface for the Latin, Greek, and Cyrillic scripts: "Brill". See and download: brill.com/brill-typeface.

ISSN 2352-0299
ISBN 978-90-04-72998-8 (hardback)
ISBN 978-90-04-74259-8 (e-book)
DOI 10.1163/9789004742598

This book is printed on acid-free paper and produced in a sustainable manner.

Contents

Acknowledgments

This volume was a long time coming. It started with discussions about exile at the annual meeting of the Southeastern Medieval Association in 2016, a session on exile at SEMA 2017, and a joint session titled "Closing the Gates: Exile and Execution," sponsored by the American Society of Irish Medieval Studies at SEMA in 2019. It morphed from a volume titled *Topology of Exile and Identity Formation* and a separate collection titled *Performing Fatal Justice: Execution in Medieval and Early Modern Society* into a project that combined both exile and execution because we realized how closely these two concepts functioned in the Middle Ages and later centuries. As the volume evolved, we had eighteen contributors who offered a rich array of essays on archaeology, literature, law, criminology, and history. Then the COVID-19 pandemic struck, and all our contributors suffered in their own ways from the isolation, the lack of access and resources, the separation, and the virus itself. Consequently, several of our contributors could not continue, but they made invaluable contributions from the start, and they deserve our thanks for their part in shaping this collection: Marisa Bueno, John Halbrooks, Kaitlin Leathers, Nolwena Monnier, Rachel E. Scott, Lorraine K. Stock, and Larry Swain. The pandemic, and the global political climate, especially in the United States after the 2016 election, had a profound effect on the way in which this volume finally emerged, and they informed how we examine these issues in the medieval context. They influenced the questions we asked and the methods we used to approach these topics. Because of the impact of global events, we owe our contributors a debt of gratitude for their patience in this process as we brought this volume into being. We would also like to thank those who supported and encouraged this project along the way, specifically Tina Boyer, Melissa Ridley Elmes, Ellen Friedrich, Mary Leech, Asa Simon Mittman, Vicky McAlister, Thea Tomaini, Mary Valante, and Malcom Vale. We are also grateful to Marcella Mulder at Brill, and the Board of Explorations in Medieval Culture for their patience and their input during this process.

Larissa Tracy's chapter emerged from her presentation, "Creating Literary Heroes: Nostalgia, National Identity and the Idea of Justice," at a special workshop on nostalgia organized by Dr. Hannah Skoda and hosted by St. John's College, Oxford in 2017. I am extremely grateful to Dr. Skoda for the invitation and her hospitality. In 2021, I was interviewed for St. Ambrose University KALA's *Relevant or Irrelevant* (ROI) Radio Program, hosted by Jay Swords and John Kealey, about this project, and that opportunity provided me with a unique sounding board for exploring these issues. I am also grateful to my family, both born and chosen, who kept me going through my own isolation during the pandemic, especially my mother, Nina Zerkich, my father, Robert Tracy, who passed away in 2022 before this project was finished, my stepmother, Marsha Tracy, Sally Cinch, Tracey and Eric Dunn, Beth Feagan, Susan Parrott, Olena Staveley-O'Carroll, and, above all, Parris Jensen—who saw me through the worst periods of lockdown and lit my way, lifted my heart, and brought me joy through most of this process.

Gila Aloni's chapter transpired from her presentation to the Medieval and Early Modern Studies group at the Center for the Humanities at the University of Miami in November 2022. I am very grateful to the director of the Center, Professor Hugh M. Thomas, for his invitation that allowed me to reshape ideas that I explored in my 2008 article "M(ons)ters in laws: Maternal Models in the Man of Law's Tale," *Medievales* [44]: 1–10. My interest in exile springs from my personal, albeit voluntary, exilic experience to France and to the U.S. I would like to take a moment to express my gratitude and appreciation to those who have supported me throughout this journey away from my homeland. I wish to remember the many conversations I had with the late philosopher, Jacques Derrida about exile as freedom. Special thanks to Leo Carruthers, Professeur émérite, Sorbonne University, for his friendship and mentorship. To my parents, thank you for your wisdom, unwavering love, and for instilling in me the values of perseverance, and dedication. To my spouse and children, thank you for being my greatest motivators. Your unwavering love and support have given me the strength and inspiration to pursue my passions. To all my friends who became my extended family, thank you for your love, support, and encouragement throughout the years. Your presence in my life has enriched me in ways that words cannot express. Finally, the deepest thank you to Larissa (Kat) Tracy, my partner in this volume, for her humor, endless phone and Zoom conversations, and perseverance.

Figures and Tables

Figures

Tables

Abbreviations

AGR	Archives générales du Royaume, Chambre des comptes (CC), 13780, f. 32v.
Belle-Mère	"De la fame qui fist estrangler son gendre" ["The Woman Who Had Her Son-in-Law Strangled"], *La Vie des pères*, The Hague, Koninklijke Bibliotheek (KB) MS 71 A 24 (Ms. k), fols. 124v–125r.
The *Consolation*	Boethius, *Consolation of Philosophy*, trans. S.J. Tester, Loeb Classical Library (Cambridge: Harvard University Press, 1973), Book I.
DN	*Diplomatarium Norvegicum*. Vols. I–XXIII. Edited by C.C.A. Lange et al. Christiania/Oslo: Norsk historisk kjeldeskrift-institutt/Riksarkivet, 1847–2011.
DS	*Diplomatarium Suecanum*. Vols. I–XI. Ed. J.G. Liljegren et al. Stockholm: KVHAA/Riksarkivet, 1829–.
EETS e.s.	Early English Text Society early series
EETS o.s.	Early English Text Society original series
Havelok	*Havelok the Dane*, Oxford, Bodleian Library, MS Laud 108, ff. 204r–219v.
Gest	*Gest of Robyn Hode*, in *Robin Hood and Other Outlaw Tales*, ed. Stephen Knight and Thomas Ohlgren, *TEAMS Middle English Texts Series* (Kalamazoo, MI: Western Michigan University Press, 2000), 80–168.
Guy of Gisborne	*Robin Hood and Guy of Gisborne* in *Robin Hood and Other Outlaw Tales*, ed. Stephen Knight and Thomas Ohlgren, *TEAMS Middle English Texts Series* (Kalamazoo, MI: Western Michigan University Press, 2000), 169–180.
MED	*Middle English Dictionary*
MGH	*Monumenta Germaniae Historica, Scriptores rerum Merovingicorum* 4 (Hanover, 1902).
MND	Gautier de Coinci's "D'une fame qui fu délivrée a Loon dou feu" ["The Woman Was Delivered From Burning at Loon"], *Les Miracles de Nostre Dame*, ed. V.F. Koenig, 4 vols. (Geneva: Droz, 1955–1970), II Mir. 26, vol. 4, 265–294.
MoLT	Geoffrey Chaucer, *The Man of Law's Tale*, in *The Riverside Chaucer*, ed. Larry D. Benson (Boston: Houghton Mifflin, 1987).
NIMEV	New Index of Middle English Verse
PL	*Patriologiae cursus completus: series Latina*, 221 vols. (Paris, 1844–64).
VDP	*La Vie des pères*, The Hague, Koninklijke Bibliotheek (KB) MS 71 A 24 (Ms. k), fols. 76r–187r.

Publisher's Note

Brill would like to note that the series editor of *Explorations in Medieval Culture* did not participate in our decision to publish the present volume due to her involvement with the project. We thank the series Board for overseeing the publication of this book and supporting our commitment to academic integrity.

Notes on Contributors

Gillian Adler
PhD, is Associate Professor of Literature and Esther Raushenbush Chair in Humanities at Sarah Lawrence College. She is the author of *Chaucer and the Ethics of Time* (Wales, 2022) and co-author of *'Alle Thyng Hath Tyme': Time and Medieval Life* (London, 2023). She is also the founder of the New York Medieval Society.

Gila Aloni
PhD, is affiliated with Association des Médiévistes Anglicistes de l'Enseignement Supérieur (Paris). Previously, she was Associate Professor at Lynn University, and an English faculty at Ransom Everglades. Her publications appear in three languages (English, French, Hebrew) on rape, gender and sexuality, hagiography, rhetoric, anti-Semitism, and Middle Eastern and Jewish Studies. She is the author of *Pouvoir et Autorité dans "The Legend of Good Women"* (2000), and more than fifteen articles including, "From Medieval to Pop Culture: An Old-World New Text, the Golem of Prague—A Traveling Monster/Hero" (*SAMLA*, 2016), and "Palimpsestic Philomela" in *Palimpsests and the Literary Imagination of Medieval England*, ed. Tatjana Silec, Raeleen Chai-Elshols, and Leo Carruthers (Palgrave, 2011). Between 2009 and 2017 she served as the associate editor of *Medieval Perspectives: Journal of the Southern Medieval Association*. Aloni's post-doctorate work includes a fellowship in 2004 in the Medieval and Renaissance Center, New York University, and a fellowship at The Center for Medieval Studies, Fordham University.

Kim Bergqvist
PhD candidate, is completing a dissertation on aristocratic insurrections, resistance, and political values in Castile-León and Sweden in the period *c.*1270–1370. Bergqvist specializes in medieval political and comparative history, history writing, genre and fictionality, and the history of gender and emotions. His research has appeared in *Collegium Medievale* and *The Medieval Chronicle*, and he is the co-editor of *Conflict and Collaboration in Medieval Iberia* (Cambridge Scholars Publishing, 2020) and *War, Diplomacy and Peacemaking in Medieval Iberia* (2021). He teaches Viking and medieval studies at DIS Stockholm.

Karen Casey Casebier

PhD, is Professor of French at the University of Tennessee at Chattanooga. Her principal area of research is the conflation of the sacred and the profane across genres of thirteenth-century French literature. She has published articles and book chapters on Chrétien de Troyes, Christine de Pisan, Marie de France, the Old French *fabliaux*, *La Vie des pères* and the Arthurian graphic novel. Her research interests include manuscript studies, bestiaries and contemporary interpretations of Arthurian literature. She is currently working on a series of unpublished, unedited miracle tales in a fourteenth-century manuscript branch of *La Vie des pères*.

Westley Follett

PhD, is Associate Professor of History at the University of Southern Mississippi, Gulf Coast where he teaches classical, medieval, and world history. He held a postdoctoral scholarship in the School of Celtic Studies at the Dublin Institute for Advanced Studies. He is the author of *Céli Dé in Ireland: Monastic Writing and Identity in the Early Middle Ages* and has numerous publications in edited volumes and journals, to include most recently *The Journal of Medieval Monastic Studies, The Oxford Handbook of Christian Monasticism,* and *Peritia: Journal of the Medieval Academy of Ireland*. He is past president of the American Society of Irish Medieval Studies.

Radosław Kotecki

PhD, is an adjunct professor at the Institute of History and International Relations, Kazimierz Wielki University in Bydgoszcz. He has published numerous essays on medieval Church and culture, and recently on clerical warfare. He is co-editor of several books including *Ecclesia et Violentia: Violence against the Church and Violence within the Church in the Middle Ages* (Cambridge Scholars, 2014) and *Between Sword and Prayer: Warfare and Medieval Clergy in Cultural Perspective* (Brill, 2018). He is now engaged in a research project on the military activity of medieval Polish bishops awarded by the National Science Centre (Poland), as well as currently preparing a monograph on religion and the conduct of war in Poland and East Central Europe in the high Middle Ages. His research interests also include legal history, especially medieval justice, king's peace, and secular and ecclesiastical penalties.

Mireille J. Pardon

PhD, is Assistant Professor of History at Berea College in Berea, Kentucky. She received her PhD in 2020 with a dissertation exploring judicial practice in fifteenth-century Bruges and Ghent. She has since published articles on the prosecution of violent crime in late medieval Flanders, the reputation of crowds in late medieval cities, and feral child narratives in early modern France. She is currently working on a book about the changing perception of homicide in fifteenth and early sixteenth-century Flanders.

Ben Parsons

PhD, is Associate Professor in Late Medieval and Early Modern Literature at the University of Leicester. He has published widely on medieval and Renaissance culture as both researcher and editor. His work has appeared in the journals *Medium Aevum, Exemplaria, Viator, Modern Philology*, and the *Chaucer Review*, and in the edited collections *Blood Matters* (UPenn Press, 2018), *Medieval and Early Modern Murder* (Boydell Press, 2018), and the *Oxford Handbook of Poetry in English* (2023). He is the co-author of the critical anthology *Comic Drama in the Low Countries, c.1450–1560* (D.S. Brewer, 2012), and author of *Punishment and Medieval Education* (D.S. Brewer, 2018), *Two Middle English Prayer Cycles* (Medieval Institute Publications, 2023), and *Introducing Medieval Animal Names* (University of Wales Press, 2025).

Bojana Radovanović

PhD, is a Classical Philologist (originally from Belgrade, Serbia). She spent two years (2020–2022) at the Radboud University Nijmegen (NL), with the working group "History of Christianity" at the Faculty of Philosophy, Theology, and Religious Studies, as a guest-researcher. She pursued the Erwin Schroedinger Postdoctoral project funded by the Austrian Science Fund (FWF), entitled "*Sicut oves in medio luporum*: Religious Landscapes, Dualist Dissent, and the 'Language of Heresy' (11th–13th centuries)" (No. J4431-G). The third and final year of her postdoctoral project is being carried out at the Institut für Mittelalterforschung in Vienna. She is a co-organizer of the monthly online "Bogomil Seminar" and is currently working on a monograph titled *Along a Less Travelled Road: Bogomil Exegesis, Social Practice and Extra-Canonical Mysticism.* Her other research interests include late Antiquity, non-Christian heritage of the medieval philosophical and theological concepts, dualist heresies in the Middle Ages, dualist legends, Slavonic apocrypha, and intercultural transmission between Byzantium and the Latin West.

Abel de Lorenzo Rodríguez
PhD, specializes in social violence in early medieval North-West Iberia (eighth–twelfth centuries), specifically crimes and punishments of North Iberian Kingdoms, under the direction of teachers Ermelindo Portela Silva and Israel Sanmartín. He has been an academic visitor in the University of Oxford and is a post-doctoral researcher at the Université Paris 1-Panthéon Sorbonne. His publications include "Voices of Destruction: Prophecy, Punishment and Prodigies in Early Medieval Hispania (5th–8th centuries)," with Marisa Bueno, in *Prophetie, Prognose und Politik. Personengeschichtliche Perspektiven zwischen Antike und Neuzeit*, ed. Ch. Hoffarth (Klostermann, forthcoming); "Rites and Riots. Re-enchanting and Legitimating Violence as a Medieval Revival in Spain and France (1936–1945)," *V Ciclo di Studi Medievali. Atti del Convegno*, 2019, among others. He has also participated in conferences at Oxford, Leeds, Florence, Barcelona, Madrid, and Porto.

Susan Small
PhD, is Associate Professor of French at King's University College at Western University, Canada. Her recent publications include "Flesh and Death in Early Modern Bedburg," *in Flaying in the Pre-Modern World: Practice and Representation*, ed. Larissa Tracy (D.S. Brewer, 2017), "The Medieval Werewolf Model of Reading Skin," in *Reading Skin in Medieval Literature and Culture*, ed. Katie L. Walter (Palgrave, 2013) and "Frontier Girl Goes Feral in Eighteenth Century France: The Curious Case of Marie-Angélique Memmie Le Blanc, the Wild Girl of Champagne," in *Making Monstrosity: Exploring the Cultural History of Continental European Freak Shows*, ed. Anna Kérchy and Andrea Zittlau (Cambridge Scholars, 2012).

Larissa Tracy
PhD, is Visiting Assistant Teaching Professor at the University of Maryland, Baltimore County, and former Professor of Medieval Literature at Longwood University. She is the author of *Torture and Brutality in Medieval Literature* (D.S. Brewer, 2012), *Women of the Gilte Legende* (D.S. Brewer, 2003) and editor of eight collections including *Heads Will Roll: Decapitation in the Medieval and Early Modern Imagination*, with Jeff Massey (Brill, 2012), *Castration and Culture in the Middle* Ages (D.S. Brewer, 2013), *Wounds and Wound Repair in Medieval Culture*, with Kelly DeVries (Brill, 2015), *Flaying in the Pre-modern World* (D.S. Brewer, 2017), *Medieval and Early Modern Murder* (Boydell Press, 2018), *Treason: Medieval and Early Modern Adultery, Betrayal, and Shame* (2019), *Medieval English and Medieval Dutch Literatures* with Geert H.M.

Claassens (D.S. Brewer, 2022), and *The Cultural History of Blood: The Medieval Era 1000–1400* (Bloomsbury, forthcoming). She has published articles on violence, fabliaux, comedy, romance, gender, hagiography and *Sir Gawain and the Green Knight*; she is also the series editor for Explorations in Medieval Culture (Brill). In 2016, she was a Visiting Scholar at St. John's College, Oxford and she has appeared on several National Geographic, Discovery, and History Channel documentaries, including *Dark Marvels* and *The UnBelievable* hosted by Dan Aykroyd.

Introduction

By Choice or by Force: Performing Final Justice through Exile and Execution

Gila Aloni and Larissa Tracy

> Go from your country, your people and your father's household
> to the land I will show you.
>
> Genesis 12.1

•••

> ROMEO: "Ha, banishment? Be merciful, say 'death,'
> For exile hath more terror in his look,
> Much more than death. Do not say 'banishment'."
> FRIAR LAURENCE: "Here from Verona art thou banishèd:
> Be patient, for the world is broad and wide."
>
> WILLIAM SHAKESPEARE, *Romeo and Juliet* (3.3.13–17)

In 2025, as the world navigates a post-pandemic landscape shaped by the lasting effects of self-imposed exile, the dynamics of exile and execution have grown more complex, driven by crises like the Russia-Ukraine war and Middle East tensions. This evolving perspective is reflected domestically as well; in March 2021, Virginia became the twenty-third American state to ban the death penalty, signaling a shift in attitudes toward state-sanctioned execution amidst global and local reckonings.[1] Virginia's action inspired other states to follow suit. Delaware repealed its death penalty statute in September 2024, building on a 2016 state Supreme Court ruling that declared it unconstitutional. Similarly, Washington State passed legislation in April 2023 to formally remove

1 Samantha O'Connell, "Virginia Becomes the First Southern State to Abolish the Death Penalty," American Bar Association (March 24, 2021): https://www.americanbar.org/groups/committees/death_penalty_representation/publications/project_blog/virginia-death-penalty-repeal/#:~:text=Ralph%20Northam%20officially%20signed%20HB2263,to%20eliminate%20capital%20punishment%20entirely. Accessed June 30, 2024.

 | DOI:10.1163/9789004742598_002

capital punishment from its laws, reinforcing a 2018 state Supreme Court decision citing racial bias. Considering that the United States is unique among developed nations in maintaining state-sponsored execution, the concurrent need for voluntary exile for the greater good puts these two concepts in stark relief. To be cut off from society, from family, from traditions, from language, and even from God, is a terrifying prospect.[2]

In the last decade, conflict, invasion, and genocide have led to a dramatic rise in the number of exiles, reshaping traditional understandings of displacement. People fleeing Russia, either as dissidents or critics of the state (many of whom are being hunted down and murdered abroad)[3] or as exiles avoiding conscription into the Russian war of conquest in Ukraine; people leaving Ukraine, whether fleeing conscription or just trying to survive; Gazans fleeing Israeli bombardment; migrants from Latin America heading north, fleeing oppressive governments or gangs; refugees seeking sanctuary in Europe from civil war in Syria or Sudan. Following Hamas's attack on Jewish communities near Israel's border with Gaza on October 7, 2023, Israel experienced an unprecedented displacement of its population.[4] Political and digital exile have also become more prevalent, as activists, journalists, and dissidents from authoritarian regimes in Belarus, Iran, and Afghanistan seek refuge abroad, using encrypted communication and remote activism to continue their efforts. In many of these cases, the exiles—voluntary or forced—face execution if they remain in their home countries. Similarly, the historical forced migration of Native Americans and the use of residential schools in Canada and the United States were deliberate efforts to erase Indigenous cultures and assert colonial

---

2 This volume was conceived in 2018 and was seriously disrupted by the COVID pandemic and the crisis in the Middle East. We originally framed our Introduction with the feeling of exile imposed by the pandemic. The COVID-19 pandemic severed people from the social networks upon which they relied and has since become a death sentence for millions. As of January 20, 2024, more than 6.9 million people have died of COVID. "Coronavirus Death Toll" (January 20, 2024): https://www.worldometers.info/coronavirus/coronavirus-death-toll/. Accessed January 20, 2024. But so many political conflicts have arisen since then, we needed to change focus. We are grateful to the reader for providing us with updated suggestions of modern exile.

3 Shaun Walker and Deborah Cole, "Kremlin admits Vadim Krasikov is a Russian state assassin," *The Guardian* (Aug. 2, 2024): https://www.theguardian.com/world/article/2024/aug/02/kremlin-admits-vadim-krasikov-is-an-russian-state-assassin; Pjotr Sauer, "Twenty years of ruthlessness: how Russia has silenced Putin's opponents," *The Guardian* (Aug. 27, 2023): https://www.theguardian.com/world/2023/aug/27/history-killing-how-russia-has-silenced-putins-opponents. Accessed January 30, 2025.

4 UN Watch, "Updated Report: UN Silent on Displaced Israelis," (July 2, 2024): https://unwatch.org/report-un-silent-on-israeli-idps/. Accessed January 30, 2025.

dominance, resulting in devastating and lasting impacts—a legacy of intergenerational trauma contributing to widespread poverty, systemic inequality, and the loss of cultural identity among Indigenous communities.[5] Both exile and execution take a variety of forms in the modern world—from the political exile of dissidents, cultural isolation among the scattered people of a diaspora, to punitive sentences of death levied by a state or a society against those who have transgressed the legal values of that culture or of authoritarian rulers.

As exile becomes an increasingly urgent issue, governments and organizations are faced with the challenge of balancing security, humanitarian needs, and ethical governance in an era marked by widespread displacement and political uncertainty. The magnitude of the modern exile experience compelled the United Nations (UN) to launch a global initiative, "The Global Commission on International Migration" (GCIM) in 2003, that compiles demographic data about territorial displacement.[6] The current reality of the biggest demographic phenomenon of the twenty-first century provides a framework for understanding the complexities of premodern exile, and vice versa. Essential to the GCIM enterprise is the foundation of terms and vocabulary related to this experience, specifically "Forced Migration" and "Assimilation." "Forced Migration" is a "migratory movement in which an element of coercion exists, including threats to life and livelihood, whether arising from natural or man-made causes."[7] The GCIM defines "Assimilation" as

> the adaptation of one ethnic or social group—usually a minority—to another. Assimilation involves the subsuming of language, traditions, values, morals and behavior or even fundamental vital interests. Although

5 Antonio Voce, Leyland Cecco, and Chris Michael, "'Cultural genocide': the shameful history of Canada's residential schools—mapped," *The Guardian* (Sept. 6, 2021): https://www.theguardian.com/world/ng-interactive/2021/sep/06/canada-residential-schools-indigenous-children-cultural-genocide-map, accessed January 30, 2025; Leyland Cecco, "Cruelty of Canada's residential schools 'unimaginable', governor general says," *The Guardian* (May 24, 2022): https://www.theguardian.com/world/2022/may/24/canada-residential-schools-kamloops-governor-general, accessed January 30, 2025; Justin Ling, "'He was just a child': dead of Indigenous residential schools haunt Canada," *The Guardian* (June 5, 2021): https://www.theguardian.com/world/2021/jun/05/canada-indigenous-residential-schools-first-nations-children, accessed January 30, 2025; Hilary Beaumont, "'We're still here': past and present collide at a Native American boarding school," *The Guardian* (May 22, 2022): https://www.theguardian.com/us-news/2022/may/22/native-american-boarding-school-sherman-indian-high-school, accessed January 30, 2025.

6 International Organization on Migration, "Migration, Violent Extremism, and Social Exclusion," *World Migration Report 2018*, https://www.iom.int/wmr/chapter-9. Accessed June 20, 2019.

7 https://www.iom.int/key-migration-terms.

> the traditional cultural practices of the group are unlikely to be completely abandoned, on the whole assimilation will lead one group to be socially indistinguishable from other members of the society. Assimilation is the most extreme form of acculturation.[8]

The tension between "Forced Migration" and "Assimilation" marks the lives of millions of people globally in many forms, such as the forced migration of Native American peoples, the Armenian exile and subsequent genocide by the Ottoman Empire in 1915, the collective punishment of the Jewish people, exiled for two thousand years before the establishment of the state of Israel in 1948 after the Holocaust, and the forced exile of the Palestinian people over the last seventy-five years because of conflict with Israel.[9]

Edward Said, whose idea of exile from Palestine formed his personal life and work, "came to see Western culture as fundamentally a creation of exiles."[10] In *Power, Politics and Culture*, Said describes his life as a series of departures and returns: "But the departure is always anxious. The return is always uncertain. Precarious."[11] Said embodies the reality of millions of people who are subjected to a variety of forces that form "the greatest single fact of the past three decades ... war, colonialism and decolonization, economic and political revolution, and such devastating occurrences as famine, ethnic cleansing, and great power machinations."[12] All of those who share the fate of "[e]xiles, émigrés, refugees, and expatriates uprooted from their lands [face the challenge of having to] make do in new surroundings, and the creativity as well as the sadness ... has still to find its chroniclers."[13] When chroniclers of exile consider

---

8 Zeynep Sahin, *Ethnicity, Nationalism, and Migration in the Middle East*: https://oxfordre.com/internationalstudies/view/10.1093/acrefore/9780190846626.001.0001/acrefore-9780190846626-e-174#acrefore-9780190846626-e-174-div1-0006. For more recent information about violence against journalists in exile, see: Joe McKendry, "'I decided to not let anybody silence my voice': The Journalists in Exile but Still at Risk," *The Guardian* (May 3. 2024): https://www.theguardian.com/media/ng-interactive/2024/may/03/i-decided-to-not-let-anybody-silence-my-voice-the-journalists-in-exile-but-still-at-risk. Accessed June 30, 2024.

9 Sahin, *Ethnicity, Nationalism*. See also: A. Fat*h*i, ed., *Iranian Refugees and Exiles since Khomeini* (Lexington, KY: Mazda, 1991) and David Marshall Lang, ed., *The Armenians: A People in Exile New Edition* (London: Unwin & Hyman, 1989).

10 Lal Vinay, Preface to "Enigmas of Exile: Reflections on Edward Said," *Economic and Political Weekly* 40.1 (2005), 30.

11 Edward W. Said, *Power, Politics and Culture: Interviews with Edward Said*, ed. Gauri Viswanathan (London: Vintage, 2004), 456.

12 Edward W. Said, *Reflections on Exile and Other Essays* (Cambridge, MA: Harvard University Press, 2000), 5.

13 Said, *Reflections on Exile*, 5.

the scale of modern migration and displacement they must take into consideration the historical perspective, "since almost by definition exile and memory go together, it is what one remembers of the past and how one remembers it that determine how one sees the future."[14] Biblical accounts of Lucifer's exile from Heaven and Cain's exile for the murder of his brother Abel, have embedded the idea of banishment in place of execution as the ultimate punishment for extraordinary crimes in the Western imagination. In Genesis, Adam and Eve's transgression results in both immediate exile and future death. They are cast out of Eden—exiled from God's direct presence and the perfection of the garden. While the sentence of death is pronounced—"for dust you are and to dust you will return" (Genesis 3:19)—it is not immediate but inevitable. Their exile is both a form of divine punishment and a harbinger of the mortal fate awaiting humanity because of their disobedience. Thus, exile and execution (or death) are interconnected: the exile marks the beginning of their separation from life as it was meant to be, and death completes this separation. Exile as both a political tool and weapon, and, in Said's terms, the historical memory of exile—as well as execution, the other side of the same punitive coin—shape modern circumstances, resonating through the human record.

Like exile, execution persists in modern society through centuries of human history. According to Amnesty International, 690 people were executed globally in 2018, excluding China where the exact numbers of those killed by the state are classified; by 2021, following the global pandemic, that number had fallen to 579, but it was still a twenty-percent increase from 2020.[15] By the end of 2021, 108 countries had completely abolished capital punishment, a number that does not include the United States where the death penalty is legal federally, in the military, and in twenty-three states, banned outright in twenty-four (including the District of Columbia), and on hold due to gubernatorial moratoriums in four.[16] On January 20, 2025, President Trump began his second term in office by signing an executive order titled "Restoring the Death Penalty and Protecting Public Safety," directing the Attorney General to "pursue the death penalty for all crimes of a severity demanding its use."[17] The order emphasizes cases involving the killing of law enforcement officers and capital crimes

---

14 Said, *Reflections on Exile*, 27.

15 Amnesty International, "The Death Penalty": https://www.amnesty.org/en/what-we-do/death-penalty/. Accessed February 24, 2023.

16 Death Penalty Information Center, https://deathpenaltyinfo.org/state-and-federal-info/state-by-state.

17 Sam Levin, "'So much of this seems vengeful': alarm as Trump recommits to death penalty," *The Guardian*, January 22, 2025: https://www.theguardian.com/us-news/2025/jan/22/trump-death-penalty?utm_source=chatgpt.com.

committed by individuals unlawfully present in the United States. It also instructs the Attorney General to ensure that states have sufficient lethal injection drugs to carry out executions.[18] This move reverses the moratorium on federal executions imposed by former Attorney General Merrick Garland in July 2021, which was enacted to review concerns about the pain and suffering associated with execution methods. In December 2024, prior to leaving office, President Joe Biden commuted the sentences of thirty-seven out of forty federal death row inmates to life imprisonment without parole, citing moral objections to capital punishment. Notably, this commutation did not include individuals convicted in high-profile cases, such as Dzhokhar Tsarnaev (Boston Marathon bomber), Dylann Roof (Mother Emanuel AME church shooter), and Robert Bowers (Tree of Life synagogue shooter), whose death sentences remain in place.[19] President Trump's recent executive order signals a clear intent to resume federal executions and expand the application of the death penalty during his second term.

While another twenty-eight countries globally have made the death penalty illegal in practice, eight use it for exceptional crimes; it is fully legal in fifty-five countries, including Iran and Saudi Arabia, as well as the United States.[20] Amnesty International classifies the death penalty as "the ultimate cruel, inhuman and degrading punishment" that "breaches human rights, in particular the right to life and the right to live free from torture or cruel, inhuman or degrading treatment or punishment."[21] In places like the United States where the death penalty is a divisive issue that elicits arguments about vengeance and the sanctity of life, arguments for and against capital punishment often echo the debates regarding execution from preceding centuries. In the modern world, exile and execution often seem at odds with each other—one preserves life, the other ends it; however, exile as an instrument of oppressive regimes or even as a by-product of internal or regional conflict serves the same purpose as execution: ridding society of those it deems undesirable.

---

18 Donald Trump, "Restoring the Death Penalty and Protecting Public Safety," The White House: https://www.whitehouse.gov/presidential-actions/2025/01/restoring-the-death-penalty-and-protecting-public-safety/; Alanna Durkin Richer, "Trump signs death penalty order directing attorney general to help states get lethal injection drugs," ABC News, January 20, 2025: https://abcnews.go.com/US/wireStory/trump-signs-death-penalty-order-directing-attorney-general-117920507.

19 Nandita Bose, "Biden commutes sentences of 37 of 40 inmates on federal death row," Reuters, December 23, 2024: https://www.reuters.com/world/us/biden-commutes-sentences-37-40-inmates-federal-death-row-2024-12-23/?utm_source=chatgpt.com.

20 Pro/Con.org, "The Death Penalty."

21 Amnesty International, "The Death Penalty."

The etymology of "exile" describes the experience of those banished from their homeland: consider the Anglo-French *essil, exil*, from the Latin *exilium*, itself from *exul, exsul* [an exile], where the prefix "ex" denotes "out of," or "exclusion from."[22] According to Roman law, *exsilium* denotes voluntary exile as an alternative to capital punishment.[23] Banishment as punishment was particularly painful "since it meant not only years of aimless wandering away from family and familiar places but also being a permanent outcast."[24] The interchangeability between exile and capital punishment suggests that displacement from one's homeland resembles the ultimate expulsion from life. Indeed, as Ovid famously put it after nine years of banishment: *Exilium mors est* [Exile is death].[25] Forced displacement not only entails the loss of physical place, of a home, it also engenders a host of existential tensions related to the inner home and identity of the exile. Medieval exiles struggled to find a place and an identity in their new surroundings while still holding on to the vestiges of who they were and the place they left. The punitive, painful, and humiliating nature of both punishments distinguishes exile and capital punishment from all other experiences. This volume explores the nature of exile and execution in medieval and early modern societies in both practice and representation—their consequences, lasting effects, impacts on communities and social standing, offering new perspectives on relations between margin and center. Binary distinctions between execution (death sentence) and exile (circumvention of the death penalty) have prevented the bulk of traditional scholarship from comprehensively describing the dynamics between these two forms of punishment during the Middle Ages. Such divisions impose an artificial structure that creates margins and boundaries in a world in which contact and travel between people and culture was (and is) more fluid, more porous, and where exile and execution often operated in tandem.

Despite persistent modern assumptions that the judicial death sentence was a frequent public spectacle performed regularly for audiences as a deterrent for a host of crimes, the reality was far less spectacular and less common. Legal systems followed strict procedures, especially after the rediscovery of Roman Law, and the new provisions permitting interrogatory torture in certain circumstances were codified by the Fourth Lateran Council in 1215. In England,

22 "exile": https://www.merriam-webster.com/dictionary/exile. Accessed 20 June 2019.

23 William Smith, ed., *Dictionary of Greek and Roman Antiquities*, 3rd ed. (London: John Murray, 1875), 136–137.

24 Edward W. Said, "Intellectual Exile: Expatriates and Marginals," *Grand Street* 47 (1993), 113.

25 See: Sabine Grebe, "Why Did Ovid Associate His Exile with a Living Death?," *The Classical World* 103:4 (2010): 491–509. See also: Raymond Huntington Coon, "Ovid in Exile," *The Classical Association of the Middle West and South* 22:5 (1927), 355–369.

Common Law developed from early legal traditions expanded upon after the Conquest but relied upon precepts like "innocent before proven guilty" and the right to a trial by jury enshrined in the *Magna Carta* also of 1215. Once found guilty by ordeal, or later by confession, the convicted could be sentenced to death according to the crime.[26] Methods of execution varied, depending on the locality and the laws in play. There are plenty of harsh and brutal executions in the records, many of which Gregory of Tours (*c.*539–594) enumerates in his *History of the Franks*, like being dragged behind a horse and then hanged, illustrated by William Fitz Osbert's execution for rebellion in 1196.[27] In Germany, the wheel was a common implement of both torture and execution, though the frequency of its use is debatable.[28] Hanging was the most common form of judicial execution for secular crimes while burning at the stake was used for spiritual transgressors accused and convicted of heresy.[29] Excruciating punishments like hanging, drawing, and quartering were generally reserved for traitors of the lower classes, while beheading was the "mercy" meted out to aristocratic offenders.[30] Execution could be summarily carried out during war, or it could be enacted in the public square after a trial. Some executions were conducted in secret to avoid public outcry. Propaganda often preceded and succeeded certain executions, as Michel Foucault argues, to demonstrate the dominance and power of the ruler and urge their subjects to obey the law.[31]

Medieval literary sources often elevate execution as a means of either condemning excessive violence and abuses of power or of reifying the authority of certain institutions. Even though hanging was used more frequently, Robert Mills points out that chroniclers often omit records of simple hangings, preferring to dwell on the rarer, but more spectacular forms of execution like flaying and equine quartering; however, many of these were only popular literary

26 See: Robert Bartlett, *Trial by Fire and Water: The Medieval Judicial Ordeal* (Oxford: Clarendon, 1986); Edward Peters, *Torture* (Philadelphia: University of Pennsylvania Press, 1985); and Larissa Tracy, *Torture and Brutality in Medieval Literature: Negotiations of National Identity* (Cambridge: D.S. Brewer, 2012).

27 Gregory of Tours, *The History of the Franks*, trans. and ed. Lewis Thorpe (London: Penguin, 1974); and Emanuel J. Mickel, *Ganelon, Treason, and the 'Chanson de Roland'* (University Park: Pennsylvania State Press, 1989), 147.

28 Mitchell B. Merback, *The Thief, the Cross and the Wheel: Pain and the Spectacle of Punishment in Medieval and Renaissance Europe* (London: Reaktion, 1999), 158.

29 Robert Mills, *Suspended Animation: Pain, Pleasure, and Punishment in Medieval Culture* (London: Reaktion Books Ltd., 2005), 9.

30 See: *Flaying in the Premodern World: Practice and Representation*, ed. Larissa Tracy (Cambridge: D.S. Brewer, 2017).

31 Michel Foucault, *Discipline and Punish: The Birth of the Prison*, trans. Alan Sheridan (New York, 1977/79), 1–5, 7–8.

motifs rather than representations of actual practice.[32] Hagiography is rife with brutal executions, especially those of virgin martyrs whose sanctity rests on not suffering while subjected to the cruelest forms of punishment. Famous traitors, like Ganelon in the *Chanson de Roland*, are subjected to unthinkable punishments like equine quartering. The Viking Bróðir who murdered King Brian Boru at the Battle of Clontarf in 1014, was eviscerated, according to the account in *Brennu-Njals saga*. Thomas Hill explains that Bróðir's execution is a means of punishing the murderer of a king where "a particularly evil man was killed in a particularly cruel way."[33] Often the narrative of exile and return includes a brutal execution scene where the usurper who displaces the exiled hero is subjected to judicial punishment that ends in a horrifying execution, as in the early-fourteenth-century *Havelok the Dane* (*c.*1295–1310) where Godard is flayed alive and then hanged. But capital punishment was relatively restricted in medieval societies to the most heinous crimes: murder, heresy, and treason—and, sometimes, not even then.[34] The death penalty was largely a later medieval phenomenon, gaining ground after the rediscovery of Roman Law in the twelfth and thirteenth centuries as a more common method of punishment in post-medieval periods.[35] Those judged guilty were more often exiled, especially in the earlier Middle Ages. This collection investigates the relationship between the exiled and the landscape, physical or psychological, into which they are (dis)placed in conversation with accounts of execution, constructed by the authorities or observers, or invented to criticize the whole system.

Medieval societies took neither punishment nor penance lightly. The loss of community and identity that resulted from exile was often considered the worst possible punishment, and it could be conceived of in a variety of ways:

---

32 See: Tracy, *Torture and Brutality*; *Flaying in the Premodern World*, ed. Tracy; and *Medieval and Early Modern Murder: Legal, Literary and Historical Contexts*, ed. Larissa Tracy (Woodbridge: Boydell Press, 2018).

33 Thomas D. Hill, "The Evisceration of Bróðir in *Brennu-Njals Saga*," *Traditio* 37 (1981): 437–44 at 438.

34 See: Nicole Marafioti and Jay Paul Gates, "Capital and Corporal Punishment in Anglo-Saxon England," *Capital and Corporal Punishment in Anglo-Saxon England*, ed. Marafioti and Gates (Woodbridge: Boydell Press, 2014); *Heads Will Roll: Decapitation in the Medieval and Early Modern Imagination*, ed. Larissa Tracy and Jeff Massey (Leiden: Brill, 2012); *Medieval and Early Modern Murder:*, ed. Tracy; and *Treason: Medieval and Early Modern Adultery, Betrayal and Shame*, ed. Larissa Tracy (Leiden: Brill, 2019).

35 Paul Hyams points out that in the twelfth century, capital punishment was rare, especially for vassals. "Henry II and Ganelon," *Syracuse Scholar* 4 (1983): 22–35 at 30 n. 16. See also: *Society's Final Solution: A History and Discussion of the Death Penalty*, ed. Laura E. Randa (Lanham, MD: University Press of America, 1997).

punitive exile, outlawry, spiritual exile (excommunication), migration (forced or voluntary), and execution (the exile of death). In the premodern world, the relationship between exile and execution was symbiotic: violate the requirements of exile and face death; submit to exile and become a martyr through execution in foreign lands; leave family, friends, community, language, and culture behind in a symbolic exercise of execution. Essentially, the act of exile could be a verdict of execution where those who were cast out of society were expected to die through starvation and deprivation, or where the act of being cast out left the exile subject to extra-judicial execution. In many cases, the community preferred exile to the final judgment of execution, but as legal and political structures expanded, execution was increasingly weaponized by rulers (and occasionally mobs) against those who threatened social institutions. The scope of medieval law changed over time; corporal punishment replaced exile for the worst crimes, and exile or forced displacement became a self-imposed mode of punishment. Once an exile was sentenced, they existed outside the law, and so mob violence or vigilante violence against them became the law. Execution and exile were thus the ultimate endgames—a sentence of death or banishment from the community carried equal weight and gravity.

In both exile and execution, society must be complicit; people must be willing to ostracize their neighbors or watch their execution, participating in the spectacle that reifies the power of the state. Exile relies on community consent to banish members from its borders, to cast out those who transgress its norm, and to shun them. However, some entered into exile voluntarily, as *peregrinatio*, wandering the world in search of divine inspiration, separating themselves from home out of need or will. *Peregrinatio*, or pilgrimage—exile as a form of spiritual observance and penance—features heavily in early Christian biographies and chronicles. But Westley Follett argues here that "*peregrinatio* as an act of penance did not likely arise from any pre-existing practice of judicial exile, but rather emerged from the confluence of Roman, biblical, and patristic ideals regarding departure from one's *patria*, and the ecclesiastical promotion of exile from one's *patria* as an alternative or spiritual equivalent to a sentence of judicial execution."[36] Working from the eighth-century text *Navigatio Sancti Brendani* (*Voyage of Saint Brendan*), Follett examines the term in an Irish context and concludes that *peregrinatio* could be applied as a form of punishment imposed for some of the worst sins, rather than simply being a voluntary act undertaken as spiritual penance.

36 Westley Follett, ""He Shall Die unto the World with Perpetual Exile": The Penitential Aspect of Insular *peregrinatio*," 21.

Exile from the spiritual community of the Church in the form of physical separation or excommunication, was also a means of severing those who transgressed from the body of the Church—a metaphor often employed in physical terms of dismemberment. In her chapter, Bojana Radovanović examines the severance trope in ninth-century Greek and Latin narratives by Hincmar of Reims (*c.*806–882; archbishop of Reims from 845), Hrabanus Maurus (*c.*780–856; archbishop of Mainz from 847), Gottschalk of Orbais (*c.*804–868), among others. She argues that in the debates regarding heterodoxy and orthodoxy, spiritual or allegorical self-exile functioned as a salutary form of spiritual quest whether it manifested in physical separation from the community of the Church or not.

The painful element of any kind of exile is lasting punishment, and thus, exile was preferable to the finality of execution. In his *Life of Charlemagne* (*c.*826–7), Einhard records the emperor's response to the treachery of his son Pippin and his fellow plotters: "All the perpetrators were sent into exile, some blinded and others unharmed, but only three conspirators lost their lives; since they had drawn their swords to avoid arrest and had killed some people, they were slain because there was no other way to subdue them."[37] In pre-Conquest England, Christian authorities were confronted with conflicting doctrines of mercy and the earthly obligation to punish criminals—one reason exile was preferred to execution.[38] As Nicole Marafioti and Jay Paul Gates explain, "the alignment of secular and spiritual priorities had long been an element of English law, as Christian clergy had been drafting English royal legislation since the turn of the seventh century."[39] To balance these demands, Archbishop Wulfstan of York (d. 1023) instituted numerous legal codes proscribing non-lethal punishments, including banishment and mutilation, for smaller offenses: "Whereas an immediate death sentence might place the soul of the condemned beyond redemption, if he lacked the opportunity or inclination to repent before his execution, a life-sparing judgment allowed even the worst offenders enough time to make their peace with God."[40] Of course, execution follows the precept of "an eye for an eye' in the laws of Hammurabi, to which rulers turned as a justification for deadly force for centuries. The Christianization of the Roman Empire after Constantine resulted in the amelioration of some of the most horrific methods of torment and execution in the

37 Einhard, *The Life of Charlemagne*, in *Einhard and Notker the Stammerer: Two Lives of Charlemagne*, ed. David Ganz, 17–44 (London: Penguin, 2008), 33.

38 Marafioti and Gates, "Capital and Corporal Punishment," 1.

39 Marafioti and Gates, "Capital and Corporal Punishment," 1.

40 Marafioti and Gates, "Capital and Corporal Punishment," 1.

Roman legal process like feeding the accused to lions or hanging them over a crowd and pouring molten lead down their throats, but the Christian emperors also preserved the jurisprudence upon which they had originally been based.[41] However, as in early-medieval England, "lawmakers did not prescribe capital and corporal punishments lightly."[42] Nor did they banish transgressors without considering the larger ramifications for the community. Late tenth-century Old English elegiac poems like *The Wanderer* and the *Wife's Lament* ruminate on the loss inherent in exile and the separation from self that occurs with being separated from home, family, and community.

In medieval Icelandic law, exile was part and parcel of outlawry; sagas like *Grettis saga*, *Gísla saga*, and *Brennu-Njals saga* feature exile as the central conflict but the finality of exile could be mitigated by travel, migration, or immigration. Sometimes, exile was limited by law to a period of years rather than being permanent. However, the prospect of exile was often worse than the alternative—death—or the status of the exile could be used to justify execution. While outlawry and fines, rather than execution, were the primary penalties under Icelandic law for serious crimes like murder, an outlaw who did not adhere to the provisions of exile could be killed with a certain amount of impunity.[43] Thus, exile was also a death sentence in circumstances where the banished was cast out without means of survival or in manner where death was likely. Capital punishment certainly existed independently of exile as the most extreme punishment for the most heinous crimes, but it was very often the last resort.

Even after the reinstitution of Roman law and the increased implementation of capital punishment for crimes like murder, heresy, and treason, exile remained a facet of premodern justice and figured prominently in the literary imagination. Like Ovid, Dante Alighieri wrote his literary masterpieces as a response to his own experience of exile. In *The Divine Comedy*, Dante describes the painful experience: "Tu lascerai ogne cosa diletta più caramente; e questo è quello strale che l'arco de lo essilio pria saetta. Tu proverai sì come sa di sale lo pane altrui, e come è duro calle lo scendere e 'l salir per l'altrui scale"

41 Edward Peters, "Destruction of the Flesh—Salvation of the Spirit: The Paradoxes of Torture in Medieval Christian Society," *The Devil, Heresy and Witchcraft in the Middle Ages: Essays in Honor of Jeffrey B. Russell*, ed. Alberto Ferreiro, 131–48 (Leiden: Brill, 1998), 135.

42 Marafioti and Gates, "Capital and Corporal Punishment," 3.

43 Jesse Byock, *Medieval Iceland: Society, Sagas, and Power* (Berkeley: University of California Press, 1988), 26, 27–28. It was a clever system where outlaws could be "in-lawed" again if they killed another outlaw. This both kept outlaws from joining up together and ensured that quite a lot of them were likely to end up dead, even if they were not executed through judicial decree. Our thanks to the anonymous reader for pointing this out.

[You shall leave everything you love most dearly: this is the arrow that the bow of exile shoots first. You are to know the bitter taste of others' bread, how salt it is, and know how hard a path it is for one who goes descending and ascending others' stairs] (Par. 17.55–60).[44] In this famous metaphor of exile as a bow and arrow, Dante manipulates the traditional image of Cupid and the arrow of love: the pain of expulsion from the beloved is that of an arrow shot by Exile; the taste of the bread, the most basic element of one's meal, is bitter when in exile; the everyday experience of going up and down stairs becomes a challenge. In her chapter, Gillian Adler considers the relationship between time and exile in Dante's *Commedia* (*c*.1308–1320) and Christine de Pizan's *Le Livre de la Cité des Dames* (*Book of the City of Ladies*) (1405). Adler argues that while Dante engages with his physical exile from Florence through the displacement of time, Christine emulates his model—not through literal exile—but by "authorizing her position in defiance of the social and intellectual, rather than physical, ostracism she faced as a female author writing within a patristic milieu."[45] Christine's exile is one of social exclusion created by misogynist attitudes in medieval French society.

An entire genre of "exile and return" narratives pivots around the exile of the central hero and their triumphant return home to claim their rightful place.[46] Texts like the twelfth-century Latin *Gesta Herewardi* (*Hereward the Wake*) and *Havelok the Dane* situate the exile of the hero within the older, more nostalgic legal traditions. Within outlaw narratives, exile and execution operate as parallel punishments for capital crimes; outlaws suffer exile or face execution as the alternative. The largely fifteenth-century Robin Hood ballads romanticize the exiled outlaw and cast him as the defender of good law and proper governance, even as he exists outside its boundaries. Here, Larissa Tracy argues that the *Gest of Robyn Hode* (*c*.1450?) and *Robin Hood and Guy of Gisborne* (*c*.1475?) evoke a sense of nostalgia, "a longing for a simpler, more idealistic past or place, often rooted in criticism of the present."[47] In these English texts, the exile employs execution—unofficially sanctioned but legally acceptable—to

44 Dante Alighieri, *The Divine Comedy*, trans. Henry Wadsworth Longfellow with an Introduction by Ellen M. Mitchell, Vol. 2, *Paradiso* XVII: 55–60 (Digireads: 2017).

45 Gillian Adler, "The Time of Exile: Historical Distance and Ethical Perspective in Dante's *Commedia* and Christine de Pizan's *Le Livre de la Cité des Dames*," in this volume, 117.

46 Rosalind Field, "The King over the Water: Exile-and-Return Revisited," in *Cultural Encounters in the Romance of Medieval England*, ed. Corinne Saunders (Cambridge: D.S. Brewer, 2005), 41–53. See also: Laura Ashe, "'Exile-and-return' and English Law: The Anglo-Saxon Inheritance of Insular Romance," *Literature Compass* 3 (2006), 300–317.

47 Larissa Tracy, "Nostalgia in Medieval English Narratives of Outlaws, Exiles, and Execution," 211.

reinforce orthodox structures of authority while also facing the possibility of that punishment in their exiled state. Tracy concludes that "by expressing the need for outlaws to literally take the law into their own hands by executing corrupt officials, these narratives criticize the failures of the medieval English political system to dole out justice fairly, disrupting the nostalgia the exile should have for their home."[48] In this context, the outlaw is the ultimate exile who wields justice denied to them.

Not every outcast, however, suffers political or even physical exile. The idea of spiritual exile underlies Geoffrey Chaucer's *Man of Law's Tale*, part of the fourteenth-century *Canterbury Tales*. Scholars have read Chaucer's Custance in *The Man of Law's Tale* as an exile from her home and family as she wanders throughout the text, journey after journey, mercilessly tossed about by the desires of others until she finally returns to her original home. However, Gila Aloni deftly argues that, in this tale, Custance is never really an exile in the way that Christianity and Islam view this condition. Thus, Aloni challenges the dominant interpretation of this narrative as one of exile and of a missionary bride on a quest for conversion, arguing that Chaucer advocates religious tolerance rather than Christian superiority. The tale, Aloni asserts, "advances a more nonsectarian worldview that can accept the value of other religious faiths rather than offering a polemic on punitive physical exile as a result of religious difference."[49]

Chaucer's satire extends beyond the imposition of exile in *The Man of Law's Tale*, targeting the corrupt figures of society who exercise potentially fatal justice for their selfish ends. Similarly, other European communities resisted the implementation of execution as a legitimate mode of punishment. Some chroniclers condemned the injustice of royally sanctioned execution, encouraging rebellion against such tyranny. In his contextual discussion of the Old Swedish *Erikskrönikan* (*The Chronicle of Duke Erik*) (c.1320), Kim Bergqvist contends that the author condemns the abuse of political power by the ruling factions, portraying these executions as nothing more than illicit and illegal political murder and favoring exile as a means of ejecting political opponents. Likewise, in Piast Poland, rulers employed execution and exile as means of enhancing their power. Banishment and execution often went hand-in-hand; they were offered as options in different political circumstances. In his contribution to this volume, Radosław Kotecki analyzes the development of the death penalty in fourteenth and fifteenth-century Piast Poland as a political weapon wielded

48 Tracy, "Nostalgia in Medieval English Narratives," 212.

49 Gila Aloni, "A Re-examination of Constance's Exile—Geoffrey Chaucer's *Man of Law's Tale* and Constance's Return Home," 149.

by rulers to exercise their authority, juxtaposed against instances of political banishment. Some rulers chose to exile their political enemies and rivals, as a political strategy meant to serve the same ends—or, in Foucault's words, reactivating power rather than enacting justice.[50]

That power rests on the gruesome spectacle of execution as much as it does on its enactment. Public execution carries significant political weight—but it was not always carried out by the authorities. Abel de Lorenzo Rodríguez discusses lapidation—stoning—as a form of public execution enacted by mobs who took part in the exercise of local justice, and the way that practice exiled those who were stoned from their communities. Reinforced by Jewish, Christian, and Muslim traditions in the early Middle Ages, stoning was a popular form of execution on the Iberian Peninsula. There, from the fifth through the twelfth centuries, stoning "was the outcome of a mob's euphoria, using the most basic, primitive, and economical instrument imaginable as a weapon for a ritualized, penitential, and even lawful performance."[51] Karen Casey Casebier examines how the Virgin Mary exercises her power by disrupting trials and executions in favor of her faithful, even in cases where the proceedings are lawful. She draws upon accounts in two collections of Old French miracle tales by Gautier de Coinci's "D'une fame qui fu delivree a Loon dou feu" ("The Woman Was Delivered From Burning at Loon") (*c.*1214–36) in *Les Miracles de Nostre Dame* and the anonymous *Vie des pères*' "De la fame qui fist estrangler son gendre" ("The Woman Who Had Her Son-in-Law Strangled") in which the Virgin intercedes to prevent execution, even when the accused is guilty. The spectacular judicial ritual of execution was not just reserved for punishing human criminals, however; nor was it simply carried out for judicial reasons. Examining archival sources of urban justice, including bailiff accounts from the Low Countries and Northern France, Mireille Pardon, considers how stripping the identity of those condemned to death—not only living people but dead bodies, falsely-made goods, and domesticated animals—rendered them not only inhuman but also transformed them into an object whose only suitable role was violent purgation by the state.

Literary examples create a disproportionate image of violence in medieval society, which contributes to a "distorted picture of medieval penal practice" and suggests that "pre-modern people were accustomed to witnessing extravagant, showy execution rituals with unremitting frequency."[52] While this may

50 Foucault, *Discipline and Punish*, 172.

51 Abel de Lorenzo Rodríguez, "*Lapidabatur a populo*: Stoning as Collective Execution and Exile in Early Medieval Iberia (Fifth–Twelfth Centuries)," in this volume, 61.

52 Mills, *Suspended Animation*, 26.

have been the case in some towns and cities at particular times in medieval Europe, "the overall picture painted by court records is that the majority of criminals unfortunate enough to be sentenced to death met more ignominious ends at the end of a rope."[53] John Bellamy points out that premodern people were not inherently violent, nor did they necessarily take any pleasure in the violence of their world: "when medieval men were cruel there was usually a good reason for it. Rarely were they brutal out of sheer sadism."[54] The execution of convicted criminals, when it happened, was not the product of some kind of medieval savagery, but rather of a serious interest in finding ways to apply the law effectively. However, the law could be abused and, even if enacted correctly, could still play into political propaganda. But the medieval landscape was not one populated by hanging corpses left to rot as a deterrent to potential criminals. Even though it was used as a political weapon (Berqvist, Kotecki), society often resisted its use, which was far from widespread in the first place.

Several narratives satirize the use of fatal justice while others condemn it outright, even when the guilt of the accused is not in doubt. The public execution of traitors sent a strong signal of justice in action, and the "gathering of crowds of ordinary people to watch and cheer at the gruesome fate of traitors was itself redolent both of the attitude of awe, respect and fear which the Crown wished to inculcate and the way in which the public at large could be attracted by or drawn into such events."[55] Accounts of executions become increasingly common later in the Middle Ages and into the early modern period. The condemned gave gallows speeches that were printed and circulated widely. Hangmen—the more common form of executioner—were often the focus of the popular imagination. In their chapters, Ben Parsons and Susan Small examine literature and art produced in response to public executions. Parsons examines *Groanes from Newgate* (1663) which concerns the natural death in his sleep of hangman Edward Dun. This satirical tract exploits Dun's status for comedic and political ends. Small investigates the controversial history of the portrait of the notorious poisoner Marie-Madeleine Dreux d'Aubray, Marquise de Brinvilliers, drawn by Charles Le Brun, First Painter to King Louis XIV, the day after her execution. Haunted by her composure, Le Brun sketched her face before she was beheaded and burned, and included an image of Edme Pirot, her confessor. He also allegedly included the image of a tiger because he saw a

53 Mills, *Suspended Animation*, 26.

54 John Bellamy, *Crime and Public Order in England in the Later Middle Ages* (London: Routledge, 1973), 66.

55 Anthony Musson, *Medieval Law in Context: The Growth of Legal Consciousness from Magna Carta to the Peasant's Revolt* (Manchester: Manchester University Press, 2001), 19.

resemblance between it and the Marquise, a claim Pirot rejects. Small's analysis of the image juxtaposed with Pirot's account of her punishment provides an extraordinary first-hand account of an execution that had far-reaching consequences, even triggering the infamous Affair of the Poisons which led to the arrest of 319 people, 36 of whom were executed. Condemnation and a sentence of execution literally cut the convicted off from society and their social identity. Exile served a similar function of severance and alienation.

Even though exile and execution were often intertwined in medieval law, custom, and practice in the Middle Ages, most scholarly studies examine *either* exile or execution—one or the other—but rarely both in tandem. William Chester Jordan's *From England to France: Felony and Exile in the High Middle Ages* examines the judicial and administrative processes involved in the "abjuration" of English subjects, treating exile in its punitive capacity as a central feature of medieval jurisprudence, but isolated from execution.[56] Like many studies on exile in the Middle Ages, Jordan's study focuses on England and France from 1180 to approximately 1350. *Exile in the Middle Ages*, edited by Laura Napran and Elisabeth Van Houts, explores a wider geographical range, devoting a section of the collection to "Secular Exile" and to the vocabulary of outlawry and exile; however, the collection focuses mainly on bishops in exile during the period of the central Middle Ages from *c.*900 to *c.*1300 in Western Europe.[57] Other scholarly works include analyses of excommunication as a spiritual exile in England,[58] political exile in Italy,[59] and temporary Anglo-Norman exile in the eleventh and twelfth centuries, where time away from the homeland allows all parties involved to reconsider their position.[60] Broader studies on crime and punishment in the medieval world, like Trevor Dean's excellent and comprehensive *Crime in Medieval Europe*, often refer to exile and execution as outcomes of judicial proceedings, but only in the

56 William Chester Jordan, *From England to France: Felony and Exile in the High Middle Ages* (Princeton: Princeton University Press, 2015), 1–7.

57 Laura Napran and Elisabeth Van Houts, eds., *Exile in the Middle Ages: Selected Proceedings from the International Medieval Congress, University of Leeds, 8–11 July 2002* (Turnhout: Brepols, 2004).

58 F. Pollock and F.W. Maitland, *The History of English Law before the Time of Edward I*, 2nd ed., 2 vols. (Cambridge: Cambridge University Press, 1898; repr. 1968).

59 R. Starn, *Contrary Commonwealth: The Theme of Exile in Medieval and Renaissance Italy* (Berkeley: University of California Press, 1982).

60 E. van Houts, "L'exil dans l'espace Anglo-Normand," in *La Normandie et l'Angleterre au Moyen Âge*, 4–7 Octobre 2001 Colloque Cerisy-la Salle, ed. by V. Gazeau (Turnhout: Brepols, 2003).

context of the larger-scope crimes or violence.[61] Several studies on capital punishment focus either on the method, like *Heads Will Roll: Decapitation in the Medieval and Early Modern Imagination*, or on the specific crime that might warrant it, like *Medieval and Early Modern Murder* or *Treason: Medieval and Early Modern Adultery, Betrayal, and Shame*, without focusing specifically on the sentence of execution or its relationship to exile as an equally viable option.[62] This volume attempts to redress that, suggesting a dialogue between the two and interrogating how these punishments were exercised in relation to each other. Building on the considerable foundation laid by earlier works, this volume seeks to bridge the gap between the two most extreme sentences—exile and execution—which featured prominently in the discourse of medieval punishment.

The interdisciplinary chapters of this volume, arranged chronologically, speak to each other about the significance of these modes of punishment to particular medieval societies, at times reflecting on both exile and execution where one feeds into the other. Not every chapter addresses exile and execution *together*, but rather, in their focus on one or the other, they illustrate the similarities between these seemingly disparate punishments. Nor is this an exhaustive study—no volume can be—but an opening for more exploration of these two concepts that share so much in determining the course of someone's life. Much remains to be done in investigating these two ideas within the wider medieval world. Beginning with Irish accounts of spiritual exile as execution in Insular *peregrination*, the essays cover a broad range of material from Old English penitential literature on spiritual exile to French courtly epics and English legendary histories, from Spanish textual evidence of executions to

---

61 Trevor Dean, *Crime in Medieval Europe 1200–1550* (Harlow: Pearson Education, 2001). On capital punishment see: Paul Friedland, *Seeing Justice Done: The Age of Spectacular Capital Punishment in France* (Oxford: Oxford University Press, 2012); Gates and Marafioti, eds., *Capital and Corporal Punishment*. See also: G. Geltner, *The Medieval Prison: A Social History* (Princeton: Princeton University, Press, 2008) and a variety of important studies on medieval violence in general, including: Hannah Skoda, *Medieval Violence: Physical Brutality in Northern France 1270–1330* (Oxford: Oxford University Press, 2013; rptd. 2015); Warren C. Brown, *Violence in Medieval Europe* (London: Routledge, 2011); Massimo Vallerani, *Medieval Public Justice*, trans. Sarah Rubin Blanshei (Washington, DC: The Catholic University of America Press, 2012), which centers on medieval Italy; and John Bellamy, *Crime and Public Order in England in the Later Middle Ages* (London: Routledge & Kegan Paul, 1973), which mainly deals with England, as does James Given, *Society and Homicide in Thirteenth-Century England* (Stanford: Stanford University Press, 1977).

62 See: *Heads Will Roll*, ed. Tracy and Massey; *Castration and Culture*, ed. Tracy; *Flaying in the Premodern World*, ed. Tracy; *Medieval and Early Modern Murder*, ed. Tracy; *Treason*, ed. Tracy; and Tracy, *Torture and Brutality*.

legal treatises governing both exile and execution in the late Middle Ages and early modern period. In their specific analysis, the essays engage with each other and address the inextricable relationship between exile and execution even when they only focus on one or the other. Because several of the chapters share source material, there is a select bibliography at the end of the volume with major sources on both exile and execution.

Thus, as this volume demonstrates, exile is one of the most pervasive aspects of the human condition—there has always been exile, and there will always be exile, and it often operates in conjunction with execution—two potentially impossible choices or no choice at all. Still, the execution of criminals certainly occupied the imaginations of medieval audiences; the art and literature of the period often depict scenes of execution that were relatively rare—or even unheard of—in judicial practice. Overall, attitudes regarding execution and exile that survive in historical, literary, and material sources indicate that exile and execution share a significance in society rather than being distinct or separate retributions.

CHAPTER 1

"He Shall Die unto the World with Perpetual Exile": the Penitential Aspect of Insular *peregrinatio*

Westley Follett

Almost fifty years ago, Thomas Charles-Edwards published a seminal article on the practice of *peregrinatio* attested among the Irish as early as the sixth century.[1] Usually translated "pilgrimage," the word *peregrinatio*, as Charles-Edwards points out, served as an umbrella term for a range of related but still distinctive activities in the early Middle Ages.[2] These include: a journey undertaken as an act of devotion to a set destination of religious significance, such as that of the seventh-century Frankish bishop Arculf who visited multiple holy sites in the Levant;[3] monastic wandering or voyaging in a variety of settings, perhaps most vividly portrayed in the eighth-century text *Navigatio Sancti Brendani* (*Voyage of Saint Brendan*);[4] departure from one's homeland or *patria* to take up the ascetic life in a foreign land, such as ascribed to the sixth-century founder of Iona, Saint Columba, who left Ireland for Britain "pro Christo peregrinari uolens" [wishing to be a pilgrim for Christ];[5] and penitential exile as expia-

1 Thomas Charles-Edwards, "The Social Background to Irish *Peregrinatio*," *Celtica* 11 (1976): 43–59.

2 See also: Elva Johnston, who describes a "spectrum of *peregrinatio*": "Exiles from the Edge? The Irish Contexts of *Peregrinatio*," in *The Irish in Early Medieval Europe: Identity, Culture and Religion*, ed. Roy Flechner and Sven Meeder (New York: Palgrave, 2016), 38–52 at 39–40; Stephanie Hayes-Healy, "'Irish Pilgrimage': A Romantic Misconception," in *Princes, Prelates and Poets in Medieval Ireland: Essays in Honour of Katharine Simms*, ed. Seán Duffy (Dublin: Four Courts Press, 2013), 241–60 at 242–4; Stephanie Hayes-Healy, "Patterns of *Peregrinatio* in the Early Middle Ages," in *Medieval Paradigms: Essays in Honor of Jeremy duQuesnay Adams*, ed. Stephanie Hayes-Healy (New York: Palgrave, 2005), 2:3–24.

3 As recounted in Adomnán, *De locis sanctis*, ed. and trans. Denis Meehan, *Adamnán's De Locis Sanctis* (Dublin: Dublin Institute for Advanced Studies, 1983).

4 *Navigatio Sancti Brendani Abbatis from Early Latin Manuscripts*, ed. Carl Selmer (Notre Dame, IN: University of Notre Dame Press, 1959).

5 Adomnán, *Vita S. Columbae*, second preface, ed. and trans. Alan Anderson and Marjorie Anderson, *Adomnán's Life of Columba* (Oxford: Clarendon Press, 1991), 6–7. See also the sermons of Columba's younger contemporary, Columbanus. Katja Ritari, "'Pilgrims in the World': Monastic Life as a Quest for Heaven in Early Medieval Ireland," in *Pilgrimage of Life: Studies in Honour of Professor René Gothóni*, ed. Riku Hämäläinen, Heikki Pesonen, Mari Rahkala, and Tuula Sakaranaho (Helsinki: University of Helsinki, 2010), 336–45. Such

 | DOI:10.1163/9789004742598_003

tion for some specific sin, as in the case of a Connachtman guilty of murder who went to Columba's Iona "ad delenda in peregrinatione peccamina" [to expiate his sins in pilgrimage].[6] Charles-Edwards gives most of his attention to *peregrinatio* as an act of ascetic renunciation, but notes that "for the Irish, [the term] *peregrinus* may be used for an exile or alien even though the exile is not in fulfilment of an ascetic ideal."[7] The fluidity of meaning accorded to *peregrinatio* in early medieval texts has complicated understanding of how the practice of penitential pilgrimage arose in the sixth century.[8] Contrary to some prior assertions, *peregrinatio* as an act of penance did not likely arise from any pre-existing practice of judicial exile, but rather emerged from the confluence of Roman, biblical and patristic ideals regarding departure from one's *patria*, and the ecclesiastical promotion of exile from one's *patria* as an alternative or spiritual equivalent to a sentence of judicial execution.[9]

The word *peregrinatio* first appears in an Irish context at quite literally the beginning of Irish history, in the *Confessio* and *Epistula* of Saint Patrick in the fifth century. Patrick had been a very unwilling exile in his youth, captured and enslaved for years in Ireland, but for him *peregrinatio* only came with his later and voluntary return to the land of his captivity. Drawing upon scripture, he says it was through the grace of God

> ut ego ueneram ad Hibernas gentes euangelium praedicare et ab incredulis contumelias perferre, ut *audirem obprobrium peregrinationis meae*, et persecutiones multas usque ad uincula et ut darem ingenuitatem meam pro utilitate aliorum.

> [that I came to the Irish peoples to preach the gospel and to bear insults from unbelievers, such that I would hear the reproach of my *peregrinatio*.

a pilgrim is known in Irish law tracts as a *déorad Dé* [exile for God] and held an honor price equivalent to that of a bishop or a local king. Charles-Edwards, "The Social Background," 53.

6 Adomnán, *Vita S. Columbae* 2.39, ed. and trans. Anderson and Anderson, *Adomnán's Life of Columba*, 154–5; I pass over yet another variety of *peregrinatio*, undertaken by Irish court scholars who went abroad in the eighth and ninth centuries, for which see: Hayes-Healy, "Irish Pilgrimage," 256–8, and Kathleen Hughes, "The Changing Theory and Practice of Irish Pilgrimage," *Journal of Ecclesiastical History* 11 (1960): 143–51.

7 Charles-Edwards, "The Social Background," 46.

8 For consideration of penitential pilgrimage in the Carolingian and post-Carolingian eras, see: Robin Ann Aronstam, "Penitential Pilgrimages to Rome in the Early Middle Ages," *Archivum Historiae Pontificiae* 13 (1975): 65–83.

9 For contrary prior assertion, see: Johnston, "Exiles from the Edge?" 41–43, and below, n. 31.

> I bore many persecutions, even chains, so that I could give up my free-born state for the sake of others.][10]

Such was his success among the Irish that even when British raiders carried away captive some of his converts, he could still exult, "Gaudeo intra meipsum: non gratis laboraui uel peregrinatio mea in uacuum non fuit" [I rejoice within myself: I have not worked for nothing, my *peregrinatio* has not been in vain].[11] Patrick appears to hold a Roman understanding of *peregrinatio* as residence away from one's natal land where the laws and customs of one's own people could offer no protection. In the early empire, a *peregrinus* [foreigner] was a non-Roman subject of the state—a Gaul, for example—who resided among Romans but lacked the privileges and protections accorded to a *civis* [citizen].[12] By the later empire, when Roman citizenship was more widely held, the term *peregrinus* could more simply mean anyone, regardless of citizenship, who was resident in a city or province other than his or her registered place of origin.[13] Patrick seems to engage with both Roman legal senses of *peregrinatio*, emphasizing the vulnerability of his position in an alien land. While he uses the term in a technical sense, the sentiment is imbued with religious purpose: his precarious status as a foreigner among the Irish was in furtherance of the work of God.

Patrick's conception of *peregrinatio* also draws from another context besides Roman law. From its early days, Christianity was infused with a sense of life on this earth as an exile, filled with longing for a true home that is not of this world. This appears to be the sentiment expressed in 1 Peter 2:11, wherein the author addresses his fellow Christians, "Dearly beloved, I beseech you as strangers and pilgrims"—*aduenae* and *peregrini*, in the Vulgate translation known to Patrick and most other churchmen and women in the Latin West. In similar fashion,

---

10 Patrick, *Confessio* 37, ed. Ludwig Bieler, *Libri epistolarum Sancti Patricii episcopi* (Dublin: Royal Irish Academy, 1993), 1:77, quoting Ecclesiasticus [Sirach] 29.30: "Minimum pro magno placeat tibi, et improperium peregrinationis non audies"; see also *Confessio* 26: "Dominus pepercit proselito et peregrino," ed. Bieler, *Libri epistolarum*, 73; cf. *Epistula* 1: "Inter barbaras itaque gentes habito proselitus et profuga ob amorem Dei," ed. Bieler, *Libri epistolarum*, 1:91.

11 Patrick, *Epistula* 17, ed. Bieler, *Libri epistolarum*, 1:99.

12 Martin Claussen, "'Peregrinatio' and 'Peregrini' in Augustine's 'City of God,'" *Traditio* 46 (1991): 33–75 at 35–36; Ralph Mathisen, "*Peregrini, Barbari,* and *Cives Romani*: Concepts of Citizenship and the Legal Identity of Barbarians in the Later Roman Empire," *The American Historical Review* 111 (2006): 1011–40 at 1013–21.

13 Wolf Liebeschuetz, "Citizen Status and the Law in the Roman Empire and the Visigothic Kingdom," in *Strategies of Distinction: The Construction of the Ethnic Communities, 300–800*, ed. Walter Pohl and Helmut Reimitz (Leiden: Brill, 1998), 131–52 at 131–5.

the author of the Epistle to the Hebrews counts Abraham, who following the command of God departed the land of his birth to dwell among the Canaanites (Genesis 12), among several scriptural examples of faithful obedience:

> Fide qui uocatur Abraham oboediuit in locum exire, quem accepturus erat in hereditatem; et exiit, nesciens quo iret. Fide moratus est in terra repromissionis, tamquam in aliena. … Juxta fidem defuncti sunt omnes isti, non acceptis repromissionibus, sed a longe eas aspicientes, et salutantes, et confitentes quia peregrini et hospites sunt super terram.
>
> [By faith Abraham, when called to go to a place he would later receive as his inheritance, obeyed and went, even though he did not know where he was going. By faith he made his home in the promised land like a stranger in a foreign country. … All of these people were still living by faith when they died. They did not receive the things promised; they only saw them and welcomed them from a distance, admitting that they were *peregrini* and strangers on earth.] (Hebrews 11:8–9, 13)

Indeed, the *peregrinus* Abraham became an exemplar of voluntary separation from *patria* as an act of ascetic renunciation. This practice resonated deeply among the early medieval Irish, as in the seventh-century *Life* of Saint Columbanus, who, inspired by Abraham, "coepit peregrinationem desiderare" [began to desire a *peregrinatio*] and so left Ireland around 590 to found monasteries in Gaul and Italy.[14]

Alongside biblical representations of *peregrinatio*, the legalistic Roman sense of the term remained relevant to late Antique and early medieval ecclesiastics. In his monumental treatise of Christian philosophy, Augustine of Hippo recasts the antithetical Roman conceptions of citizen and *peregrinus* to depict Christians as both citizens of the City of God and *peregrini* on earth; *peregrinatio* is thus a life of faithfulness spent hoping for a return to the heavenly home.[15] Closer to Patrick's day, Gallo-Roman bishop Sidonius Apollinaris demonstrates how both legalistic and Christian understandings of *peregrinatio* could intertwine. In 477, Sidonius was expelled from his see at Clermont following the surrender of that city to Euric, king of the Visigoths, and confined

14 Jonas of Bobbio, *Vita Columbani abbatis* 4, ed. Bruno Krusch, *Ionae vitae Sanctorum Columbani, Vedastis, Iohannis*, *Monumenta Germaniae Historica* [hereafter MGH], *Scriptores rerum Merovingicorum* 4 (Hanover, 1902), 70.

15 Claussen, "'Peregrinatio' and 'Peregrini,'" 33–75.

to a fort not far from Carcassonne in southern Gaul. In a letter to fellow-bishop Faustus of Riez, he remarks that

> per officii imaginem uel, quod est uerius, necessitatem solo patrio exactus, hoc relegatus uariis quaquauersum frangor angoribus, quia patior hic incommoda peregrini, illic damna proscripti.
>
> [through a pretense of duty or, more truly, necessity, I was expelled from my native land, and banished from it I am crushed by differing torments at every turn, because here I suffer the hardships of a *peregrinus*, there the forfeitures of one proscribed.][16]

Thus far, Sidonius demonstrates a secular conception of *peregrinatio* inasmuch as he had been turned out from his homeland in the Auvergne and subjugated to the rule of the Goths, to whom he was a foreigner with no protections as a Roman citizen. In these respects, he had something in common with Patrick, who as a Briton in Ireland lacked the status of a free-born Irishman and could lay no claim to the rights of his own *patria*.[17] Sidonius continues, however, asking Faustus to pray for him so that "non remaneamus terreni, quibus terra non remanet, inchoemusque ut a saeculi lucris, sic quoque a culpis peregrinari" [we may not persist in earthly cares, we for whom the earth no longer remains, and that we may begin to estrange ourselves also from the sins of the world as we are from its riches] (9, 3.4:135–6). With this remark, Sidonius conflates his forced impoverishment and departure from Clermont with his desire for separation (*peregrinari*) from worldly concerns and sins. His *peregrinatio* was not just a political exile; it became an opportunity to alienate himself from the things that were displeasing to God. Thus, by the latter part of the fifth century, the term *peregrinatio* had clearly become multivalent. It continued to signify the legalistic sense of a foreign residency—that is, a departure, willing or compelled, from one's *patria* to reside among another people as an alien lacking the rights of one native born. But it could also signify a spiritual estrangement, whether in the metaphorical sense of the Christian experience of life on earth away from the kingdom of God, or as an actual separation from a place, people, or things, with the expectation of obtaining a spiritual benefit.

---

16 *Epistulae* book 9:3.3, ed. André Loyen, *Sidoine Apollinaire, Tome III: Lettres* (Paris: Les Belles Lettres, 1970), 135–6; on the place of his confinement, see 8:3.1; for subsequent citations, book, chapter and page numbers are given in parentheses.

17 Patrick, *Epistula* 10, ed. Bieler, *Libri epsistolarum*, 1:96.

By the sixth century, western churchmen—and, it appears, Insular churchmen earliest among these—found further spiritual purpose in *peregrinatio* as a penitential remedy for sin. One of the canons of the brief text known as *Sinodus luci uictorie* (*Synod of the Grove of Victory*), believed to have been a council of the early British Church,[18] stipulates that "qui mechator matris est, .iii. annis cum peregrinatione perenni" [he who defiles his mother, (must do penance for) three years with perpetual pilgrimage].[19] As with Patrick and the earlier sources, here too *peregrinatio* means departure from home to reside as a stranger among people who are not one's own, but, whereas the apostle of the Irish left Britain for evangelical purposes, the *Sinodus luci uictorie* imposes departure from home as an act of contrition for a specific sin. In such a context *peregrinatio* might reasonably be taken to mean "penitential exile." As an act of penance assigned by a confessor, it is meant to be reformative rather than punitive like a sentence of judicial exile mandated by a legal code.

Admittedly, the terminology that the earliest penitential sources employ sometimes blurs the distinction between penitential exile and judicial exile, complicating modern scholars' efforts to understand the origin of the former. Other British-authored texts from the sixth century do not speak specifically of *peregrinatio* or *peregrini* but rather use words such as *exilium* [exile], as if confessors were judges in law courts. According to the *Sinodus aquilonalis Britaniae* (*Synod of North Britain*), "monachus consecrata furatus anno, et altero cum fratribus peniteat; si autem iterauerit, exilium patietur" [a monk who has stolen consecrated things shall do penance for a year (in confinement), and another year with his brethren; but if he repeats the offense he shall suffer exile].[20] Similarly, one who steals foods after three prior offenses "iugi exilio sub alio abate peniteat" [shall do penance in permanent exile under another abbot] (4:66–67). Probably a bit later than the *Sinodus aquilonalis Britaniae* is the *Penitentialis Vinniani* (*Penitential of Finnian*), attributed to a sixth-century British cleric named Uinniau residing in Ireland, where he was known as Finnian. This work prescribes that a cleric guilty of fornication who then compounds the sin with the murder of the resulting child

18 John McNeill and Helena Gamer, *Medieval Handbooks of Penance* (New York: Columbia University Press, 1938, rpt. 1990), 169–70; James Kenney, *The Sources for the Early History of Ireland: Ecclesiastical* (New York: Octagon, 1929, rev. 1966), 239.

19 *Altera sinodus luci uictorie* 6, ed. and trans. Ludwig Bieler, *The Irish Penitentials* (Dublin: Dublin Institute for Advanced Studies, 1975), 68–69.

20 *Sinodus aquilonalis Britaniae* 3, ed. and trans. Bieler, *The Irish Penitentials*, 66–67.

> extorris existat de patria sua donec impleatur numerus .vii. annorum et ita iudicio episcopi uel sacerdotis suo officio restituatur. Si autem non occiderit filium, minus peccatum se eadem penitentia.
>
> [shall be an exile from his own country, until a period of seven years is completed, and so by the judgement of a bishop or a priest, he shall be restored to his office. If, however, he has not killed the child, the sin is less, but the penance is the same.][21]

Similarly, a cleric who slays his neighbor is "exterrem [*sic*] fieri de patria sua" [to become an exile from his country] for ten years, seven of which "in alia urbe" [in another city] (i.e. ecclesiastical settlement). After that time,

> si bene egerit et comprobatus fuerit testimonium abbatis siue sacerdotis cui commissus fuerit, recipiatur in patria sua et satis faciat amicis eius quem occiderat et uicem pietatis et oboedientie reddat patri et matri eius si adhuc in corpore sunt et dicat: "Ecce ego uobis pro filio uestro; quecumque dixeritis mihi faciam." Si autem non satis egerit, non recipiatur in aeternum.
>
> [if he has done well and is approved by the testimonial of the abbot or bishop to whom he was committed, he shall be received into his own country and make satisfaction to the friends of him whom he slew and compensate his father and mother, if they are still in the flesh, by filial piety and obedience and say: "Lo, I am in the place of your son; I will do for you whatever you tell me." But if he does not fulfil his obligation he shall not be received back for ever.] (23:80–84)

In the above examples, the terms *exilium* and *extorris* plainly signified a departure from one's *patria* specifically as an act of penance, rather than a sentence of judicial exile mandated by a legal code. The requirement that the exiled penitent must be supervised by an abbot or bishop underscores the reformative purpose of penitential exile. The confessor assigns penitential exile in the hope of the sinner's spiritual rehabilitation and eventual restoration to his or

21 *Penitentialis Vinniani* 12, ed. and trans. Bieler, *The Irish Penitentials*, 78–79; for subsequent citations, chapter, and page numbers are given in parentheses.

her community.[22] Understanding the intent of *peregrinatio* as penitential exile is an important step toward apprehending the origin of the practice.

Each of these British-authored texts, the *Sinodus aquilonalis Britaniae*, the *Sinodus luci uictorie*, and the *Penitentialis Vinniani*, influenced subsequent penitential works produced by Irish ecclesiastics.[23] The seventh-century *Paenitentiale Cummeani* (*Cummean Penitential*) ascribed to Cumméne Fota, possibly the abbot of Clonfert, quotes *Sinodus aquilonalis Britaniae* on the penance of exile under another abbot for a re-offending food thief, and *Sinodus luci uictorie* on the imposition of *peregrinatio perennis* for the sin of maternal incest.[24] The probably seventh-century *Tres canones Hibernici* (*Three Irish Canons*), as they are known to modern scholars, advise "dura penitentia in peregrinatione" [hard penance in *peregrinatio*] for offenses relating to the desecration or theft of sacred objects and for the apprehension, wounding, or slaying of one in service to a bishop.[25] The *Paenitentiale Columbani* (*Penitential of Columbanus*) relies extensively upon *Penitentialis Vinniani*, for example with the requirement that a cleric who has "ruina maxima ceciderit et filium genuerit, septem annis peregrinus in pane et aqua paeniteat" [fallen to the depth of ruin and begotten a child, let him do penance as a *peregrinus* for seven years on bread and water].[26] Similarly, for one who has slain his neighbor, "x annis exul paeniteat; post hos recipiatur in patriam" [let him do penance for ten

22 See also: *Sinodus aquilonalis Britaniae* 1, ed. and trans. Bieler, *The Irish Penitentials*, 66–67: "cum mulier uel cum uiro peccans quis expellatur ut alterius patriae cenubio uiuat, et peniteat confessus .iii. annis clausus, et postea frater illius altari subiectus ... doctoris iudicio peniteat" [one who sins with a woman or with a man shall be sent away to live (in a monastery) of another country, and shall do penance, after he has confessed, for three years in confinement (i.e. as an ex-communicant); and afterwards, as a brother re-admitted to the altar ... he shall do (further) penance at the discretion of his spiritual director].

23 The possibly British, sixth- or early seventh-century *Paenitentiale Ambrosianum* (*Ambrosian Penitential*) was also influential; see: Ludger Körntgen, *Studien zu den Quellen der frühmittelalterlichen Bußbücher* (Sigmaringen: Thorbecke, 1993), 80–86, with an edition at 258–70 (cf. mention of *exules* in 2.6 at 260). See also: Rob Meens, "The Irish Contribution to the Penitential Tradition," in *The Irish in Early Medieval Europe: Identity, Culture and Religion*, ed. Roy Flechner and Sven Meeder (London: Palgrave, 2016), 131–45 at 133 and 135.

24 *Paenitentiale Cummeani* 1.12 and 2.7, ed. and trans. Bieler, *The Irish Penitentials*, 112–13 and 114–15; for subsequent citations, chapter, section, and page numbers are given in parentheses; cf. *Sinodus aquilonalis Britaniae* 4 and *Sinodus luci victorie* 6, ed. and trans. Bieler, *The Irish Penitentials*, 66–67 and 68–69.

25 *Tres canones Hibernici* 1–3, ed. and trans. Bieler, *The Irish Penitentials*, 182–3.

26 *Paenitentiale Columbani* B 2, ed. and trans. Bieler, *The Irish Penitentials*, 98–99; cf. *Penitentialis Vinniani* 12, ed. and trans. Bieler, *The Irish Pentitentials*, 76–79.

years in exile; after these, let him be restored to his native land], providing that the murderer *satis faciat* [makes satisfaction] to the relations of the victim and offers filial piety to the victim's parents, if they are still living. If he does not do this, *Paenitentiale Columbani* likewise directs, "nunquam recipiatur in patriam" [let him never be restored to his native land], and then uniquely adds, "sed more Cain *uagus et profugus sit super terram*" [but like Cain let him be a "wanderer and fugitive upon the earth"] (Genesis 4:12).[27] The example of Cain, *uagus et profugus super terram*, is a striking counterpoint to the example of Abraham, *peregrinus et hospes super terram* (Hebrews 11:13). While both figures may be said to have been exiles insomuch as each departed his natal land and kin, never to return, they differed significantly. Cain's removal from society was no act of penance but rather punishment for his crime of fratricide; he was a *profugus*, not a *peregrinus*. Abraham, on the other hand, departed his *patria* as an act of faithful obedience and ascetic renunciation, making him an example of righteous *peregrinatio* that even saints would emulate.[28]

What remains unclear is how the Insular churchmen responsible for the early medieval penitentials first came to regard *peregrinatio* specifically as a remedy for sin.[29] For the authors of the *Penitentialis Vinniani* and *Paenitentiale Columbani*, the provision of satisfaction to the injured party was an important component of penitence, as in the case of the murderer who must offer recompense to the victim's kin and render filial piety to the parents in the place of their murdered son. This insistence on restorative justice has parallels in early medieval legal practice. Among the Franks and pre-Conquest English, the payment of a compensatory fine for an unjustified killing was termed *wergild*; the Irish knew it as *éraic*, and the obligation of filial piety to parents they called *goire*.[30] In light of such prescriptions, some scholarship has supposed that the

27 *Paenitential Columbani* B 1, ed. and trans. Bieler, *The Irish Penitentials*, 98–99; cf. *Penitentialis Vinniani* 23, ed. and trans. Bieler, *The Irish Pentitentials*, 80–83.

28 Jonas of Bobbio, *Vita Columbani abbatis* 4, ed. Krusch, *Ionae vitae Sanctorum*, 70.

29 Bernhard Kötting suggested that it was the ascetic character of *peregrinatio* (*Wallfahrt*) that gave rise in the sixth century to its perception "als Frucht der Gesinnung, als Bußübung zu betrachten, zumal wenn während der Reise das Fasten als aszetische Leistung geübt wird" [as a fruit of the spirit, as an exercise of penance, especially if fasting is practiced as an ascetic feat during the trip]. But it appears that when he speaks of *peregrinatio* he has in mind pilgrimage in the traditional sense, as *ad limina*, a set journey to a destination of religious significance, rather than a departure or exile from one's *patria* to live as a stranger in a foreign land; *Peregrinatio Religiosa: Wallfahrten in der Antike und das Pilgerwesen in der alten Kirche* (Münster: Regensberg, 1950), 329–30 at 330.

30 Fergus Kelly, *A Guide to Early Irish Law* (Dublin: Dublin Institute for Advanced Studies, 1988), 125–6 (*éraic*), 80 (*goire*); ed. and trans. Bieler, *The Irish Penitentials*, 243 n.10.

origin of *peregrinatio* as penance stemmed from pre-existent practices of judicial exile.[31] This requires careful consideration.

Certainly, exile was an important feature of Roman law. In the late Republic, permanent exile was the usual sentence for capital convictions.[32] By the late Empire, however, a time of heightened imperial concern for law and order, exile was prescribed for a wider range of crimes.[33] The Theodosian Code, a fifth-century compilation of earlier legal material, stipulates exile (*deportatio*) for certain sexual and marital offenses, various crimes against property, a range of official misconduct, desertion from civil service, malicious calumny, and a host of other misdeeds.[34] After the Council of Nicaea in 325, the sentence of exile could also befall clerics and theologians whose doctrinal views were deemed heretical, as was the case with the Briton Pelagius and his followers, exiled from Rome in 418 and from all Italy in 425.[35] In 429, Germanus, bishop of Auxerre, contended against the Pelagian heresy in Britain, where some of the exiles had evidently fled, and on a second trip in the 440s he accomplished the expulsion of the remaining Pelagians there.[36] Interestingly, in none of the examples above do the sources use the words *peregrinatio/peregrinus/peregrinari* in reference to judicial exile, whether it was imposed for criminal activity or for heresy. Perhaps a distinction is thus possible: in a late antique context, a *peregrinus* is one who departs his or her *patria* willingly, even if in contrition,

31 Johnston, "Exiles from the Edge?" 41–43; Charles-Edwards, "The Social Background," 56; Jonathan Sumption, *Pilgrimage: An Image of Mediaeval Religion* (Totowa, NJ: Rowan and Littlefield, 1975), 101.

32 Gordon Kelly, *A History of Exile in the Roman Republic* (Cambridge: Cambridge University Press, 2006), 40.

33 Julia Hillner, *Prison, Punishment and Penance in Late Antiquity* (Cambridge: Cambridge University Press, 2015), 196–7.

34 Clyde Pharr (trans.), *The Theodosian Code and Novels and the Sirmondian Constitutions* (New York: Greenwood Press, 1952), 246 at § 9.25.3 (rape), 343 at § 12.1.6 (marriage to slaves), 76–77 at § 3.16.1–2 (divorce without sufficient cause), 100 at § 4.22.2 (unlawful confiscation), 149 at § 8.30.16–17 (desertion), and 255 at § 9.39.2 (calumny), as a few examples among many. In this volume, see: Bojana Radovanović, "Exile and Excommunication in the Trope of Severance from the 'Body of the Church' in Ninth-Century Greek and Latin Texts."

35 *De constitutionibus imperatorum in causa Pelagianiae haeresis*, ed. Jacques-Paul Migne, *Patriologiae cursus completus: series Latina* [hereafter *PL*], 221 vols. (Paris, 1844–64), 48:385; Prosper of Aquitaine, *Contra collatorem* 21:2, ed. Migne, *PL* 51.271; Mar Marcos, "Anti-Pelagian Legislation in Context," in *Lex et Religio. XL Incontro di Studiosi dell'Antichiá Cristiania*, ed. Instituo Patristico Augustinianum (Rome: Institutum Patristicum Augustinianum, 2013), 317–44 at 340–1.

36 Constantius of Lyon, *Vita S. Germani* 27, ed. and trans. René Borius, *Constance de Lyon: Vie de Saint Germain d'Auxerre* (Paris: Les Éditions du Cerf, 1965), 173.

in the hope that pilgrimage or exile will redound to his or her spiritual benefit, as opposed to the *exsul* whose departure is punitive and compelled by a judicial sentence. Such an understanding accords well with the contrast noted above between the *peregrinus* Abraham and the *profugus* Cain.

Judicial exile is unevenly attested in the earliest law codes promulgated by Germanic kings. It appears in neither the Code of the Salian Franks produced by Clovis (d. 511),[37] nor the Burgundian Code issued by Gundobad (d. 516),[38] nor in the codes of early English kings Aethelbert (d. 616), Hlothhere and Eadric (d. 685 and 686 respectively), and Wihtred of Kent (d. 725),[39] and only once in the seventh-century Code of the Ripuarian Franks, which lists it as the punishment for kin-slaying and incest.[40] In marked contrast to these, the Visigothic Code, dated in its extant form to the reign of Recceswinth (d. 672), prescribes exile for a range of offenses, including incestuous and adulterous marriages, the contracting of marriage with avowed virgins and widows or penitent women, divorce, the abandonment of a freeborn child, the unjustified killing or maiming of a slave, high-status deserters and objectors to military service, failure to defend the king against scandal, heresy, and, most frequently mentioned, the violation of various restrictions imposed upon Jews.[41] One might initially suppose that the prevalence of judicial exile among the Visigoths reflects a greater degree of Romanization among them than was the case with other Germanic peoples. Given, however, that most of the offenses warranting judicial exile would have been of particular concern to the Church, surely Christianization was at least as significant an influence upon the Visigothic Code as Romanization. In other words, contrary to the

37 *Pactus legis Salicae*, ed. Karl Eckhardt, MGH, *Legum sectio I*, *Leges nationum Germanicarum*, Vol. 4, part 1 (Hannover, 1962); trans. Katherine Drew, *The Laws of the Salian Franks* (Philadelphia: University of Pennsylvania Press, 1991).

38 *Liber constitutionum siue lex Gundobada*, ed. Ludwig Rudolf von Salis, MGH, *Legum sectio I*, *Leges nationum Germanicarum* 2:1 (Hannover, 1892); trans. Katherine Drew, *The Burgundian Code: Book of Constitutions or Law of Gundobad* (Philadelphia: University of Pennsylvania Press, 1972).

39 Frederick Attenborough, *The Laws of the Earliest English Kings* (Cambridge: Cambridge University Press, 1922).

40 *Lex Ribuaria* 72:2, ed. Franz Beyerle and Rudolf Buchner, MGH, *Legum sectio I*, *Leges nationum Germanicarum* 3.2 (Hannover, 1954), 124.2; trans. Theodore Rivers, *Laws of the Salian and Ripuarian Franks* (New York: AMS Press, 1986), 204.

41 *Liber iudiciorum sive Lex Visigothorum edita ab Reccessvindo rege* 3:5.2, 3:6.2, 4:4.1, 6:5.12, 6:5.13, 9:2.8, 9:2.9, 12:2.2, 12:2.14, 12:3.1–27 passim, ed. Charles Zeumer, MGH, *Legum sectio I*, *Leges nationum Germanicarum* 1 (Hannover, 1902), 160.17, 168.20, 193.25, 276.10–11, 278.30, 371.30, 373.8, 375.6, 413.10, 421.5, 422.9, 430–54; trans. Samuel Scott, *The Visigothic Code (Forum Judicum)* (Boston: The Boston Book Company, 1910), 107, 115, 135, 223, 226, 326, 327, 328, 365, 371–2, 382–408.

assertion that secular judicial notions shaped the practice of *peregrinatio*, it is more probable that the tenets of spiritual and penitential *peregrinatio* helped form late and sub-Roman judicial views of exile.

Turning to the Irish evidence for judicial exile, the earliest relevant legal sources are later than the first appearance of *peregrinatio* in Insular penitentials, making it difficult to argue that penitential exile among the Irish arose out of an older, native practice of judicial exile. The Roman legal evidence is older, but one may reasonably question how much imperial jurisprudence could have shaped the use of exile in Ireland, which was never part of the Roman empire. There are better grounds for believing, rather, that Christian considerations similarly influenced early Irish thinking on the subject, much as suggested above in regard to the Visigothic evidence. *Córus Bésgnai* (*Ordering of Discipline*), an Old Irish text that forms part of the eighth-century legal compilation known as the *Senchas Már* (*Great Tradition*),[42] mentions *ailithre*, which can mean "pilgrimage," but as the text's modern editor Liam Breatnach translates, here it is "exile" or, more specifically, "penitential exile." It is listed as one of several justifiable reasons for the abandonment of one's ancestral church, "mád ailithre beres a anmcharae fair" [if it be exile which his confessor prescribes (as a penance) for him].[43] Two other *Senchas Már* tracts mention a form of punishment wherein the offender was cast adrift in a small boat, either to perish at sea or to wash up on some farther shore.[44] One of these texts, informally known as "the *Fuidir*-tract," refers to a category of "semi-freeman" or *fuidir*, namely, the "fuidir cinad o muir" [*fuidir* of an offense from the sea].[45] This was an individual "who has been cast adrift on the sea for some offense and is

42 On the date of the *Senchas Már*, see: Kelly, *A Guide*, 245.

43 *Córus Bésgnai*, on which see: Liam Breatnach, *A Companion to the Corpus Iuris Hibernici* (Dublin: Dublin Institute for Advanced Studies, 2005), 290, and Kelly, *A Guide*, 267; §75 and §83[B], ed. and trans. Liam Breatnach, *Córus Bésgnai: An Old Irish Law Tract on the Church and Society* (Dublin: Dublin Institute for Advanced Studies, 2017), 42–45, also 236–7 and 244–5.

44 On the sentence of setting adrift, see: Pamela O'Neill, "Landmarks of Another Kind: Carved Stones, Setting Adrift and Early Irish Law," *Australian and New Zealand Law and History eJournal* (2006), Paper no. 8; Mary Byrne, "On the Punishment of Setting Adrift," *Ériu* 11 (1932): 97–102; and Whitley Stokes, ed., *Tripartite Life of Patrick* (London: Eyre and Spottiswoode, 1887), clxxiv. For consideration of the practice in a wider context, see: J.R. Reinhard, "Setting Adrift in Medieval Law and Literature," *Proceedings of the Modern Language Association of America* 56 (1941): 33–68.

45 *Fuidir*-tract, see: Breatnach, *A Companion*, 294, and Kelly, *A Guide*, 271; §7, ed. Rudolf Thurneysen, "Irisches Recht," *Abhandlungen der Preussischen Akademie der Wissenschaften: Jahrgang 1931, Philosophisch-Historische Klasse* 2 (Berlin: Akademie der Wissenschaften, 1931): 1–90 at 65, with commentary at 74–75.

then taken into servitude on being washed ashore," as Fergus Kelly observes.[46] A gloss found in one manuscript witness of the tract offers *fingal* [kin-slaying] as an example of an offense meriting such a punishment, even if it was unintentional.[47] The later commentary on another *Senchas Már* tract, *Bretha for Macślechtaib* (*Judgments on Categories of Sons*), specifies casting adrift as the sentence for an unintentional or inadvertent homicide committed *fri neimhedh* [against a privileged place], or more specifically *ré h-eclais* [before a church]—that is, on church grounds.[48] This tract, similar to the pastoral context of the passage in *Córus Bésgnai* which mentions the confessor, *anmcharae* [soul-friend], who prescribes exile, clearly indicates the ecclesiastical milieu that shaped early Irish legal thinking.[49]

The above consideration of the Latin and vernacular evidence for judicial exile, viewed in light of the reformative intent of *peregrinatio*, provides compelling reasons to doubt that penitential exile developed from pre-existent practices of judicial exile, and to suspect that the former rather influenced the early medieval implementation of the latter. The specific instructions on how to carry out the Irish sentence of casting adrift add to this suspicion. Returning to the commentary on *Bretha for Macślechtaib*, there was some expectation that one so condemned might survive the experience:

> Is ed dleghar in duine do chur for muir ina cintaibh anfoit nó indeithbire torbha, maine uilet seoit aici, ₇ a chur for muir in airet is leir geilsciath ₇ lon menaighte ina ucht ₇ ordu tri ndornd ina laimh do dingbhail na neathetad de. acht mas isin fearann cetna rocuired he, is a beith amal cach nduine ndligtech isin fine, uair is e dia ruccustar breith fair. mas a

46 Kelly, *A Guide*, 219, where the passage is referenced as "Heptad 72," and 33–35; see the glosses to the *Fuidir*-track, ed. Thurneysen, "Irisches Recht," 65.

47 Thurneysen (ed.), "Irisches Recht," 74.

48 *Bretha for Macślechtaib*, ed. Daniel Binchy, *Corpus Iuris Hibernici* (Dublin: Institute for Advanced Studies, 1978), 109.8–10 with punctuation added but otherwise no attempt at normalization: "damadh re hecclais doneith foghal, robiadh peannait di re taeb a chur for muir. A tidhnacul ina cinaidh nó a breith i cliabh aensluaiste" [if it were in front of a church that he had committed the assault, penance would result from it in addition to his being cast upon the sea. His being delivered from his liability or (else) his carrying away in a boat of a single paddle]. Translation is my own, but see also: Byrne, "On the Punishment," 99, and O'Neill, "Landmarks of Another Kind." See: Breatnach, *A Companion*, 300, and Kelly, *A Guide*, 270.

49 On *anmchairdes* [soul-friendship], see: Westley Follett, "On Women, Blood, and Soul-friendship," in *Gablánach in scélaigecht: Celtic studies in honour of Ann Dooley*, ed. Sarah Sheehan, Joanne Findon, and Westley Follett, (Dublin: Four Courts Press, 2013), 53–68 at 60–66.

fearann eile dorala he, is a dilse daibh nó co tucthar cumal dar a cheann ⁊ comhraind bairce dligthighe ar in cumail sin.

[it is fitting the person be cast upon the sea for his crime of negligence or inadvertent injury, unless he has sufficient chattels (i.e. he is able to pay the *éraic* fine), and his being put upon the sea as far out as a white shield (on the shore) remains visible and a provision of gruel in his lap and a portion (of meat) of three hand-widths in his hand for keeping the birds away from him. But if he is washed ashore in the same territory, he is like any legally restricted person in the kin group, because it is God who has passed judgment on him. If it has put him at another (kin group's) territory, he is forfeit to them until a *cumal* is paid for his security and a share of the boat legitimate for that *cumal.*][50]

The glosses and commentary on *Córus Fine* (*Ordering of the Kin Group*), a now fragmentary tract not part of the *Senchas Már* collection but likely written around the same time, offer similar details regarding a "fer a cliab aenṡluaisti" [man of a boat of a single paddle],[51] and also prescribe setting adrift a son who is born of incest.[52] Such allowances imply that the punishment of setting

50 *Bretha for Macṡlechtaib*, ed. Binchy, *Corpus Iuris Hibernici*, 109.10–16, with punctuation added but no attempt at normalization; translation is my own, but see also: Byrne, "On the Punishment," 99, and O'Neill, "Landmarks of Another Kind."

51 *Córus Fine*, ed. Binchy, *Corpus Iuris Hibernici*, 744.32–34, with punctuation added but no attempt at normalization: "MAD FER A CLIAB AENLUAISTI, .i. Duine seo curtar a cliab aenluaiste amach for muir ina cintaib anfoit nó inndethbiri torba, in airet is leir geilsciath for muir, lon menaidhe aenaidhce lais, ⁊ geann orda tri ndornd ina laim ac dingbail aithide in mara de; acht mas isin crich-sin feil dorala é, is a beth amal cach mac indligtec isin fine" [IF IT BE A MAN IN A BOAT OF A SINGLE PADDLE, that is, a person who is put in a boat of a single paddle out on the sea for his crime of negligence or inadvertent injury, as far out as a white shield remains visible from the sea, a provision of gruel for one night with him, and a wedge(?)-portion of three hand-widths in his hand for warding off sea birds from him. But if he is washed ashore in the same territory, he is like every legally restricted son in the kin group]. Translation is my own, but see also: Byrne, "On the Punishment," 98–100, and O'Neill, "Landmarks of Another Kind." See: Breatnach, *A Companion*, 235–9, and Kelly, *A Guide*, 270.

52 *Córus Fine*, ed. Binchy, *Corpus Iuris Hibernici*, 744.28–31, with no attempt at normalization: "MAD MAC SCRINE, .i. Mac so dorinne re coibdelaig ina richt bodein; ⁊ is ed dlegar a cur i scrin lethair ar muir in eret bus leir gelsciath ar muir; acht masin ferann-sin fein dorala aris é, is fognum fuidhre uadha do macaib na primmna, ⁊ a beth amal gac mac indligthec isin fine" [IF IT BE A SON OF A COFFER, that is, a son who is begotten on a kinswoman in her own guise; and it is fitting he is put in a leather coffer on the sea as far out as a white shield will be visible on the sea; but if he is washed ashore in the same territory, he gives the service of a *fuidir* to the sons of the first wife, and he is like every legally restricted

adrift was not intended to be a sentence of certain death but rather a variety of *ailithre*, that is, exile from the kin group or *fine*. The practice suggests some reticence to employ execution in capital cases.

The reluctance of early Irish jurists to impose the death sentence in at least some instances might mean that the sentence of casting adrift was originally a penalty urged by ecclesiastics in lieu of capital punishment.[53] Supporting this view, the Old Irish ecclesiastical tract *Cáin Adomnáin* (*Law of Adomnán*), promulgated at the Synod of Birr in 697 and primarily concerned with ensuring the protection of non-combatants, includes a provision that a woman who deserves death for one of a range of offenses might be set adrift instead:

> Ar is ed bás dlegair do banscáil dia marbad fir nó mná, nó di thabairt neime dia n-abbalar, nó di loscad, nó di fochlaid ecalse .i. cor in nói óinṡlúaisti for murchreth hi fairrge do techt le gaeth di thír. Long menathcha do breith lee. La Día brithimnacht furi ísin.
>
> [For a woman deserves death for killing a man or a woman, or for giving poison whereof death ensues, or for burning, or for digging under a church, that is to say, she is to be put in a boat of one paddle at (the distance of) a *muirchrech* (i.e. as far out as a white shield on the shore remained visible) upon the ocean to go with the wind from land. A vessel of meal and water to be given with her. Judgment upon her as God deems fit.][54]

The similarity of this ecclesiastical legislation to the later directions given in the commentaries for *Bretha for Macṡlechtaib* and *Córus Fine* is plainly evident, again indicating that one tradition drew upon the other. *Cáin Adomnáin*, however, provides context missing from the others that equates setting adrift at sea

son in the kin group]. Translation is my own, but see also: Byrne, "On the Punishment," 98–100, and O'Neill, "Landmarks of Another Kind."

53 As first proposed by Byrne, "On the Punishment," 100; Kelly, *A Guide*, 219–20. For further commentary, see: John Ryan, "The Cáin Adomnáin," in *Studies in Early Irish Law*, ed. Rudolf Thurneysen, Nancy Power, Myles Dillon (Dublin: Hodges, Fidges and Co., 1936), 269–76 at 270–1, and O'Neill, "Landmarks of Another Kind."

54 *Cáin Adomnáin* 45, ed. and trans. Kuno Meyer, *Cáin Adamnáin: An Old-Irish Treatise on the Law of Adamnan* (Oxford, 1905), 30–31; regarding *murchreth* (recte *muirchrech*), see: Byrne, "On the Punishment," 98, who provides the manuscript gloss: "isi im[urro] muirch[reth] in airet [is leir] for muir [sciath] gel for [tir]" [a *muirchreth*, moreover, is as far out at sea as a white shield on land is visible], and Pamela O'Neill, "Old Irish *Muirchrech* 'Sea-Boundary,'" *Ériu* 67 (2017): 1–10.

with judicial execution.[55] This implies that out of a humane desire to avoid the taking of life, the matter was best left to God. As the commentary on *Bretha for Macślechtaib* similarly phrases it, "is e dia ruccustar breith" [it is God who has passed judgment]. Early Irish laws (and literature) attest to capital punishment, most often in the form of hanging, but it does not figure prominently.[56] The clerical sentiment behind these passages in *Cáin Adomnáin* and the *Bretha for Macślechtaib* commentary may be the reason why.

A striking hagiographical correspondence to the ruling from *Cáin Adomnán* situates the practice of setting adrift in a more overtly penitential context. In Muirchú's *Vita Patricii* (*Life of Patrick*), dated to the second half of the seventh century, Patrick encounters a pagan bandit named Macc Cuill. When his plot to deceive and kill the saint is exposed, Macc Cuill professes his belief, accepts baptism, and asks that Patrick "iudica ergo quantum debuerit pro tanto ac tali cremine" ["pass judgment, therefore, and state how much is due for such a great and wicked crime"].[57] Patrick demurs, however, saying, "Non possum iudicare, sed Deus iudicabit" ["I cannot judge, but God will judge"] (1.23 [22]:104–5). He then directs Macc Cuill to depart the land of the Irish in a boat made of one hide, without rudder or oars, and with himself fasting, dressed in a single, short garment with the emblem of his sin (*insigne peccati*) upon his head,[58] and his feet bound in fetters with the key cast into the sea. In this manner, Providence would pass judgment upon Macc Cuill, who was left to the mercy of the wind and the waves (1.23 [22]:104–5), as stipulated in *Cáin Adomnáin*. The decision of the Divine Judge is seemingly evident in that Macc Cuill does not perish at sea but rather washes up on the Isle of Man. The sentence, presumably, was for him to remain there in exile as a *fuidir cinad o muir* [semi-free man of an offense from the sea], in the language of the *Fuidir*-tract. Yet as Muirchú frames the tale, Macc Cuill was a penitent; his distinctive dress and the emblem of his sin on his head literally marked him as such. On the Isle of Man, he came under the direction of two missionary bishops, reflecting the insistence that a

55 On the issue of setting women adrift as a literary motif in Geoffrey Chaucer's *Man of Law's Tale* and whether that qualifies as exile or not, see in this volume: Gila Aloni, "A Re-examination of Constance's Exile—Geoffrey Chaucer's *Man of Law's Tale* and Constance's Return Home."

56 Kelly, *A Guide*, 217, but see also: Stokes, *Tripartite Life*, clxxiv.

57 Muirchú, *Vita S. Patricii*, 1.23 (22), ed. and trans. Ludwig Bieler, *Patrician Texts in the Book of Armagh* (Dublin: Dublin Institute for Advanced Studies, 1979), 102–5. For subsequent citations, chapter and page numbers are given in parentheses.

58 Perhaps a tattoo? See: W. Mark Gustafson, "*Inscripta in Fronte*: Penal Tattooing in Late Antiquity," *Classical Antiquity* 16 (1997): 79–105, who observes that in the later Roman Empire penal tattooing typically accompanied a sentence of judicial exile and hard labor.

penitential exile must be supervised. His redemption was complete when he eventually succeeded them in the episcopacy. Much as Abraham's departure from his *patria* became a hallmark of ascetic renunciation, Macc Cuill's departure from his *patria* signified the renunciation of his former life—each experienced a metaphorical death, leaving behind all they had known, followed by a spiritual rebirth, a new existence in a land shown them by God.

Although there is little cause to attribute the sixth-century Insular development of penitential pilgrimage to older practices of judicial exile, this does not mean that early medieval Irish hagiographers were uninformed of secular jurisprudence, even if it had not yet been written down in their day. Muirchú's account of Macc Cuill shows some awareness, and Adomnán's *Vita Columbae* (*Life of Columba*), dated to near the end of the seventh century and prior to the writing of the earliest Irish legal tracts, evinces still more. In the first of two illustrative examples,[59] Adomnán relates the story of a man who was guilty of both fratricide and incest with his mother. Displaying his prophetic knowledge of events far away, Columba informs his monks that "in hora aliquod inauditum in mundo peccatum perpetratum est, pro quo ualde timenda iudicialis uindicta" ["in this hour a sin unheard-of in this world had been committed, for which the judicial penalty must be very terrible"].[60] A few months later, a boat bearing the sinner pulls up on the shore of Iona. Columba has no desire to receive the unhappy fellow, but then learns that the wretch has commenced a coercive fast against him, effectively compelling the saint to see him. Columba reluctantly goes down to the beach, where the man immediately kneels before him and "leges penetentiae expleturum se promisit, iuxta sancti iudicationem" [vowed that he would perform what the laws of penance required, according to the decision of the saint] (1.22:48–51). Columba replies,

> Si .xii. annis inter Brittones cum fletu et lacrimis penetentiam egeris, nec ad Scotiam usque ad mortem reuersus fueris, forsan deus peccato ignoscat tuo.
>
> [If you do penance among the Britons with wailing and weeping for twelve years, and do not return to Ireland until your death, perhaps God will condone your sin.] (1.22:50–51)

59 See also: Adomnán, *Vita S. Columbae*, 1.30 and 1.36, ed. and trans. Anderson and Anderson, *Adomnán's Life of Columba*, 56–59 and 64–67.

60 Adomnán, *Vita S. Columbae*, 1.22, ed. and trans. Anderson and Anderson, *Adomnán's Life of Columba*, 48–49; for subsequent citations, book, chapter, and page numbers are given in parentheses.

As in the story of Macc Cuill, judicial punishment and penitence here seem intertwined. Columba is aware of the *iudicialis uindicta* [demands of justice], but since the would-be penitent succeeds in gaining an audience with the saint, these appear to be subsumed under the *leges penitentiae* [laws of penitence]. Accordingly, the seemingly contrite man is consigned to twelve years of penance "cum fletu et lacrimis" [with wailing and weeping] among the Britons, presumably under the watchful care of an abbot, but even after that, he must remain exiled from his *patria* to his dying day. Only then might he hope to attain God's forgiveness. For all that, however, the sinner does not fulfil the penance he promised and returns to Ireland where he is killed by his enemies, just as the saint further prophesied.

Later along in *Vita Columbae* is the story of Librán, a layman from Connacht who arrives at Iona "ad delenda in peregrinatione peccamina" [to expiate his sins in *peregrinatio*] (2.39:154–5). As Librán himself explains to Columba, he had killed a man and was then taken and held in chains as one condemned to death, in accordance with Irish legal practice. However, a wealthy relation of his had purchased his release, also in keeping with Irish law, and thereby redeemed his life.[61] In gratitude, Librán had sworn an oath that he would serve his kinsman for the remainder of his days. But after only a short while, "seruire homini dedignatus et deo potius obsecundare mallens" [disdaining to be a servant of man, and choosing rather to obey God], he had broken his vow of servitude and fled. Having made the journey now to Iona, where he hoped to become a monk, "omnia sua confessus peccata leges penitentiae flexis in terram genibus se impleturum promisit" [he confessed all his sins, and promised, kneeling on the ground, that he would do all that the laws of penance required] (2.39:154–5). Raising the fugitive up, Columba imposes a penance of seven years on the nearby island of Tiree, after which Librán is to return to Iona, where he could approach the altar and receive the Eucharist once again. Accepting all this, the *penitens* [penitent] *peregrinus*, as Adomnán terms him, departs for the monastery at Tiree, where he completes seven full years of penance. He then returns to Iona as instructed and is restored to communion (2.39:156–7).

At this point, the *leges penitentiae* seem to have been satisfied; however, Columba now directs Librán to go back to Ireland to make satisfaction to his kinsman from whom he fled as a runaway bondservant, and then to fulfil the duties of filial service which he owes to his aged parents but has long withheld. All this the man does, and when he eventually returns to Iona, free and clear

61 See: Kelly, *A Guide*, 97–98, 215.

of all legal obligation, Columba welcomes him and accepts his vow. Finally a monk, Librán is sent by the abbot to reside in the same monastery "in quo prius .uii. annis penitens domino seruiit" [in which he had formerly served the Lord as a penitent for seven years] (2.39:156–61). There are several salient points to this interesting story, which in truth deserves more attention than possible here. Columba once again exhibits sensitivity to what in the previous story were termed the *iudicialis uindicta* [demands of justice]. As fugitive from justice, Librán's life is lawfully forfeit. But in as much as he removes himself from the arena of secular jurisprudence and, as a *penitens peregrinus*, appeals to an ecclesiastical authority, his case is settled in accordance with the *leges penitentiae*. Columba thus imposes the ecclesiastical equivalent of a secular judgment of death, a penitential *peregrinatio* under the direction of an abbot.

A shared characteristic of these hagiographical depictions of penitential exile is the penitents' emotional displays of contrition: "with wailing and weeping," as Adomnán puts it. From very early times, penance was associated with the rituals of mourning. In the third century, Tertullian describes the act of penance as a rite performed in a church in the context of the celebration of the Eucharist. Wearing sackcloth and ashes, the fasting penitent, barred from communion, prostrated himself before the priests, confessed his sin with groaning and weeping, and then, kneeling before the altar, asked all the faithful present to petition God on his behalf to hear his supplication for pardon.[62] Caesarius of Arles drew a distinction between lesser sins (*peccata minuta*) and greater sins (*peccata capitalia*), preaching that for redemption from the former, charitable works might suffice. These, however, were not enough for capital sins, "sed addendae sunt lacrymae, rugitus et gemitus, continuata et longo tempore protracta jejunia ... in luctu et in tristitia multo tempore permanentes" [but tears and crying, and groaning must be added, as also continuous fasting which is extended over a long time ... continuing a long time in grief and sadness].[63] "Lugeamus exstinctam nostram animam" [Let us mourn for our soul when it is dead], he advises, "quomodo alienam carnem mortuam plangimus" [in the

62 Tertullian, *De paenitentia* 9, ed. and trans. Charles Munier, *Tertullian: La Pénitence*, Sources Chrétiennes 316 (Paris: Les Éditions du Cerf, 1984); see: Guy Stroumsa, "From Repentance to Penance in Early Christianity: Tertullian's *De paenitentia* in Context," in *Transformations of the Inner Self in Ancient Religions*, ed. Jan Assmann and Guy Stroumsa (Leiden: Brill, 1999), 167–78 at 175–8.

63 Caesarius of Arles, *Sermo* 179.6–7, ed. Germain Morin, *Sancti Caesarii Arelatensis sermones*, 1.2, Corpus Christianorum Series Latina 104 (Turnhout: Brepols, 1953), 724–9 at 727–8; for subsequent citations, sermon, chapter and page numbers are given in parentheses; trans. Mary Magdeleine Mueller, *Caesarius of Arles: Sermons, Volume 2 (81–186)* (Washington, D.C.: Catholic University Press, 1964), 454.

same way in which we bewail the dead body of another] (179.6–7:727–8). The perception of penitential exile as a kind of death, an ecclesiastical equivalent to judicial execution, makes such mournful behavior all the more appropriate. The penitent *peregrinus* is, in effect, one condemned. A passage from the Irish-authored *Paenitentiale Cummeani* illustrates this concept quite well:

> Qui homicidium odii meditatione facit, relictis armis usque ad mortem mortuus mundo uiuat Deo. Si autem post uota perfectionis, cum peregrinatione perenni mundo moriatur.
>
> [He who commits murder through nursing hatred in his mind, shall give up his arms until death, and, dead unto the world, shall live unto God. But if it is after vows of perfection, he shall die unto the world with perpetual exile.] (4.5–6:118–21)

This means that one who has taken monastic vows, *vota perfectionis*, and then out of abiding hatred (i.e. premeditation) commits murder is consigned to life-long penitential exile (*peregrinatio perennis*). He shall thus become dead to the world—or certainly to the world that he knew, his *patria*. In secular society, the unjustified and premeditated taking of human life might be answered with judicial execution. But such a punishment could hardly be countenanced in a monastic context, shaped by the theology that no sin is beyond the reach of God's mercy. *Peregrinatio perennis* might thus have been regarded the ultimate form of penance for especially grievous sins. To borrow the words of Caesarius of Arles, it was the most demonstrable way to "mourn for our soul when it is dead."

The authors of early Insular texts that speak of penitential exile did not write in ignorance of secular jurisprudence, but the extant sources do not support the claim that penitential *peregrinatio* derived from pre-existent practices of judicial exile. Penitential exile rather stemmed from late Roman and sub-Roman views on the hardship of departing one's *patria* to live as a stranger among foreigners and from scriptural and patristic views on the spiritual merit of renouncing one's home and people. With the development of penitential taxonomies in the sixth century, it is not hard to see how *peregrinatio* was included with fasting and other hardships as expiation for sin, rather than simply remaining an ascetic endeavor that one took on in the manner of Abraham, Sidonius Apollinaris, or Patrick. Its notions of vulnerability, trust in the judgment of God, and mournful contrition assured that *peregrinatio* as exile had a valued place in the confessor's toolbox, imposed for some of the worst sins that penitential authors and hagiographers could imagine. The ecclesiastical perception of *peregrinatio* as a metaphorical death transferred to a Christianized secular society that permitted the exile of criminals as an equivalence to their execution when circumstances were fitting.[64]

64 This chapter benefited significantly from the constructive criticism of the editors of this book and, especially, Dr. Phyllis Jestice at the College of Charleston. Any errors it contains are of course my own.

CHAPTER 2

Exile and Excommunication in the Trope of Severance from the "Body of the Church" in Ninth-Century Greek and Latin Texts

Bojana Radovanović

> *... propter incredulitatem fracti sunt.*
> *Tu autem fide stas ... si permanseris in bonitate, alioquin et tu excideris*
>
> ... because of unbelief they were broken off. But thou standest by faith ... if thou abide in goodness, otherwise thou also shalt be cut off"
>
> Rom. 11:20, 22

∵

Critics have long understood the ways in which ninth-century Carolingian and Byzantine authors described and differentiated the faithful from the unfaithful as a function of the underlying necessity to exercise control over the social body.[1] Ninth-century authors in both contexts used the trope of amputation, deeply rooted in the early medieval projects of pursuing social unity and consolidating Church and state authority, to conceptualize exile for heretics. This trope was grounded in the scriptural and early Christian narratives, but some ninth-century literature contained a contrasting motif which also resurged from the scriptural and early Christian narratives: that of allegorical spiritual self-exile as a salutary form of spiritual quest.

In these ninth-century narratives, the trope of severance of the putrid body part—and the sequence of events leading up to it—transposed the different

1 Richard Broome, "Pagans, Rebels and Merovingians: Otherness in the Early Carolingian World," in *The Resources of the Past in Early Middle Ages*, ed. Clemens Gantner, Rosamond McKitterick, and Sven Meeder (Cambridge: Cambridge University Press, 2015), 155–171; Walter Pohl, "Social Language, Identities and the Control of Discourse," in *East and West: Modes of Communication*, ed. Evangelos Chrysos and Ian Wood (Leiden: Brill, 1999), 127–141.

 | DOI:10.1163/9789004742598_004

facets of exile into the symbolic plane, in a representational procedure that was influenced by theological, historical, and political events. The severance trope also framed the contours of the semantic field of allegorical exile in ninth-century Greek and Latin narratives, since allegorical exile coexisted with other forms of exile since the early era of the established Church from the reign of Constantine.[2] Not all the early medieval authors who spoke of exile actually suffered exile in the physical sense: at times, they drew on much older exilic traditions stemming from more ancient authors and texts, including classical and Scriptural sources. At the same time, descriptions of exile in these texts were also shaped heavily by contemporary theological debates in both contexts.[3] In ninth-century Francia and Byzantium, several significant doctrinal debates arose over redefining the means of combatting religious dissenters.[4] In the Carolingian realm, as well as in Byzantium, the struggle against heresy became essential to the unity of the Empire. The orthodox faith was defended by Hincmar of Reims (*c.*806–882; archbishop of Reims from 845), Hrabanus Maurus (*c.*780–856; archbishop of Mainz from 847), and others.[5] Specifically, the Predestination debate appeared in Francia in the years approaching the middle of the century, carried by Gottschalk of Orbais (*c.*804–868), as well as Hincmar and Hrabanus Maurus. The core of this controversy lay in Gottschalk's refuted doctrine of twin predestination, according to which some people were

2 See for example: Paul J. Alexander, "Religious Persecution and Resistance in the Byzantine Empire of the Eighth and Ninth Centuries: Methods and Justifications," *Speculum* 52.2 (April 1977): 238–264.

3 Cf. Jan Felix Gaertner, "The Discourse of Displacement in Greco-Roman Antiquity," in *Writing Exile: The Discourse of Displacement in Greco-Roman Antiquity and Beyond*, ed. Gaertner (Leiden: Brill, 2007), 1–3; David Ganz, "Theology and Organization of Thought," in *The New Cambridge Medieval History II, c. 700–900*, ed. Rosamond McKiterick (Cambridge: Cambridge University Press, 1995), 758–785 at 783–785.

4 Cf. Mayke de Jong and Irene van Renswoude, "Introduction: Carolingian Cultures of Dialogue, Debate and Disputation," *EME* 25.1 (2017): 6–18; Warren Pezé, "Doctrinal Debate and Social Control in the Carolingian Age: The Predestination Controversy (840s–60s)," *EME* 25.1 (2017): 85–101; see also: Hans-Werner Goetz and Ian Wood, "The Many Facets and Methodological Problems of 'Otherness,'" in *Otherness in the Middle Ages*, ed. Hans-Werner Goetz and Ian Wood (Turnhout: Brepols, 2021), 11–36; James T. Palmer, "The Otherness of Non-Christians in the Early Middle Ages," in *Christianity and Religious Plurality*, ed. Charlotte Methhuen, Andrew Spicer, and John Wolffe (Woodbridge: Boydell, 2015), 33–52; Hans-Werner Goetz, *Die Wahrnehmung anderer Religionen und christlich-abendländisches Selbsverständnis im frühen und höhen Mittelalter (5.–12. Jahrhundert)* (Berlin: Akademie Verlag, 2013), 1:1–31; Ian Wood, "The Pagan and the Other: Varying Presentations in the Early Middle Ages," *Networks and Neighbours* 1 (2013):1–22; Christine Caldwell Ames, *Medieval Heresies: Christianity, Judaism, and Islam* (Cambridge: Cambridge University Press, 2015), 112–130.

5 Walter Ullman, *The Carolingian Renaissance and the Idea of Kingship* (London: Methuen, 1969), 140–144.

predestined for eternal blessing and others for eternal damnation. As a consequence, Gottschalk was labelled a heretic during the Synod of Mainz in 848 and sentenced to life-long imprisonment.[6]

The heralds of the anti-heretical polemical literature in ninth-century Byzantium were Theodore the Studite (759–826), and Patriarchs of Constantinople Nicephorus (806–815) and Photius (858–867; 877–886). Theodore the Studite, abbot of the Studion monastery and a renowned figure in theological disputes of the end of the eighth and the first decades of the ninth century (759–826), was thrice banished: first, between 795/6 and 798 to Thessalonica; then in 809 on canonical grounds upon the decisions of the so-called Moechian Synod to the Princes' Islands, and, lastly, in 815–821, on doctrinal grounds (during the second Iconoclast period) to Bythinia and Smyrna. During his time spent in exile, Theodore attempted to protect the Christian flock from the official position of the Church, which he considered erroneous. His attitude towards the official ecclesiastical climate of those days could indeed be perceived as dissenting.[7] The Iconoclast controversy over the use of religious images encompassed two periods in the history of Byzantium: the first between *c.*726 and 787, and the second between 814 and 842. The second period of the Iconoclastic controversy hit the Byzantine Empire in the first half of the ninth century, creating turmoil as well, which is echoed in the writings of both Theodore and Patriarch Photius.[8]

Some of the texts produced in the context of these turbulent social, political, and theological situations include the epistemological works of Hincmar, Hrabanus Maurus, Pope Nicholas I (858–867), Theodore the Studite, and Photius; Hincmar's *De una et non trina Deitate*, *De divortio Lotharii regis et Theutbergae regine*; Hrabanus's *De clericorum institutione ad Heistulphum Archiepiscopum*; Photius's treatise against the Manichaeans, *Contra Manichaeos*; Gottschalk's

6 Cf. Pezé, "Doctrinal debate"; Warren Pezé, "Le virus de l'erreur: Essai d'histoire sociale sur la controverse prédestinatienne à l'époque carolingienne" (PhD Dissertation, University of Paris, 2014); Matthew Gillis, "Gottschalk of Orbais: A Study of Power and Spirituality in a Ninth-Century Life" (PhD Dissertation, University of Virginia, 2009). Another important debate of the epoch which included Gottschalk was the short upsurge of the Trinitarian controversy in the mid-850's. Cf. Gillis, "Gottschalk of Orbais," 282–290.

7 Cf. Vladimir Baranov, "Constructing the Underground Community: The Letters of Theodore the Studite and the Letter of Emperors Michael II and Theophilos to Louis the Pious," *Scrinium* 6 (2010): 230–259 at 236.

8 Cf. Peter Brown, "A Dark-Age Crisis: Aspects of the Iconoclastic Controversy," in *Doctrine and Debate in the East Christian World, 300–1500*, ed. Averil Cameron and Robert Hoyland (Farnham: Ashgate, 2011), 237–270; Kathryn Ringrose, "Monks and Society in Iconoclastic Byzantium," *Byzantine Studies* 6 (1979): 130–151. Other controversies of the epoch included the Moechian controversy, the Filioque controversy, and the Photian Schism.

and Theodorus's poetry; homilies of Photius, and the *Liber de rectoribus Christianis* of Sedulius Scottus. All of them attest to a climate in both the Frankish and Byzantine contexts in which the ruling ecclesiastical and political circles considered the discourses of "outsiders" dangerous.[9] In situations where the Carolingian and Byzantine societies were unbalanced by doctrinal controversies, anti-heretical struggles were often motivated by an urge to re-establish a state of social unity and harmony.

Since the fourth century, the Church sought solutions to doctrinal questions from the ruling structures, especially in the aftermath of the Edict of Thessalonica in 380, which declared Nicene Christianity the state religion of the Roman Empire.[10] In the first half of the fourth century, Eusebius, bishop of Caesarea (265–339), saw Constantine the Great (r. 306–337) as a pillar of orthodoxy, because it was to him that "... τὸν ἐπὶ πάντων Θεὸν τῶν ἐπὶ γῆς τὴν βασιλείαν παρασχεῖν" [God had bestowed the rulership of the earth].[11] Accordingly, Constantine was portrayed as "τῶν ἐκτὸς ὑπὸ θεοῦ καθεσταμένος, ἐπίσκοπος ἂν εἴην" [the supervisor of the external affairs of the Church, appointed by God] (*De Vita imperatoris Constantini*, 4:24, 1172AB),[12] and this concept was applied in the Theodosian Code (*Codex Theodosianus*) and Justinian Code (*Corpus Iuris Civilis*).[13] Justinian's *Leges Novellae* brought to the fore and explained the God-established dyarchy of the emperor and of the patriarch, smoothly

9 Cf. Daniela Müller, "Our Image of 'Others' and Our Own Identity," in *Iconoclasm and Iconoclash: Struggle for Religious Identity*, ed. Willem J. van Asselt, Paul Van Geest, Daniela Müller, and Theo Salemink (Leiden: Brill, 2007), 107–123 at 107–110, 115–118.

10 These doctrinal debates already arose at the First Council of Nicaea (325) and the First Council of Constantinople (381) and mainly revolved around Arianism, Apollinarism, Sabellianism, as well as incongruities regarding the questions related to the Holy Spirit; cf. Henry A. Myers, *Medieval Kingship*, in cooperation with Herwig Wolfram (Chicago: Nelson-Hall, 1982), 18–19.

11 Eusebius of Caesarea, *De Vita imperatoris Constantini*, ed. Jacques-Paul Migne, PG 20: 909–1252 (Paris: Imprimerie Catholique, 1857–1866), 4: ch. 29, col. 1180AB. Page numbers follow in parentheses; Cf. Meyers, *Medieval Kingship*, 24–25.

12 Cf. John Meyendorff, *Byzantine Theology: Historical Trends and Doctrinal Themes* (New York: Fordham University Press, 1974), 82.

13 *Theodosiani libri XVI cum constitutionibus Sirmondianis et leges novellae ad Theodosianum pertinentes*, ed. Theodor Mommsen and Paul Meyer (Berlin: Weidmann, 1905; Reprint 1954, 1970); Iacobus Gothofredus, *Codex Theodosianus 16,8,1–29*, Übersetzt und bearbeitet von Renate Frohne, Europäische Hochschulschriften, 3:453 (Frankfurt am Main: P. Lang, 1991); *The Theodosian Code And Novels And the Sirmondian Constitutions: A Translation with Commentary, Glossary, and Bibliography*, trans. Claude Pharr (Princeton, NJ: Princeton University Press, 1952); *Corpus Iuris Civilis. 2, Codex Justinianus*, ed. Paul Krueger (Berlin: Weidmann, 1954).

aligning with Justinian's theory of "symphony" between Church and state.[14] Priesthood and imperial dignity were considered the two greatest gifts which God granted men to administer divine and human affairs.[15] Both the Theodosian and Justinian Codes, organized in the form of a compilation of Roman Law in the fifth and sixth centuries, had a great impact on medieval policies, laws, and theology. The endeavors to eradicate heterodox doctrines were often based upon the Theodosian and Justinian Codes, as well as upon the decisions of the Ecumenical Synods and the writings of the Church Fathers.[16] Importantly, these codices officialized the Christian religion and refuted other belief systems and spiritual practices. The Theodosian and Justinian Codes provided formative elements and legal regulations for the treatment of heretics, which more frequently included exile, rather than execution, as punishment.

Book 16 of the Theodosian Code focuses on heresies and includes examples of exile as the primary punishment for heretics. It refers to each heterodox doctrine as *secta* [sect] and indicates that those who performed anything which was judged as "quod sit catholicae sectae contrarium adversumque"[17] [contrary and opposed to the Catholic sect] were subject to penalties.[18] According to the Theodosian Code, enemies of the Church have to be punished: "Omnes haereses omnesque perfidias, omnia schismata superstitionesque gentilium, omnes catholicae legi inimicos insectamur errores" [We prosecute all heresies and all perfidies, all schisms and superstitions of the pagans and false doctrines inimical to the Catholic faith] (Theodosian Code, 16.5.63, 462).[19] Disturbers of the Church's peace, particularly those who attempted to agitate against Church regulations, are also to be treated as traitors and severely punished: "… seditionis auctores pacisque turbatae ecclesiae, maiestatis capite ac sanguine sint supplicia luituri" [authors of sedition and as disturbers of the peace of the Church … shall pay the penalty of high treason with their lives and blood] (Theodosian Code, 16.4.1, 449).[20] The Theodosian Code dictates that religious

---

14 Cf. Meyendorff, *Byzantine Theology*, 83.

15 *Novella VI*, *Corpus juris civilis*, ed. Rudolfus Schoell (Berlin: Weidmann, 1928), 3:35–36, cited from Meyendorff, *Byzantine Theology*, 213.

16 Cf. Willemien Otten, "The Texture of Tradition: The Role of the Church Fathers in Carolingian Theology," in *The Reception of the Church Fathers in the West*, ed. Irena Backus (Leiden: Brill, 1997), 1:3–50; Meyendorff, *Byzantine Theology*, 20–23, 79–90.

17 *Theodosiani Libri*, ed. Mommsen and Meyer, 870; Theodosian Code, 16.5.44, 458. Hereafter, page numbers are given in parenthesis.

18 The here-translated Latin adjective *catholica* as "Catholic" refers to the universal/ecumenical Church, that is, to the Nicene creed.

19 *Theodosiani Libri*, ed. Mommsen and Meyer, 877.

20 *Theodosiani Libri*, ed. Mommsen and Meyer, 853.

privileges are reserved for the adherents of the Nicene creed only (Theodosian Code, 16.5.1, 450),[21] marks heretics unambiguously as outcasts, and defines their heterodoxy as a public crime: "… quia quod in religionem divinam committitur, in omnium fertur iniuriam" [… since that, what has been committed against the divine Christian worship inflicts injury to everyone] (Theodosian Code, 16.5.40.1, 457). Similarly, the Justinian Code prescribes that those who oppose the *vera fides* [true faith] are to be alienated from communion and from the Church for committing a crime against it, bringing detriment to all, as well as committing a crime against the public.[22]

Framing crimes against the Church as threats to the body politic in both Codes reflects an early medieval world-view in which Church and state were considered one body, whose head was Christ.[23] This theological frame of mind was rooted in the thought of Aurelius Augustine (354–430), bishop of Hippo (396–430), and its ensuing reception, which came to be called "political Augustinism,"[24] underlining the fact that Augustine considered obedience one of the highest virtues.[25] Ruler theology in ninth century Francia took shape at the Synod of Frankfurt (794), which officially elevated the king above the pope. Namely, Charlemagne was acclaimed as *rex et sacerdos* [king and priest] and heresy was deemed to be the primal enemy of the Frankish state.[26] The letter of Pope Gelasius I (492–496), composed in 494 and addressed to Emperor Anastasius I (r. 491–518), was read on that occasion:

21 *Theodosiani Libri*, ed. Mommsen and Meyer, 855.

22 *Codex Justinianus*, http://www.thelatinlibrary.com/justinian/codex1.shtml, accessed December 27, 2019, 1.5.4.1, and 1.1.8.30; *Codex Justinianus*, ed. Krueger, 51.

23 Cf. Thomas F.X. Noble, *Images, Iconoclasm, and the Carolingians* (Philadelphia: University of Pennsylvania Press, 2009), 358.

24 For more extensive information, see: Karlfried Froehlich, *Biblical Interpretation from the Church Fathers to the Reformation* (Farnham: Ashgate, 2010), 239–260; Henri-Xavier Arquillière, *L'augustinisme politique. Essai sur la formation des théories politiques au Moyen Âge* (Paris: Vrin, 1934; Reprint, 1955).

25 Augustine of Hippo, *De civitate Dei*, ed. Bernard Dombart and Alphonse Kalb, CCL 48 (Turnhout: Brepols, 1955), 14, 12, 434; see: Augustine, *De civitate Dei*, ed. Dombart and Kalb, 85–90; on medieval concepts of Christ-centered kingship, see: Ernst Kantorowicz, *The Kings's Two Bodies: A Study in Medieval Political Theology* (Princeton: Princeton University Press, 1957), 42–86.

26 Cf. Janet L. Nelson, "Religion in the age of Charlemagne," in *The Oxford Handbook of Medieval Christianity*, ed. John Arnold (Oxford: Oxford University Press, 2014), 490–514; Ullmann, *Carolingian Renaissance*, 43–70; Pezé, "Virus de l'erreur," 237–238; Heinrich Fichtenau, *The Carolingian Imperium*, trans. Peter Munz (Oxford: Basil Blackwell, 1957), 58.

> Duo quippe sunt, imperator auguste, quibus principaliter mundus hic regitur: auctoritas sacrata pontificum et regalis potestas, in quibus tanto gravius est pondus sacerdotum, quanto etiam pro ipsis regibus hominum in divino reddituri sunt examine rationem.[27]
>
> [Two elements, August Emperor, go into the means for ruling this world: the sacred authority of the pontiffs and the regal power. In their exercise, the responsibility of priests is heavier, all the more so because they must render an account before the divine judgment for the kings themselves.]

This letter laid the groundwork for ever more elaborate concepts of medieval ruler theology in the centuries to come, as it became a reference point in the debates encircling the sacerdotal *auctoritas* [authority] and imperial *potestas* [power]. This text, in fact, became the basis for later conceptions of the relationship between the ruler and the Pope, which would often be referred to throughout the entire early medieval period.[28]

A few decades later, the charge of the *imperium Christianum* [the Church and kingdom] was accorded to Louis the Pious in the *Admonitio ad omnes regni ordines* (*Admonition to All Ranks of the Kingdom*) of 825.[29] Consequently, the Council of Paris in 829 (where the letter of Pope Gelasius I was read again) laid the foundations for medieval political theory. This began the era of Carolingian ruler-symbolism, emphasizing the connection between the ruler and the Church and the impermeable bond between the two powers,

27 Cf. Pope Gelasius, *Concordantiam Discordantium Canonum Seu Decretum Gratiani*, ed. Jacques Paul Migne, PL 187 (Paris: Imprimerie Catholique, 1844–1855), 9–1870 at 458D–459B; Bronwen Neil and Pauline Allen, *The Letters of Gelasius I (492–496): Pastor and Micro-Manager of the Church of Rome* (Turnhout: Brepols, 2014), 73–80; Myers, *Medieval Kingship*, 54; Ullmann, *Carolingian Renaissance*, 89; see: Mayke de Jong, *The Penitential State: Authority and Atonement in the Age of Louis the Pious, 814–840* (Cambridge: Cambridge University Press, 2009), 176 n. 134.

28 Cf. Myers, *Medieval Kingship*, 54; Ullmann, *Carolingian Renaissance*, 89, 56–7; for more detailed information on the concept of secular and sacred authority in the Carolingian time, see: John Michael Wallace-Hadrill, "The Via Regia of the Carolingian Age," in *Trends in Medieval Political Thought*, ed. Beryl Smalley, 22–41 (New York: Blackwell, 1965); Joseph Canning, *A History of Medieval Political Thought: 300–1450* (New York: Routledge, 1996), 36–39; cf. Robert L. Benson, "The Gelasian Doctrine: Uses and Transformations," in *La notion d'autorité au Moyen Âge: Islam, Byzance, Occident. Colloques internationaux de la Napoule: Session des 23–26. Octobre 1978*, ed. George Makdisi, Dominique Sourdel, and Janine Sourdel-Thomine (Paris: Presses universitaires de France, 1982), 13–44.

29 Cf. *Admonitio ad omnes regni ordines*, ed. Alfred Boretius, MGH Capititularia regum Francorum 1:303–307 (Hannover: Hahn, 1883); see: Gen. 14:18–19.

ecclesiastical and royal.[30] These two persons—the primary authorities of the world order—were understood to work cohesively and in harmony, with the patriarch looking after the souls of the people, and the emperor responsible for the well-being of his subjects. Moreover, theology, history, and politics became more pronouncedly intertwined: theological debates which arose in the ninth century were conducted in respect to the historical and political contexts in which they were embedded.

In an analogous way, ninth-century medieval political theory gave bishops a predominant role in mediating between God and the ruler and a responsibility for maintaining cohesion in the realm, since the negligence of this office could provoke social disorder and scandal.[31] It was the bishop who, together with the king, represented the image of God on earth.[32] For example, in his *De divortio Lothari regis et Theutbergae reginae* composed in 860, Hincmar severely criticizes neglectful bishops for causing a lack of discipline in the population.[33] Following the Theodosian Code, a former bishop was to be apprehended for having acted against the public security or public peace, and sentenced to exile (Theodosian Code, 16.2.35, 446).[34]

Augustine, who refuted heresies in numerous works, giving an impetus and direction to the textual treatment of heresies in the following centuries, argues that the sin was greater for someone who had once been in the Church and deserted it than for the person who had never been a part of it.[35] He maintains that those who fall into heresy or into non-Christian superstitions—including

---

30 See: Ullmann, *Carolingian Renaissance*, 43–64.

31 Jong, *Penitential State*, 176–183.

32 Cf. Affeldt, *Weltliche Gewalt in der Paulusexegese*, 75; Georges Dumézil, *Jupiter, Mars, Quirinus. Essai sur la conception indo-européenne de la société et sur les origines de Rome* (Paris: Gallimard, 1941), 81f.

33 Hincmar of Reims, *De divortio Lotharii regis et Theutbergae reginae*, ed. Letha Böhringer, MGH Concilia 4, Suppl.1, 99–261 (Hannover: Hahn, 1992), 261. See my forthcoming article, "The Cohesive Force of Hierarchy in the Carolingian Era: The Interpretation of Romans 13:1–7 by Hrabanus, Hincmar, and Gottschalk," in *Social Cohesion and its Limits/Identity and Religion*, ed. Walter Pohl and Andreas Fischer (Vienna: Institut für Mittelalterforschung).

34 *Theodosiani Libri*, ed. Mommsen and Meyer, 847.

35 Some of the most influential of Augustine's works on heresies include: *De baptismo contra Donatistas libri septem*, ed. Migne, PL 43: 107–244; *Adversus Quinque Haereses*, ed. Migne, PL 42: 1099–1116; *Contra Epistolam Manichaei*, ed. Migne, PL 42: 173–206; *Contra Sermonem Arianorum*, ed. Migne, PL 42: 683–708; *Contra Sermonem Arianorum*, ed. Max Josef Suda, CSEL 92 (Vienna: Verlag der österreichischen Akademie der Wissenschaften, 2000), 1–126; *De Gestis Pelagii*, ed. Migne, PL 44: 319–360; *De Haeresibus*, ed. Migne, PL 42: 21–50; *De Haeresibus*, ed. Roel Vander Plaetse and Clemens Beukers, CCL 46 (Turnhout: Brepols, 1969).

the heresiarchs, founders of heresies—fall out of the body of Christ, and are exiled from it.[36] Augustine also insists that these dissenters become part of a new body, the body of the devil, in opposition to the body of the Church. Hence, the devil is the head of the impious ones who constitute his body and are doomed to eternal fire; on the other hand, Christ, the head of the Church, leads those who shall enter into heavenly glory.[37] Augustine underscores the notion that the Church, according to the apostolic teachings, represents the body of Christ, which is also called his spouse. Thus, Christ "Corpus ergo suum multis membris diversa officia gerentibus, nodo unitatis et charitatis tanquam sanitatis astringit" [... binds his body together, which is constituted of many members endowed with diverse functions, by means of unity and charity—thus reflecting (its) well-being].[38] Augustine thus intrinsically connects the *corpus Christi* [the body of Christ] and *membra Christi* [the limbs of Christ].[39] In a similar tone, Jerome (*c.*347–419/20), Augustine's near contemporary, warns of the *putridas carnes* [putrid flesh] that should be cut off.[40] This implies that the severance of the unbelievers from the body of the Church—potentially through exile—was necessary, as the putrid body part represented an imminent threat of contamination to the entire body of believers.

In ninth-century Francia, Hrabanus Maurus stressed the importance of abiding in the "body of the Church," aligning the symbolism of unity with the Eucharist. According to a passage from his *De clericorum institutione* (*c.*819), those who comprise part of Christ's body should live; one must strive not to become separated from it and alienated from salvation.[41] Hrabanus describes believers as *membra corporis Christi* [limbs of the body of Christ] who should stay jointly bound;[42] in contrast, he compares sinners to the limbs of sinners, modeled after the image of Judas.[43] The Eucharist "aeternam societatem capitis membrorumque suorum significat ... Quicunque enim ejus particeps fuerit, id est, Christo capiti membrum associatus fuerit in regno coelesti" [represents

36 Augustine, *De civitate Dei*, ed. Migne, 21.741–742; Augustine, *De civitate Dei*, ed. Dombart and Kalb, 21.794–796.

37 Augustine, *De doctrina Christiana*, ed. Klaus-Detlef Daur and Joseph Martin, CCSL 32 (Turnhout: Brepols, 1962), 114.

38 Augustine, *De Doctrina Christiana Libri Quatuor*, ed. Migne, PL 34:0015–0122 at 1:25.

39 Augustine, *Enarrationes in Psalmos*, ed. Migne, PL 37:1033–1967 at 1842.

40 Jerome, *Commentarii in Sophoniam Prophetam*, ed. Migne, PL 25:1337–1388A at 1:1351D.

41 Hrabanus Maurus, *De clericorum institutione ad Heistulphum Archiepiscopum Libri Tres*, ed. Migne, PL 107: 293–420A at 1:ch. 31, 321C; cf. *Hrabanus Maurus, De Institutione clericorum: Über die Unterweisung der Geistlichen* I, ed. Detlev Zimpel (Turnhout: Brepols, 2006).

42 Cf. Hrabanus, *Epistolae*, ed. Ernst Dümmler, MGH Epp. 5, 379–516 (Berlin: Weidmann, 1898–1899), 481–487: *fides recta* versus *haec secta*.

43 Hrabanus, *De clericorum institutione*, ed. Migne, 1: ch. 31, 319D.

the eternal food and drink and community constituted by the head and its limbs … Whoever participates in it, will represent a limb of Christ the head in the heavenly kingdom].[44] Hrabanus also accentuates the role of the sacraments: "In virtute enim sacramenti omnia membra capiti suo conjuncta et coadunate … nos in corpus Christi convertimur dum oboedienter et pie vivimus" [It is through virtue of the sacraments that all the limbs become fused and attached with the head … We get transformed in the body of Christ if we lead a life of piety and obedience] (*De clericorum institutione*, 318 A). The principle of obedience is described as a ligature, attaching the limbs of the "body of the Church" together in unity.[45] Consequently, Hrabanus sees Gottschalk through that lens and condemns his doctrine of twofold predestination as being new, perverted, and heretical.

In the ninth century, the Eastern and Western churches constituted one Christian Ecumene. In Byzantium, just as in Francia, Church and state were also viewed as organisms with two equally important rulers at their heads: the Emperor and the Patriarch.[46] Byzantine literature includes similar symbols of bodily unity.[47] In his *Contra Manichaeos*, written around 871–872, Photius describes the importance of the Eucharist: "Ὁ δὲ τρισαλιτήριος πάλιν τόν τε ἀτιμίαις ὑπάγοντα τὸ σῶμα καὶ αἷμα Χριστοῦ τοῦ θεοῦ ἡμῶν καὶ τὸν τῆς μετοχῆς αὐτῶν ἔξω διαμένοντα τῷ ἀναθέματι παρετίθετο" [The most wicked of all is the person who brings the body and blood of Christ to defamation, and he, who does not participate in the Eucharist, is to be anathematized].[48] Photius elaborates on the limbs which make the unity of the "body of the Church" and on the severance of the limbs, which: "… Χριστοῦ τῆς κεφαλῆς διασπομενά τε καὶ ἀποφθειρόμενα" [… had been torn apart and disconnected from Christ, the head of the Church].[49] In numerous letters composed during his exiles, Theodore spread his opinions, addressing pivotal issues on which he diverged from the key ecclesiastics of his time. In one of his letters addressed to Naucratius,

44 Hrabanus, *De clericorum institutione*, ed. Migne, 1: ch. 31, 317AD. Page numbers are given in parenthesis.

45 Cf. Celia Chazelle, "The Eucharist in Early Medieval Europe," in *A Companion to the Eucharist in the Middle Ages*, ed. Ian Levy, Gary Macy, and Kristen Van Ausdall, 205–250 (Leiden: Brill, 2012), 206–208.

46 Despina Stratoudaki White, *Patriarch Photios of Constantinople: His Life, Scholarly Contributions, and Correspondence Together with a Translation of Fifty-two of His Letters* (Brookline, MA: Holy Cross Orthodox Press, 1981), 139–155, 193–194; Photius, *Epistolarum Libri Tres*, ed. Migne, PG 102: 585–1000, 1:Ep. 14, 742D–764D at 764AD.

47 Cf. Kenneth Parry, *Depicting the World: Byzantine Iconophile Thought of the Eighth and Ninth Centuries* (Leiden: Brill, 1996), 178–190.

48 Photius, *Contra Manichaeos*, ed. Migne, PG 102: 15–0264 at 56AB.

49 Photius, *Epistolae*, ed. Migne, 1: Ep. 14, 756CD.

Theodore also depicts heretics as severed from the body of Christ: ... ἑαυτοὺς ἀπέρρηξαν τοῦ σώματος τοῦ Χριστοῦ, τοῦ κορυφιακοῦ θρόνου, ἐν ᾧ Χριστὸς ἔθετο τάς κλεῖς τῆς πίστεως[50] [... who have cut themselves off the body of Christ, of the most-high throne, in which Christ has placed the keys of faith]. In the Byzantine Empire, as in Francia, the Eucharist represented both the body of Christ and the embodiment of the unity of the Church and believers.[51] As reflected in the early Christian theological texts, the Eucharist ensures unity of the body of the Church. The Pauline introduction of the allegorical portrayal of Christ's body as the Church was sublimely elaborated upon in the metaphor of Christ's mystical body consisting of the members of the Church. This imagery found its most refined apogee in the fourth-century Syriac Christian hymnography, heralded by Aphrahat and Ephrem the Syrian.[52]

Furthermore, severance from the "body of the Church" and the Eucharist often represents the first stage in the sequestration of heretics in these texts. Major theologians in both the Frankish and the Byzantine contexts not only stressed the necessity of severing heretics from the "body of the Church" to protect its spiritual well-being, but also emphasized the role of the Eucharist as a way for the faithful to physically, as well as symbolically, be united in the Church and in the body of Christ.[53] Because the Church represented Christ's body and the Bride of Christ, the participants in the Eucharist were understood to be enlivening both their genuine connection with Christ and their bond with Ecclesia, thus solidifying and strengthening the social body of believers.[54]

Conversely, to be excluded from the liturgy was understood as a form of spiritual and social alienation at the same time. As Theodore explains in one of his epistles, if a person cultivates contacts with heretics, or obtains their benediction, or simply maintains relations with them, he or she is forbidden to participate in the Eucharistic service, for a more or less long period—sometimes

---

50 Theodore the Studite, *Epistolarium libri duo*, ed. Migne, PG 99: 903–1679, 2:Ep. 53, 1281–1284 at 1281A. Page numbers follow in parenthesis.

51 Cf. Meyendorff, *Byzantine Theology*, 206–210.

52 Cf. Robert Murray, *Symbols of Church and Kingdom: A Study in Early Syriac Tradition* (Piscataway, NJ: Gorgias Press, 2004), 86–93; Jean Daniélou, *Primitive Christian Symbols*, trans. Donald Attwater (Baltimore: Helicon Press, 1964), 58–70.

53 Ganz, "Theology and Organization of Thought," 777–780. Deliberations on the nature of the Eucharist influenced even the court of Charles the Bald. Paschasius Radbertus also wrote extensively on the issue of the presence of Christ's flesh and blood in the Eucharist service.

54 Paschasius Radbertus, *Liber de corpore et sanguine Domini*, ed. Migne, PL 120: 1267–1350, 1284 BD–1285A.

even until his or her death.[55] The penance should last, implies Theodore, "ἕως ἂν ἀναλάμψῃ ἡ τῆς ὀρθοδοξίας αἰθρία" [until the serenity of the orthodox faith re-emerges] (*Epistolae*, 2, 1148C).[56]

According to Hincmar's *De Una et non trina Deitate* (856–857), "Pastoralis tamen necessitas habet … separare ab ovibus sanis morbidam … ut omnes velimus salvos fieri …"[57] [It is necessary for the ecclesiastics to exclude the diseased sheep from the flock, since we wish all to be saved] (*De una et non trina Deitate*, 483A). Hincmar underlines the severity of this exclusion from the ecclesiastical unity: "Quisquis autem a catholica Ecclesia fuerit separatus … hoc solo scelere, quod a Christi unitate disjuncuts est, non habebit vitam, sed ira Dei manet super eum" [He, who is excluded from the catholic Church, is by this very crime disjoint from the unity in Christ, and he shall not live, but the wrath of God will stay upon him] (*De una et non trina Deitate*, 483B).[58] In another metaphoric formulation, he insists that it is of the utmost importance to sever the roots so the crooked branches can dry out.[59] One specific example of dissent upon which Hincmar focuses his analysis is that of Gottschalk. In his *De Una et non trina Deitate*, Hincmar states—just as Hrabanus did—that Gottschalk must be expelled from the Eucharist. He should be punished, like every impious, obstinate, insolent, or disobedient monk, according to St. Benedict, who established the precepts of monastic discipline.[60] Gottschalk should be segregated from the healthy limbs of the body of Christ, Hincmar argues, to prevent him from harming the rest of the body. In other words, he should be exiled from the community of the Church—a living execution of sorts.

In the following section of the narrative, Hincmar expands on the reasons that have led him to judge Gottschalk guilty for his doctrine on double predestination, segregate him from the participation in the body and blood of Christ, and excommunicate him.[61] In Hincmar's view, sinners represent the limbs on the Devil's body, and the Devil wishes to harm God's body: "… qui illud inaestimabile Domini corpus violare praesumit" [attempts to defy the body of the

55 Theodore the Studite, *Epistolae*, ed. Migne, 2: Ep. 32, 1205AB (referring to John Chrysostom); Ep. 11, 1148C; Ep. 95, 1348C.

56 Theodore the Studite, *Epistolae*, ed. Migne, 2: Ep. 11, 1148C.

57 Hincmar, *De una et non trina Deitate*, ed. Migne, PL 125:473–0618 at 483A. Page numbers are given in parentheses.

58 The here-translated Latin adjective *catholica* as "catholic" refers to the universal/ecumenical Church, that is, to the Nicene creed.

59 Hincmar, *De una et non trina Deitate*, ed. Migne, 501CD.

60 Hincmar, *De una et non trina Deitate*, ed. Migne, 615BC.

61 Hincmar, *De una et non trina Deitate*, ed. Migne, 616AD.

Lord].[62] Therefore, Christians cannot live without communion with God and the remission of sins. Consequently, those who enter into communion with "the Prostitute" become one in body with her, different from those who enter into communion and unity with God.[63] After comparing Gottschalk to Simon the Magician, Hincmar addresses the core issue of double predestination that led to Gottschalk's condemnation, and expresses his opinion that anyone who evangelizes without the benediction of the Holy Spirit and six ecclesiastical councils is to be anathematized.[64] Furthermore, anyone who acts outside the frame of the scriptural tradition and the tradition of the Church Fathers is to be condemned and separated from the community by exile or imprisonment, so that he will not endanger the others.[65] In other words, Hincmar emphasizes the importance of unity: unity of the Church, as well as of the empire, by foregrounding the precept that there is only one faith, one baptism, one kingdom, one Church, and one Christian law.[66]

To further justify his approach to heresy, Hincmar refers to the actions undertaken by the Ecumenical synods to condemn heresies in the past, which served as a precedent for any heresy that might have emerged. Hincmar quotes the eighteenth act of the Sixth Ecumenical Synod (680/1), to which Gottschalk also alludes in his interpretation of the Trinitarian issue, that clearly states and defines the concept of "anathema." The Synod determined that those who accepted and taught a doctrine of faith other than the ones proclaimed by the Ecumenical councils, and those who altered the symbol of faith, were to be expelled from the Church, anathematized, and subject to exile.[67]

Byzantine authors who tackled the topic of religious dissent also stressed the importance of the Eucharist and the danger of being disconnected from it, often in strikingly similar terms. In a long letter written during his first exile, Photius mentions the "members/limbs of Christ ... with which we are united ... being both torn asunder and utterly destroyed," quoting 1 Cor. 12:12–27.[68] He does not refer explicitly to heretics here, but rather to the members of the Church. Furthermore, he writes that discord in the Church provokes serious

62 Hincmar, *Hincmari archiepiscopi Remensis epistolae*, ed. Ernst Perels, MGH Epp. 8:1–228 (Berlin: Weidmann, 1939), Ep. 127, 66, l. 27–29.

63 Hincmar, *Epistolae*, ed. Perels, Ep. 125, 62, l. 2.

64 Hincmar, *De una et non trina Deitate*, ed. Migne, 495BC.

65 Hincmar, *De una et non trina Deitate*, ed. Migne, 495CD.

66 Hincmar, *De divortio Lotharii regis*, ed. Böhringer, 236: ... *unus dominus, una fides, unum baptisma, unus deus et pater omnium ... unum regnum, una Christi columba, videlicet sancta ecclesia, unius Christianitatis lege, regni unius et unius ecclesiae.*

67 Hincmar, *De una et non trina Deitate*, ed. Migne, 528AB.

68 Cf. Stratoudaki White, *Patriarch Photios of Constantinople*, Ep. 8, 149.

consequences, resulting in "... ἐν ἐκκλησίᾳ δὲ διασπορὰν τῶν μελῶν καὶ τῆς κατὰ τὴν εὐσέβειαν ἁρμονίας ἔκλυσιν" [the scattering of her members and the dissolution of harmony which attends piety].[69] The heretics are torn away from the Lord's body, the Church: "... τὰ μέλη αὐτοῦ τῆς νύμφης ἐκκλησίας ἀποσπαράξας μέλη τῆς πόρνης παρασυναγωγῆς ἀπεργάζεται" [and they do not represent the members of the "body of the Church" any more, but become the members of the "harlot conventicle" instead] (162, l.21–22). Those drawn to impious heresies or those who fall into schismatic madness are "... τοῦ κυριακοῦ σώματος τῆς ἐκκλησίας διασπώμενος" [torn apart from the Church, Lord's body] (162, l.16–17, 19–20).[70] Theodore was strongly opposed to capital punishment, preferring exile or excommunication. In the early ninth century, the Armenian Paulicians posed a threat to the doctrinal stability of the Christian Church of Constantinople. Prominent theologians started writing on the danger of this heresy, and the ecclesiastical and state authorities looked for ways to deal with it.[71] Emperor Michael I Rangabe (r. 811–813) decreed that the Paulicians be subjected to capital punishment.[72] However, sometime between 815 and 818, Theodore found himself exiled for the third time and composed a letter in which he underlines the importance of non-violence, repeating the words from the Gospel of Matthew that "all that take the sword shall perish by the sword."[73] In another epistle composed a few years later, Theodore refers to St. John the Chrysostomos's homilies on the Gospel of Matthew and to St. Denys the Areopagite whilst insisting that the heretics should not be put to death, thus expressing his condemnation of death penalty: "... εἰ δὲ οὐ τύπτειν δεῖ σχολῇ γοῦν αὐτοὺς κτένειν ... ὅτι μαχαίρᾳ ἡ 'Εκκλησία οὐκ ἐκδικεῖ" [... should not be punished, and by no means killed, because the Church should not take vengeance by a sword] (*Epistolae*, 2, 1485 AD).

Likewise, the Theodosian Code emphasized deportation and/or exile as a punishment for several sins against the Church, rather than execution. The Code specified deportation explicitly as the punishment, for "Deportatione dignus est, qui nec generali lege admonitus nec competenti sententia emendatus et fidem catholicam turbat et populum" [the person who disturbs both the

69 Photius's Sixteenth homily, *Photius. The Homilies of Photius Patriarch of Constantinople*, trans. Cyril Mango (Cambridge, MA: Harvard University Press, 1958), 275; Photius, *Homilies*, ed. Vasileios Laourda (Thessaloniki: ΠΑΡΑΡΤΗΜΑ, 1959), 161, l.9–13. Page numbers are given in parentheses.

70 Cf. 1 Cor. 6:16.

71 Cf. *The Chronicle of Theophanes*, trans. Harry Turtledove (Philadelphia: University of Pennsylvania Press, 1982), 174–175.

72 Cf. *Chronicle of Theophanes*, 495; Photius, *Contra Manichaeos*, ed. Migne, 77A.

73 Cf. Mt. 26:52.

Catholic faith and the people and if he has failed to heed the admonition of the general law] (Theodosian Code, 16.4.3, 449).[74] The Theodosian Code clearly demonstrates that the adherents to heresies and other religions were often sentenced to exile.[75] Furthermore, those who polluted the divine (Christian) teaching with sacrilegious rites were also to be sent into exile, in some cases to solitary islands.[76] The Code states that heretics should be expelled beyond the city boundary, *extra moenia urbis*, and it also proscribes exile for "pagans" who offer sacrifices to demons.[77]

Like the *Codex Theodosianus*, the Justinian Code also calls for heretics to be expelled beyond the city walls.[78] According to the Code, heretics bear different names, but perform the equivalent sacrilege and are, therefore, mutually connected by their crimes.[79] The Code deems non-Christian rites criminal and requires corporal punishment followed by perpetual exile to be imposed on the owners of houses in which these rites have been performed.[80] Both the Theodosian Code and the Justinian Code clearly exemplify an urge to sequestrate heretics from the inhabitants of the Ecumene, in both the geographical and spiritual sense. The practice of banishing heretics grew more habitual and current after the exile of Arius during the first Council of Nicaea in 325, as the authorities started to normatively and legally sanction the resurging heresies.[81]

In cases of heresy, repentance was a penultimate process upon which the execution of penance—which often included exile—depended.[82] In the early

74 *Theodosiani Libri*, ed. Mommsen and Meyer, 854; cf. *Theodosiani Libri*, ed. Mommsen and Meyer, 875; Theodosian Code, 16.5.57, 461.

75 *Theodosiani Libri*, ed. Mommsen and Meyer, 863–864; Theodosian Code, 16.5.25, 454.

76 *Theodosiani Libri*, ed. Mommsen and Meyer, 872–873; Theodosian Code, 16.5.52, 5, 459.

77 *Theodosiani Libri*, ed. Mommsen and Meyer, 864–865; 904; Theodosian Code, 16.5.29, 455; 16.10.21, 475–476.

78 *Codex Justinianus*, 1.5.5.1; *Codex Justinianus*, ed. Krueger, 51.

79 *Codex Justinianus*, 1.5.8.2; *Codex Justinianus*, ed. Krueger, 52.

80 *Codex Justinianus*, 1.11.8.1; *Codex Justinianus*, ed. Krueger, 63.

81 Cf. Edward Peters, ed., *Heresy and Authority in Medieval Europe: Documents in Translation* (Philadelphia: University of Pennsylvania Press, 1980), 1–12; Robert F. Gorman, "Persecution and Exile in the Patristic Period: Athanasian and Augustinian Perspectives," *Journal of Refugee Studies* 6.1 (1993), 40–55 at 43–46.

82 The extensive bibliography on the exhaustive topic of medieval repentance include: Claudia Rapp, "Spiritual Guarantors at Penance, Baptism and Ordination in the Late Antique East," in *A New History of Penance*, ed. Abigail Firey (Leiden: Brill 2008), 121–148; Rob Meens, "The Historiography of Early Medieval Penance," in *A New History of Penance*, ed. Abigail Firey (Leiden: Brill, 2008), 73–96; Mayke De Jong, "Transformations of Penance," in *Rituals of Power: From Late Antiquity to the Early Middle Ages*, ed. Frans Theuws and Janet L. Nelson (Leiden: Brill, 2000), 185–224; Mayke de Jong, "Power and

Middle Ages, the exclusion from communion followed public acknowledgment of sin. During the reign of Louis the Pious, many political opponents were banished, including Wala, Benedictine abbot of Corbie (*c.*755–836), who suffered exile twice: in 814 (after which he was rehabilitated in 822) and for the second time in 830.[83] His banishment was related to the turbulent events of the 820s; the year 827 brought some undesired turmoil into the Carolingian realm, mainly provoked by the incursions of the Bulgarian and Slavonic tribes in Pannonia and the unsuccessful raids against the Saracens in the Spanish March. Louis the Pious convened councils in 829 aimed at finding a solution that would bring peace to the realm and—in tune with the very foundations of Carolingian ruler theology—appease God's anger. Consequently, Wala and Einhard (*c.*770–840) composed a *correctio*, acts of repentance based upon extracts from the Bible and the Church Fathers, as required by the Emperor.[84] The Council of Paris held in 829 tackled the question of negligence of office, implying that bishops and king's ministers were a possible cause of God's anger.[85] Moreover, Louis the Pious applied public penance in the form of monastic exile, as a demonstration of royal discipline.[86] In the aftermath of rebellion, the culprits would also be subjected to internal exile by being sent to monasteries.[87]

In a letter written in response to the Bulgars' conversion in the heat of the Filioque controversy about the inclusion of the "Son" in refence to the Holy Spirit, Pope Nicholas describes exile as a type of penance.[88] He compares the penance of exile to the severance of limbs, since the *exilés* should be placed outside the society (and by implication, outside the hierarchy) that banished him. The comprehensive section of this epistle tackles different forms of exile: by quoting scriptural verses (e.g. Gen. 12:1,4), Nicholas distinguishes between *exilium* and *fuga*—*exilium* as voluntary departure, as with Abraham, whereas *fuga* corresponds to flight, or an imposed departure.[89]

Humility in Carolingian Society: The Public Penance of Louis the Pious," *EME* 1 (1992): 29–52; Cyrille Vogel, *Les "Libri Paenitentiales"* (Turnhout: Brepols, 1978).

83 Cf. Jong, *Penitential State*, 123–127.

84 Jong, *Penitential State*, 171–174.

85 Jong, *Penitential State*, 40.

86 Jong, *Penitential State*, 232–234; Jong, "Power and Humility in Carolingian Society."

87 Jong, *Penitential State*, 29, 23.

88 Pope Nicholas I, *Epistolae*, ed. Ernst Perels, MGH Epp. 6: 257–690 (Berlin: Weidmann, 1925), Ep. 99, 576, l. 40–41.

89 Nicholas, *Epistolae*, ed. Perels, Ep. 99, 579, l.1–11; cf. Gaertner, "The Discourse of Displacement in Greco-Roman Antiquity," 1–3.

Dedicated to the growth of the seed of *fides recta* [the true faith] among the newly-baptized Bulgars as a counterbalance to idolatry, and hoping to prevent their potential relapse, Nicholas refers to St. Paul's epistle to remind them that those *qui foris sunt* [who are outside] do not represent St. Paul's concern.[90] He employs the term *alienus* in a similar sense in reference to Photius, who started his career as a layman. The notion of *alienus*—foreigner; he who is outside—becomes the key-word in Nicholas's rhetoric of theological positioning and self-representation.[91] In another letter, also composed at the peak of the Photian Schism, Nicholas expounds on the lay and clerical ranks in his condemnation of Photius's election, having argued that Photius ascended from a lay rank and reached the patriarchal office too swiftly.[92] With these words, Nicholas implicitly connects the status of foreigner and layman in affairs pertaining to the ecclesiastical cursus. In this way, he frames dissent as a refusal to accept the norm, a defiance of the authorities proscribing the norm, as well as an affront to order, convention, and tradition in a wider sense.

At the same time, however, discourses of self-representation in this period also drew on more allegorical or poetic conceptions of exile derived from the early Christians, who saw themselves as outsiders and foreigners. Paul's epistles include several instances of exilic self-identification: "… et confitentes quia peregrini et hospites sunt super terram" [… and confessing that they are pilgrims and strangers on the earth];[93] "Carissimi obsecro tamquam advenas et peregrinos abstinere vos a carnalibus desideriis quae militant adversus animam … Ergo jam non estis hospites, et advenæ: sed estis cives sanctorum, et domestici Dei" [Dearly beloved, I beseech you as strangers and pilgrims, to refrain yourselves from carnal desires which war against the soul … Now therefore you are no more strangers and foreigners; but you are fellow citizens with the saints, and the domestics of God].[94] Whereas secular forms of exile functioned mainly as political and social banishment, voluntary exile—intertwined with the early Christian ascetic tradition—was understood by its theorists and practitioners within the semantic field of pilgrimage and monasticism, as spiritual

90 Cf. 1 Cor. 5:12, 13; Nicholas, *Epistolae*, ed. Perels, Ep. 99, 582, l. 40, and 583, l. 20–22.

91 Cf. Dion C. Smythe, "Insiders and Outsiders," in *A Companion to Byzantium*, ed. Liz James (Oxford: Wiley-Blackwell, 2010), 67–80; Michael Goodich, "Foreigner, Foe and Neighbor: The Religious Cult as a Forum for Political Reconciliation," in *Meeting the Foreign in the Middle Ages*, ed. Albrecht Classen (New York: Routledge, 2002), 11–26.

92 These events marked the upsurge of the so-called Photian Schism; cf. Nicholas, *Epistolae*, ed. Perels, Ep. 98, 564, l.8–11.

93 Epistle to Hebrews, 11:13, to note only some.

94 Douay-Rheims Bible, 1 Petr. 2:11; Ephes. 2:19.

exile from the world.[95] Thus, in the early Middle Ages, exile took two forms: as punishment, since heretics were frequently exiled, or as a search for the divine realm on earth, an idea rooted both in Scripture and in Augustine's observation that we are all foreigners and *peregrini sumus* [pilgrims on earth].[96]

Being essentially metaphorical, this hermitic notion of exile, which emerged in the deserts, could be transposed onto other allegorical structures, including and especially the medieval tradition of *navigatio* [seafaring]. The ascetic practice of self-exile was understood to resemble a sea journey with all its "tempests" or, further West in the Christian *Oikoumene*, the Irish *peregrini* navigating in search of the Otherworld, with the sea reflecting the desert of the Byzantine ascetics.[97] The legend of St. Brendan describes a pious monk who abandoned his everyday life and embarked on a sea-journey. He was later consecrated as abbot and enjoyed the company of numerous followers after his voyage, which allowed him to see the Otherworld: Paradise as well as Hell.[98] Some apocryphal texts, like the *Visio Pauli* in which St. Paul finds himself on a ship on his journey to Rome, include the metaphor of the sea.[99] In Byzantium, prose authors like Photius employed this well-known metaphor of the stormy sea to symbolize the troubles of life.[100] The motif of the sea and the sea-journey is also present in the poems of Theodore the Studite. He compares life to navigation—*εὔπλους βίος*. Theodore opens the poem by addressing

---

95 See: Philip Sheldrake, *Living Between Worlds: Place and Journey in Celtic Spirituality* (London: Darton, Longman, and Todd, 1995).

96 In his *De civitate Dei*, Augustine recurred numerous times to the terms *peregrinatio* and *peregrini*. See: Martin A. Claussen, "'*Peregrinatio*' and '*Peregrini*' in Augustine's '*City of God*,'" *Traditio* 46 (1991): 33–75. Cf. Peter Brown, *Augustine of Hippo: A Biography* (Berkeley: University of California Press, 1975), 312–329, esp. 314; Augustine, *Sermo XX, de Verbis psalmi XXXVIII*, in *Sancti Aurelii Augustiniani Opera Omnia, post Lovaniensium theologorum recensionem*, 10, ed. Monachorum ordinis Sancti Benedicti (Paris: Montrouge, 1841), 908.

97 Cf. Sebastian I. Sobecki, *Sea and Medieval English Literature* (Woodbridge: Boydell Press, 2007), 21–22, 25–40, 48–55; Jude S. Mackley, *The Legend of St. Brendan: A Comparative Study of the Latin and Anglo-Norman Versions* (Leiden: Brill, 2008); Dorothy Whitelock, "The Interpretation of *The Seafarer*," in *Early Cultures of Northwest Europe*, ed. Cyril Fox and Bruce Dickins (Cambridge: Cambridge University Press, 1950), 261–272; Sebastian I. Sobecki, "The Interpretation of the Seafarer: A Re-examination of the Pilgrimage Theory," *Neophilologus* 92.1 (2008): 127–139. See Follett in this volume.

98 Cf. Mario Esposito, "An Apocryphal 'Book of Enoch and Elias' as a Possible Source of *Navigatio Sancti Brendani*," *Celtica* 5 (1960): 192–206.

99 Carl Schmidt, *Acta Pauli, nach dem Papyrus der Hamburger Staats- und Universitäts—Bibliothek* (Hamburg: Veröffentlichungen aus der Hamburger Staats-und Universitäts-Bibliothek, 1936).

100 *Homilies of Photius*, 110; Photius, *Homiles*, ed. Laourda, 52, l.15–22.

mortals, Ἄνδρες βροτοί, inciting them to "φύγωμεν ἐκ κόσμου πλάνου" [flee the deceits of this world]. The only concern for a monk, according to Theodore, is reaching a tranquil harbor where the burdens of pain will cease.[101] Carolingian authors also made frequent associations between seafaring and metaphorical exile, especially in poetic works: "Exul ego diuscule / Hoc in mare sum, domine" [For some little time I have been an exile, On this sea, Lord].[102]

This potent image of spiritual exile as a form of seafaring connected to the allegorical representation of the state as a ship, and of the ruler as its captain. This complex metaphor stemmed from classical antiquity: Cicero refers to the image of the state-ship, describing the ruler of the state as *gubernator*.[103] This became a common trope, exemplified by the mid-ninth century treatise composed by Sedulius Scottus, *Liber de rectoribus Christianis*.[104] Sedulius employs the designation *gubernator* for a ruler;[105] Gottschalk uses the same metaphor for Christ.[106] Similarly, praising the accomplishments of Emperor Constantine, Eusebius described him as a κυβερνήτης [pilot] in charge of the σκάφος [vessel] of the state.[107] Thus, the concept of self-exile was not only connected to the ascetic renunciation of worldly pleasures and pursuits; it also sprang out of Early Christian notions of the exiled state, intrinsically related to the aspiration to flee worldly aspirations and regain the state of paradise.

This terminology was still *en vogue* in the Carolingian epoch.[108] Corresponding with the later ninth-century applications of this topos to the actual situations of the epoch, the body of the Church was imagined as a ship carrying men through a storm. This idea was present in earlier Christian theological treatises:

---

101 Cf. *Theodoros Studites. Jamben, auf verschiedene Gegenstände*, ed. and trans. Paul Speck (Berlin: De Gruyter, 1968), 116.

102 Translation in Gillis, "Gottschalk of Orbais," 275, note 168; cf. Gottschalk of Orbais, *Ut quid iubes*, in *Godescalci Carmina*, ed. Ludwig Traube, MGH PLAC 3: 723–738 (Berlin: Weidmann, 1896), 9:732; Marie-Luise Weber, *Die Gedichte des Gottschalk von Orbais* (Frankfurt am Main: P. Lang, 1992), 150.

103 Cf. Scharer, *Herrschaft und Repräsentation*, 171–174; on the prevalent influence of Cicero in Sedulius's texts, but also in Einhard, see especially notes 335 and 336 on the page 171.

104 Cf. Anton Scharer, *Herrschaft und Repräsentation*. Habilitationsschrift an der Geistwissenschaftlichen Fakultät der Universität Wien (University of Vienna, 1998), 171–175; Sedulius Scottus, *Liber de rectoribus Christianis*, in *Sedulius Scottus*, ed. Siegmund Hellmann (München: C.H. Beck, 1906); Robert W. Dyson, ed., *Sedulius Scottus, De Rectoribus Christianis* (Woodbridge: Boydell Press, 2010).

105 Cf. Hellmann, *Sedulius Scottus*, ch. 9, 47.

106 Cf. Gottschalk, *Christe rex regum*, in *Godescalci carmina*, ed. Traube, 728.

107 Eusebius, *De Laudibus Constantini Oratio in ejus Tricennalibus Habita*, ed. Migne, PG 20:1316–1440 at 2: ch. 7, 1356BC, cf. Myers, *Medieval Kingship*, 24.

108 Cf. Scharer, *Herrschaft und Repräsentation*, 173, note 345; 174, note 346.

for example, in the Pseudo-Clementine homilies, dated to the fourth century.[109] The turbulent sea represented the problems encountered in the worldly existence of the faithful, whereas Christ—the helmsman—served as a guide leading the soul out of temptation. Early medieval exile took different forms (voluntary or involuntary, physical or allegorical), and was deeply connected to the ways in which the Christian Church and its heralds—the leading theological authors of those times—related to heretics and political opponents. Exile was, on the one hand, severance from the "body of the Church," representing the last stage in anti-heretical procedures and ultimately designed to reinforce the unity of the state, Church and individual on the micro- and a macro-level. Ninth-century authors used the trope of amputation for heretics, a trope that sprang out of the early medieval endeavors for achieving social unity and consolidating Church and state authority. At the same time, the trope of allegorical spiritual self-exile as a salutary form of spiritual quest was also inherited from scriptural and early Christian narratives.

109 Daniélou, *Primitive Christian Symbols*, 58–9. Moreover, the comparison of the state to the ship reaches back to the Hellenistic and Jewish literature, see: Daniélou, *Primitive Christian Symbols*, 61–2.

CHAPTER 3

Lapidabatur a populo: Stoning as Collective Execution and Exile in Early Medieval Iberia (Fifth–Twelfth Centuries)

Abel de Lorenzo Rodríguez

Et in veteri quidem lege quicumque sacerdotibus
non obtemperasset aut extra castra positus lapidabatur a populo

Under the old law he who disobeyed the priests
was put outside the camp and stoned by the people

JEREMIAH OF STRIDON, *Ad Heliodorum, monachum*, 14.8, transmitted via *Polycarpus*, 4:35, 12

⁖

Throughout the penal history of Hispania and neighboring areas up to the late Middle Ages, diverse social groups—parricides, heretics, apostates, perjurers, adulterers, traitors, and murderers—were stoned to death as punishment either for their grave crimes and legal transgressions or for their religious practices and customs. Stoning functioned as a form of capital punishment within Jewish, Christian, and Muslim traditions, but also as a deterrent, exiling people from their communities. It is difficult to establish a connection between these diverse groups in early medieval Iberia, but stoning is found within all three. Except for a few legal traditions in which it was explicitly codified (the Jewish, Visigothic, Islamic traditions), lapidation was a legally ambiguous capital punishment that might or might not involve a trial beforehand. Even if it was inconsistently institutionalized, however, stoning was a form of public vengeance considered judicial by the community mandating the execution.[1] It was the outcome of a mob's euphoria, using the most basic, primitive, and

1 See: Deuteronomy 17:6, "On the evidence of two witnesses or of three witnesses the one who is to die shall be put to death; a person shall not be put to death on the evidence of one witness."

 | DOI:10.1163/9789004742598_005

economic instrument imaginable as a weapon for a ritualized, penitential, and even lawful performance. The use of stoning on the Iberian Peninsula dates to the pre-Roman communities in northern Hispania, but the practice persisted centuries after the Roman Empire, reinforced by Jewish, Christian, and Muslim traditions in the early Middle Ages.

The ritual of stoning involved not just killing the criminal but also driving them out of the community in two ways. First, lapidation could be commuted by exile in some circumstances. Secondly, it was performed outside the camp or city, cutting off the person from their community before death. In this way, stoning could be considered a form of extermination in the original sense of the verb *exterminare* [*ex-* (prefix) *terminare* (verb)]: both a way to eliminate the criminal and to drive them beyond the boundary, expel, banish.[2] Like exile, lapidation was a way of erasing a person from the community. Also, like exile, it was popular and cheap because it did not require spending money on executioners or materials for a scaffold.

Lapidation was a *real* punishment, not solely against the worst crimes, like murder, but also against those that carried deep implications of moral subversiveness in various categories: parental (parricide), sexual (female adultery), religious (simulated conversions), and political (royal traitors). Stoning was a profoundly physical form of punishment, but it was also metaphorical, deeply symbolic: especially those forms of stoning that did not hurt the body because it was already dead or absent. Postmortem stoning punished the place of the tomb, or the resting-place of human remains, cursing them. Other ceremonies, ecclesiastic punishments motivated by the rituals of excommunication or fulmination, entailed staging a dramatic expulsion of spiritual enemies from the Christian community, like lapidated souls.

The earliest reference to stoning in Iberia appears in the writings of the geographer Strabo (64 BCE–24 CE) who describes the penal customs of northern locals in the peninsula from the Pyrenees to Galicia: "τελοῦσι δὲ καὶ ἀγῶνας γυμνικοὺς καὶ ὁπλιτικοὺς καὶ ἱππικούς, πυγμῇ καὶ δρόμῳ καὶ διακροβολισμῷ τοὺς δὲ πατραλοίας ἔξω τῶν ὀρῶν ἢ τῶν ποταμῶν καταλεύουσι" [Those who are condemned to death they hurl from precipices; and the parricides they

2 Late Middle English (in the sense "drive out"): from Latin *exterminat-* "driven out," from the verb *exterminare*, from *ex-* "out" + *terminus* "boundary." *Dictionary of Medieval Latin from British Sources* (Turnhout: Brepols, 2020). Also *exterminare* as *Exterminus, qui est extra terminus, exsul, expulsus*, or *Exterminium, as existium strages*, Du Change dictionary. *terminum auferre vel exul<e>m facere, quasi extra terminos ponere et eicere et proprie de exulibus dicitur .i. destruire, essiller, banir, mettre et geter hors des termes*, Firmin Le Ver Dictionary, Both references from *Database of Latin Dictionaries* (Brepols).

stone to death out beyond their mountains or their rivers].[3] Like the Romans and the *poena cullei* [penalty of the sack], the Callaicans, the Asturians, the Cantabrians, and even the Vasconians seem to have reserved their cruelest punishment for parricides—those who kill parents or near relatives—because, unlike throwing someone off a cliff, stoning is not a quick death. Strabo implicitly contrasts the natives of Hispania and his own Greco-Roman civilization. The Greek geographer compares these penal customs to the archaic practice of throwing people to their death found in Greek and Roman penal codes no longer in use during his time. According to Eva Cantarella in her discussion of capital penalties and Greek literature, Plato also preferred symbolic stoning for parricides in his ideal Republic, even though stoning was not institutionalized in Greece. The northerners of Hispania enacted the punishment the same way.[4]

Strabo's seminal text establishes two key points later mentioned in early medieval Iberia. First, stoning required the collective participation of the community—often relatives or witnesses to the crime. Second, stoning was carried out in specific public places that were at odds with the sacred or communal territory, taking the culprits outside the city walls, and, thus, outside the physical limits of common public space. Strabo's references to ὀρῶν [mountains] and ποταμῶν [rivers] have been interpreted by Juan Santos and Juan de Churruca not only as sacred landscape marks, but also as the bounds of the community, suggesting that stoning implied exile. Like Jewish, Greek, or Roman stoning, in Hispania, this form of execution was kept outside sacred places or territorial boundaries because it was considered a stain or blemish that must be avoided.[5] These two characteristics of lapidation—geographic distance and public participation—were constant elements throughout the

3 Strabo, *Geography*, 3:3,7 in *Geography, Volume 2: Books 3–5*, ed. Horace Leonard Jones, Loeb Classical Library 50 (Cambridge, MA: Harvard University Press, 1923), 77. For a general overall of lapidation in Greece and Rome see: Arthur Stanley Pease, "Notes on Stoning among the Greeks and Romans," *Transactions and Proceedings of the American Philological Association* 38 (1907): 5–18.

4 Roman poena cullei punished parricide, like stoning because it avoided contact with the parricide or *patraloías*, one guilty of murdering a family member. José Carlos Bermejo Barrera, *Mitología y mitos de la Hispania prerromana II* (Madrid: Akal, 2005), 30–33. Eva Cantarella, *I supplizi capital in Grecia e a Roma*, (Milano: Rizzoli, 1991), 80 and Michel Gras, "Cité grecque et lapidation", in *Du châtiment dans la cité. Supplices corporels et peine de mort dans le monde antique. Table ronde de Rome, 9–11 novembre 1982* (Rome: École Française de Rome, 1984), 75–89.

5 Juan de Churruca Arellano, "Estrabón y el País Vasco, I: contexto de la información, marco geográfico y los montañeses de la cordillera cantábrica," *Iura Vasconiae* 2 (2008): 751–848 at 823–824.

centuries, differentiating stoning from any other form of punishment. The penal tradition of stoning was known, practiced, and remembered through stories of martyrs from the Jewish tradition, religious revivals, Visigothic laws, and the extrajudicial collective violence that emulated the law in Iberia.

The first facts regarding stoning that emerge after Strabo's descriptions in Iberia relate to religious competition on the island of Minorca starting in the fifth century. Bishop Severus (*c.*350–450) recorded two incidents of stoning in his *Epistula Seueri* (*Letter on the Conversion of the Jews*), describing the events that led to the conversion of Jews on the island in 418. On certain occasions, the violent conflict between the Jewish and Christian communities of Severus led to clashes within the Jewish community. In the first incident, a group of Jewish women tried to stone Christians as well as Jews who wanted to assemble in the synagogue on Saturdays (93–94). Taking advantage of the situation, a Christian was caught breaking into the synagogue to steal but he was nearly stoned to death, which Severus compared to the story of Achan's stoning in the Book of Joshua (Joshua 7, 20–26).[6]

There, Achan is sentenced to death by stoning alongside his family and goods after stealing the spoils of war belonging to Yahweh [**see Figure 3.1**]. Not only is he stoned to death, but his family's remains are also burned and then covered with large stones to memorialize the incident and his sins. Severus compares the Christian thief to Achan not only because of their shared crime (looting), but also because of the form of punishment sought by the community against the looter (94). Overall, the stoning attempts, the comparison with Achan, and the rise of the cult of Stephen's relics show what Carlo Ginzburg has called a *funzione antiebraica* [anti-Jewish function].[7] Stephen was martyred by stoning to death; in the *Letter*, Jews repeat the punishment against the looter, linking Severus's epistle with the martyr as well as contemporary problems in the dioceses.

6 "Sed antequam ad synagogam perveniremus, quaedam Iudaeae mulieres (ordinatione, credo, Domini) audaciam praesumentes, ut scilicet nostrorum lenitas incitaretur, lapides in nos ex superiori loco immanissimos iactare coeperunt" [But before we reached the synagogue, certain Jewish women (by God's arrangement, I suppose) acted recklessly, and, doubtless to rouse our people from their gentleness, began to throw huge stones down on us from a higher spot]. *Severus of Minorca: Letter on the Conversion of the Jews*, ed. and trans. Scott Bradbury (Oxford: Oxford Clarendon Press, 1996), 91. Hereafter, page numbers are given in parentheses.

7 On Severus of Minorca and his problematic interpretation of historic reality, see: Carlo Ginzburg, *Il filo e le trace: Vero, falso, finto* (Milano: Feltrinelli, 2006), 51. Bradbury notes that "Stephen, as John of Jerusalem observed, was the 'first to wage the Lord's wars against the Jews,' and Severus, who became bishop at about the time that the relics arrived, quickly enlisted Stephen as a divine patron in his campaign." Bradbury, *Severus of Minorca*, 44.

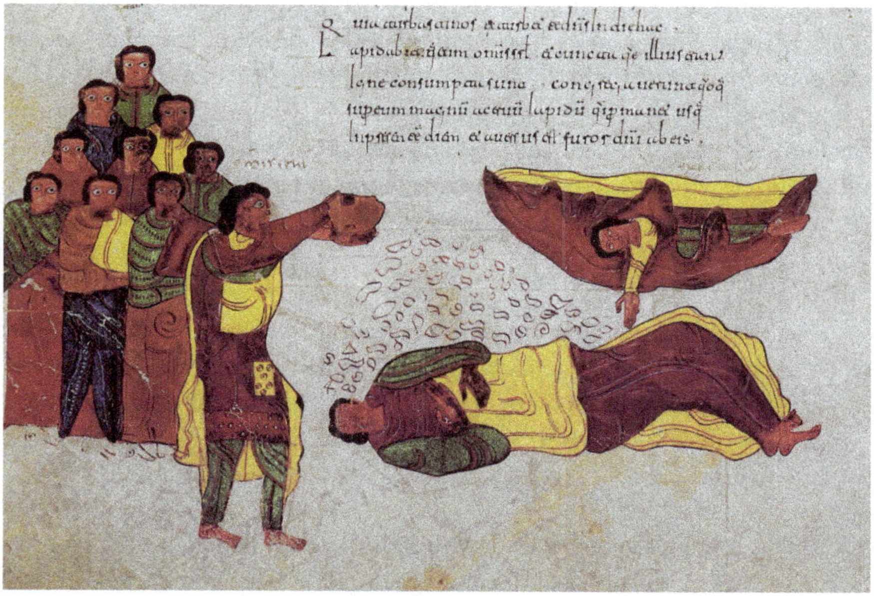

FIGURE 3.1 Stoning of Achan. Detail of *Codex Biblicus Legionensis*, known as *León Bible of 960*, fol. 91v

There are similar issues around the use of stoning in very different circumstances two centuries later, during the Gothic rule in Iberia. The *Liber Iudicum* [Book of Judges] is a compilation of laws ratified by the Visigothic kings from Euric (466–487) up to the last legal modifications of Ervig (680–687), decades before the collapse of the Visigothic Kingdom in Hispania in 711.[8] The Visigothic kings of the seventh century focused most of their interest on the laws relating to the conversion of the Jews to Nicene Christianity. After the conversion of the royal family of King Reccared from Arianism to Catholicism in 585, converting the Jews became part of a larger strategy of consolidating

8 P.S. Scott, ed., *The Visigothic Code* (*Forum Iudicum*) (Boston: Boston Book Company, 1910). Quotations of the Latin version are from the edition of Karl Zeumer, *Leges visigothorum* (Hannover: Impensis Bibliopolii Hahniani, 1902), translated into Spanish and revised in *El libro de los juicios* (*Liber Iudiciorum*), ed. Rafael Ramís Barceló and Pedro Ramís Serra (Madrid: Agencia Estatal del Boletín del Estado, 2015). Book, chapter, and page are given in parentheses. For a general overview on anti-Jewish persecution in the Visigothic Kingdom, see: Roger Collins, *Early Medieval Spain: Unity in Diversity 400–1000* (London: Macmillan, 1983), 129–146.

and unifying the realm. King Sisebut (612–621) intensified the persecution of Jewish people, forcing mass conversion under the threat of corporal, judicial, and economic punishments for those who disobeyed. The first account of Jews being stoned appears thereafter, promulgated by Chintila (636–639) during the fourth Council of Toledo in *placitum* [agreement] with the Jewish communities. Recceswinth (653–672) popularized one of the most severe laws, condemning those who broke the new laws against Jews to the most severe capital punishments in the *Liber*:

> Hec de sinu fortissimarum legum sententia emanat ad puniendam perfidiam Iudeorum, ut, quicumque aut superioribus vetita legibus aut suis ineca placitis temerare voluerit vel frustrare presumserit, mox iusta sponsionem ipsorum gentis sue manibus aut lapide perimatur aut igne crematur.
>
> [This sentence emerges from within the severest laws in order to punish the Jews' perfidy, that if anyone should wish to violate or dare to trespass the prohibitions enjoined by the above-mentioned laws or the oaths derived from them, he shall be immediately either stoned to death or burnt in fire.] (*Liber Iudicum*, 7:2, 11.417)

The oath sworn to King Recceswinth in 654 by the Jews of Toledo stated that transgressors, refusing to convert, would receive the same capital punishments, and the community would execute them. According to Recceswinth, the steps marked by Chintila in the past: "qui ex nobis horum omnium vel unius transgressor inventus fuerit, aut a nobis ignibus vel lapidibus perimatur" [if any of us should be discovered to be a transgressor of all these or even of one of them, either he shall be destroyed by us by fire or by stoning] (*Liber Iudicum*, 12:2, 17.426). Recceswinth left the commutation of capital punishment to the free will of royal clemency. This was something of a false opportunity, however, considering that it is likely that stoning or burning alive were much less common than the more profitable forfeiture and exile.

In the Visigothic context, subjecting Jews who refused conversion to stoning was grounded in an interpretation of ancient Jewish laws and was an attempt to re-enact them. Both the purpose of the punishment and the manner of its execution closely resembled earlier Hebrew traditions. Hebrew law of Deuteronomy (13:6–10) prescribes stoning in cases of blasphemy and apostasy, and if the instigator is a family member, the relatives throw the first stones.[9] According to the logic of *contrapasso* or mirror punishment—the punishment fitting the crime—every crime was related to a punishment, so stoning was meant to take a Jewish person back to biblical origins by bringing forth his own Hebraic penal traditions. In the *Liber Iudicum*, not all crimes had mirror punishments, only a few, like arson, where the arsonist was burned alive. Jews, however, were subjected to a few forms of *contrapasso*, including burning or stoning for false conversion or castration for circumcision. During forced conversion, the Christian legislators and kings not only appropriated a Hebraic punishment but also inverted its original purpose. While stoning or other forms of punishment were originally used by the Hebrew communities to prosecute religious dissent and strengthen the Jewish faith, in the case of the *Liber Iudicum* (12:2, 11) Christian and Visigothic rulers used the same mechanism to destroy the Jewish communities. According to Felix Dahn, making close relatives participate in an execution was an additional sign of cruel irony (*grausame Ironie des Fanatismus*).[10] This could be defined as a type of penal syncretism, a concrete branch of cultural and legal syncretism, demonstrating how two or more different penal traditions interweave to produce a combination of both. Rather than voluntary syncretism, however, Visigothic rulers and legislators coercively appropriated Jewish traditions, requiring the participation of the offender's own community in their punishment. Thus, the Christian community did not punish Jews, but converted Jews who punished the non-converted.[11]

---

9 "If thy brother, the son of thy mother, or thy son, or thy daughter, or the wife of thy bosom, or thy friend, which is as thine own soul, entices thee secretly, saying, let us go and serve other gods, which thou hast not known, thou, nor thy fathers. But thou shalt surely kill him; thine hand shall be first upon him to put him to death, and afterwards the hand of all the people. And thou shalt stone him with stones, that he dies; because he hath sought to thrust thee away from the Lord thy God, which brought thee out of the land of Egypt, from the house of bondage," (Deut. 13: 6–9).

10 Felix Dahn, *Westgothische Studien: Entstehungsgeschichte, Privatrecht, Strafrecht, Civil und Straf Prozess und Gesammtkritik der Lex Visigothorum* (Würzburg: Stahel, 1874), 55. P.D. King notes that the law is reminiscent of the comedy of innocence (*unschuldskomödie*), an expiatory ritual between executioner and victim. *Law and Society in the Visigothic Kingdom* (Cambridge: Cambridge University Press, 1972), 133. On the "comedy of innocence," see: Walter Burkert, *Homo necans: The Anthropology of Ancient Greek Sacrificial Ritual and Myth* (Berkeley: University of California Press), 16.

11 Cecil Roth gives many other examples from later centuries in which the stoning of the Jews became a liturgical tradition due to anti-Semitic propaganda in Spain, Italy, and France. According to the *Sentence from the Ordinary of St. Vincent of Chalons*: "Judaei lapidantur a clero et populo eo quod lapidaverunt Jesu" [the Jews were stoned by the clergy

However, stoning was not just related to Jewish traditions. Nearby, in the Merovingian kingdoms, there are references to this form of execution among Christians. Around the year 480, a Roman mob stoned Victorius for his lecherous behavior with women.[12] Victorius had been duke in Septimania under Visigothic king Euric (440–484) and later left for Rome. Two coetaneous references more specifically explain the ritual of lapidation. Gregory of Tours describes the executions of Parthenio and Chundo, where both were bound by the hands to a stake or column and then stoned to death. In the first case, the Franks killed Parthenio because they objected to taxes during the reign of Theodebert I (500–548). In the second case, Chundo, chamberlain of King Childebert I (497–558), was stoned for treason after losing a duel.[13]

A decade after King Recceswinth, King Ervig amended certain Visigothic laws over the right to punish, making them softer, including those relating to the Jewish community.[14] Under Recceswinth, supposed Jewish transgressions were punished by stoning or burning, but under Ervig that punishment was no longer considered appropriate: "Deus mortem non vult nec letatur in perditione vivorum, pro eo quod in se peremptionis continet morentium" [this law which prescribes the penalty to be inflicted for the transgressions of the Jews shall be hereafter considered of no validity and effect; for the reason that God does not desire the death of His creatures or rejoice in their perdition] (*Liber Iudicum*, 12:3, 1.431). The Visigothic king substituted the punishment of stoning and burning alive for exile and prison, as well as the confiscation of property. This change in the character of penitential punishment from capital to corrective may have been a strategy of Visigothic monarchy to temper the turbulent last decades of the seventh century.[15]

---

and people because they stoned Jesus]. Quoted in Cecil Roth, "The Eastertide Stoning of the Jews and Its Liturgical Echoes," *The Jewish Quarterly Review, New Series*, 35.4 (1945): 361–70.

12 Gregorio Turonensis, *De Historia Francorum* 2:20, in Brehaut, *Gregory of Tours*, 36.

13 Gregorio Turonensis, *De Historia Francorum*, 3:36: "vinctis postergum manibus, ad colomnam lapidibus obruerunt" [tying his hands behind his back, they stoned him to death beside a column]; Gregorio Turonensis, *De Historia Francorum*, 10:10 in Brehaut, *Gregory of Tours*, 71, 235: "vinctusque ad stipitem lapidibus est obrutus" [he was caught and tied to a stake and stoned].

14 Céline Martin, "Ervig and Capital Penalties: The Way of Exile," in *Framing Power in Visigothic Society: Discourses, Devices, and Artifacts*, ed. Eleonora Dell'Elicine and Céline Martin (Amsterdam: Amsterdam University Press, 2020), 133–158.

15 Biaio Saitta, *L'Antisemitismo nella Spagna visigotica* (Roma: L'Erma di Bretschneider, 1998), 57–59, 78. Juan Gil, "Cristianos y judíos en la Hispania del siglo VII," *Hispania Sacra* 30 (1977): 9–10; Wolfram Drews, "Barbarians and Jews in Early Medieval Spain: Shifting Constellations of Religion and Identity," in *Barbarian and Jews: Jews and Judaism*

King Sisebut, who forced the Jewish community to accept baptism, wrote in his *Vita Desiderii* about the life and martyrdom of Bishop Desiderius of Vienne (d. 607). In this account, stoning is described as an excessive punishment worthy only of tyrants and violent kings. Sisebut describes Desiderius as a member of a noble Roman family who ascends to the highest local ecclesiastical powers. After Desiderius reaches the episcopate of Vienne, a noblewoman, Justa, in alliance with King Theuderic (595–613) and his grandmother Brunhilda (543–613), accuses him of trying to kidnap her, and, as a result, Desiderius is exiled. However, Justas's repentance later provokes Desiderius' forgiveness and his return to Vienne, expelling his rival in the bishopric, Domnulus. Nevertheless, Theuderic and Brunhilda order Desiderius executed, events recounted for the first time by Sisebut, who possibly took advantage of the bishop's martyrdom as a geopolitical excuse to speak out against his northern neighbors.[16] According to the hagiographic account, a series of disagreements between Desiderius and the Merovingian kings provokes a clash that leads first to the bishop's exile but ends in his execution, which concludes with stoning: "Desiderium moribus nostris infestum et operibus inimicum lapidus ictibus uerberatum multoque genere penarum afflictum animaduerti complacuit" [It pleases us to see Desiderius, critic of our life and enemy of our deeds, stoned and afflicted with all manner of tortures] (16).[17] Sisebut describes a mob descending and raining stones on Desiderius under direct orders from Theuderic. The bishop finally meets his death when his neck is broken:

---

in the Early Medieval West, ed. Yitzhak Hen and Thomas F.X. Noble (Turnhout: Brepols, 2018), 47–67.

16 Jacques Fontaine, "King Sisebut's Vita Desiderii and the Political Function of Visigothic Hagiography," in *Visigothic Spain: New Approaches*, ed. Edward James (Oxford: Clarendon Press, 1980), 93–129.

17 All quotations from the Latin version of *Vita vel Passio Sancti Desiderii a Sisebuto rege composita* are from Juan Gil, *Miscellanea Wisigothica* (Seville: University of Seville Press, 1972), 53–88; English translations are from A.T. Fear, *Lives of the Visigothic Fathers* (Liverpool: Liverpool University Press, 2011), 1–15. Hereafter, page numbers are given in parentheses. This martyrdom account focuses on the relationship between the bishop and king, framing it within the context of problematic competition between the ecclesiastics and the aristocrats in the Merovingian kingdoms. In this case it seems that both Justus, as a nobleman, and Domnulus, as a rival bishop, represent a faction opposed to and in competition with Desiderius. Even though the kings apparently agree to exile Desiderius in a monastery after deposing him, he still suffers public execution. See also: Paul Fouracre, "Why Were So Many Bishops Killed in Merovingian Francia?' in *Bischofsmord im Mittelalter*, ed. Natalie Fryde and Dirk Reitz (Berlin: Vandenhoeck & Ruprecht, 2003), 13–35, esp. 17.

> Horum execranda pernicies furore ministrante arma nequissimo rapuit atque super martyrem Xpi imbrem lapidum cor saxeum fudit. Quem cum missilia preterirent dira furentium iacula et in partem aliam cursum flecteret silicum natura durissima ipseque fragor lapidationis Dei famulo famulatum exhiberet. (*Vita vel passio sancti Desiderii*, 18.65)
>
> [This accursed band, vile madness giving them their arms, seized and their stony heart poured a rain of stones over the martyr of God. The terrible missiles flung by the madmen missed him: the harsh nature of flints turned aside in its flight, and the very sound of the stoning showed itself to be the servant of the servant of God.] (*Life and Martyrdom of Saint Desiderius*, 12)

Sisebut's account of Desiderius' martyrdom inspired future *Lives* that vary slightly in the motives and form of execution. In the seventh-century *Chronicle of Fredegarius*, the prime instigator is Brunhilda, who sentences the bishop to death by making him return from exile, but not before explaining that the kingdom of Theuderic and his children was destroyed by the divine hand as vengeance.[18] In the seventh-century *Carmina Sangallensia*, the executioners appear to be a group completely composed of plebeians: "Esse sibi patrem domino tractante tonantem/ plebs furibunda pium certat lapidare magistrum" [Noisily they dragged him, and the angry plebeians wanted to stone the master].[19]

The stoning of a bishop was not completely unusual considering previous incidents that strongly resemble Desiderius' case. Sisebut's account of the bishop was inspired by similar events from contemporary Merovingian France. Stoning bishops as punishment is also found in ancient apocryphal texts like the *Visio Pauli* that condemns bishops to stoning in Hell for neglecting widows and orphans.[20] In his *Historiae*, Gregory of Tours describes the accusations of having illicit relations with a woman and fathering her child

---

18 "Brunechilde sanctum Desiderium de exilium egressum lapidare praecipit," *Fredegarius. Chronicarum*, 4:32 in Bruno Krusch, *Scriptores rerum Merovingicarum* (Hannover: Monumenta Germaniae Historica, 1888), 2:133.

19 *Carmina Sangallensia*, 7:5 in Ernst Dümmler, *Poetae latini aevi Carolini*, (Berlin: Monumenta Germaniae Historica, 1884), 2:482.

20 J.K. Elliot, *The Apocryphal New Testament. A Collection of Apocryphal Christian Literature in an English Translation* (Oxford: Oxford University Press, 2005), 635. *Visio Pauli* says, "a bishop, who did not give just judgements or show compassion to widows and orphans is stoned, receiving 'retribution according to his Works,'" Jil Harries, *Law and Empire in Late Antiquity* (Cambridge: Cambridge University Press, 1999), 147.

against Bishop Brice of Tours (377–444), the disciple and successor of Martin of Tours (316–397). This provokes the wrath of the townspeople, who demand the bishop be stoned: "Qua de re surrexit omnis populus Toronorum in ira, et totum crimen super episcopum referunt, volentes eum unanimiter lapidare" [At this news the entire population of Tours rose in its anger. They laid the whole guilt on their Bishop and as one man wanted to stone him to death].[21] Even the wonders he performs in his defence, like speaking with a newborn or carrying lit coal on his clothing, are in vain. Unlike Desiderius, Brice is spared stoning but suffers exile from Rome. In his epistle to an adulterous monk, the fifth-century Iberian writer Bachiarius warns future monks that lapidation is the punishment for breaking celibacy.[22] Other examples of a mob trying to carry out a sentence of this kind include Praetextatus of Rouen (d. *c.*580) and Caesarius of Arles (470–542), both threatened with public stoning during judicial proceedings by Visigothic king Alaric II (485–507). As with other cases, Bishop Caesarius has to choose between exile or a death sentence, but proves his innocence, avoiding stoning.[23] Apart from cruel kings, queens, and furious mobs, the executioners might be demons, following the logic of hagiography as with Saint Emilian, according to the *Vita Sancti Aemiliani* by Braulius of Zaragoza (590–651), the same writer who legally promoted the first Gothic reference about stoning Jewish people. After Emilian exorcises a demon confusing and harassing people in the house of Senator Honorius, the demon attempts to retaliate by stoning the saint, who walks away miraculously unharmed. The reliquary housing his remains (*c.*1060) depicts Emilian stopping the demon's stones with one hand while blessing Honorius' house with the other.[24]

---

21 Gregorius Turonensis, *De Historia Francorum*, 2:1 in Ernest Brehaut, *Gregory of Tours. History of the Franks* (New York: Norton, 1969), 22.

22 "Legislator praecepit (Levit 20:10), ut qui uxorem alterius macularet, cum ipsa lapidaretur pariter; et ideo non permittit conjugium" [the lawyer sentenced that anyone who committed adultery with women will be stoned, and this way the law does not allow marriage]. Bachiarius monachus, *Epistula ad Ianuarium seu De lapso* in Jose Carlos Martín-Iglesias, *Bachiarius monachus. De fide, Epistula ad Ianuarium, Epistulae II* (Turnhout: Brepols, 2019).

23 Against bishop of Rouen, Praetextatus "a multitude of Franks raised an angry shout and wished to break through the church doors as if to drag the bishop out and stone him; but the king prevented them," Gregorio Turonensis, *De Historia Francorum*, 5:18 in Brehaut, *Gregory of Tours*, 119. In the case of Caesarius, "Accusatorem vero eius lapidare rex praecepit. Iamque cum lapidibus populi concurrentes, subito ad aures eius iussio regis pervenit," *Cyprianus, Firminus, Viventius*. *Vita Caesarii Arelatensis*, 1:24 in Bruno Krusch, *Scriptores rerum Merovingicarum* (Hannover: Monumenta Germaniae Historica, 1896), 3:466.

24 Somes pieces of these ivory reliefs are preserved in Yuso Monastery, San Millán de la Cogolla and referred to in *Vita Sancti Aemiliani*, 17 en Fear, *Lives*, 32.

Imitation of earlier models through storytelling or representation is an important facet of the development of hagiography and early medieval clerical historiography.[25] Hagiographies and chronicles featuring lapidation tended to draw analogies between the first martyrs and more recent examples of slain Christians, contributing to an interpretive model that framed any form of penal violence as martyrdom—even though it was linked with social and competitive struggles, not just with religious purposes. In the case of stoning, the most widespread narrative models were those of Saint Stephen and Saint James, Christ's brother.[26] Through image and word, they helped to spread—and, partly, to popularize—the ancient penal tradition. The executions of these two saints appear prominently in antiphonaries and sacramentals like the *Liber Sacramentorum* and the *Liber Commicus*, used in Hispanic liturgy, dating to the first Hispano-Goths or Mozarabs. The reference to Stephen in *Liber Sacramentorum* is much more succinct than in other liturgy books: "qui sancto martiri tuo Stephano post ictus lapidem, regnum tribuisti/ Quique eum lapidari permisit ab impiis, non patiatur uos lacerari ullo modo ab iniquis" [Saint Stephen, your saint and martyr, who after his stoning, gave him your kingdom / May the one who allowed him to be stoned by the wicked not suffer you to be destroyed in any way by your enemies].[27] The *Officium in diem Sancti Stephani* [*Saint Stephen's Divine Office*] of the Visigothic-Mozarab antiphonary of the Cathedral in León (*c.*910–970) also recounts Stephen's martyrdom, but in a more detailed manner in line with the Acts of the Apostles: "impetum fecerunt unanimiter adversus Stephanum et falsi testes deposuerunt vestimenta sua et eicientes eum extra civitate lapidabant illum" [the perjurers together blamed Stephen, and they unclothed him and stoned him out of the city].[28] The holy day celebrating Saint James the Just occurs soon after Stephen's holy day and frames the terms of trial and punishment in a similar way.[29] Lastly, the *Liber Commicus* quotes specific biblical passages where people are sentenced

25 See: Erich Auerbach, *Mimesis: The Representation of Reality in Western Literature* (Princeton: Princeton University Press, 2003).

26 Shelly Matthews, *Perfect Martyr. The Stoning of Stephen and the Construction of Christian Identity* (Oxford: Oxford University Press, 2010). See also: Shelly Matthews, "The Need for the Stoning of Stephen," in *Violence in the New Testament*, ed. Shelly Matthews and Leigh Gibson (New York: T&T Clark, 2005), 124–139.

27 Marius Férotin, *Le Liber mozarabicus sacramentorum et les manuscrits mozarabes* (Paris: Firmin-Didot, 1912), col. 59–60. English translation in Andrew Kurt, "Lay Piety in Visigothic Iberia: Liturgical and Paraliturgical Forms," *Journal of Medieval Iberian Studies*, 8 (2016), 1–37 at 23.

28 Louis Brou and José Vives, *Antifonario visigótico mozárabe de la Catedral de León* (Barcelona: CSIC-Instituto Enrique Flórez, 1959), 95–98.

29 Férotin, *Le Liber mozarabicus*, col. 66.

to death in successive incidents, such as the adulterer and the Pharisees (John 7:53–8:11), the warning from the disciples of Christ about the Jews' desire to stone him (John 9:1–52), and the later attempt to stone a blasphemer (John 10:31).[30] In all these cases, works including the divine office suggest that lapidation was not merely an old-fashioned tradition linked to ancient law.

These representations supported a mentality that justified any moment of collective violence, since they were understood as a return to the primal persecution of martyrs. As the churchmen remembered their predecessors, they created false portrayals of violence that obscured the real reasons behind each conflict.[31] This, at least, is Eulogius of Cordoba's explanation in his *Documentum martyriale* and his *Memoriale sanctorum* [*Martyrial Document / Memorial of the Saints*] (*c.*850–859), in which he writes about those executed or persecuted through stoning during the mid-ninth century revolts by a faction of the *Dhimnies* Christians in Cordoba: "They (the children) don't stop harassing us, throwing stones at our backs."[32] Almost 300 years later, the clergy did not lament the stones thrown under the order of the Muslim qadis, but the revolts within the Christian kingdoms.

From 1111 to 1136, rebellions in Sahagún, Santiago de Compostela, and Lugo put the leaders of these towns at serious risk, whether they were abbots or bishops. Peasants and nobles converged in these revolts, but the rights of a new group emerged—the bourgeoisie—who came into conflict with the ecclesiastical jurisdictional lords. This urban revolt was related to the civil war for the throne of Leon and the confrontation with Aragon. During the rebellion in Sahagún, the abbot was summarily tried in the council of the rebels and charged with treason, homicide, theft, and witchcraft. The rebels' first choice was stoning, which they defined as a shameful punishment: "vnos le llamauan traidor, otros omeçida, otros ladrón, otros maléfico e malfechor, otros digno de

30 Justo Pérez de Urbel, Atilano González Ruiz-Zorrilla, *Liber Commicus* (Madrid: CSIC, 1950), 268, 299, 303, 312.

31 See: Paul Fouracre, "Why Were So Many Bishops Killed in Merovingian Francia?" in *Bischofsmord im Mittelalter*, ed. Natalie Fryde and Dirk Reitz (Berlin: Vandenhoeck & Ruprecht, 2003), 13–35: "In Spain, the type of martyr venerated remained that of the Late Antique hero of the age of persecutions" (32).

32 *Memoriale sanctorum*, liber 1:21: "the saints were beaten, flogged, stoned, and sold." *Documentum Martyriale*, 6 in Juan Gil, *Corpus scriptorum Muzarabicorum*, vol. 2 (Madrid: Instituto Antonio de Nebrija, 1973). Eulogio's interpretation is interesting considering that years before the revolt of Arrabal (818) in Córdoba, which has little to do with *exempla* of primitive martyrs, the community used stoning as the severest punishment against authority. See: Federico Corriente, *Ibn Hayyan. Crónica de los emires Alhakam I y Abdarrahman II entre los años 796 y 847. Almuqtabis II-1* (Zaragoza: Instituto de Estudios Islámicos y del Oriente Próximo, 2001), 70–71.

ser apedreado" [ones named him treacherous, murder, robber, others malefic and wrongdoer, and others worthy to be stoned].[33] Others preferred hanging, burning, and even sparing the condemned to humiliate him. In the heat of the argument, one of the conspirators, Bernardo, decided to kill the abbot himself with a knife, but was detained because the rebels argued that the abbot should be communally executed.

This was not the last time the monks of Sahagún were in danger of being stoned to death. Years after the first great revolt, around 1123, another dispute nearly resulted in the stoning of the monastery granary keeper—one Bernardus—at the hands of the inhabitants of Grajal de Campos. Thirty years later, in a document dated 1152, the infanta Sancha Raimúndez (*c.*1100–1159), sister of King Alphonse VII, presided over a trial for two incidents dating back two decades. The toll needed to use the road or the bridge (*portatico*) was the final reason for the confrontation between the Grajals and the monks of Sahagún: the Grajals refused to pay and broke the mill's dam in protest, while the monks maintained their fiscal privilege granted by Alphonse VII until the groups finally clashed. Bernardus addressed the Grajals accompanied by Martinum Fernandiz, and the Grajals attempted to kill both men. Bernardus made a quick escape on horseback while Martinum was almost stoned to death; he would have died had it not been for the intervention of one of the Grajals' neighbors. During the trial more than twenty years later, Martinum himself recounted the incident in detail.[34] The distance between the facts, documents, and the trial reveal a pattern of violence between the community of Grajal and the Sahagún monks that blew up during the stoning attempt against the granary keeper.

33 Antonio Ubieto Arteta, *Crónicas anónimas de Sahagún* (Zaragoza: Anubar, 1987), 69. There are accounts of stones being used not only during popular revolts but also in war. During the confrontations of Alphonse VI in the *taifa* of Zaragoza, and due to the treason of Rueda who governed Albufac in 1083, many knights were killed with only stones. See: *Historia Roderici uel gesta Roderici Campidocti*, 18 in Emma Falque, Juan Gil, A. Maya, *Chronica hispana saeculi XII* (Turnhout: Brepols, 1990), 1:56. In the supposed confirmation of 978 during the founding of the monasteries de San Cosme and San Damián de Covarrubias (Castilla), there is a reference to weapons such as spears, shields, and rocks in the event of a confrontation between neighborhoods. See: Luciano Serra, *Cartulario del Infantado de Covarrubias* (Valladolid: Cuesta, 1907), 21.

34 "Et ipsi continuo vituperantes cellerarium, miserunt lapides contra eum et voluerunt eum capere et interficere" [and they always insulted the granary keeper, throwing stones against him and wanted to catch and kill him]. José A. Fernández Flórez, *Colección diplomática del Monasterio de Sahagún, (1110–1199)* (León: Centro de Estudios e Investigación "San Isidoro," 1991), 4:238. It is not surprising that the Grajal village was involved in the attack on the abbot decades before the rebellion of Sahagún. See: Ubieto Arteta, *Crónicas anónimas*, 37.

The same year that the abbot of Sahagún escaped being stoned by his vassals, in Santiago de Compostela Archbishop Diego Gelmírez (served 1100–1140) experienced a similar attack at the hands of rebellious bourgeoisie. According to the *Historia Compostellana*, written under the patronage and the memory of Gelmírez, Queen Urraca also suffered stoning in a public shaming.[35] In this 1116 incident, the stoning was not disguised behind a mock trial as in Sahagún; it was the result of a public uprising, but it was not the last attempt against Bishop Gelmírez.

The revolts that affected the Iberian Kingdoms during the twelfth century continually jeopardized the *ordo clericalis*, putting their lives at risk not only through reforms but with a series of destabilizing attacks on their power. In the aforementioned cases, attempts on the bishop or abbot by kings, counts, or relatives disguised sedition: they were attempts to execute extrajudicial violence outside the established legal power, while also imitating penal violence. Since the *Liber Iudicum* included stoning as a punishment for the Jews and against adulterers, it became a shameful way to punish and persecute powerful figures. By punishing their lords in this shocking manner, the rebels of Sahagún and Santiago drew on a clear penal inspiration, arguing that their lords deserved being stoned to death.

In 1136, in compliance with King Alphonse VII, the canons pursued a conspiracy against Gelmírez with the sole objective of stoning him, which he survived despite his advanced age. The *Historia Compostellana* and the cathedral chartulary (*Tumbo A*) commissioned by the archbishop, both recount the story in a legal declaration.[36] In stark contrast to what occurred in Sahagún during the revolt against the abbot, the rebels did not allow Gelmírez to choose his method of execution. The rebels in Santiago, under the command of Uilelmus Siginides, prioritized the various modes of execution but lapidation was the first choice.[37] In fact, they planned to stone the archbishop and stab his

35 *Historia Compostellana*, 2:53 in Emma Falque Rey, *Historia Compostellana* (Turnhout: Brepols, 1988), 321. For the events relating Gelmírez's administration of the diocese, see: Richard A. Fletcher, *Saint James's Catapult: The Life and Times of Diego Gelmirez of Santiago de Compostela* (Oxford: Clarendon Press, 1984), 223–253 and Ermelindo Portela Silva, *Diego Gelmírez (c. 1065–1140): el báculo y la ballesta* (Madrid: Marcial Pons, 2016).

36 In Falque, *Historia Compostellana*, 3:46–47, 504–511 and in the cartulary of Tumbo A (doc. 102) the confiscation of Juan Lombardo's property by the king is documented a few years after the events: "Ut eum occiderent, armis et lapidibus armati et muniti, diabolico spiritu inspirante," in Manuel Lucas Álvarez, *Tumbo A de la Catedral de Santiago* (Santiago de Compostela: Seminario de Estudos Galegos, Cabildo de la S.A.M.I. Catedral, 1998), 215–216.

37 The *Historia Compostellana*, 3:46–47 cites other methods such as stabbing or shooting with arrows, but stoning is the most popular way to eliminate the bishop. The events are recalled in Falque, *Historia Compostellana*, 3:53, 522 and 3:54, 527.

followers.[38] The rebels collectively tried stoning the bishop from his chambers all the way to the cathedral's altar. The bishop escaped by taking refuge behind the bars of the altar, under lock and key. According to Pedro Marcio, however, the mob took advantage of the construction scaffolding inside the cathedral, climbed up, and began pouring stones down on him from above, injuring the archbishop's back and striking him on the ear.[39] The altar bars deflected the furious stoning but he would have not survived had the women of Santiago not clamored for an end to the violence. After recovering from the assassination attempt, the archbishop publicly accused the aggressors in the council of Burgos that same year, which led to the excommunication of Guillermo and his conspirators. In fact, the assembly of prelates encouraged Alphonse VII to employ corporal punishment, because he alone had the authority to add capital punishment to the canonical sentence of exile. Gelmírez subordinated himself to the king to appease Alphonse's murderous intentions.

Similarly, in the *Historia Compostellana* (Chapter 54, Book 3), Marcio draws a direct parallel to evangelic Scripture by comparing the bishop's story to the Jewish attempt to stone Christ.[40] In the Gospel according to Saint John, Christ argues with the Jews and defends his existence prior to Abraham, eliciting an attack on him with stones (John 8:46–59). Consequently, Christ leaves the Jews. In the *Historia Compostellana*, Marcio aligns the bishop with Christ both by emphasizing the similarities of the events (both figures run away from danger) and by stressing that the bishop pardoned those involved in the attack. This is not the only reference to Gelmírez and the ancient law of stoning, and to its use in biblical times. In the collection of canons of the *Polycarpus* (*c.*1110), written by Gregory of San Crisógono and dedicated to Gelmírez, a letter of Jerome of Stridon quotes the ancient law of stoning to explain that anybody who disobeys the priest will be taken outside the town and stoned by the people.[41] This

38 Falque, *Historia Compostellana*, 3:47, 508.

39 Falque, *Historia Compostellana*, 3:47, 510. Pedro Marcio is the author of the third and final book of the bishop's life. See: Falque, *Historia Compostellana*, 16–17. The comparison of stoning to rain recalls the rhetorical device of hail used heavily in accounts of the miracles of Saint Zoilo. See: Patrick Henriet and José Carlos Martín-Iglesias, "Le dossier hagiographique de Zoïle de Carrión dans le manuscrit Madrid, BNE,11556 (XIIe siècle): Étude et édition," in *Estudios de filología e historia en honor del profesor Vitalino Valcárcel*, ed. Íñigo Ruiz Arzalluz (Vitoria: País Vasco University, 2014), 429–459 at 454.

40 Falque, *Historia Compostellana*, 3:54, 527.

41 "Et in veteri quidem lege quicumque sacerdotibus non obtemperasset aut extra castra positus lapidabatur a populo" [Under the old law he who disobeyed the priests was put outside the camp and stoned by the people], *Polycarpus*, 4:35, 12. The reference is from Jeremiah of Stridon, *Ad Heliodorum, monachum* 14.8 in Philip Schaff and M.A. Freemantle, *Jerome: The Principal Works of St. Jerome* (New York: Christian Literature Publishing

account foreshadows the trials Gelmírez faced to strengthen his power during the first half of the twelfth century.

There are other references to the public attempted murder of prelates in the kingdom of León and Galicia. In 1159, a royal messenger and five canons from the city of Lugo were chased, cornered, and assassinated in the cathedral for demanding properties and taxes owed to the Church. This triggered the flight of Bishop Juan and his possible exile in Rome. In 1161, the bishop and the city briefly reconciled, but only until Pentecost. After that, the bishop and his servants were stoned and their homes destroyed, without fatalities, in a revolt. A conspiracy or brotherhood, allegedly in collusion with King Ferdinand II (1155–1188), carried out these attacks.[42] According to other authors such as Antonio García Conde and Amador López Valcárcel, the availability of stones in an unfinished cathedral facilitated the lapidation of church officials, as was the case in 1136 in Santiago when the presbyters attacked the archbishop leading to their excommunication.[43] Thus, parallel to the petrification of wealth in the great Romanesque buildings of this period and their expensive, ornate stonework, there arises at the same time a petrification of punishment: the same figures who promoted the construction of churches were attacked with their materials.[44]

Stoning was used not just in conflicts between prelates and furious lay people. Clashes also occurred between monastic or episcopal communities, as in a case in Coimbra, Portugal between 1180 and 1190. A dispute over an inheritance (*uilla Paucam*) brought before the bishopric Miguel País Salomao

Co., 1892). About the *Polycarpus* see the edition in Uwe Horst, *Die Kanonessammlung Polycarpus des Gregor von S. Grisogono. Quellen und Tendenzen* (München: Monumenta Germaniae Histórica, 1980), 297.

42 The references to the attempts against the bishop's life in Lugo are in a lost pontifical document by Urban III from 1184 that was kept in the Galician cathedral and is known only thanks to the writing of seventeenth-century author Juan Pallares y Gayoso, *Argos Divina Sancta María de Lugo de los Ojos grandes, Fundación, y Grandezas de su Iglesia, Sanctos naturales, Reliquias, y Venerables Varones de su Ciudad, y Obispado, Obispos y Arçobispos que en todos Imperios la gouernaron* (Santiago de Compostela: Imprenta de Benito Antonio Frayz, 1700), 378.

43 See the appendix of chapter 11 of the Third Lateran Council (1179), Antonio García Conde and Amador López Valcárcel, *Episcopologio lucense* (Lugo: Diócesis de Lugo, 1991), 199–202.

44 On the petrifying of wealth in the eleventh and twelfth centuries in medieval Europe, especially Iberia, see: *Monográfico: La petrificación de la riqueza: construcción e identidad en la Península ibérica e Italia, siglos XI–XIII, Studia historica. Historia medieval* 39 (2021): 3–240. See also: *Petrifying Wealth: The Southern European Shift to Masonry as Collective Investment in Identity, c.1050–1300*, a European Research Council Advanced Grant (GA N° 695515).

(1162–1176) of Coimbra led to a conflict between the monastery of Santa Cruz and the canons from the Cathedral of Santa Maria de Coimbra, resulting in a hail of stones from both the monks and the canons. Years later, witnesses confirmed the events, with the help of a few interrogations by Pope Innocent III (1198–1216). Gunsaluus Garsias, one of the witnesses, testified that the canons stoned the buried bodies in the church but also the monks located inside the monastery of Santa Cruz. During the trial, thirteen other witnesses corroborated the accounts, explaining that the mutual stoning between the canons and the monks of Santa Cruz occurred during an inheritance dispute.[45] The confrontation exploded between the cathedral and the monastery over the possession of property, in addition to the appropriation of the taxes which had caused conflict between the bishops and the monks in the city for decades.

Parody sometimes dominates representations of the persecution of prelates depicting them as new martyrs. The *Tractatus Garsiae* (1099–1116) describes the archbishop of Toledo and his companion García, on their way to Rome, as facilitating corruption in the pontifical court of Urban II. The tract jokes about this persecution comparing it with ancient, stoned martyrs: "Hiis ergo molaribus lapidatus est pontifex Romanus, hiis gladiis sectus eat, hiis malignis spiritibus temptatus est, hiis occisionibus interemptus est" [With such stones was the Roman pontiff stoned, with such swords was he cut, with such malignant spirits was he tempted]. The Pope was not literally stoned, this is simply a rhetorical assessment of Vatican corruption; the weapons for this persecution were the exquisite delicacies and the jewels of the pontifical corruption.[46] When García says *lapidatus* [stoned], he means that Urban II was bribed, painting a sarcastic portrait of the consequences of battles for profits, goods, and domains between Hispanic dioceses, the Cluny intermediation, and the papal finances.

---

45 The declaration of Gunsaluus Garsias' sentence: "fratres Sancte Crucis et altaria sua et corpora tan vivorum quam mortuorum tam regum quam canonicorum suorum lapidaverunt canonici Sancte Marie" [The monks of Santa Cruz stoned the bodies, dead or alive, canons or kings and the altar of the church of Santa Maria]. Other witnesses corroborated this version, stating or clarifying that the stoning was mutual. See: Avelino de Jesus da Costa, *Bulário português. Inocêncio III (1198–1216)* (Coimbra: Instituto Nacional de Investigação Cientifica, 1989), 141–149.

46 *Tractatus Garsiae*, 2:163–165 in Rodney M. Thomson, *Tractatus Garsiae, or The Translation of the Relics of SS. Gold and Silver* (Leiden: Brill, 1973), 24–25. See also the comments and translation into Spanish in Maurilio Pérez González, *La Garcineida: estudio y edición crítica con traducción* (León: University of León, 2001). Alberto González García, "El papa Urbano II y el origen de la Garcineida," *Anuario de Estudios Medievales*, 43.2 (2013), 609–647.

Stoning also figured prominently in communities that brought Christianity and Islam together. The main and most well-known conflict in medieval Iberia involved the advances of the northern peninsular Christian kingdoms in contact and integration with the Islamic communities of Al-Andalus, many of the latter governed by Christian rulers yet allowed to maintain their religious and legislative peculiarities. One such case was the conquest of the *taifa* of Valencia (later, kingdom) by Rodrigo Díaz de Vivar (1043–1099)—El Cid—after his exile by Alphonse VI of León and Castilla (1040–1109). During the diplomatic and family negotiations with the *qadi* [judge] of Valencia and Toledo, Ibn Yahhaf killed Al-Qádir in 1092 because of his contacts with Alphonse VI and El Cid. Ibn Yahhaf became the new qadi of Valencia until the arrival of El Cid in the capital of the *taifa*.

Upon capturing the city of Valencia in 1094, El Cid prosecuted Ibn Yahhaf and extorted large sums of gold and goods in exchange for his life. However, while the various chronicle accounts agree on this point, they diverge in their descriptions of his punishment. According to the *Anonymous Chronicle of Taifa's Kings* (c.1150–1175), closer to events both in terms of chronology and accuracy, El Cid ordered Ibn Yahhaf to be burned at the stake, after requesting all his wealth.[47] A later, and more interesting, version is that recounted by King Alphonse X, also known as "the Wise King" (1221–1284), in his *First General Chronicle*, which states that the execution involved stoning, not burning alive.[48] In this account, El Cid, acting as judge, asks the people of Valencia what they should do *segunt su ley* [according to his law]—that is, Islamic law—to Ibn Yahhaf for the charge of murdering his lord. The *alfaqui* [Islamic law cleric] recommends stoning against Ibn Yahhaf and 130 supporters of his cause, in accordance with Islamic jurisprudence. The complexity of the categories of punishments implies that El Cid, despite being a Christian and vassal

47 Felipe Maíllo Salgado, *Crónica Anónima de los reyes de Taifas* (Madrid: Akal, 1991), 53. The *Historia Roderici uel gesta Roderici Campidocti* does not refer to any of the events. See: Emma Falque, Juan Gil, and A. Maya, *Chronica hispana saeculi XII*, vol. 1 (Turnhout: Brepols 1990).

48 *... et después, el otro jueues, mando que se llegasen todas las gentes de los moros en el alcaçar, et asentosse en su estrado muy noblemiente, et todos antel, et mando que aduxiessen a Abeniaf et los otros presos que eran con el. Et desi dixo a aquel alfaqui a quien fizieron alcalle, et a los otros omnes buenos, que judgassen que muerte meresçien, segunt su ley, por que mataron a su señor, segunt ha contado la estoria. Et ellos dixieron: señor segunt nuestra ley deuen ser apedreados. Et el Çid mandolos luego matar desta guisa. Et eran con Abeniaf CCC et XXX*. Ramón Menéndez Pidal, *Primera Crónica General de España*, (Madrid: Seminario Menéndez Pidal, 1977), 2:591. For more information about El Cid and his time, see: Ramón Menéndez Pidal, *La España del Cid*, (Madrid: Plutarco, 1929), translation by Ramón Menéndez Pidal, *The Cid and his Spain* (New York: Routledge, 2016), 357–364.

of a Christian King, had to act according to the law of his subjects and defer to the people in their jurisprudence; the Christian warrior only sanctions a capital sentence issued by others.

Christian expansion in the Andalusian domains thus involved a form of penal syncretism with both the Islamic and Jewish communities.[49] Before the fall of Valencia to El Cid, the city of Toledo and its *taifa* were given to Alphonse VI in 1085. A few decades later, in 1118, his grandson Alphonse VII (1105–1157) gave Toledo the sanctioned privilege to lapidate anyone who committed homicide in the city of Toledo itself or in the surrounding five-mile area.[50] This punishment also qualified as *morte turpissima* [a humiliating, ugly, dishonorable death]. If the accusation against the murderer was doubtful, the jurisdiction allowed them to be judged according to the Christian *Liber Iudicum*.[51] To be inside or outside the city in cases of bloody crime could mean the difference between death by stoning or not, but in any case, the space of execution matters.

Despite their earlier tradition, Hebrew communities very rarely used stoning as punishment. Only a few references to *responsa*—legal responses to specific cases—survive in Iberia. For example, the Jewish judge Ibn Abittur (Yosef ibn Abitur ben Satan, d. 970) explained that his family name, Satan, originated from the four capital sentences imposed by his grandfather (circa 9th century):

> In view of the fact that a gaon has insulted us because of our appellation. … Know Your Reverence that my grandfather's grandfather, our Lord have mercy on them, was powerful in Sepharad, although he was not able to discern the degrees between Torah and other teachings, he imposed four death sentences in Spain, which would not have been possible except in the Diaspora. And because he was a scourge to scourge the wicked, he was called 'whip of man'.

---

49 Adulterers, apostates, and sodomites could be punished this way. See: Christian Lange, *Justice, Punishment and the Medieval Muslim Imagination* (Cambridge: Cambridge University Press, 2008), 58, 66–67 and Delfina Serrano Ruano, "Stoning as Punishment of Illegal Sexual Relations (*Zina*) in the Heart of the Maliki School: Doctrine, Legal Practice and Individual Attitudes in the Face of the Crime," *Al-Qantara*, 26.2 (2005): 449–473.

50 Deposition 25 under the charter of 1118 affirms: "Quod si aliquis aliquem hominem occiderit intus Toleti, aut foras infra quinque milliarios in circuitu eius, morte turpissima cum lapidibus moriatur" [If anyone kills someone inside the city of Toledo or within five miles, the murder will be executed with an awful death, stoning]. See: Alfonso García-Gallo, *Los fueros de Toledo* (Madrid: Instituto Nacional de Estudios Jurídicos), 478.

51 Disposition 27 of local laws (*fuero*). García-Gallo, *Los fueros*, 478.

Later, Joseph ibn Migash (1077–1141) refers to a stoning carried out during Yom Kippur, prompting the thirteenth-century exile Judah Asher Ben Yehiel to express surprise at the power of the Jewish communities in Castile.[52]

The reason for using this penalty may lie, again, in reappropriating punishments of Jewish origin. In his *Book of Tradition*, Abraham ibn Daud of Toledo (*c.*1110–1181) recounts the internal schism among Hebrew communities after Alphonse VI expelled the Karaite Jewish faction, rather than allowing their execution by their peers—other Jews: "Nasi R. Joseph b. Ferrizuel, surnamed Cidellus ... suppressed them even beyond their former lowly state. He drove them out of all the strongholds of Castille except for one, which he granted them, since he did not want to put them to death (in as much as capital punishment was not administered at the present time)."[53] The Karaite were a Jewish sect that believed only in the written Torah and rejected the oral Torah. The narrative does not refer to the type of execution, but among Hebrew communities, stoning would have been likely. Once again, the story also establishes a relationship between this likely stoning and exile. In his *Partidas* (*Legal Code*) (*c.*1250), more than a century later and, perhaps confirming actual dynamics, King Alphonse X of Castilla prohibited the Jewish communities from "stoning, hurting, or killing" those Jews who converted to Christianity.[54] In this case, the convert's murderers would be burned, an example of a Gothic revival of the *Liber Iudicum*, 12.2,17.

Execution by stoning and exile were intimately related during this period. Not all forms of capital punishment were performed outside communities but stoning to death was one of them. Jewish, Roman, Greek, Muslim, and Christian tradition endured in medieval Iberia, inspired by well-known Patristic and legal arguments which understood extermination in a double sense: to put end to the human life and to exile (out-of-the-borders). For example, the transformation of death penalties into exile, as with the last stages of Visigothic anti-Jewish legislation or the exile of Karaite Jews from the kingdom of León-Castilla. In hagiography, Saint Desiderius was condemned first to exile,

---

52 Judit Targarona, "Breves notas sobre Ibn Abitur," *Miscelánea de estudios árabes y hebraicos. Sección de hebreo*, 31 (1982), 53–85 at 69. Ephraim Kanarfogel, "Capital punishment," in *Medieval Jewish Civilization: An Encyclopedia*, ed. Norman Roth (New York, London: Routledge, 2003), 134–136.

53 Jaime Bages, *Abraham ben David. Sefer-Ha-Kabbalah* (*Libro de la tradición*) (Granada: El defensor, 1922), 68. English version in Gerson D. Cohen, *Abraham Ibn Daud, The Book of Tradition* (*Sefer Ha-Qabbalah*), (Philadelphia: The Jewish Publication Society of America, 1967), 95 and notes in 144.

54 The same *Partida* (7:24, 6) again mentions the "death or stoning" executed by the Jews. See: José Sánchez Arcilla, *Las Siete Partidas* (Madrid: Reus, 2004), 961–962.

then forgiven, but at last executed by stoning. In the eleventh and twelfth centuries, plenty of cases emerged in which churchmen were exiled, murdered, or menaced with stoning. Sometimes stoning did not serve as a method of execution, but as an extreme measure to enforce expulsion from the community like the case of archbishop Diego Gelmírez and the abbot of Sahagún monastery (and his monks). In Toledo, if a murder was committed inside the city (up to 5 miles out), the murderer would be stoned to death, reflecting a very deep relationship between punishment, identity, and place because only those murders executed inside city and neighboring areas deserved death by stoning. Ultimately, as stoning was marginalized in the Iberian world, it was understood as a method of execution with a violent and mixed heritage that crossed cultural boundaries and recapitulated the punishments of the ancient past.

CHAPTER 4

Judicial Authority and Marian Mercy in Gautier de Coinci's "D'une fame qui fu delivree a Loon dou feu" and *La Vie des pères*' "Belle-Mère"

Karen Casey Casebier

As stories of divine interventions made on behalf of undeserving sinners, medieval miracle tales highlight the role of grace and mercy in salvation by demonstrating God's love for sinners. Yet they also underscore the Virgin Mary's broad intercessory powers to intervene on the behalf of her faithful.[1] Mary's discretionary powers are central to judicial miracles, where she wields her spiritual authority to correct or prevent miscarriages of justice. Judicial miracles become controversial, however, when the Virgin intervenes in cases involving capital punishment, because she demonstrates a bias towards her faithful that disrupts trials and executions, thereby sparing even those guilty of serious spiritual and criminal offenses.

One illustration of Mary's exercise of divine authority to amend the prescription and practice of medieval courts is the miracle of the woman who was saved from burning, represented in two collections of Old French miracle tales by Gautier de Coinci's "D'une fame qui fu delivree a Loon dou feu" ("The Woman Was Delivered From Burning at Loon") (c.1214–36) [hereafter MND] and the anonymous *Vie des pères*' "De la fame qui fist estrangler son gendre" ("The Woman Who Had Her Son-in-Law Strangled") [hereafter *Belle-Mère* for the individual tale or VDP for the whole work].[2] As the VDP's title suggests,

1 "The miracles always seek to communicate Mary's power and mercy, the strength of her care and protection, and the eternal rewards of devotion to her." Adrienne Williams Boyarin, Introduction, *Miracles of the Virgin in Middle English: A Broadview Anthology of British Literature*, ed. and trans. by Adrienne Williams Boyarin (Petersborough, Ontario: Broadview Press, 2015), 9–15 at 11. The most common miracle plot involves sinners who find themselves in desperate situations and appeal to the Virgin, who provides a miraculous rescue because of the supplicant's faithful service to her. Clarissa Atkinson, *The Oldest Vocation: Christian Motherhood in the Middle Ages* (Ithaca, NY: Cornell University Press, 1991), 133.

2 "D'une fame qui fu delivree a Loon dou feu," in *Les Miracles de Nostre Dame*, ed. L.F. Koenig, 4 vols. (Geneva: Droz, 1955–1970), 2 Mir. 26, 4:265–294. Gautier de Coinci's version was composed *c.*1214–36. All references to this work will be abbreviated as *MND*, and all translations are my own. Lines numbers are given in parentheses. "De la fame qui fist estrangler son gendre," *La Vie des pères*, The Hague, Koninklijke Bibliotheek (KB) MS 71 A 24

 | DOI:10.1163/9789004742598_006

the narrative is a salacious *exemplum* of contract murder and vengeance that recounts the story of a mother-in-law who gets along so well with her son-in-law that there are rumors of an adulterous, incestuous affair. To repair her reputation, the eponymous character hires two men to murder her son-in-law. When her crime is discovered, the Belle-Mère is tried and sentenced to burning, but the Virgin responds to the woman's crisis, sparing her an ignominious public execution; she returns home to die after a short period of penance.

As both spiritual lesson and secular entertainment, the Marian miracle tale appealed to a broad spectrum of medieval society.[3] As a subset of miracle tales, judicial miracles conform to the traditional representation of the Virgin as an important, accessible saint who intercedes for those who find themselves in desperate situations, and this representation is remarkably stable across different vernacular literatures. Nonetheless, Mary's intervention in legal affairs capitalizes on the drama inherent to capital cases, deliberately evoking the social context of the miracle tale. Comparing different variants of the same tale not only provides critical insight into contemporary beliefs regarding popular spirituality, but also reveals how sensational crimes may have been tried and sentenced in medieval courts, and how judicial miracle tales might function as nuanced commentaries on the limitations of temporal justice. Indeed, Hannah Skoda's study of violence in thirteenth- and fourteenth-century France asserts that although contemporary literary texts should not be read as "mirrors of society," medieval literature remains a valuable source of information on interpersonal violence in medieval society because these texts "engaged with social norms, problematized them, and embodied the dialogue between those norms, the composers and the audiences who read, listened to, and

(MS k), fols. 124v–125r; Brussels, Bibliothèque Royale de Bruxelles (KBR) MS 9229–30 (MS i), fols. 123r–124r; and Paris, Bibliothèque de l'Arsenal (Ars.) MS 5204 (MS d), fols. 148r–148v. Unless otherwise noted, all references refer to MS k, the oldest manuscript in this branch. All references will be abbreviated as *VDP*, and all translations are my own. Following the tradition of abbreviated titles in the critical edition of the First-Third *Vies*, this tale will be referred to as *Belle-Mère* when discussing the individual tale, and *VDP* for the whole work. Note that the manuscript sigla and the order of the *VDP* were first established by Edouard Schwan, "*La Vie des anciens pères*," *Romania*, 13 (1884): 233–63 and are still in use. Félix Lecoy adds new manuscripts and sigla but otherwise follows Schwan. Introduction to *La Vie des pères*, ed. Félix Lecoy, 3 vols. (Paris: Société des anciens textes français, 1987–1999), 1:ix–xxiv. The Old French *VDP* should not be confused with William Caxton's 1495 Middle English translation (1977), which is based on the Latin *Vitae sanctorum patrum*, although Caxton does claim kinship with the Old French collection.

3 Boyarin, Introduction, 12.

watched them."[4] In the *MND*, Gautier de Coinci criticizes the abuses of ecclesiastical justice, whereas in *Belle-Mère*, the *VDP*-poet promotes the wisdom of the secular court in ceding to Mary's mercy, but both variants demonstrate the superiority of the celestial court to render justice by virtue of its consideration of the sinner's spiritual well-being.[5]

When Mary uses her spiritual authority to overturn the decisions of ecclesiastical or royal courts, the judicial miracle represents a subversive challenge to judicial authority because the celestial court operates both above and outside the law, in ways that frequently contradict contemporary legal prescription and practice in both ecclesiastical and secular courts.[6] Indeed, when the Virgin exercises her discretionary intercessory powers for the benefit of her faithful, earthly judicial authorities rarely question the decision of the celestial court, even when divine mercy exonerates the guilty, commutes a harsh sentence, or applies the maximum penalty under the law.

The Virgin's role in executions is especially problematic within the context of judicial practice because her exercise of divine mercy suspends the *ordo iudiciarius* [trial procedure], thus undermining its legitimacy. In medieval cases involving capital punishment, court officials interpreted miracles as signifying that the offender was either innocent or that death was too harsh a penalty for the crime.[7] Indeed, Claude Gauvrard argues that in failed executions, "le miracle prouve l'innocence de l'accusé" [the miracle proves the accused's innocence].[8] Therefore, judicial miracle tales that rescind or commute the prescription of earthly courts constitute both imaginative displays of the Virgin's power and mercy towards her faithful as well as social criticism

4 Hannah Skoda, *Medieval Violence: Physical Brutality in Northern France 1270–1330* (Oxford: Oxford University Press, 2013), 13. See also Natalie Zemon Davis, who proposes that narratives of fictional events were constructed to fit legal and societal norms in *Fiction in the Archives: Pardon Tales and Their Tellers in Fifteenth-Century France* (Stanford: Stanford University Press, 1990).

5 Although issues of community play a critical role in the narrative, I restrict the discussion here to questions pertaining to trial procedure, the jurisdiction and application of royal and canon law, and the procedures and customs related to public execution.

6 David A. Flory cautions on the limits of the sociohistorical applications of literature in "The Social Uses of Religious Literature: Challenging Authority in the Thirteenth-Century Marian Miracle Tale," *Essays in Medieval Studies* 13 (1996): 61–69 at 64. See also: David A. Flory, *Marian Representations in the Miracle Tales of Thirteenth-Century Spain and France* (Washington, D.C.: Catholic University of America Press, 2000).

7 Trevor Dean suggests that miracles could be interpreted as evidence that the prescribed punishment was not commensurate to the crime, regardless of its legality, in *Crime in Medieval Europe: 1200–1550* (Harlow: Pearson Education 2001), 136.

8 Claude Gauvard, *De grace especial: Crime, état et société en France à la fin du Moyen Age* (Paris: Publications de la Sorbonne, 1991), 180.

of contemporary legal practice. In effect, Mary's protection of condemned criminals nullifies any attempt to bring them to justice through established legal procedures, ecclesiastical or secular, and invites the audience to contrast the infallible and expeditious procedures of God's grace and mercy with the imperfect operations of medieval courts.

As is common with vernacular miracle tales, the miracle of the woman who was saved from burning enters Old French literature as a retelling of earlier Latin texts, and most of the scholarly record concentrates on the transmission of the tale.[9] Gautier de Coinci produced the first vernacular version in the first half of the thirteenth century, in which he asserts that Mary's interference in the Belle-Mère's execution corrects the harsh (yet entirely legal) punishment meted out by an overzealous ecclesiastical court. This version inspired several fourteenth-century prose retellings of the tale, as well as a play, and although the narrative has not inspired much scholarly study, there are a few references to this miracle in linguistic and stylistic studies.[10] The next known vernacular variant appears nearly one hundred years later, in an unedited interpolation

9 Joseph Morawski, "Mélanges de littérature pieuse," *Romania* 61.3–4 (1935): 145–209 at 201–02, lists the Latin versions of this tale: Guibert de Nogent, *A Monk's Confession: the Memoirs of Guibert de Nogent*, ed. Paul J. Archambault (University Park, PA: Pennsylvania State University Press, 1996); Herman de Laon, *De miraculis sanctae Mariae Laudunensis*, ed. Alain Saint-Denis (Paris: CNRS éditions, 2008); Vincent de Beauvais, *Le Speculum Historiale de Vincent de Beauvais*, ed. M. Taraye (Paris: Champion, 1999); and Jacobus de Voragine, *Legenda aurea: vulgo Historia lombardica dicta*, ed. Johann Georg Theodor Graesse, 3rd ed. (Breslau: Koebner 1890, 1st ed. 1845) [Repr. Osnabruck: O. Zeller, 1969], ch. 131, para. 10 at 594–95.

10 The sheer number of extant fourteenth-century variants suggests that this was a popular miracle tale. Jean le Conte's collection of Marian miracles includes a prose version: Jean le Conte, *Miracles de Nostre-Dame (fin XIVe siècle), Edition critique, d'après le ms. BNF fr. 1806*, ed. Pierre Kunstmann and Yen Duong (Ottawa: University of Ottawa Press, 1998); as does Jean Miélot's fifteenth-century compendium: *Miracles de Nostre Dame collected by Jean Miélot, secretary to Philip the Good, duke of Burgundy, Reproduced in facsimile from Douce manuscript 374 in the Bodleian Library for John Malcolm of Poltalloch with text, introduction and annotated analysis by George F. Warner, M.A*, ed. George F. Warner (Westminster: Nichols and Sons, 1885). Both prose versions are based on the *VDP* (Mierowski, "Mélanges de littérature pieuse," 175–78). The miracle was also dramatized in the late fourteenth century: *Une Femme que Nostre Dame garda d'estre arse*, in *Les Miracles de Nostre Dame par personnages*, ed. Gaston Paris and Ulysse Robert, 8 vols. (Paris: Firmin Didot, 1876–93), 4:175–235. Skoda's comments on the play highlight the ambivalence of violence, and she also suggests that the miracle tale is based on a real incident that took place in 1096 (*Medieval Violence*, 239–42, n. 19 at 239). For the *MND* variant, see: Tony Hunt, *Miraculous Rhymes: The Writing of Gautier de Coinci* (Woodbridge: D.S. Brewer, 2007); Gérard Gros, "Prière et poésie selon Gautier de Coinci,"in *La Spiritualité des écrivains*, ed. Olivier Millet (Geneva: Droz, 2008), 17–34.

of miracle tales within a fourteenth-century manuscript branch of the *VDP*, an eclectic collection of thirteenth-century devotional literature that highlights the role of repentance, confession, and penance in salvation and includes several miracles of the Virgin, one of which is *Belle-Mère*.[11] The *VDP*-poet presents a very different account of the woman's trial and failed execution in which municipal court officials immediately recognize the miracle and release the condemned to her family, so that the dispassionate response of the municipal court and its officials presents customary law as more just and discerning than canon law. Comparing the two versions suggests that the tension between the two types of law can only be resolved by divine intervention, since neither ecclesiastical courts nor secular courts deliver what the celestial court determines to be a just punishment for the Belle-Mère's crime.

---

11 This particular tale has never been the object of scholarly study. The narrative roughly follows Gautier de Coinci's version but draws other details from the *Legenda aurea* and Alfonso X, el Sabio's Galician-Portuguese miracle collection. "Como Santa Maria guareceu a moller que fezera matar seu genrro polo mal prez que ll' apõyan con el, que non ardeu no fogo en que a meteron," in *Cantigas de Santa Maria*, ed. Walter Mettmann, 3 vol. (Madrid: Clásicos Castalia, 1986–89), Cantiga 255, 3:13–17; Morawski proposes Herman de Laon's Latin version as the model for this tale ("Mélanges de littérature pieuse," 202).

As a collection of devotional literature, the *VDP* has a complex history with respect to both compilation and composition. The *VDP* began with 42 tales (*c.*1215–30) but was expanded twice during the thirteenth century to include 32 additional tales, mostly miracles of the Virgin. To distinguish the original collection of 42 tales from its later expansions, Schwan divided this work into the First, Second and Third *Vie des pères* at the turn of the twentieth century ("*La Vie des anciens pères*"). Lecoy dates the Second *Vie des pères* to *c.*1241–1250 and the Third *Vie des pères* to 1252, and observes marked instability in the order and content of the Second and Third *Vie des pères* (introduction to *La Vie des pères*, 1:xxiii). For additional discussion on the composition of *La Vie des pères*, see: Adrian Tudor, "The One That Got Away: The Case of the Old French *Vie des pères*," *French Studies Bulletin*, 55 (1995): 11–15.

The fourteenth-century manuscript branch that contains *Belle-Mère* includes an interpolation of ten miracle tales that are inserted in the exact order and in the same place in all three manuscripts, which date to *c.*1325–27. *Belle-Mère* is Miracle 7 in this series. Both the narrative structure and the thematic content of these new tales conform to the existing structure and content of *La Vie des pères*, although they may be distinguished from earlier additions by both this *VDP*-poet's modest literary talents and their brevity. As new tales not previously associated with the collection, the attention to form, thematic content and placement within the manuscript branch is highly suggestive of a fourth *Vie des pères*. Morawski describes this manuscript branch in his study of interpolations of miracle tales within compilations of pious literature ("Mélanges de littérature pieuse," 147, 194–205). For the dating and production of this manuscript branch, see Mary and Richard Rouse, *Manuscripts and Their Makers: Commercial Book Producers in Medieval Paris 1200–1500*, 2 vols. (London: Harvey Miller, 2001), 1:191–202.

Both poets emphasize variable aspects of judicial practice and procedure, but they also reveal disparities in the treatment of the crime and the criminal, from its discovery to the dramatic suspension of the sentence, precisely because of the two different courts and systems of justice. In both versions, the outcome of the miracle tale remains the same, but each highlights different judicial actors, both ecclesiastical and secular, during a period in which the actual rule of law was neither uniform nor monolithic. In France, legal matters during the thirteenth and fourteenth centuries were increasingly settled by customary law, which was progressively subject to royal jurisdiction. Ecclesiastical and royal courts shared overlapping jurisdictions for some types of crimes, but in reality, canon law and civil law both complemented and competed with one another during this period; they served the same communities but offered alternative solutions to similar legal situations.[12] After the late twelfth century, ecclesiastical courts exercised broad jurisdiction over all immoral behavior by virtue of their classification as sinful acts. Moreover, they claimed exclusive jurisdiction over sex crimes and marital infractions, inextricably linking the social context of the Belle-Mère's predicament with the evolution and standardization of medieval law. While the *MND* illustrates how the case might have been handled by ecclesiastical law, contrasting a spiritually corrupt ecclesiastical court with the Virgin's grace and mercy, the *VDP* promotes a positive image of customary law by demonstrating that the swift justice of municipal courts readily submits to the decision of the superior, celestial court to which the criminal has appealed.

Gautier de Coinci begins his version of the tale by accumulating narrative details that encourage the audience to accept the veracity of the miracle. The incident takes place in Chïevi, near Laon (*MND*, 28), and he lists the first names of every family member in the household (*MND*, 29–35) as well as several court officials (*MND*, 25, 182, 262). He also identifies the Belle-Mère as the mayor's wife (*MND*, 29), whereas in the *VDP*, the husband is simply referred to as *li barons* [the baron] (*VDP*, fol. 124v, col. C), a term that implies nobility. Since the Belle-Mère occupies an important social position in the community, her crime represents a threat to both the social order and the common good.

The young couple lives together in the family home (*MND*, 39; *VDP*, fol. 124v, col. A), and although Gautier de Coinci describes the Belle-Mère as *cortoyse et sage* [courtly and wise] (*MND*, 41), he underscores the scandalous nature of community gossip: "A dire pristrent mout de genz / Qu'il tenoyt la fille et la

12 James A. Brundage, *Medieval Canon Law* (London: Longman Group Limited, 1995), 97 and James A. Brundage, *Law, Sex, and Christian Society in Medieval Europe* (Chicago: University of Chicago Press, 1987), 319 and 481.

mere" [Many people started to say that he was having daughter and mother] (*MND*, 48–49). In contrast to Gautier de Coinci's neutral tone in reporting the rumors, the *VDP* specifically characterizes the woman's relationship to her son-in-law as beyond reproach, so that her violent crime against him appears to be out of character:

> Et la mere tant l'en ama
> Que *la* mere l'en difama,[13]
> Et disoit fause renommee,
> Que de son gendre estoit amee,
> Folement et d'amour vilainne. (*VDP*, fol. 124v, cols. A–B)
>
> [And the mother loved him so much that she was slandered because of it, and false rumours were told that she was loved passionately by her son-in-law, in a shameful way.]

The *VDP*-poet makes it clear that this is a lie intended to besmirch the Belle-Mère's reputation, emphasizing the woman's *bonne amour* [wholesome love] (*VDP*, fol. 124v, col. B) that others have mistaken for adultery and incest:

> Car c'est la coustume mondainne
> De parvertir en mal les biens.
> Mes cele n'i penssoit a riens,
> Fors qu'en tout bien, en toute honnour,
> S'entramoient de bonne amour. (*VDP*, fol. 124v, col. B)
>
> [Because it is human nature to pervert good into evil. But she didn't think anything of it, except that they should love one another with a wholesome love, with all honor and respect.]

Since a medieval woman's reputation was closely linked to chastity before marriage and fidelity afterwards, rumors of sexual misconduct provide the protagonist with a motive for murder.[14] The portrait of the Belle-Mère as a vir-

13 *l'en* (MS k); This line is corrected from MS i (fol. 123v, col. A) and MS d (fol. 148r, col. B) for grammatical reasons.

14 Dean suggests that "a woman's sexual conduct must be characterized by a complete absence of impropriety" (*Crime in Medieval Europe*, 116). According to Brundage, finding a married woman alone with a man other than her husband constituted sufficient proof of adultery for some medieval courts (Brundage, *Law, Sex, and Christian Society*, 519).

tuous woman who is the victim of malicious gossip also inspires sympathy for her, since the crime contrasts sharply with the initial image of the protagonist as a model mother-in law and an upstanding member of the community.

When she learns that the community has accused her of a *crime de moeurs*, Gautier de Coinci highlights the Belle-Mère's emotional response:

> Mout heit sa vie et mout la blasme.
> Tant dolante est, tant plainne d'ire
> Ne seit que faire ne que dire.
> Tant durement est destorbee
> Que durement jor et nuit bee
> Pense et repense et subtelie
> Comment ceste grant vilenie
> Abatre puist et esfacier. (*MND*, 54–61)

> [She hates her life very much, and curses it frequently. She is so sorrowful [and] so full of anger that she does not know what to do or say. She is so distraught that all night and day, aghast, she thinks and ponders and plots of how she might demolish and expunge this great injury.]

In contrast, the *VDP*'s version suggests that her obsession with slander renders her susceptible to demonic influence:

> Pour poi ne devint forsenee,
> Et si la l'anemi temptee.
> L'ire qui l'aguillonne et point,
> Qui la mis en dampnable point
> Li fet braser .i. tel afaire
> Que li tournera a contraire. (*VDP*, fol. 124v, col. B)

> [She was on the verge of madness when the enemy tempted her. Anger goads and pricks her, and has put her in a damnable situation; she is so consumed by the matter that it will turn everything upside down.]

In both versions, the devil wastes little time in suggesting murder (*MND*, 71–75; *VDP*, fol. 124v, col. B), a solution that appears logical to the protagonist in her fragile mental state. Gautier de Coinci's version foreshadows the Belle-Mère's strategy to restore her reputation by introducing the devil as "[Cielz] qui Caÿm fist murtrir Abel" [[He] who caused Cain to murder Abel] (*MND*, 63), but the *VDP*-poet describes a generic demonic temptation. The trope of demonic torment or temptation is a hagiographic commonplace, but in the *VDP*, it frequently precedes spectacular falls from grace that endanger the protagonist's soul.[15] More importantly, when those with otherwise blameless characters suddenly commit grievous sins, the devil's influence not only minimizes the protagonist's responsibility for sinning, but also engenders sympathy in the audience for them. Thus, the Belle-Mère chooses contract murder to end the malicious gossip: "Deuz fors ribaus li a fait penre / Et louer pour murtrir son genre" [She hired two strong scoundrels to take her son-in-law and murder him] (*MND*, 87–88). The *VDP*-poet adds that she hired the murderers for ".xl. soulz" [40 *sous*] (*VDP*, fol. 124v, col. B), a pecuniary detail that contradicts the *VDP*'s characterization of the woman as emotionally unstable by highlighting her ability to reason.[16] As a willing participant in her fall from grace, the Belle-Mère's flagrant sinning emphasizes her responsibility for the young man's murder, since it can in no way be interpreted as a crime of passion, but it also nullifies the sympathetic response from the audience that the demonic temptation motif typically inspires. Moreover, the realistic detail of payment for this service underscores her violent intent, so that the miracle is unequivocally performed on behalf of a sinner.

Within the social context of this tale, the devil is an effective counsellor, albeit a poor one. Since demonic influence was cited as a legal defense in up to 48% of medieval crimes in the late-fourteenth century, the *VDP*-poet's insistence on demonic temptation would have resonated with the audience both as a hagiographic motif and as a criminal defense strategy.[17] In addition, Skoda argues that emotion was a critical element in women's crime, and that their presumed inability to control their emotions usually resulted in more lenient punishments for some types of violent crime.[18] While the Belle-Mère's anger and her gender would typically mitigate her punishment, however, both her

15 Notable examples include "Ivresse," in *VDP*, 1:169–82, in which a saintly hermit commits the sins of drunkenness, fornication and murder following nightly visits from the devil, and "Nièce," in *VDP*, 2:150–69, in which a hermitess breaks out of her cell to become a prostitute.

16 Cf. "xx solidos" in Jacobus de Voragine's *Legenda aurea* (ch. 131, para. 10 at 594). Forty *sous* is the rough equivalent of $2000, not adjusted for inflation. The value of medieval coins varied somewhat according to weight and purity, and varied widely depending on where the coins were minted. Jeffrey L. Singman, *Daily Life in Medieval Europe* (Westport, CT: Greenwood Press, 1999), 59.

17 Gauvard, *De grace especial*, 297.

18 Skoda cites infanticide as a prominent example (*Medieval Violence*, 228), concluding that women's crimes were often treated leniently during this period (*Medieval Violence*, especially Ch. 6). Likewise, Trevor Dean maintains that "[violence] is not a part of the social or cultural construct of femininity," noting that only 4% of women asked for pardons for

social status and the nature of the crime counteract the possibility of a light sentence. In scandalous crimes that involved prominent families, offenders frequently suffered the full consequences of their actions, since punishments were meant to serve as deterrents as well as correctives.[19] As a noblewoman who killed a male family member to defend her reputation, the Belle-Mère's best possible legal outcome relies on her appeal to Mary.

As for the crime itself, both versions of this tale unequivocally characterize the son-in-law's death as murder by virtue of contract killing and concealment of the body.[20] In addition, Gautier de Coinci's version employs the term *murtrir face* [to do murder] (*MND*, 74) to describe the contract murder, whereas the *VDP*-poet chooses the expression *fere occirre* [to have [him] killed] (*VDP*, fol. 124v, cols. B–C).[21] The deliberate use of legal terminology to describe the young man's violent death strengthens the social context of this tale by making the woman's trial and execution more credible, since prescribing the maximum penalty for prominent members of the local community reflects contemporary beliefs on how to restore social order after scandalous crimes.[22]

Gautier de Coinci depicts the murder as particularly heinous, recounting the crime in salacious detail. First, the Belle-Mère pretends to be ill and asks her "bialz doz fiex" [good, sweet son] (*MND*, 103) to fetch her some wine from the cellar (*MND*, 103–05):

> Si tost com chiet entre les leuz,
> Pris et saisi l'ont entr'auz deux.

violent crimes during the reign of Charles VI (1389–1422) and that only 20% of Lyon's convicted felons were women (*Crime in Medieval Europe*, 77).

19 Brundage, *Law, Sex, and Christian Society*, 519.

20 A nearly universal characteristic of medieval murder is that murder occurs at night, or there is an attempt to hide the body after death. Pieter Spierenberg, *A History of Murder: Personal Violence in Europe from the Middle Ages to the Present* (Cambridge: Polity, 2008), 53. See also: *Medieval and Early Modern Murder: Legal, Literary and Historical Contexts*, ed. Larissa Tracy (Woodbridge: Boydell Press, 2018).

21 The other witnesses also employ these verbs (MS i, fols. 123v, col. B-123v, col. C and MS d, fols. 148r, col. C-148v, col. A).

22 Skoda's analysis of the French lexicon of homicide includes nouns such as *homicide* and *trahison* as well as verbs such as *tuer, ocir, murtrir, mourir* and *mettre a mort* (*Medieval Violence*, 30). Although Skoda insists that the choice of language further refined the type of homicide (*Medieval Violence*, 31), Gauvard's study concludes that the legal terms used to describe various types of homicides in the thirteenth century may be misleading. Punishment was at the discretion of the judge, but the severity of sentences suggests that courts increasingly distinguished between manslaughter and murder in the thirteenth century, with special emphasis on pleas of self-defense whose mitigating circumstances usually resulted in lighter penalties (Gauvard, *De grace especial*, 799–806).

Sa lasse gorge li estrangnent
Tant qu'il le tüent et estaingnent.
Ne li ont fait ne sanc ne plaie.
La torteruele qui fressaie
En peu de tanz est devenue
Tout coyement, a mousche mue,
En son lit reporter leur fait. (*MND*, 111–19)

[As soon as he entered the [cellar], they took him and seized him between them. [Then] they strangle his poor neck until they kill him and extinguish [his life]. They did not shed any blood, nor cause any wound. In a short time, the frightened turtledove became entirely calm, quiet as a mouse, [and] they placed him in his bed.]

The scene ends when the murderers take the young man upstairs, staging his body so that he will appear to have died in his bed, "por mielz couvrir ce grant mesfait" [to better hide this great crime] (*MND*, 120).

In contrast to this detailed account of the murder, in *Belle-Mère*, the protagonist leads her son-in-law to the cellar on an unknown pretext, where "li murtrier l'ont lors estranglé" [the murderers then strangled him] (*VDP*, fol. 124v, col. B).[23] She then takes steps to conceal her crime by moving his body upstairs, but unlike Gautier de Coinci, the *VDP*-poet describes the woman's actions without authorial intervention, allowing the audience to come to the conclusion that she is attempting to disguise murder as a sudden calamity: "La fame la porte errant / Ou lit sa fille com dormant, / Et de robes moult bien couvert" (*VDP*, fol. 124v, cols. B–C) [The woman immediately carries [the body] to her daughter's bed, as though he were sleeping, tucking him in properly with blankets]. As in the *MND*, the Belle-Mère next asks her daughter to wake him for lunch, when the latter discovers her husband dead in their bed (*MND*, 146–164; *VDP*, fol. 124v, col. C). Here, the *VDP*-poet conveys both the daughter's discovery of the body and her sorrow in six verses (*VDP*, fol. 124v, col. C),[24] but Gautier

23 Cf. Philippe de Beaumanoir, *The Coutumes de Beauvaisis of Philippe de Beaumanoir*, ed. and trans. F.R.P. Akehurst (Philadelphia: University of Pennsylvania Press, 1992), §1956 at 715–16, in which the wife lets her husband's killers into the family home to murder him in the bath.

24 In the *VDP*, murder appears to be the purview of women. In *Inceste*, a new mother commits infanticide to hide the sin of incest ("Inceste," in *VDP*, 2:228–45). *Sénéchal* features a double-murder, in which the queen first murders the eponymous seneschal who seduces her prior to the wedding and next murders her cousin, a virgin whom she had placed in the king's bed on her wedding night to hide her own sexual misconduct ("Sénéchal," in

de Coinci includes a lengthy discovery scene emphasizing the daughter's grief (*MND*, 150–71).

These straightforward accounts of the young man's death are rendered more complex because each poet alludes to the hagiographical register either prior to or during the murder. The *VDP*-poet points out that the Belle-Mère hired the men to "Fere occirre / Son gendre, et livrer a martire" [to kill her son-in-law and deliver him to martyrdom] (*VDP*, fol. 124v, col. B), and although the characterization of his murder as martyrdom is rather tenuous, the use of *martire* highlights the son-in-law's innocence in the matter of adultery. In Gautier de Coinci's more precise description of the victim, he refers to animals associated with specific saints, both of whom represented fidelity and chastity in the medieval imagination. When the young man unwittingly descends to his death, the poet refers to him as *li doz aigniauz* [the sweet lamb] (*MND*, 110), an animal that frequently accompanies Saint Agnes in medieval iconography, and which is traditionally interpreted as a symbol of Christ in the New Testament. The poet also evokes Saint Alexis when he calls him *la torteruele* [the turtle-dove] (*MND*, 116) as he is strangled.[25]

These symbolic borrowings from the hagiographical lexicon amplify the son-in-law's innocence in adultery by aligning him with saints reputed for their fidelity and chastity. Thus the brutal strangulation of the victim, followed by the literal and figurative secrecy of posing the body to imitate a natural death, casts the Belle-Mère as the diabolical mastermind of the murder plot. Demonic suggestion neatly explains her drastic transformation from virtuous housewife to murderess. In the contemporary legal context, although the protagonist has the presence of mind to plan the murder and attempt to conceal her role in it, an insanity defense, by virtue of demonic influence, eliminates the aspect of premeditation that defines violent death as murder in French

---

VDP, 2:84–107). The motif of contract murder to cover a non-existent sin is therefore in keeping with the general themes of the collection, since it expands the repertoire of murder tales.

25 John the Baptist greets Jesus as the "Lamb of God" when he baptizes him (John 1:29, 1:36). Citations from the Bible refer to the *Biblia sacra iuxta vulgatam versionem* (Stuttgart: Württembergische Bibelanstalt, 1969–75). All translations refer to the *The Bible*, Authorized King James Version (Oxford: Oxford University Press, 1998). For detailed discussion of Saint Agnes's lamb as a symbol of chastity, see: Louis Réau, *Iconographie de l'art chrétien*, 3 vols. (Presses Universitaires de France, 1955–59), 3:33. Contemplating her impending widowhood, Alexis' bride uses the turtledove to signify her fidelity and chastity when the saint abandons her on her wedding night. *La Vie de Saint Alexis: texte du ms. A*, ed. T.D. Hemming (Exeter: University of Exeter Press, 1994) *laisse* 52 at 931–41. For additional examples of the turtledove in hagiographic literature, see: Florence McCulloch, "Sainte Euphrosine, Saint Alexis, and the Turtledove," *Romania* 98 (1977): 168–85.

customary law.[26] If she is nearly mad (*VDP*, fol. 124, col. B), her intent is to quell malicious gossip and the crime is merely a means to achieve it; neither court has the authority to condemn her because demonic suggestion has inspired an act of insanity. Indeed, Mary's miraculous intervention in the *dénouement* will correct the flawed decision of both courts by preventing her execution.

After the murder, the two narratives diverge. In *Belle-Mère*, removing the son-in-law from the family home causes the rumors of illicit sexual conduct to cease (*VDP*, fol. 124v, col. C). As a consequence, the community begins to speculate about the young man's sudden death suspecting foul play: "Tuit dient que despourveüe; / Mort que l'en apele soudainne / L'ot ocis, qui moult est vilainne" [Everyone says that it was unexpected; death that calls one suddenly had killed him, which is a crying shame] (*VDP*, fol. 124v, col. C). But while the community is preoccupied with new gossip, the Belle-Mère's confession, inspired by her own guilty conscience, hastens the discovery of the crime:

> Mes cele qui fist la folie
> Si ne le puet oublier mie,
> Car conscience le remort;
> Set que par lui a prise mort. (*VDP*, fol. 124v, col. C)
>
> [But she who committed this folly can hardly forget about it, because her conscience torments her; she knows that he died because of her.]

Wracked by guilt, she goes to the parish priest, who hears her confession and assigns an unknown penance (*VDP*, fol. 124v, col. C). This is not unusual in the *VDP*, whose tales consistently highlight the role of repentance, confession, and penance in salvation, but the Belle-Mère's confession and the priest's subsequent actions pose a theological quandary when her confessor fails to adhere to the principle of secrecy. The element of secrecy was considered essential to the act of confession because it was believed that sinners would cease to confess their sins if priests did not maintain discretion; it was a principle of confession that those who confessed their sins should be able to do so without

26 Hannah Skoda, Conclusion, *Medieval and Modern Murder*, Tracy, 594–610 at 601. For the definition of murder as a premeditated act of violence that results in death, as well as the association of murder with treachery, see: Philippe de Beaumanoir, *The Coutumes de Beauvaisis*, § 825–827 at 303. See also: Gauvard, *De grace especial*, 800–01.

"fear of loss of family, reputation, or life."[27] The *VDP*-poet underscores the Belle-Mère's presumption of the secrecy of confession, noting that:

> Et cele ne se douta point
> Que il de sa confession[28]
> Deüst ja fere mencion,
> Comme courtois non deüst il. (*VDP*, fol. 124v, col. C)
>
> [And she didn't once suspect that he might ever make her confession known, since this would not be proper.]

Here, she confesses the sin of murder to the priest, then undertakes an undefined penance to atone for it, but the *VDP*-poet introduces a corrupt cleric into this scene:[29]

> Mes il fu si fol et si vil,
> Que la femme plus vil en tint,
> Et la despit dont il avint,
> ....
> Li prestres mauvais, ce me semble. (*VDP*, fol. 124v, col. C)
>
> [But he was so foolish and mean, rife with the worst intentions because of the contempt that he had for her ... It seems to me this is a bad priest.]

The *VDP*-poet's unequivocal condemnation of this character reflects the extent of his spiritual corruption. Theologians placed a great value on confession:

---

27 Karma Lochrie, *Covert Operations: The Medieval Uses of Secrecy* (Philadelphia: The University of Pennsylvania Press, 1999), 26. The practice of confession and penance dates from the sixth century, and by the thirteenth century, the principle of what came to be called the "seal of confession" was already well established. Thus, the seal of confession was an established religious custom when the Fourth Lateran Council of 1215 formalized what was already common practice; Canon 21 outlines the role and responsibilities of the priest in administering confession. Lochrie summarizes this complex theological issue by explaining that the priest's role in confession was to uncover the sin and interrogate the sinner until a full confession had been heard, then to give absolution and assign penance (*Covert Operations*, 27–29).

28 This line omits elision to preserve octosyllabic verse. Please note that although there are numerous hypersyllabic lines in the poem, notes on the meter will be reserved only for that which interferes with ease of reading.

29 This character also appears in Jacobus de Voragine's *Legenda aurea* (ch. 131, para. 10 at 594).

priests who revealed their parishioner's sins publicly risked being removed from office to perform perpetual penance in a monastery.[30] Thus his violation of the seal of the confession by relating the Belle-Mère's sin to the community, and specifically to her son-in-law's family, is in keeping with the *VDP*-poet's characterization of him as a bad priest (*VDP*, fol. 124v, col. C): "Ce mal mot fu tost avant mis / Raconté fu tost as amis / Et aus parens a celui gendre" [This bad report was immediately spread about; it was soon told to the friends and relatives of this son-in-law] (*VDP*, fols. 124v, col. C–125r, col. A).

Ironically, the priest who violates the secrecy of confession imitates the behavior of his parishioners, whose false rumors of adultery and incest incite the woman to commit murder to preserve her reputation in the first place. In their role as confessors, priests were meant to function as spiritual physicians, and are often described as such in confessional manuals, but rather than healing the sinner's soul, this priest reproaches the Belle-Mère for her behavior, then exposes her sin in order to punish her.[31] When the Belle-Mère's confessor denounces her by repeating her sincere confession, his actions pose an institutional and a practical problem because he violates canon law. More importantly, his public declaration of her eyewitness testimony turns her sin into a criminal act by simulating a *fet notoire* [common knowledge of the facts].[32]

30 Thomas Aquinas argues that priests should exercise the same discretion as God when receiving confession (Henry Charles Lea, *A History of Auricular Confession and Indulgences in the Latin Church*, 3 vols. (Philadelphia: Lea Brothers, 1896), 1:412. Oscar D. Watkins notes that an earlier theologican, Burchard, the Bishop of Worms, who assigned the first penance for violating the secrecy of confession, underscores in the *Corrector* that priests should take care not to repeat the sins that are confessed to them (Oscar D. Watkins, *A History of Penance*, 2 vols. (New York: Burt Franklin, 1961) 2:736). This is noteworthy because, as Book 19 of the *Decretum*, Burchard's *Corrector* is sometimes considered a penitential in its own right; this chapter was almost always copied with the *Decretum* during the eleventh and twelfth centuries, and Burchard's work frequently appeared alongside other legal texts pertaining to canon law. The manuscript transmission suggests that canon law and penitentials were not mutually exclusive (John Burden, "Reading Burchard's *Corrector*: Canon Law and Penance in the High Middle Ages," *Journal of Medieval History* 46:1 (2019): 77–97. Regardless of the debate pertaining to Burchard's theological thought, Pope Innocent III maintains that the revelation of sin by a confessor is a graver sin than that which was revealed to him (Lea, *A History of Confession*, 1:420). Moreover, the element of secrecy was so strict that priests were not to betray sinners in either word or deed (Watkins, *A History of Penance*, 2:748–49).

31 "[Confession] stresses the healing of the sinner's soul, rather than exposure and punishment of the sickness" (Lochrie, *Covert Operations*, 26). Lochrie cites Alain de Lille's *Liber poenitentialis* as an example of the motif of priest as spiritual physician (*Covert Operations*, n. 50 at 233).

32 Legally, a *fet notoire* required the eyewitness testimony of six or more persons of good reputation. F.R.P. Akehurst, "Name, Reputation, and Notoriety in French Customary Law,"

Although it would constitute hearsay in modern judicial systems, medieval criminal proceedings could be instituted with the sworn testimony of as few as two credible witnesses, and the criminal's confession was taken as undisputed proof that a crime had been committed.[33] The priest's public disclosure of the Belle-Mère's crime leads directly to her trial and failed execution because the legal procedure known as *plena probatio* [full proof] required only that the accuser provide oral testimony and proof of confession, both of which are given here by the priest.[34] According to customary law, criminal cases began on the basis of *mala fama* [notoriety], and proof through presumption could be established thereafter by the "serement de bonnes gens" [the testimony of honest persons].[35] Since the minimum requirement for guilt was common knowledge of a crime and the sworn testimony of citizens of good character, the confessor acts as person of *bonne renomee* [good character], an unimpeachable witness who makes the Belle-Mère's actions a prosecutable crime, even as he simultaneously reveals himself to be a corrupt cleric who commits a serious religious infraction that damages the sinner's reputation and puts her in mortal danger.[36]

The priest's verbal offense is also problematic because it recalls the specter of blood feuds during a period when French law favored reconciliation between families. By reporting the Belle-Mère's misdeed to the community instead of a court official, and specifically to the victim's relatives, he escalates the potential consequences of the murder from interpersonal violence to community conflict by creating conditions favorable to vengeance, a sentiment that the victim's family will later express during the execution episode.[37]

---

in *Fama: The Politics of Talk and Reputation in Medieval Europe*, ed. Thelma Fenster and Daniel Lord Smail (Ithaca: Cornell University Press, 2003), 75–97 at 84.

33 All that was necessary to instigate, try, and convict a defendant in a *per notorium* [by notoriety] case was public complaint and eyewitness testimony, with or without the criminal's confession. The procedure known as *plena probatio* [full proof] required the testimony of two witnesses (Brundage, *Medieval Canon Law*, 132).

34 Brundage proposes that the increased reliance on sworn testimony as proof of criminal activity was an innovation of canon law beginning in the late twelfth century (*Law, Sex, and Christian Society*, 319–20). The scriptural basis for eyewitness testimony is found in Matt. 18:16, Deut. 18:15 and 2 Cor. 13:1.

35 Akehurst, "Notoriety in French Customary Law," 84. On *mala fama*, see: Thelma Fenster and Daniel Lord Smail, Introduction, *Fama*, ed. Fenster and Smail, 1–11 at 3. See also: Gauvard, *De grace especial*, 135.

36 Akehurst, "Notoriety in French Customary Law," 77–85.

37 Gauvard reports that homicide was the principal motive for private justice, occurring in more than 80% of cases (*De grace especial*, 755–56).

For now, they reject private justice and observe correct legal procedure.[38] The Belle-Mère seeks refuge in the parish church, but her son-in-law's relatives forcibly remove her, hauling her before the *prévot* [provost] (*VDP*, fol. 125r, col. A), who sentences her to death by burning.[39] The *VDP*-poet sums up the trial in two verses: "L'en la mist engiehinne fort / Et condempnee fu a mort" [They tortured her vigorously and condemned her to death] (*VDP*, fol. 125r, col. A). Since she now confesses publicly in court to what she had previously confessed privately in church, the sinner's private penance is recast as a criminal's public restitution.

In the *VDP*, criminal proceedings begin on the basis of *mala fama* and conclude in *plena probatio*, and the Belle-Mère's *processus per notorium* [trial by notoriety] takes place in a municipal court.[40] In contrast, Gautier de Coinci's miracle takes place in the ecclesiastical court, underscoring the broad judicial powers of ecclesiastical law to bring criminals to justice through the practice of *processus per inquisitionem* [trial by investigation].[41] Here, the *vidame* acts upon his personal suspicion of foul play in the young man's death, arrests the Belle-Mère and her entire family in Chïevi, and hauls them before the bishop's consistory court in Laon. As deputies of the bishop, ecclesiastical court officials such as *vidames* could take action against suspected offenders without a formal accusation or denunciation. Specifically, they could summon witnesses and interrogate them if they believed that a crime had been committed.[42]

Both variants illustrate cases that are initiated on the basis of *mala fama*, and both feature clerical villains, but because the *VDP*'s "bad priest" acts alone

38 During this period, justice relied on the victim or family member to register a formal complaint and ask a judge to summon the accused (Akehurst, "Notoriety in French Customary Law," 85), so that the aggressive action of the victim's relatives anticipates contemporary legal procedure to prevent the Belle-Mère's escape. Gauvard's study indicates that flight was a traditional means of avoiding prosecution and occurred in up to 70% of homicide cases. However, since flight also allowed time to demand a pardon or to negotiate a peace between families, it was actually helpful to avoid blood feuds that further disrupted the social order (*De grace especial*, 166).

39 Habitual criminals, convicted criminals, thieves and murderers did not benefit from sanctuary laws. In fact, the Parlement de Grenoble declared in 1457 that the removal of murderers from places of sanctuary did not violate the principle of sanctuary (Dean, *Crime in Medieval Europe*, 111).

40 In Alfonso's Cantiga 255, the trial also takes place in a municipal court, before a magistrate (ll. 55–72).

41 Brundage, *Medieval Canon Law*, 147. Pope Innocent III authorized judges to use this novel form of action in a decretal of 1199, which was formalized as an established procedure of criminal law by the Fourth Lateran Council of 1215 (Canon 8 and Canon 10.5.124).

42 Brundage, *Medieval Canon Law*, 148. Cf. the role of the *juge d'instruction* or *accusateur public* in the modern French legal system.

in violating canon law, the audience views the character in opposition to the morally neutral proceedings of the municipal court. As the sole bad actor, the corrupt cleric is an aberration whose disregard for the salvation of his parishioners misrepresents the majority of parish priests, who exercise good pastoral care. Conversely, Gautier de Coinci's account of the Belle-Mère's trial constitutes a strong critique of ecclesiastical justice because he multiplies the number of clerical officials and places the trial in an ecclesiastical court, which contrasts God's grace and mercy towards sinners with the harsh penalties prescribed by the law.

In *Belle-Mère*, the *VDP*-poet describes the sole clerical character as *fol* [foolish] and *vil* [mean] (*VDP*, fol. 124v, col. C) because he is corrupt, but Gautier de Coinci populates the ecclesiastical court with cruel officers. The poet introduces the *vidame* as "Si tres sage homme / Se plus ne fust crüex que sages" [A very intelligent man who was as cruel as he was wise] (*MND*, 184–85). He then adds that he is a man whose heart is so hardened that "Ja n'eüst d'omme ne de fame / Pitié" [He never had any mercy on men or women] (*MND*, 188–89). When news of the young man's sudden death and hasty burial spreads from Chïevi to Laon (*MND*, 177–79), it arouses the *vidame*'s suspicions. He arrives at the church just in time to interrupt the funeral, and Gautier de Coinci reinforces his previous depiction of the character by stating that he is "com hom trop crüeuz en justise" [a man of very harsh justice] (*MND*, 210). After examining the body, the *vidame* declares that a murder has been committed (*MND*, 217) because the deceased's throat is *noir et taint* [black and discolored] (*MND*, 215).

If the cursory proceedings of *Belle-Mère*'s municipal court assume that the audience possesses the relevant knowledge of secular judicial procedure, Gautier de Coinci's account illustrates the workings of the bishop's consistory court in great detail, and the attitudes of the court officials towards the criminal are just as important as the depiction of court procedure. To learn the truth of the young man's death, the *vidame* arrests the grieving family, transports them to Laon (*MND*, 218–23) and begins an *apprise* in which he puts everyone to the question (*MND*, 224). As part of the *ordo iudiciarius*, an *apprise* was less formal than an *enqueste*, which involved multiple witnesses and oral arguments and required a full trial. More importantly, an *apprise* could be instigated solely on the basis of *mala fama* or a *fet notoire*, meaning that it required less evidence than an *enqueste*.[43] During the *apprise*, which quickly draws an audience of ten thousand people (*MND*, 226–28) the *vidame*'s principal method of questioning is judicial torture: "mout les fait batre et mesmener" [[He] has them soundly

43 For further discussion of the differences between the *apprise* and the *enqueste*, see: Akehurst, "Notoriety in French Customary Law," 87–88, and Skoda, *Medieval Violence*, 34.

beaten and brutalized] (*MND*, 224). Although Ron Akehurst argues that "torture was not much used in thirteenth-century France to extract confessions," judicial torture was permitted and practiced in both ecclesiastical and customary law.[44] Moreover, Gautier de Coinci's choice of investigative techniques vividly illustrates the *vidame*'s cruelty: The use of interrogatory torture may be a legal means to extract criminal confessions, but the brutalization of the suspects in a naked display of ecclesiastical power places the Belle-Mère's trial squarely within the context of an abuse of judicial authority.[45]

Nonetheless, judicial torture has the desired effect, for as soon as the Belle-Mère observes the condition of her husband and daughter, she is moved by the Holy Spirit to proclaim their innocence and her own guilt:

> Ces innocens ne tüez mie,
> Car couppes n'ont en cest affaire.
> Moy ardoir faites et desfaire,
> De moy justise faites penre,
> Quar je murtrir fis mon biau genre.
> Par moy gist il, li las, em biere.
> Homecide sui et murtriere. (*MND*, 240–46)
>
> [Do not kill these innocents, because they are blameless in this affair. Burn me, and put an end to me, [or] hang me [and] justice will be done, because I had my good son-in-law murdered. He lies on the bier because of me, poor boy. I am a killer and a murderer.]

Having confessed her crime, the Belle-Mère is imprisoned pending sentencing (*MND*, 249–52). In fact, there is little for the court to do other than debate "comment ses cors sera destruis" [how her body will be destroyed] (*MND*, 252). Although numerous crimes were punished by confiscation of property or banishment of the offender, the contract murder of a relative warranted capital

44 Akehurst, "Notoriety in French Customary Law," 93. Judicial torture was also subject to strict regulations: it should be applied moderately, on a single occasion, and questioning was limited to a subject's known or suspected offenses. In addition, confessions that were elicited under judicial torture were subject to subsequent ratification (Dean, *Crime in Medieval Europe*, 15). Moreover, Larissa Tracy points out medieval perspectives on the use of interrogatory torture to enact justice were far from homogeneous. In France, an ordonnance of Louis IX legalized judicial torture in 1254, and by the fourteenth century, "torture was the routine procedure for serious crimes." *Torture and Brutality in Medieval Literature: Negotiations of National Identity* (Cambridge: D.S. Brewer, 2012), 7.

45 For a full discussion of the uses and abuses of judicial torture, see: Tracy, *Torture and Brutality*.

punishment.[46] *Les Coutumes de Beauvaisis* provides a pertinent parallel, in which a woman hires two men to kill her husband at home during his bath.[47] In this case, the woman lets her hirelings into the family home, where they lie in wait for their victim. She then claims that her husband had been attacked by armed assailants, offering a nicked club as proof that he tried to defend himself from the intruders' swords, but neither the club nor the body corroborates her testimony. As soon as the judge threatens torture, she confesses and receives a sentence of burning. In the miracle tale, Gautier de Coinci indulges in dramatic irony by having the Belle-Mère suggest potential punishments for her crime, including burning, in her confession (*MND*, 242).

In contrast to the swift justice of the *VDP*'s municipal court, Gautier de Coinci's ecclesiastical court includes judicial debate to determine the appropriate punishment, and he introduces additional court officials whose zeal for punishment not only portrays the court as cruel, but also contradicts the official position of canon law, which preferred penance to punishment in order to rehabilitate the sinner.[48] Although canon law does not regulate murder, Gautier de Coinci exercises the poet's right to dramatic license by setting the trial episode in the bishop's consistory court. However, since rumors of adultery are the Belle-Mère's motive for murder, and adultery was believed to lead to other sinful acts, the Church's sweeping claims to exclusive jurisdiction over sex crimes explains their involvement in this case.[49]

Gautier de Coinci describes the prosecutor who calls for the Belle-Mère to be burned (*MND*, 273–75) as a man whose *grant scïence* [vast knowledge] (*MND*, 264) is not tempered by the Holy Spirit (*MND*, 265–66). Like the *vidame* who is known for his *crüeuz en justise* [harsh justice] (*MND*, 210), the prosecutor also has a reputation for recommending the maximum penalty: "trop fu crüeuz, sauve sa grace" [[He] was very severe [and] spared his mercy] (*MND*, 267). Thus, it is not surprising that he argues for the death penalty without considering God's grace and mercy (*MND*, 268–71). The poet harshly criticizes ecclesiastical justice at the end of the trial episode. Although the death penalty is in full

46 Gauvard, *De grace especial*, 256, and Skoda, *Medieval Violence*, 45. Murder, heresy and treason constitute notable exceptions.

47 Philippe de Beaumanoir, *The Coutumes de Beauvaisis*, §1956, 715–16. Philippe de Beaumanoir offers this case as an example of a judge's probity, so that it provides support for cases tried *per inquisitionem* in customary law.

48 Although reformers would later insist that punishments serve as both deterrents as well as correctives, the principal goal of canon law was the rehabilitation and salvation of the offender (Brundage, *Medieval Canon Law*, 151).

49 Brundage, *Law, Sex, and Christian Society*, 388.

compliance with the range of sentences provided by contemporary customary law, the poet's sympathies clearly reside with the condemned:

> Encore li clers fist pis dou lai
> Qui si crüeument la juja.
> Mal est jugiez qui mal juge a:
> La lasse ou clerc ot felon juge. (*MND*, 284–87)
>
> [The cleric who judged her so harshly was worse than a layman. He who has a bad judge is poorly judged: the poor woman had an evil judge in that cleric.]

After the trial, the court informs the victim's family, heretofore absent from the *MND*, that "l'orde murdriere mettre en rost" [the filthy murderer will be burned] (*MND*, 296). The Belle-Mère is then bound and led in procession to the place of execution, but the *vidame*, urged by the crowd, reluctantly grants her request to stop in the church for confession (*MND*, 302–08), where she publicly declares her guilt. Last requests prior to imminent death are not unusual, but the *vidame*'s reluctance to grant one reinforces the portrait of a cruel ecclesiastical court that prioritizes the punishment of sinners over the salvation of their eternal souls. Moreover, Trevor Dean argues that crowds played an active role in executions and suggests that judicial authorities were particularly sensitive to appeals from the crowd for mercy that could either halt an execution or reduce the punishment.[50] Within the context of execution, the *vidame*'s hesitation to grant the Belle-Mère's request for final confession foreshadows his dismissal of the miracle when it occurs.

In the church, Gautier de Coinci highlights the woman's sincere repentance, rendered even more credible by the shedding of tears (*MND*, 336, 338–39): "Ne croy qu'a piece voyés mais / Fame de tele repentance" [I don't believe I've seen a woman of such repentance in quite some time] (*MND*, 326–27). In fact, some members of the crowd are so moved by her confession that they plead for mercy: "De pitié pleurent clerc et lai / Gaires n'i a grant ne petit / Qui em plorant pour li ne prit" (*MND*, 332–34) [Clerics and laymen alike begged for

50 Dean, *Crime in Medieval Europe*, 135–36. Patricia Turning maintains that the nature of executions as public spectacles not only provided restitution to the survivors of violent crimes, but that it bound the community together by restoring law and order. "A Case of Mariticide in Late Medieval France," in *Medieval and Modern Murder*, ed. Tracy, 511–40 at 517. Turning also comments on the role of the crowd in granting official reprieves from capital punishment by relating several examples from fourteenth-century Toulouse (515–16).

mercy—There was hardly anyone, lord or peasant, who did not ask for it while weeping]. After her initial confession under judicial torture, the poet consistently refers to the Belle-Mère as *la lasse* [the poor [woman]] (*MND*, 249, 301, 309, 506), *la lasse fame* [the poor woman] (*MND*, 380, 389), or *la lasse dolante fame* [the poor, sorrowful woman] (*MND*, 233, 357). This sympathetic portrait of remorse is rendered more poignant by the act of public weeping, and her *chaudes larmes* [hot tears] (*MND*, 338) are a physical proof of contrition that evokes the motif of *contrition larmoyante* [tearful repentance].[51] In his discussion of the trope, Jean-Charles Payen asserts that public acts of confession and repentance in devotional literature have the most impact when they are associated with grievous sins, concluding that "le repentir est d'autant plus frappant que le pécheur est plus enfoncé dans sa faute" [Repentance is all the more striking when the sinner is deeply mired in sin].[52] Unfortunately, both the Belle-Mère's confession and her prayer that burning on earth will allow her to escape the fires of hell (*MND*, 341–45, 370–73) are frequently interrupted by the *vidame*'s impatient demands to get on with the execution (*MND*, 330–31, 352–56, 399). Like the mercilessness of the prosecutor (*MND*, 267), the *vidame*'s unmitigated zeal for the Belle-Mère's death underscores his cruelty because he ignores the pleas of the community, as represented by the crowd, to commute the death sentence.

Within the context of public confession and sincere repentance, the Belle-Mère's willingness to suffer the ignominious death of the body to save her soul corresponds to contemporary beliefs concerning the spiritual benefits of this mode of execution. The sentence of death by burning was reserved for the most heinous crimes, such as sodomy, incest, or infanticide, because the elimination of the body was required to purify the soul. Burning was also the primary mode of execution for heresy for the same reasons, even though the gendered dimension of medieval execution reveals that women were often burned for crimes for which a man would be hanged.[53] Here, the Belle-Mère willingly accepts her sentence because burning is a means of spiritual purification, and Gautier de Coinci suggests that execution is the ultimate act of penance:

---

51 Jean-Charles Payen, *Le Motif du repentir dans la littérature française médiévale (des origines à 1230)* (Geneva: Droz, 1967), 515–16.

52 Jean-Charles Payen, *Le Motif du repentir*, 532.

53 Dean, *Crime in Medieval Europe*, 124, and Skoda, *Medieval Violence*, 227. Dean points out that while male murderers received sentences of hanging, the preferred method for executing women in France was burning; they were rarely hanged (*Crime in Medieval Europe*, 124–25).

> Par le torment de ceste flame,
> Par ceste mort pesme et honteuse,
> Haute pucele gloriëuse,
> Dou feu d'enfer m'eschive et garde. (*MND*, 370–73)
>
> [Deliver me and keep me from the fires of hell, high and glorious Lady, by [virtue of] the torment of these flames, by this horrible and shameful death.]

However, Gautier de Coinci deliberately complicates this interpretation by identifying the place of execution as the "liu de son martire" [the place of her martyrdom] (*MND*, 382). Just as he highlights the victim's innocence by evoking specific saints during the murder episode (*MND*, 110 and 116), the poet's use of the hagiographical lexicon to characterize the place of execution as a place of martyrdom further refines the extent of the ecclesiastical court's cruelty by portraying the sentence of burning as an overreach of judicial authority. More importantly, when Gautier de Coinci portrays the Belle-Mère as a victim of judicial abuse, he extends the lexicon of martyrdom from the innocent victim to the guilty murderer, so that the conflict between ecclesiastical law and the heavenly court places the execution episode squarely within the hagiographical context.

Indeed, only divine intervention can prevent a miscarriage of justice, and Gautier de Coinci augments the role of grace in salvation by amplifying the hagiographical motifs associated with virgin martyrs when the execution begins. Although the general tendency in thirteenth-century devotional literature is to amplify the *merveilleux*, these narratives also emphasize the role of the sinner in securing their own salvation.[54] While in the church, the Belle-Mère begins her prayer with the formulaic expression "Aiez pitié de ma misere" ["Take pity on my wretchedness"] (*MND*, 315), and the Virgin hears her plea. After the execution begins, some members of the crowd pray for mercy, moved by her penitence and humility:

> Cil qui cuers ont doz et devoz,
> Quant par tout voyent feu et flamme,
> Em plorant prïent Nostre Dame
> Qu'ele ait pitié isnelement

54 Payen, *Le Motif du repentir*, 542.

De celi qui si doucement
A sa douceur s'est commandee. (*MND*, 406–11)

[When they see the fire and the flames everywhere, those who have tender and devout hearts pray to Our Lady while weeping, that she would immediately have mercy on she who had so gently given herself over to her care.]

Others heckle and take an unseemly pleasure in her punishment:

Cil qui n'ont pas sainne pensee
Et qui felon sont de corage
Entor le fu mainnent grant rage.
Souvent li crïent s'ele a chaut,
C'est a bon droyt, ne leur en chaut. (*MND*, 412–16)

[Those who have evil thoughts and bad intentions gather around the fire with great anger. They often cry out that if she's feeling warm, it's only right—it's nothing to them.]

The poet places the victim's family in this second group when he relates their disappointment that the Belle-Mère is still alive:

Quant li parent le mort la voient,
Qui sanz dotance bien cuidoient
Que toute fust arse et bruïe,
Mout est leur joye esvanuïe.
Com cil qui gaires ne l'ont chiere,
Huçant li vont: "Orde murtriere!
Ainsi n'eschaperez vos pas.
Arse serez isnelpas,
Par la bouele et par les plaies!" (*MND*, 441–49)

[When the dead man's relatives see her, whom they believed without a doubt to have been completely burned and roasted, it greatly diminishes their joy. As though she were someone whom they had never held dear, they go towards her screaming: "Filthy murderer! You will not escape your fate! You will be burned on the spot, with logs and kindling!"]

In the church, the crowd's universal demands for mercy fall on the *vidame*'s deaf ears (*MND*, 332–34), but in these passages, Gautier de Coinci divides the witnesses to the execution into two distinct parties. Good Christians who desire mercy for the condemned now address their prayers to the Virgin Mary to deliver the Belle-Mère (*MND*, 406–11). The crowd's prayers for divine intervention in the *MND* are ambiguous, because they do not specify what form Mary's intercession should take, which contrasts with *Belle-Mère*, where sympathetic onlookers specifically call for the woman's release from the scaffold (*VDP*, fol. 125r, col. A). Gautier de Coinci creates dramatic tension in this scene by including hecklers whose hearts are presumably hardened by their own sin and vigorously concur with the decision of the ecclesiastical court (*MND*, 412–16). In particular, the victim's family, to whom restitution is owed, is beside themselves with joy (*MND*, 454), and their eagerness for her punishment aligns them with the *vidame*, the prosecutor, and the ecclesiastical court.

In this fashion, Gautier de Coinci sets the stage for a miracle by providing a detailed description of the scaffold that prevents her execution from being interpreted as a simple equipment failure, but since he has already named the place of execution as a place of martyrdom (*MND*, 382), he reinforces the hagiographical aspects of the miracle by recounting what happens to the woman's body in painstaking detail. First, they bind the Belle-Mère to the stake with *grosses cordes* [thick ropes] (*MND*, 392), and then they light the wood and charcoal on all sides (*MND*, 401–402). In fact, the fire is so great that a neighboring building catches fire and collapses (*MND*, 420–21), but the condemned suffers no ill effects: "N'ele ne brait n'ele ne crie, / Ainz samble que soit endormie" [She neither cries out nor screams, so it seems like she is sleeping] (*MND*, 435–36). The *VDP*-poet describes her ordeal in similar terms: "Longuement i fu drue et sainne / Sanz sentir angoisse ne painne" [She stayed [in the fire] for a long time, hale and hearty, feeling neither pain nor anguish] (*VDP*, fol. 125r, col. A).

Gautier de Coinci reports that her hair is not even singed (*MND*, 438–39), making the execution episode specifically recall virgin martyrs like Christine, who also fail to burn.[55] Moreover, he strengthens the link to hagiographical

55 Saint Christine survives both burning on the wheel and five days locked inside a furnace. Gautier de Coinci, *La vie de sainte Cristine, Edition critique d'après le manuscrit f. fr. 817 de la Bibliothque national de France*, ed. Olivier Collet (Geneva: Droz, 1999). Cf. Saints Eulalie, Lucy and Agnes, who also fail to burn. "La Cantilène de Sainte Eulalie," ed. Brigitte L.M. Bauer and Jonathan Slocum, The University of Texas at Austin Linguistics Research Center, 2020, https://lrc.la.utexas.edu/eieol/ofrol/40; Jacobus de Voragine, *Legenda aurea* (ch. 24, 97–100). See also Saints Lucy and Agnes, Jacobus de Voragine,

literature and heightens the drama by having the fire create substantial collateral damage while leaving its intended victim unharmed. Much like Saint Catherine, who shatters the wheel upon which she was condemned to be broken with a touch, killing several spectators, the Belle-Mère's fire spreads to nearby homes (*MND*, 403–405).[56] But rather than invoking such inimitable models of sanctity, the poet cites the biblical miracle of Daniel to reinforce a general notion of divine protection (*MND*, 573–77).[57] Most importantly, he specifically credits the Virgin Mary with the failed execution (*MND*, 466–68), so that in her mercy, the condemned "ne sent ne feu ne flame" [feels neither fire nor flame] (*MND*, 478).

Both narratives add an additional hagiographic motif by offering an alternative mode of execution when the condemned fails to burn.[58] Gautier de Coinci describes an outraged family member who adds straw, thatch and wood to the pyre (*MND*, 450–53), but to no avail. In the *VDP*, the victim's family goes much further. Neither appeased nor impressed by the miracle, the victim's relatives attack the condemned with "maint glaive et mainte lance" [many swords and spears] (fol. 125r, col. A).[59] Like Gautier de Coinci's spiritually hardened clerics, the victim's family acts with "grant cruaute par malveillance" [great cruelty, out of malice] (*VDP*, fol. 125r, col. A), compounding their misguided attempt to circumvent Marian mercy.

In the *MND*, the Belle-Mère finally asks the *vidame* to cede to divine justice:

"Seignor, seignor," ce dist la fame,
"Quant par les preces de la dame
Qui dame et roÿne est des cielz
Espargnie m'a li doz Diex,

Legenda aurea (ch. 4, para. 1 at 31–32 and ch. 24, para. 1 at 115). However, it seems likely that Gautier de Coinci would have worked from earlier Latin texts (see n. 9), or that he followed oral tradition in adding a hagiographic gloss to the Belle-Mère's ordeal.

56 Jacobus de Voragine, *Legenda aurea*, ch. 172, 789–97. See also the life of Saint Agnes, in which the flames spare the saint, but kill the executioners. Jacobus de Voragine, *Legenda aurea*, Ch 24, para. 1 at 115.

57 Hananiah, Mishael, and Azariah were cast into a fiery furnace by Nebuchanezzar for refusing to worship false idols; witnesses report seeing a fourth figure in the flames who is 'like the Son of God' (Daniel 3: 25).

58 Saints Christine, Eulalie, Agnes, and Catherine are ultimately beheaded. Gautier de Coinci, *La vie de sainte Cristine*; "La Cantilène de Sainte Eulalie "; Jacobus de Voragine, *Legenda aurea*. Saint Lucy is fatally wounded by a sword blow to her throat but does not die until after she has taken communion (Jacobus de Voragine, *Legenda aurea*).

59 This episode parallels Jacobus de Voragine's *Legenda aurea* (ch. 131, para. 10, 595).

Espargniez moy, si ferez bien.
....
Car Diex me garde par sa grace
Et par les preces de la dame
A cui j'avo mon cors et m'ame." (*MND*, 511–15, 518–20)

["Lord, Lord," said the woman, "when our merciful Lord has pardoned me by the prayers of she who is the Lady and the Queen of heaven, you would do well to pardon me [too] ... Because God keeps me in his grace, and because of the prayers of the Lady to whom I pledged my body and my soul."]

The crowd immediately acknowledges the miracle, and begins to weep and praise God and Mary for their mercy towards her (*MND*, 523–26), and the public's reaction to the miracle is mirrored in the *VDP*: "Hommes et fames qui la erent / A merveille se merveillierent" [The men and women who were there marveled at the miracle] (*VDP*, fol. 125r, col. A). Unfortunately, in Gautier de Coinci's version, the court officer only recognizes the miracle when the condemned points out that one is taking place (*MND*, 527–28). Like the onlookers who take pleasure in the Belle-Mère's execution, the *vidame*'s adherence to the letter of the law fails to consider the woman's contrition or the role of demonic suggestion, factors that would typically mitigate the sentence of burning. Moreover, he is as insensitive to public appeals for mercy as he is to the miracle unfolding before him.

The execution scene is handled differently in *Belle-Mère*, where the municipal court shows both wisdom and discernment in acknowledging the miracle. As in the *MND*, the *VDP*-poet invites comparisons with the hagiographical register by highlighting the physical damage to the sinner's body. When the *prévot* hears the crowd beg for mercy and recognizes the signs of a miracle, he immediately halts the execution and commands the crowd to do no further harm to the condemned: "et que nul plus mal ne li face" (*VDP*, fol. 125r, col. A). During the Belle-Mère's physical examination, the *prévot* confirms the miracle when he sees that no sign of burns mar her body, despite the visible extra-judicial sword wounds made by victim's family:

Mes sus lui ne parut cuiture
Ne trace nisune d'arsure;
Bien est voirs les places paroient
Que des lances faites estoient. (*VDP*, fol. 125r, col. B)

[But there were no burns on her, nor any trace of burning, [although] the wounds that the lances had made could be clearly seen.][60]

The *prévot* then declares that the condemned is "comme par miracle espurgee" [purified by virtue of miracle] (*VDP*, fol. 125r, col. B). Here, the *VDP*-poet's wording of the verdict is critical. Typically, equipment failures during executions were considered proof of the accused's innocence, but the use of *espurgier* emphasizes the Belle-Mère's guilt, because it means *to purge, to clean* or *to purify*, so that the court dismisses the case without absolving her of the crime to which she has, after all, confessed.[61] Moreover, the use of this verb, with its narrow interpretations, further aligns the execution episode with the hagiographical register, precisely because it also appears in saints' lives such as *La Vie de Sainte Marguerite* and *La Vie de Saint Alexis*.[62]

In contrast, Gautier de Coinci's miracle minimizes the legal context of the miracle, releasing her from the stake without declaring a formal pardon. The Belle-Mère begins and ends her speech by proclaiming that she has been spared "'par les preces de la dame'" ["by the prayers of our Lady"] (*MND*, 512, 519), framing the miracle as the manifestation of the crowd's direct appeal to the heavenly court for Marian mercy. The *vidame* then asks her to descend from the stake, and both he and the crowd verify that her body and clothing show no signs of fire damage (*MND*, 548–51, 556–65). He also begs the Belle-Mère's forgiveness, which is granted (*MND*, 536–42), before everyone returns to the church for formal prayers and thanksgiving to the Virgin, which is a typical response in miracle tales.

In the epilogue, Gautier de Coinci maintains that this miracle demonstrates "Que granz chose est de penitence" [that penitence is a mighty thing] (*MND*, 683), and he insists all sins may be forgiven, provided the sinner repents by making confession, performing penance, and showing contrition (*MND*, 680–87). Although he cites Saint Augustine's *Livre de Confession* (*MND*, 688–93), the poet also highlights Saint Gregory's admonitions that the sinner's tears inspire God's grace and mercy (*MND*, 694–702). Belle-Mère's sincere repentance, made evident by her tears of contrition, provides a theological

60 The physical examination parallels Jacobus de Voragine's *Legenda aurea* (ch. 131, para. 10, 595). The Spanish magistrate is equally discerning of the miracle, although the execusion episode unfolds without a physical examination in Alfonso's Cantiga 255 (ll. 134–41).

61 See n. 7 and 8 (Dean, *Crime in Medieval Europe*, 136 and Gauvard, *De grace especial*, 180). Frédéric Godefroy, *Dictionnaire de l'ancienne langue française et de tous ses dialectes du IXe au XVe siècle*, 10 vol. (Paris: F. Vieweg, 1880–95) s.v. *espurgier*; here vol. 3, 556.

62 Godefroy, *Dictionnaire de l'ancienne langue*, s.v. *espurgier*; here vol. 3, 556.

justification for the miracle that commutes the ecclesiastical court's unduly harsh sentence.

While the *VDP*-poet also emphasizes the importance of repentance, confession, and penance in salvation, the prologue of *Belle-Mère* frames the miracle as a theological debate between the merits of penance, enacted through corporal punishment, and sincere repentance, which takes place in the soul. Rather than focusing on the woman's trial and execution as an example of the abuse of judicial authority, the *VDP*-poet posits his version of the miracle within the context of the divisive debate between two competing theological notions, salvation by grace or salvation through works. These positions are embodied respectively by Mary and Christ, so the celestial court claims jurisdiction over the Belle-Mère's case from the beginning.

The *VDP*-poet depicts Christ as a judge of sinners in the first two lines: "Dous Jhesucrist veult miex pugnir / *Le* las cors que l'ame honnir" [Sweet Jesus Christ would rather punish the weak body than dishonor the soul] (*VDP*, fol. 124v, col. A).[63] He then tempers the image of Christ meting out punishment by underscoring the grace imparted to sinners by the Virgin Mary:

> Plainne est de si grant amistié,
> Que tantost a dame pitié
> Dont li cuers du cors se repent.
> Tantost a sa merci le prent,
> Et pugnir le cors senglement,
> Par metre l'ame a sauvement. (*VDP*, fol. 124v, col A)
>
> [The Lady has such great loving kindness that she immediately takes pity on people who repent with all their heart. As soon as she takes them into her mercy, she punishes only the body, permitting the soul to be saved.]

Belle-Mère's prologue distinguishes the miracle as an *exemplum* that illustrates the merits of punishing the body to save the soul, so that Mary's intervention resolves contemporary theological debates between grace and works. The Belle-Mère's attitude towards her own execution is also more nuanced in the *VDP*. Although she is willing to undergo earthly punishment, she specifically asks the Virgin to spare her both a shameful death and a painful death:

---

63 *les* (MS k); This line is corrected from MS i (fol. 123v, col. A) and MS d (fol. 148r, col. A), for grammatical reasons. The poet's language echoes the position of medieval canon law, in which the goal of physical punishment is the rehabilitation and salvation of the offender (Brundage, *Medieval Canon Law*, 151).

Devant son ÿmage requist
....
Qu'ele la gart de mort vilainne;
Et se il l'en convient la painne
De mort souffrir, si qu'a l'ame,
L'en soit alegement a la dame. (*VDP*, fol 125r, col. A)

[Before her image she asked … that [Mary] keep her from a shameful death; and if she must suffer the pain of death, even unto the soul, that it might be eased by the Lady.]

In addition to underscoring her fear of execution, the condemned woman's request highlights the prologue's debate over the merits of penance, in the form of public execution, and repentance, which is a private matter.

The *VDP*'s execution episode generally follows that of Gautier de Coinci. However, two notable differences are the emotional response of the victim's family and the municipal court's rapid response to the miracle. Although the family follows secular legal procedure in bringing their complaint to the *prévot*, Mary's intervention thwarts their desire for temporal justice. But like the miracle itself, when the victim's relatives attempt to execute the Belle-Mère (*VDP*, fol. 125r, col. A), their actions subvert the *ordo iudiciarius*, too. In the *MND*, the relative who stokes an already raging fire is not an ecclesiastical court official, but his irregular actions attempt to ensure that the prescribed punishment of execution is carried out (*MND*, 450–53); the family submits to the ecclesiastical court's verdict. Gautier de Coinci thus reveals the tension between ecclesiastical law and divine mercy. In *Belle-Mère*, although the family's rejection of the miracle defies the decision of the municipal court, the introduction of interpersonal vengeance into the execution episode actually reaffirms the temporal authority of secular law by aligning its judicial authority with that of the celestial court. The *prévot* defers to a higher court of appeals when he acknowledges the miracle and halts the execution, and the victim's family acts in defiance of both secular law and Marian mercy. Celestial and secular authority are in harmony.

Thus, even though both courts recommend the same sentence, the *VDP*'s municipal court proves more discerning than its ecclesiastical counterpart in the *MND*. The ecclesiastical court officials in the *MND* display an un-Christian desire for earthly punishment that blinds them to the spiritual benefits of repentance, confession, and penance. Indeed, they are so fixated on the objective of carrying out the sentence that they repeatedly ignore the legitimate appeals of the crowd for mercy until the condemned herself asks the *vidame* to recognize Mary's divine authority (*MND*, 509–20). Both the officers and the mode of execution are depicted as excessively harsh and brutal; the miracle not only contrasts God's grace and mercy towards sinners with the ecclesiastical court's disregard for the spiritual well-being of convicted criminals, but also culminates in a spectacular display of the Virgin's discretionary powers. In the *VDP*, the family's desire for vengeance parallels the cruelty and brutality of the ecclesiastical court, but the municipal court officials act with wisdom and discretion. In ceding to the miracle, secular law acknowledges and enforces divine justice, because although this failed execution does not signify the accused's innocence, the formal declaration of a miracle by a representative of the municipal court in the *VDP* transforms the execution of a confessed murderess into a quasi-hagiographic test of faith and devotion (*VDP*, fol. 125r, col. B). In both versions, the Belle-Mère's guilt is never in question, but both the ecclesiastical court's zeal for capital punishment and the family's attempt to overturn secular and celestial judgements demonstrate the imperfect nature of temporal law codes. In addition to resolving the *VDP*-poet's debate over the spiritual merits of punishing the body to save the soul, both narratives reveal the superiority of mercy, which clearly favors the rehabilitation of sinners.

The reformative effect of mercy is best demonstrated by what happens to the protagonist after the miracle. Mary's divine intervention in the Belle-Mère's execution does not prevent her actual death, but it does prevent a shameful one, as she specifically requests in *Belle-Mère* (*VDP*, fol. 125r, col. A). In the *MND*, the protagonist dies three days after the failed execution (*MND*, 659–62), allowing Gautier de Coinci to employ a final hagiographical trope, but the *VDP*-poet delays her sentence for an indefinite period of time.[64] After she returns to her family, the Belle-Mère becomes a model of sanctity, renews her commitment to Mary, and leads a life of constant prayer as a living testament to God's mercy and grace towards sinners:

> Sa repentance et ses grans plours
> Li a abregie ses doulours.
> Briefment la du siecle apelee;
> Em penitance est trespassee,

64 The time period of three days is a common hagiographical motif that aligns the saint with Christ, who rose from the dead after three days (Mark 8: 31, Matt. 27: 63). Ironically, although this motif is not present in *Belle-Mère*, it occurs elsewhere in the *VDP*, most notably in saints' lives within the First *VDP*. Cf. *Thaïs*, in *VDP*, 1:72–90, where the *meretrix* dies three days after a hermit dreams of her in Paradise (2653–54).

A la loenge et a l'onnour
De la mere nostre seingnour. (*VDP*, fol. 125r, col. B)

[Her repentance and her many tears eased her pain [and] she was soon called from the world. She passed away in penitence, to the glory and honour of the mother of our Lord.]

Like Gautier de Coinci (*MND*, 683 and 694–702), the *VDP*-poet also insists on the role of penance and genuine remorse in the woman's salvation. Mary's intervention in legal affairs does not exonerate the sinner, but the Virgin's stay of execution does permit her to follow repentance with penance, thereby expiating the sin of murder before she dies.

Both variants of the miracle tale question the validity and authority of temporal justice in both ecclesiastical and secular courts because of abuses of judicial authority, thereby demonstrating the fallibility of human judgement. Dean suggests that miracles could be interpreted as evidence that the prescribed punishment was not commensurate to the crime, regardless of its legality.[65] This is especially true in the *MND*, where Gautier de Coinci consistently criticizes the brutality of the ecclesiastical court and its officers, but it is also valid in the *VDP*, where the woman's trial and execution rests on the immoral, if not illegal, *ex-confessio* revelations of a corrupt cleric. Mary's intervention on behalf of her faithful servant demonstrates the limitations of human justice and highlights the moral inferiority of earthly courts, precisely because the Belle-Mère does not escape death as her punishment. Gautier de Coinci criticizes an ecclesiastical court whose officers are so spiritually corrupted by their desire to punish sinners that they neither mitigate the sentence nor perceive the miracle that the Virgin grants in response to the Belle-Mère's sincere confession and tearful repentance. In *Belle-Mère*, the officer of the municipal court follows the *ordo iudiciarius* when the execution is disrupted by the miracle, but the victim's family subverts customary law when they reassert their moral, but no longer legal, right to restitution, revealing these characters to be as lustful for punishment as the *MND*'s ecclesiastical court.

Whether the case is tried *per notorium* or *per inquisitionem*, both versions of the miracle tale deem the courts inadequate, illustrating how Mary's spiritual authority is superior to temporal justice. The *VDP* illustrates the wisdom (and perhaps the superiority) of secular law when the *prévot* acknowledges the

65 Dean, *Crime in Medieval Europe*, 136.

miracle and cedes his royal authority to heavenly judgement. Even so, however, it is only through Mary's divine authority that social and spiritual order is restored. When the Virgin commutes the Belle-Mère's sentence of public execution to a short period of penance followed by a natural death, Mary's judicial intervention reveals a nuanced response to the law, tempered by grace and mercy.

CHAPTER 5

The Time of Exile: Historical Distance and Ethical Perspective in Dante's *Commedia* and Christine de Pizan's *Le Livre de la Cité des Dames*

Gillian Adler

In the Middle Ages, the hardships of exile stemmed from the loss of not only place, but also time. Exile disconnected the individual from the daily routines of the original community and threatened to destroy memories of home that were structural to identity-formation. If a sense of space and place played a role in the act of recollection, as Augustine formatively suggested when he described "campos et lata praetoria memoriae, ubi sunt thesauri innumerabilium imaginum de cuiuscemodi rebus sensis invectarum" [the fields and the grand palaces of [his] memory where there are treasure stores of countless impressions], then physical estrangement could diminish the faculty of remembrance, even forcing the exile to forget aspects of the former self.[1]

The relationship between exile and the perception of time is at the heart of Dante's *Commedia* (*c.*1308–1320) and Christine de Pizan's *Le Livre de la Cité des Dames* (*Book of the City of Ladies*) (1405) [hereafter *Cité des Dames*], two literary visions of the late Middle Ages. Nevertheless, the exile's intertwining losses of place and time might be better conceived of as a philosophical distance that catalyzes ethical perspectives on time. In both Dante's and Christine's opening passages, the protagonists—literary surrogates for the authors themselves—confess feeling a sense of estrangement; both narratives commence without supplying a clear reason for the characters' exile, or the specification of the community from which they come, which gives the impression of a prolonged stasis of suffering. However, these characters soon begin educational journeys that reframe exile, a forced distance, as a singular opportunity to develop a totalizing perspective on time. Typically, as Mark Phillips writes, "historical distance refers to the growing clarity that comes with the passage of time," and is the "equivalent of visual perspective."[2] Indeed, in a linear scheme of time, one's vision of the past matures with each year that passes, since the

1 St. Augustine, *Confessions*, vol. 2, trans. William Watts (Cambridge, MA: Harvard University Press, 1912), Book 10:8. Hereafter, book and page numbers are given in parentheses.

2 Mark Phillips, *On Historical Distance* (New Haven: Yale University Press, 2013), 1.

 | DOI:10.1163/9789004742598_007

individual's particular point in time is always increasingly distantiated from a given historical moment. Yet, exile effectively substitutes for time-passage in the *Commedia* and the *Cité des Dames*, granting the protagonists a distanced viewpoint from which to see, divine-like, the past, present, and future of the world they once inhabited. The unique perspectives they activate in their state of displacement amount to *re*visions—in the sense of seeing the world anew, correcting the punitive connotations of their marginalization, and editing the existing historical writings. If Dante achieves this revision first in his *Commedia* in response to his own physical exile, Christine emulates Dante's literary modes in the *Cité des Dames*, authorizing her position in defiance of the social and intellectual ostracism she faced as a female author writing within a patriarchal milieu.

Time constitutes one of these literary modes. Both Dante and Christine deliberately deploy anachronisms to highlight the causal relationship between exilic distance and a totalizing perspective, creating visionary worlds that intermingle figures from diverse temporalities: mythological, Biblical, ancient, and medieval. This collapse of temporal boundaries suggests that the protagonists who traverse these worlds envision different times simultaneously, thus turning their fragmentary view of time into a comprehensive vision. Moreover, both Dante and Christine visualize the collapse of boundaries as a way to organize these diverse figures according to their ethical similarities, rather than their particular epoch. By spatializing their universal histories, they stress the shared experience of the protagonists and other exiles throughout time, exiles who transformed their displacement into heroic, foundational, creative, or visionary production. These genealogies of exile legitimize the meaning of the outsider's position in the broader temporal scheme, countering the original sense of exile as punishment.

This model of exilic kinship also reveals how the authors of the *Commedia* and the *Cité des Dames*, who themselves experienced different forms of displacement, might have used their visions to transcend their circumstances. According to Nick Havely, Dante's exile from Florence in 1302, a political sentence linked to civil divisions between the dominant factions within the city, led him to wander across central and northern Italy in the years 1302–1312.[3] Florentines forced to leave their native city often were similarly restive and, as Fabrizio Ricciardelli writes, "suffered the worst fate, because they could be received or rejected, depending on their social class and wealth."[4] The

3 Nick Havely, *Dante* (Oxford: Blackwell, 2007), 26.

4 Fabrizio Ricciardelli, *The Politics of Exclusion in Early Renaissance Florence* (Turnhout: Brepols, 2007), 24.

FIGURE 5.1 Dante's *Divine Comedy* (1444–1450)
© THE BRITISH LIBRARY BOARD. YATES THOMPSON 36, F. 159R.
DANTE BANISHED FROM FLORENCE AND SENT INTO EXILE

punishment of exile was all the more severe because, "according to Florentine public law … civil rights were not considered innate to human beings, but were acquired by becoming a citizen of the state," implying that "the loss of citizenship … entailed the cancellation of political and property rights, strictly connected to an individual's freedom to act."[5] Exile obviously dramatically influenced, if not inspired, Dante's literary composition [**Figure 5.1**]; John Took made the point precisely by writing that "exile meant fashioning afresh his presence in the world as a poet, pedagogue and ultimately prophet," and highlighting various textual moments in the *Convivio*, the *De vulgari eloquentia*, and the *Commedia* to underscore Dante's struggle with nomadic life in his writings after exile.[6]

Christine did not suffer Dante's political disenfranchisement or his compulsory absence from home, even if in earlier years the challenge of moving from Venice to Paris to accompany her father, the famous astrologer Tommaso da Pizzano, in his transition to the royal world of Charles V's court (just before 1368), might naturally have brought challenges. Nevertheless, financial difficulties colliding with the deaths of family members created a sequence of losses. Christine's family suffered economic hardship after King Charles's sudden and premature death, but perhaps more poignantly, Christine's husband died when

5 Ricciardelli, *The Politics of Exclusion*, 3.
6 John Took, *Dante* (Princeton, NJ: Princeton University Press, 2020), 55.

she was only twenty-five, leaving her abruptly dispossessed, denied her share of inheritance as a result of customary prejudices against women.[7] Her sense of solitude must have become all the more pronounced by the death of her father, which eliminated a second source of financial help, as well as a source of intellectual encouragement.[8] The exile that at least partly inspired Dante to write the *Commedia* compares to the economic losses and family deaths that urged Christine to write—as a way to gain an income, to support her family, and to protest the pecuniary damages that she suffered and that diminished her children's inheritances [**Figure 5.2**].[9] According to Charity Cannon Willard, "writing verse gave Christine an outlet for her grief, her loneliness, and the pain caused by the financial burdens that were her lot."[10] Whether or not Christine's experience conditioned her preoccupation with displacement may remain uncertain, but in the *Cité des Dames*, she nevertheless begins with a premise in which, despite her education, her sex prevents her admission to a learned circle of clerical authorship. This premise continues a struggle Christine expressed only a few years before she composed the *Cité des Dames* through her fervent participation in the famous Quarrel of the Rose, a long series of letters exchanged between Christine and male scholars at the University of Paris over the ethical nature of Jean de Meun's continuation of *Le Roman de la Rose*. The letters provide evidence that, in addition to facing financial strain, Christine contended with a coterie of elite academic men who based their relegation of women to an inferior moral and intellectual position on misogynistic interpretations of scripture.[11] Christine not only boldly interjected her voice into a debate traditionally conducted by men, but also more enduringly insisted upon a woman's right to partake in academic discourse. Although Christine—that is, the Christine-*je* of the *Cité des Dames*—possesses the literacy, skill, and knowledge of male authors, being a woman makes her feel as if she is the object of their scrutiny and, thus, an intellectual exile.

---

7 Charity Cannon Willard, *Christine de Pizan: Her Life and Works* (New York: Persea Books, 1984), 35, 39–40. See also: Nadia Margolis, *An Introduction to Christine de Pizan* (Gainesville: University Press of Florida, 2011), 8.

8 See Charlotte Cooper-Davis, *Christine de Pizan: Life, Work, Legacy* (London: Reaktion, 2021), 8.

9 Margolis, *An Introduction to Christine de Pizan*, 8. See also: Sophie Bourgault and Rebecca Kingston, "Introduction," in Christine de Pizan, *The Book of the City of Ladies and Other Writings*, ed. Sophie Bourgault and Rebecca Kingston and trans. Ineke Hardy (Indianapolis, IN: Hackett Publishing Company, 2018), xi.

10 Willard, *Christine de Pizan*, 53.

11 See, for instance, Christine's letter to Jean de Montreuil in June or July of 1401, in Christine de Pizan et al. *Debate of the Romance of the Rose*, ed. and trans. David F. Hult (Chicago: The University of Chicago Press, 2010), 50–52.

FIGURE 5.2 Christine de Pizan in her study (detail), for *The Queen's Manuscript* (*c.*1410–1414)
© THE BRITISH LIBRARY BOARD. HARLEY 4431, F. 4R

This principle of belonging and not belonging, of being equal to the dominant group in theory yet simultaneously the target of the group's scorn, initiates Christine's re-education in the story of the *Cité des Dames*, which is accomplished in part through the construction of a literary genealogy in which Christine, despite solitude, can feel connected with other exiles. Like the *Commedia*, the *Cité des Dames* draws on exilic and visionary paradigms as it envisions a community that extends place and time, affirming the sense of physical, but also temporal belonging. Jo-Marie Claassen describes three stages of exile in terms of temporal orientation: "Exiles either look to the *past*, describe their *present*, or express hopes for a better *future*."[12] As exile-types who consider their position in relation to the past, present, and future, Dante and Christine seek to represent all time in their poems, placing a special emphasis on hope and faith in a future different from their own. Through this reconstitution of time, the *Commedia* and the *Cité des Dames* achieve what Claudio Guillén sees as a literary enactment of "counter-exile"; that is, "they triumph over the separation and thus can offer wide dimensions of meaning that transcend the earlier attachment to place or native origin."[13]

The meaning of exile to Dante and Christine developed out of early medieval understandings of spiritual pilgrimage. While in the legal and political contexts of antiquity, *exul* and *peregrinus* designated the individual banished by Roman law,[14] exile developed unexpectedly positive significations within early religious discourse. In the writings of the Church Fathers, the term *peregrinus* came to evoke the sense of the modern English "pilgrim," rather than "exile," as it was used to describe the individual who wanders on earth in search of God—that is, who enlists his soul on a spiritual *peregrinatio*.[15] When St. Augustine tells God that he knows Him only vaguely, he describes himself

12 Jo-Marie Claassen, *Displaced Persons: The Literature of Exile from Cicero to Boethius* (Madison: University of Wisconsin Press, 1999), 3.

13 Claudio Guillén, "On the Literature of Exile and Counter-Exile," *Books Abroad*, 50.2 (1976): 271–280 at 272.

14 For the definition of *exul* or *exsul* in the ancient context, see: Adolf Berger, *Encyclopedia Dictionary of Roman Law* (Clark, NJ: The Lawbook Exchange, 2004), 464. According to Berger, *exilium* indicated "a compulsory departure from the country if given as a punishment," though "voluntary exile was tolerated in the case of a person sentenced to death in a criminal trial," 463. For the legal context in which *peregrinus* and *peregrinatio* were originally used, see: M.A. Claussen, "'Peregrinatio' and 'Peregrini' in Augustine's 'City of God,'" *Traditio* 46 (1993), 33–75 at 35–37.

15 For a discussion of Augustine's spiritual figuration of *peregrinatio*, see: Manuela Brito-Martins, "The Concept of *peregrinatio* in Saint Augustine," in *Exile in the Middle Ages: Selected Proceedings from the International Medieval Congress, University of Leeds, 8–11 July 2002*, ed. Laura Napran and Elisabeth van Houts (Turnhout: Brepols, 2004), 83–94

as *peregrinor*, reflecting on his predicament of being "mihi sum praesentior quam tibi" [closer to himself than to God] (*Confessions* 10:5). He expresses an ontological problem described by Margaret W. Ferguson in her discussion of the Christian metaphor for mortal experience: "the metaphysical exile is defined as flawed because he is absent from an original unity of being" and is "defined negatively with reference to what he is not."[16] Yet, Augustine's consciousness of this "unlikeness" also intensifies his inward pilgrimage through anamnesis.[17] According to M.A. Claussen, Augustine's sense of the peregrine derived partly from Plotinus's notion that "the wise person ... spends his life seeking his true *patria* ... expressing an alienation from and disenchantment with the world."[18] The view of exile as a necessary precondition for finding God revises the association between exile and tragedy in Genesis, inasmuch as willfully casting oneself out of the secular community begins to enact penance for original sin, the sentence received by Adam and Eve when God expelled them from Eden and weakened their natures, rendering them "mortales et ignari et carne subditi" [mortal, and ignorant, and in bondage to the flesh].[19]

Not long after Augustine, the early medieval author Boethius endeavored to find spiritual meaning in exilic experience after being imprisoned and forced to await a death penalty by Emperor Theodoric of the Ostrogothic Empire. Boethius's *Consolation of Philosophy* [hereafter the *Consolation*] (524 CE), an allegorical vision, begins with the author-persona's lament on the injustice of his punishment, depriving him of his family, social affiliations, political position, and material possessions. These circumstances constitute the first form of exile in the *Consolation*: a displacement from the physical community and a loss of all earthly belongings. Boethius thus articulates his plight by railing against capricious Fortune: "Dum levibus male fida bonis fortuna faveret, / Paene caput tristis merserat hora meum ... fallacem mutavit nubila vultum" [While fortune favored me— / How wrong to count on swiftly-fading joys—... her clouded, cheating face is changed].[20] The personification of Fortune as a

---

at 85. In this volume, see: Westley Follett, "'He Shall Die unto the World with Perpetual Exile': The Penitential Aspect of Insular *peregrinatio*."

16 Margaret W. Ferguson, "Saint Augustine's Region of Unlikeness: The Crossing of Exile," *The Georgia Review* 29.4 (1975): 842–864 at 843.

17 Ferguson, "Saint Augustine's Region of Unlikeness," 850.

18 Claussen, "'Peregrinatio' and 'Peregrini,'" 38.

19 St. Augustine, *On the Freedom of the Will*, trans. Carroll Mason Sparrow (Charlottesville: University of Virginia, 1947), 3:130.

20 Boethius, *Consolation of Philosophy*, trans. S.J. Tester (Cambridge, MA: Harvard University Press, 1973), Book 1:Metr. 1.17–18, 19. Hereafter, book, meter (Metr.) or prose (Pr.), and page number are given in parentheses.

deceptive agent, who tricks human beings into mistaking the ephemeral for the eternal, helps Boethius dramatize his victimhood because it so clearly locates the cause of his suffering outside himself.

Boethius's complaint in Book 1 is precisely what prompts Lady Philosophy, an emanation of both knowledge and divinity, to enlighten him and, specifically, to reframe his exilic dilemma. While Boethius bemoans his banishment from Theodoric's court, Lady Philosophy worries about Boethius's more important spiritual exile from himself, which recalls Augustine's self-understanding as a *peregrinor* who has lost touch with his own essence and thereby with God. She holds her pupil accountable for this estrangement, telling him, "'Nam quoniam tui oblivione confunderis, et exsulem te et exspoliatum propriis bonis esse doluisti'" ["For because you are wandering, forgetful of your real self, you grieve that you are an exile and stripped of your goods"] (*Consolation* 1:Pr. 6.42–44). Lady Philosophy's message diminishes the value Boethius places on the mutable, earthly goods in Fortune's control, and urges him to look inward for knowledge and contentment. Performing the role of a spiritual physician, she diagnoses Boethius's ignorance of his true exile as a sickness and offers to help him through the stages of anamnesis with her medicines, which, if administered properly, can ultimately help Boethius recognize exile as a state of mind, rather than a site of punishment. Emphasizing his confusion between the physical and metaphysical, she tells Boethius, "'Hic ipse locus quem tu exilium vocas, incolentibus patria est; adeo nihil est miserum nisi cum putes contraque beata sors omnis est aequanimitate tolerantis'" ["This place itself, which you call a place of exile, is home to those who live here. So nothing is miserable unless you think so, and on the other hand a man who bears all with contentment, finds every state a happy one"] (*Consolation* 2:Pr. 4.61–64). Lady Philosophy thus locates hope in the possibility of disassociating alienation from spatiality.

In Books 4 and 5 of the *Consolation*, Lady Philosophy continues her reform efforts by stressing Boethius's potential to develop insight into divine operations. Although he complains of a physical distance and loss, he is asked to contemplate the moral phenomenon of distance from God and thus to pluralize his understanding of exile. This realization, she argues, will enable Boethius to develop self-possession amid mutability, as well as the philosophical separation from earthly concerns necessary to embrace the supreme good, God. In a Neoplatonic metaphor, Lady Philosophy thus promises Boethius wings to transport him to the eternal home: "'Sunt etenim pennae volucres mihi / Quae celsa conscendant poli'" ["For I have wings swift flying / Which can ascend the heights of heaven"] (*Consolation* 4:Metr.1.1–2). Not only will Boethius recognize the heavens as his true home, prompting him to admit, "'Haec ... memini, patria est mihi'" ["This ... I remember, is my native land"], but also, in a gratifying vengeance, he will leave behind his antagonists in a state of worldly exile: "'Quos miseri torvos populi timent / Cernes tyrannos exules'" ["Those tyrants wretched peoples fear as fierce / You will see as exiles"] (*Consolation* 4:Metr.1.25, 29–30). Lady Philosophy here couples the idea of Boethius's future sight or discernment (*cernes*) with his new insight: that the harsher state of exile is not the forced separation from contentious worldly politics or a material way of life, but instead the alienation from God and thus from oneself. She lays the groundwork for his philosophical conversion, as well as her concluding disquisition on God's totalizing vision. Deploying the same terminology she used to describe Boethius's perceptive potential, Lady Philosophy teaches about the providential eye: "'Quae tamen ille ab aeterno cuncta prospiciens providentiae *cernit* intuitus'" ["Yet that regard of providence which looks forth on all things from eternity sees this"] (*Consolation* 5:Pr. 2.27–28). Repeatedly combining the language of togetherness, eternity, vision, and distance, she establishes the principle of the *totum simul*, God's ability to see all things at once, and relates it to Boethius's own exilic distance from worldly affairs.[21] Although immersion within time makes it impossible to see all temporal parts at once, as God does, the exile, who is, in a sense, removed from time by virtue of a distance from the place of earthly origin, develops an eye similar to this simultaneous vision. If the crowning *telos* of Lady Philosophy's consolatory education is perspectival transformation, then the hypothetical scenario in which Boethius cultivates a divine-like ability to see past, present, and future as a continuous whole makes exile a uniquely rewarding experience for a human being, despite the circumscriptions of earth. The *Consolation* unsurprisingly bestows upon future writers a rich lexicon of spatial, temporal, and visionary metaphors with which to explore a philosophical approach to exile.

Dante's *Commedia* and Christine's *Cité des Dames* reveal the late medieval inheritance of Boethius's message, equating distance and the perception of time. These works adapt not only Boethian metaphor but also Boethian narrative form and sequence to reframe exile as an authorizing experience. Like the *Consolation*, the *Commedia* and the *Cité des Dames* begin with the crisis of exile and proceed with visionary educations in which the protagonists learn to cultivate a temporal and philosophical distance with which to overcome their

21 The phrase *tota simul* appears in the following teaching: "Aeternitas igitur est interminabilis vitae tota simul et perfecta possession, quod ex collatione temporalium clarius liquet" [Eternity, then, is the whole, simultaneous and perfect possession of boundless life, which becomes clearer by comparison with temporal things] (Boethius, *Consolation* 5:Pr. 6. 9–11).

initial sense of displacement. The opening segments of both works are marked by the characters' anxious reflections, as well as the trope of blindness as a metaphor for their lack of self-knowledge and historical insight. For instance, the famous opening lines of Canto 1 of *Inferno* intertwine the language of darkness, displacement, turmoil, and hazy vision, allegorizing Dante's condition of spiritual failure: "Nel mezzo del cammin di nostra vita / mi ritrovai per una selva oscura, / ché la diritta via era smarrita" [When I had journeyed half of our life's way, I found myself within a shadowed forest, for I had lost the path that does not stray] (*Inf.* 1.1–3).[22] The *selva selvaggia* [savage forest] is *aspra et forte* [dense and difficult], placing Dante, like the downcast protagonist of the *Consolation*, in a state of *la paura* [fear] and *la pieta* [anguish], producing tears so audible they eventually draw the beneficent attention of a council of holy women (*Inf.* 1.5, 1.6, 2.106). In the *Cité des Dames*, Christine not only cries but also overtly admits her state of confusion, though here it is the bookish tradition, rather than the *podestà* of Florence, that "exiles" her and makes her despair. Alone in her study, Christine encounters Matheolus's late thirteenth-century *Liber lamentionum*, which draws on classical and patristic scholarship to justify a commonly held misogynistic belief, "que la femme est foncièrement mauvaise et portée au vice" [that the behavior of women is inclined to and full of every vice] (*CD* 1.1). As she reflects on a body of writings by men that underpin Matheolus's perspective, she narrates, "Toute à ces réflexions, je fus submergée par le dégoût et la consternation, me méprisant moi-même et le sexe féminin tout entier, comme si la Nature avait enfanté des monstres" [As I was thinking this, a great unhappiness and sadness welled up in my heart, for I detested myself and the entire feminine sex, as though we were monstrosities in nature] (*CD* 1.1).[23] Christine then complains that God created her as a woman: "je me désespérais que Dieu m'ait fait naître dans un corps féminin"

---

22 All citations of Dante's *Commedia* are from Giorgio Petrocchi's edition, *La commedia secondo l'antica volgata* (Milan: Mondadori, 1966–67). All translations of the *Commedia* are from Allen Mandelbaum, *The Divine Comedy of Dante Alighieri: Inferno* (New York: Bantam, 1980); *The Divine Comedy of Dante Alighieri: Purgatorio* (New York: Bantam, 1982); *The Divine Comedy of Dante Alighieri: Paradiso* (New York: Bantam, 1984). Canto and line numbers are given in parentheses. Citations and translations of Dante's *Convivio* are from Andrew Frisardi, *Dante: Convivio* (Cambridge: Cambridge University Press, 2018). Book, chapter, and line numbers are given in parentheses.

23 All in-text citations come from Christine de Pizan, *La Cité des Dames*, ed. Thérèse Moreau and Éric Hicks (Paris: Stock, 2000). All translations are by Earl Jeffrey Richards in Christine de Pizan, *The Book of the City of Ladies* (New York: Persea, 1982, 1988). Book and chapter numbers are given in parentheses.

[I considered myself most unfortunate because God had made me inhabit a female body in this world] (1.1). Christine's protest against the very body she inhabits dualistically makes her an exile within her own flesh; she implies that the female body alienates her from a superior culture of masculinity, to which her mind and spirit might otherwise be suited to belong. Seeing exile from herself as a condition into which she has been born, she allusively recalls the Expulsion of Adam and Eve from Paradise, the original exile of Genesis which destined women to suffer in the physical body. Yet, this emotional response to the authorities whose works she reads is satirical and purposeful in the scheme of her larger project. Christine recalls her prior error—*en* [*sa*] *folie* [in [her] folly]—to distinguish her perspective in "exile" from her present view, and, by collapsing her particular plight with that of the entire feminine sex, she prepares her female readers to become disabused of false discourses that denigrate women's intellects and bodies (1.1).

Reinforcing the sense of Boethian inheritance, the tears and blurry sight of these crestfallen narrators soon invite the response of holy women and allegorical guides, who initiate profound visions of heterochronic universes, comprised of figures from throughout time. The seemingly linear and ordinary worlds of solitary experience, in which the protagonists long for their past joys and lament their present trials, are replaced by visionary realms that defy chronology and temporal unity. Between the two works, the new definition of exile first appears in the early cantos of Dante's *Purgatorio*, the second canticle of the *Commedia*. While the *selva oscura* [shadowed forest] of *Inferno* 1 encapsulates the sense of exile as an ostracizing and frightening experience, *Purgatario* 1 and 2 tie exile to the themes of community, freedom, and futurity (*Inf.* 1.2). From the shores surrounding Mount Purgatory, Dante and Virgil hear music emanating from a small boat swiftly nearing the island from across the ocean. The verse *In exitu Isräel de Aegypto*, sung in unison by souls arriving to begin their arduous ascent on Purgatory, comes from the Latin Vulgate Psalm 113, and literally concerns the Israelites' exodus from Egypt (*Purg.* 2.46). The song allegorizes the universal pilgrimage of the soul from the bondage of human flesh to God, marking exile as the starting point for *peregrinatio*. Dante's gloss of Psalm 113 in *Convivio* summarizes this figurative interpretation of the verse:

> sì come vedere può in quello canto del Profeta che dice che nell'uscita del popolo d'Israel d'Egitto Giudea è fatta santa e libera: che avegna essere vero secondo la lettera sia manifesto, non meno è vero quello che spiritualmente s'intende, cioè che nell'uscita dell'anima dal peccato, essa sia fatta santa e libera in sua potestate. (*Conv.* 2.1.7)

> [as one can see in that song of the Prophet which says that in the exodus of the people of Israel from Egypt, Judea is made holy and free. Although plainly true in terms of the letter, no less true is the spiritual sense: that in its exodus from sin the soul is made holy and free in its power.]

In *Purgatorio*, the helmsman of the ship, who "parea beato per iscripto" [seemed to have blessedness inscribed upon him], enacts Dante's secondary meaning as he makes the sign of the holy cross after the souls finish their incantation, blessing the start of their pilgrimage before sailing back to Ostia, where more souls await his transport (*Purg*. 2.44). The scene underscores the paradoxical kinship of these newcomers, who, hallowed by their helmsman, band together on the shores of Purgatory in the spirit of their shared displacement.

This scene of encounter in ante-Purgatory attributes spiritual value to Dante's historical exile both by allegorically linking Dante to the Hebrew exiles of Old Testament history and by featuring him among the exilic souls who ascend Mount Purgatory. Dante fits himself within an Exodus model at various moments in *Purgatorio*; in Canto 11, he identifies himself with the souls who repent for their pride when he records the Pater Noster, "Dà oggi a noi la cotidiana manna" [Give unto us this day the daily manna], but symbolically replaces "bread" with the Biblical "manna" to recall the sustenance God provided to the Israelites after their exodus from Egypt (*Purg*. 11.13). In Canto 2, exile is also a universal plight that fosters bonds among souls. The disoriented countenance of the recent arrivals reassures Dante and Virgil, the outlanders who have just arrived from Hell, demonstrating their own willful participation in this exilic kinship. Virgil asks them for directions at the first gesture in which they seem to orient themselves to their new temporary home: "'Voi credete / forse che siamo esperti d'esto loco; / ma noi siam peregrin come voi siete'" ["You may be convinced that we are quite familiar with this shore; but we are strangers here, just as you are"] (*Purg*. 2.61–3). His characterization of Dante and himself as *peregrin*, one of numerous instances of the word in the *Commedia*, emphasizes their connection to these new souls and reinforces the affinity between exile and spiritual pilgrimage found in Boethius's *Consolation* and Augustine's *On the Freedom of the Will*. Similarly, the language of return in this canto symbolizes the Augustinian revisions of spiritual exile as an opportunity to recover the self and discover God. When Dante's former friend Casella, now a purgatorial soul, next asks Dante why he travels through the middle region of the afterlife, Dante responds, "'Casella mio, per tornar altra volta / là dov' io son, fo io questo vïaggio'" ["My own Casella, to return again to where I am, I journey thus"] (*Purg*. 2.91–2). Dante's cryptic phrase first serves the purpose of reminding Casella that, unlike the other souls as well as Virgil, he is still mortal, anticipating his posthumous return to Purgatory. His exilic path toward God is thus unique; rather than consistently assimilating himself to the penitential crowd, as Yeo Wei Wei writes, Dante "asserts his difference and singularity" through references to his embodiment, which distinguish him as an extraordinary, divinely chosen mortal figure.[24] Furthermore, Dante's use of *tornar* implies his vision of himself as an exile who wanders inwardly.[25] The entire phrase, "per tornar altra volta" evokes not only the idea of a physical return to the region, but also the same remembrance of self that is critical to Boethian and Augustinian anamnesis, reinforcing the view that exile can incentivize a recovery of knowledge and cultivate a stabilizing self-possession.

Whereas *Inferno* casts the damned souls into an eternal exile from God and, accordingly, from themselves, in *Purgatorio*, the souls begin to bridge the gulf between themselves and God. Although the Christian notion of original sin implies that exile coincided with the Expulsion and the foundation of the temporal human world, ever-situating mortal life in exile, the bands of upward-moving souls in Purgatory, both nomadic and unified in preparation for heavenly ascent, are a reminder that the spiritual peregrine works toward the purification of sin. Dante effectively stresses the possibilities and spiritual richness of Purgatory through his ethical approach to time in this canticle. Although Purgatory is the only temporary Otherworld in Dante's tripartite vision of the afterlife, where to be temporary is to exist briefly in time, the souls operate not according to the apparent linear calendrical and chronological time of earthly experience, but instead according to the moral rules of purgation. For instance, the number of years a particular soul spends on different terraces of Mount Purgatory is relative, depending on the penance they must enact for their prior sins on earth: "tempo per tempo si ristora" [time must pay for time] (*Purg*. 23.84). Dante thus must intermingle souls from diverse epochs, as this principle clashes with any expected sequence within history: Virgil and Sordello, the thirteenth-century troubadour, embrace upon recognizing their mutual origins in Mantua, and Hugh Capet, tenth-century King of the Franks, appears to condemn his successors moments before Dante and his guide encounter the first-century poet Statius on the same terrace of Purgatory.

24 Yeo Wei Wei, "Embodiment in the *Commedia*: Dante's Exilic and Poetic Self-Consciousness," *Dante Studies* 121 (2003): 67–93 at 84.

25 The verb "tornar" is used repeatedly throughout the *Commedia* as a reminder of the exilic subtext of Dante's journey. For instance, when Dante speaks with Farinata, who describes the banishment of the Guelphs from Florence, Dante's rejoinder includes the verb "tornar": "'S'ei fur cacciati, ei tornar d'ogne parte,'/rispuos' io lui, 'l'una e l'altra fiata;/ma I vostri non appreser ben quell' arte'" (*Inf.* 10.49–51).

Not merely naïve historicism, the anachronisms suggest Dante's ability to perceive the Boethian *totum simul*, reinforcing the potential of exile to catalyze a temporal distance and more comprehensive view of time. Imitating Lady Philosophy's picture of God seeing the whole of creation from the high tower of eternity, a spatial symbol of the totalizing visionary experience that extends the distance between the providential eye and history, Dante mixes temporalities so as to indicate his divine-like perspective in exile.

Underscoring the affinity between exilic distance and visionary insight, the prophets Dante encounters within the Otherworldly regions of the *Commedia* address the subject of exile with the weight of Biblical divination. Because the fictional date of Dante's journey in the *Commedia* occurs a few years before the exile in which Dante wrote the poem, prophetic characters beginning with Brunetto Latini in *Inferno* can prefigure Dante's particular displacement to varying degrees of moral success. Brunetto correctly prophesies Dante's exile, though his damned position prevents him from seeing in the divinely perspicacious way of another prophet, Cacciaguida (Dante's great-great-grandfather), in *Paradiso*. Brunetto links exile to poetic fame, revealing his exploitative, and thus flawed, view of exile: "'La tua fortuna tanto onor ti serba'" ["Your destiny reserves for you such honor"] (*Inf.* 15.70). Although Dante praises Brunetto for teaching him "'come l'uom s'etterna'" ["how man makes himself immortal"], this teacher's existence in Hell is a reminder that one does not join God by achieving mortal fame (*Inf.* 15.85). As Giuseppe Mazzotta writes, "the pilgrim's experience is meant to show that man can become eternal, can transcend the fragmentation of time ... not through the illusory project of man's own making, as Brunetto would want it, but through God's grace."[26] Dante essentially rewrites Brunetto's interpretation of the glory that comes with exile through both Cacciaguida and Beatrice, who nurture Dante's own ability to "see" time from a new perspective. In *Paradiso*, in the heaven of Mars, Cacciaguida predicts Dante's exile in response to Dante's request to know the future of Florence: "'tal di Fiorenza partir ti convene'" ["so must you depart from Florence"] (*Par.* 17.48). Cacciaguida warns the pilgrim of coming hardships, but concludes his speech with the reassurance that exile will be coupled with immortality: "'Non vo' però ch'a' tuoi vicini invidie, / poscia che s'infutura la tua vita / vie più là che 'l punir di lor perfidie'" ["Yet I'd not have you envying your neighbors; your life will long outlast the punishment that is to fall upon their treacheries"] (*Par.* 17.98–99). The poet, rather than the treacherous city, will endure time. As Mazzotta writes, "from Cacciaguida's eternal, synchronic perspective,

26 Giuseppe Mazzotta, "Dante and the Virtues of Exile," *Exile in Literature*, ed. María-Inés Lagos-Pope (Cranbury, NJ: Associated University Presses, 1988), 49–71 at 51.

the earthly city [of Florence] is viewed through the Augustinian paradigm of the eschatological cities of Jerusalem and Babylon … part of the world of finitude."[27] Cacciaguida's prophecy thus anticipates Dante's removal from an earthly world governed by capricious fortune, evoking not only Augustine's view but also the salutary terms in which Lady Philosophy reframes Boethius's exile, and reinforces how "the notion of moral time is Dante's attempt to escape out of time, not through some conviction that time is unreal, … but because it has no ontological stability."[28] As an intercessor in Dante's education on exile, Cacciaguida, like Lady Philosophy, teaches that only through exile will the subject come to perceive larger historical patterns and become unencumbered by the vicissitudes of earthly time that otherwise cloud perspectives.

While Dante ironically only addresses the topic of his political exile when he composes *Paradiso*,[29] it is also in this most theological and divinely-centered canticle that he develops the virtuous implications of his banishment. Dante's dialogue with Beatrice in the Heaven of the Fixed Stars suggests that the spiritual meaning of his exile increases as he becomes integrated with the community of God. Here, when St. James requests a gloss on the meaning of hope, Beatrice responds by singling out Dante, as if to eclipse a response by Dante that might present him as arrogant:

> La Chiesa militante alcun figliuolo
> non ha con più Speranza, com' è scritto
> nel Sol che raggia tutto nostro stuolo:
>
> però li è conceduto che d'Egitto
> vegna in Ierusalemme per vedere,
> anzi che 'l military li sia prescritto. (*Par*. 25.52–57)
>
> [There is no child of the Church Militant who has more hope than he has, as is written within the Sun whose rays reach all our ranks: thus it is granted him to come from Egypt into Jerusalem that he have vision of it, before his term of warring ends.]

27 Giuseppe Mazzotta, *Dante, Poet of the Desert: History and Allegory in the* Divine Comedy (Princeton, NJ: Princeton University Press, 1979), 128.

28 Mazzotta, *Dante, Poet of the Desert*, 130.

29 Wei Wei notes that Dante uses "'exile' in its political sense on two occasions in the *Paradiso*, where previously it had evoked the state of one who is outcast from God's kingdom, severed from God's love" ("Embodiment in the *Commedia*," 86).

As Peter S. Hawkins argues, the focus of this canto "is not the uniqueness of James but of Dante: his extraordinary pilgrimage from Egypt to Jerusalem before death, his ascent to this *campus stellae* in Gemini ... and, most strikingly, his singular possession of the virtue James himself exemplifies."[30] When Dante next glosses the virtue, he describes it as "uno attender certo / de la gloria futura" [the certain expectation of future glory], which reiterates the connection Beatrice makes between his exilic condition and both earthly and spiritual success (*Par.* 25. 67–8). Because Beatrice intervenes to present his pilgrimage as a reenactment of holy exiles, Dante has little need to protest the charges of his historical condition.

Temporality and prophecy represent marked points of continuity between Dante's *Commedia* and Christine's *Cité des Dames*, and in fact Christine nuances Dante's literary modes of exile, restoring the position of the female reader from marginalization. Returning to Christine's opening regrets over being born a woman, exile manifests in this narrative both as an ostracism from the tradition of male authorities who belabor their messages on the inferiority of female nature, and as Christine's impression of her alienation from the female body she inhabits. Yet, over the course of her visionary journey, Christine learns to cultivate a philosophical distance with which to reexamine her place in the scheme of human time and divine timelessness. In the *Cité des Dames* as well as the *Commedia*, exile represents a starting point for foundation; yet, Christine uses the parallel with the *Commedia* to draw attention to her revision of Dante's sometimes morally binary visions of female characters and to recuperate female identity, along with the reputation of all women. The *Cité des Dames* imitates the sequence in which Dante encounters Virgil, discovers the aid of divine intercessors, and embarks on a visionary journey, even explicitly paralleling the three allegorical ladies who arrive in Christine's study to help her (Dames Raison, Droiture, and Justice) to the Trinity of Beatrice, St. Lucy, and the Virgin Mary, who grant Dante access to spiritual learning in the form of his otherworldly quest. Like Dante's heavenly intercessors, Raison, Droiture, and Justice express concern that Christine weeps because she has forgotten her essence and overlooked the error of misogynistic writings. Raison's references to exile, correction, and return recall Beatrice's request to Virgil to help Dante in *Inferno*; she insists on Christine's "ressort de *corriger* les hommes et les femmes lorsqu'ils se fourvoient et de les *remettre* dans *le droit chemin*" [duty to straighten out men and women when they go astray and to put them back on the right path], echoing Beatrice's expression of fear that Dante "è impedito /

30 Peter S. Hawkins, "Self-Authenticating Artifact: Poetry and Theology in 'Paradiso' 25," *Christianity and Literature* 41.4 (1992): 387–394 at 388.

sì nel cammin" [is so hindered on his way] and "non sia già sì smarrito" [has gone so far astray] that she arrives too late to intervene (CD 1.3, *Inf.* 2.62–3, 65; my italics). In a repetition of not only Beatrice towards Dante but also Lady Philosophy towards Boethius, Raison sees Christine's present form of exile as an impediment to the kind of self-knowledge that would appease her anxieties and help her cultivate self-possession within the mutable sublunary world. Hence, Raison holds a mirror, symbolic of *le fond de son âme* [self-knowledge], to direct Christine inward, and preoccupies herself with the task of reframing Christine's peripheral position as an opportunity for new insight (CD 1.3). If, before Raison's arrival in her solitary bedchamber, Christine considers herself at odds with her female body, Raison must facilitate Christine's reconciliation with exile by helping her re-acclimatize herself to the female body. Unlike Dante's quest, Christine's mission locates the problem in the stigmatized gendered body, its own site of exile.

The educational process that unfolds in the *Cité des Dames* nurtures Christine's development of an exilic consciousness: not simply an acceptance of distance, but a recognition of how the marginalized position ethically lengthens perspectives on time, as if such perspectives were a rung nearer to divine omniscience. Raison's role is especially seminal: by encouraging Christine to see herself more clearly, she helps her envision all female history anew, as a revision of male-authored or "male-seen" female histories. Raison's mirror, functionally akin to the Pool of Narcissus in Guillaume de Lorris's *Roman de la Rose*, reflects the ideological world of the text, but whereas the pool of the *Rose* instigates the narrator's quest for love and uncovers his amorous subjectivity, Raison's jewel-studded mirror reflects an essential truth about the nature of women, and thus about the past, present, and future of the female sex, providing Christine with the element that is forever lost in exile: time. Like the medieval allegory of Prudence, who possesses three "parts" (*memoria*, *intellegentia*, and *providentia*),[31] and who is sometimes illustrated holding a mirror in an evocation of the Latin phrase *Nosce te ipsum* [Know yourself],[32] Raison shows Christine how she fits within time and even grants her control over time through the reflection of her future city. Raison's lessons may represent the first stage in the protagonist's education, but, unlike Lady Philosophy's gradual administering of medicines, which begin tenderly before strengthening, these

31 See: John Burrow, "The Third Eye of Prudence," in *Medieval Futures: Attitudes to the Future in the Middle Ages*, ed. J.A. Burrow and Ian P. Wei (Woodbridge: Boydell Press, 2000), 37–48 at 39.

32 See: Judy Kem, "Allegorical Images of the Cardinal Virtue Prudence in the Works of the Rhétoriqueurs," *Romance Notes* 28.3 (1988): 177–185 at 183.

lessons powerfully shatter the misogynistic tradition to initiate Christine's vision of an urban world of moral and accomplished women. She helps Christine understand that, peering into the mirror from the margins, she is no longer lost in the visual limitations of the present moment.

Collectively, the allegorical ladies teach Christine the stories of women from different historical epochs by arranging them based on their ethical exemplariness, as well as skills and forms of sagacity, rather than on any particular historical sequence. These instructors offer brief explanations of how each one contributed to humanity. Some of the women, including Dido, an example of prudence, attentiveness, and constancy in love, and Medea, a model of both great learning and romantic devotion, are even described on multiple occasions to underscore the different ways in which they altered the course of history. Allegory is the didactic mode of the *Cité des Dames*: to revise history, the narrative plot centers on the construction and populating of an eternal city, which safeguards all of these women. Thus, each instructor alternates between recounting narratives and advising her on the building project; the more stories they share, the closer the city comes to completion, at which point the women noted can enter its walls. This pattern of moral instruction, historical revision, and architectural making is exemplified by Raison's introduction of Queen Semiramis in her catalog of female rulers. The revision of Semiramis, who in medieval historiography is notorious for her incestuous relationship with her son Ninus,[33] but who in the *Cité des Dames* becomes a fortifier of Babylon, narratively aligns with the concrete images of urban foundation: Raison equates the tale of Semiramis with "la première pierre des fondations" [the first stone ... in the foundation] (CD 1.16). This allegorical coincidence of rewriting and building starkly corrects Boccaccio's defamation of Semiramis as ruined by her unnatural sexuality and lustfulness in *De Claris Mulieribus* (*c*.1355–59).[34]

The women upon whom they focus are expected to enter the city after the writing and building process concludes, fully realizing Christine's exilic vision of time. According to Droiture, the divinely-endorsed city should offer them refuge and community: "'avec l'aide de Dieu nous achèverons rapidement la construction des hauts palais royaux et des nobles hôtels, où pourront résider perpétuellement et à tout jamais les dames de grand renom, éminentes et illustres, à qui seront destinées ces demeures'" ["thanks to divine virtue, we

33 See: Elizabeth Archibald, "Sex and Power in Thebes and Babylon: Oedipus and Semiramis in Classical and Medieval Texts," *The Journal of Medieval Latin* 11 (2001): 27–49.

34 Boccaccio, *Famous Women*, trans. Virginia Brown (Cambridge, MA: Harvard University Press, 2001), 2:8–11.

will soon finish building the lofty royal palaces and noble mansions for the excellent ladies of great glory and fame who will be lodged in this City and who will remain here perpetually, forever more"] (*CD* 2.1). The emphasis on timelessness emerges particularly through Droiture's change of the sense of *hôtels*, which here means not temporary guest houses, but instead permanent residences. Later, as the walls of the city are nearly complete, Droiture anticipates an influx of women into the space: "'Voici donc que s'ouvre l'ère d'un nouveau royaume de Féminie'" ["Now a New Kingdom of Femininity is begun"] (*CD* 2.12). Storytelling thus amounts to the creation of an urban landscape that spatializes eternal time as a testament to the enduring virtues of its inhabitants.

Before the building process even begins, Christine's guides predict the formidable and everlasting nature of this city, evoking the heavenly city of Augustine's *De civitate Dei*. Raison tells Christine, "'ta Cité sera d'une beauté sans pareille et demeurera éternellement en ce monde'" ["your City will be extremely beautiful, without equal, and of perpetual duration in the world"], and, reminding her of her historical readings, she contrasts it with the earthly cities of Troy, Thebes, and the Amazon kingdom, inevitably vulnerable to destruction: "'avec le temps, ces villes s'écroulèrent et tombèrent en ruine'" ["over time these cities fell and have fallen into ruin"] (*CD* 1.4). The verb *s'écrouler* and the phrase *en ruine* visualize the rubble of these legendary places, stressing the contrast between fall and renewal in the *Cité des Dames*. Indeed, interweaving the language of eternity and temporality, Raison attends to how Christine's exile positions her to partake in the eternal vision; repeating the temporal indicator *jamais*, she assures Christine that *her* city will be special precisely because it will escape the arbitrary turns of Fortune and the pattern of rise and fall that afflict time-bound civilizations. Speaking as a prophet, she tells Christine, "je t'annonce que *jamais* la Cité que tu fonderas avec notre aide ne sombrera dans le néant; elle sera au contraire à *jamais* prospère, malgré l'envie de tous ses ennemis; on lui livrera maints assauts, mais elle ne sera *jamais* prise ni vaincue" ["I prophesy to you ... that this City, which you will found with our help, will never be destroyed, nor will it ever fall, but will remain prosperous forever, regardless of all its jealous enemies. Although it will be stormed by numerous assaults, it will never be taken or conquered"] (*CD* 1.4). Through the repeated antithesis between "never" and "will," between the impossibility and guarantees of the future city, Raison divorces the sacred time of the city from the cyclical patterns of worldly empires and makes Christine a central guarantor of its imperviousness. In this attempt to differentiate this city from prior and most often male-run civilizations, the *Cité des Dames* underscores Edward Said's point that exiles exploit their difference not through "composure and serenity," but instead through "an intransigence ... willfulness, exaggeration, [and] overstatement."[35] As in Dante's *Paradiso*, which, as Said writes, "bears traces of the vindictiveness and severity of judgment embodied in the *Inferno*,"[36] the certainty with which Raison asserts the superiority of Christine's city to prior cities, and thus of her vision of female history in contrast to male-authored accounts of women, produces the same impression that the *Cité des Dames* takes subtle revenge through the discourses of time and exile.

Within the frame, the stories of the women intended to populate the city feature historical exiles who transcend their original communities and thereby give credence to Christine's new sense of displacement. Like the *Commedia*, which salvages Dante's post-exilic identity by analogizing his plight to that of the Israelites, the *Cité des Dames* aligns Christine with powerful women who faced exile or marginalization, emphasizing their resilience rather than their victimhood. Raison first motivates Christine to help build the city by alluding to the prophet Moses, who was himself an exile under God's angry injunction to him, "Neither will you yourself go in there," referring to the forbiddance against his entrance into the Holy Land (Deut. 1:37). Like Moses, responsible for the Israelites, Christine is tasked with shielding women from misogynistic assailants. Despite the future condition of the city as eternal, Raison once more stresses the timeliness of providing deliverance, as if to deter Christine from idleness: "Mais *l'heure* est venue d'ôter cette juste cause des mains de Pharaon" ["Now it is *time* for their just cause to be taken from Pharaoh's hands"] (*CD* 1.3). Although *l'heure* is here translated as "time," it more precisely invokes the context of novel timekeeping mechanisms in Christine's lifetime; Christine's awareness of the relatively new mechanical clock, which she associates with the allegory of Temperance in the *Epistre d'Othéa*, suggests that Raison mentions *l'heure* hyperbolically to persuade Christine's mission. Moreover, the mention of Moses underscores the value Christine places on the ethics of her solitude. According to John D. Barbour, "Moses is alone when he first receives God's call, and he spends forty days alone on Mount Sinai at the time he receives the Torah," which exemplifies how "solitude is an important factor in the prophets' marginal position in Israel, shaping their critical perspective and their sensitivity to injustices suffered by the less powerful and by outsiders."[37] This allusion highlights the unexpected spiritual and moral privilege of Christine's experience as an outsider to the conventional community of discourse. It is through

35 Edward Said, *Reflections on Exile and Other Essays* (Cambridge, MA: Harvard University Press, 2000), 182.

36 Said, *Reflections on Exile*, 182.

37 John D. Barbour, *The Value of Solitude: The Ethics and Spirituality of Aloneness in Autobiography* (Charlottesville: University of Virginia Press, 2004), 11–12.

this position that Christine not only affiliates with other alienated and subordinated women throughout history but also establishes her voice as one that can gather their stories into a unifying narrative, a metaphor for turning the fragments of time into an eternity. Analogous to Moses's displacement, which conditions his leadership, Christine's exilic distance equips her to cultivate a power to see and to write.

The *Cité des Dames* also aligns Christine recuperatively with Dido, the Carthaginian queen of Virgilian fame, in delineating her space and establishing the lines of her city, underscoring women's post-exilic resilience. According to Marilynn Desmond, Dido serves various positive functions and is one of the most radical examples of Christine's revisionary approach to history.[38] Her portrayal contravenes both Augustine's and Dante's condemnatory approach to Dido, subverting the idea of Dido as an embodiment of female lust, punished by *la bufera infernal* [the hellish hurricane] and *l'aere maligno* [the malignant air] of the second circle of *Inferno*, and as the object of male desire in *Confessions*, where Augustine remembers how, in his boyhood, "flebam Didonem extinctam feroque extrema secutam" [dead Dido [he] bewailed, that killed herself by falling upon the sword] (*Inf.* 5.31, 86).[39] Christine's *Cité des Dames* follows the traditional narrative of Dido's experience by portraying her as the builder of Carthage; however, she suggests that the queen's leadership skills and prudence hinge on her exile, evoking Christine's own connection with Dido, since she, too, confronts marginalization through the allegorical construction of the Cité des Dames. Thus, while the author refutes Dante's vision of Dido, she pursues a Dantean strategy of associating herself positively with an exile to redeem herself from the margins to which she has been cast. After recounting the story of King Pygmalion's cruelty and murder of Sychaeus, Christine writes of Dido, originally named Elissa, "Voyant que sa vie était en grand danger, son bon sens lui conseilla de quitter le pays et de s'en aller au loin. Cette decision prise, elle réfléchit courageusement à ce qu'elle ferait et s'arma de courage et de force pour mener son entreprise à bien" [Realizing that her life was in great danger, Elissa's own prudence prompted her to leave her homeland and to go into exile. Having considered this question, she courageously reflected

---

38 According to Desmond, "Christine would have been aware of the standard versions of Dido as an abandoned woman undone by desire," in *Reading Dido: Gender, Textuality, and the Medieval* Aeneid (Minneapolis: University of Minnesota Press, 1994), 216. For a discussion of medieval and Renaissance treatments of Dido, see: John Watkins, *The Specter of Dido: Spenser and Virgilian Epic* (New Haven, CT: Yale University Press, 1995), 30–61.

39 St. Augustine, *Confessions*, 1.13. This moment is treated in great detail in Marjorie Curry Woods, *Weeping for Dido: The Classics in the Medieval Classroom* (Princeton, NJ: Princeton University Press, 2019), 26–27.

on what she should do and armed herself with strength and constancy to put her intended undertaking into effect] (*CD* 1.46). The *bon sens*, or prudence, of Dido, which recalls Raison's time-reflecting mirror, implies her ability to use her foresight to make ethical judgments about future actions. Thus, although the French word *loin* indicates physical distance, Christine implies once more the exile's superior perspective on time, as well as space. By separating herself from King Pygmalion and the land of Tyre over which he ruled, Christine acts on her foresight about both the potential dangers of her continued residence there and about the alternative possibilities of justice and ruler in Carthage. On the subject of exile, Christine distinguishes between Dido and Ovid, who, Raison teaches, "se fut empressé de retomber dans les désordres qui l'avaient déjà fait condemner" ["was called back from exile and failed to refrain from the misdeeds for which his guilt had already punished him"] (*CD* 1.9). Unlike Ovid, who, when unable to continue enjoying the pleasures of his pre-exilic life, indulged in the pleasures of the flesh and slandered women, Dido uses her exilic position productively to create a kingdom characterized by *le droit et la justice* [the rule of law and justice], thereby demonstrating her concern not with selfish pleasure but instead with the common profit, a sign of a virtuous leader in the late medieval legal framework (*CD* 1.46).

The temporality of the *Cité des Dames* is essential to Christine's ethical vision in exile, recalling Boethius and Dante's similar emphasis on the moral value of the periphery. From her liminal viewpoint, Christine can see the women of the city, from separate temporalities, within the same all-encompassing frame, implying her philosophical, divine-like distance. Although anachronism has sometimes been perceived as a naïve historicism and irresponsible rejection of the traditional sequences of history, in the *Cité des Dames* the collapse of temporal boundaries helps Christine create a universal history for women and visualize this history for the readers. Raison effectively aligns Christine's line of sight with that of the reader: "Cela, tu peux la verifier toi-même par les chroniques, en comptant les années qui séparent ses débuts de la conquête du monde par Alexandre le Grand" ["you yourself can see from the various epochs given in charts in different history books how much time elapsed from their founding until after the conquest of Alexander the Great"] (1.19). Christine's vision reveals a more productive image of the past than the one she understood to be true at the beginning of the narrative; this vision indicates the extensive time a female-run kingdom can span, juxtaposing the longevity of the female warrior dynasty with Alexander's singular *conquête*. While Christine perceives a sequence in history, her ability to envision the *totum simul* serves a more ethical and purposeful value. As an exile, Christine has the potential to leverage her outsider status into a moral position from which to champion the stories of women, and from this position, "time" appears most generous to women when it is organized anachronistically, rather than linearly. Christine's vision of the city amounts to an ethical transformation because it makes visible the supreme good—in this case, a clearer and more accurate portrait of female excellence.

Like Dante, Christine only underscores the power of her vision of time by integrating exemplary prophets—beyond Moses—into her account of history. These women emphasize the truth-value of her allegory. For instance, Droiture's lessons begin with the divine-like sibyls, who envision the future: "'Sibylle' signifie, en effet, 'celle qui connaît la pensée de Dieu'" ["for saying 'sibyl' means 'knowing the thinking of God'"] (*CD* 2.1). The female prophets often save civilizations from servitude, underscoring the connection between the ability to see time more insightfully and ethical decision-making. Droiture calls attention to Deborah, who prophesied the deliverance of the Israelites from servitude to the king of Canaan, and to Elizabeth, the cousin of the Virgin Mary, who foresaw the Immaculate Conception. Other women constitute the guarantors of earthly civilizations, including Antonia, who saw a sign of Justinian's future as emperor of Constantinople. Allotting narrative space and time to the women who foreshadowed the fates of men reminds readers of the gaps in other histories that overlook their instrumental roles and implicitly calls attention to the way in which Christine's prophecy in the *Cité des Dames* serves as a counterpoint to the male-authored historiographies that contend with hers.

As if to align the structure of her narrative with that of the entire *Commedia*, Christine uses the third section to focus on the saintly ladies, under the queenship of the blessed Virgin Mary, in a triumphant spiritualization of the new urban landscape. Arranging the portraits of Old Testament, New Testament, and saintly women, such as Judith and Saint Catherine of Alexandria, Justice in this final section emphasizes the idea of providence: how the juxtaposition of women from different temporalities has, in fact, been divinely preordained. Thus, the Virgin Mary replies to Justice's encomium to her: "cette chose est voulue depuis toujours par Dieu la Père, prédestinée et ordonnée par la Sainte Trinité" ["this arrangement was present in the mind of God the Father from the start, revealed and ordained previously in the council of the Trinity"] (*CD* 3.1). *Toujours*, meaning "from the start" but also carrying the sense of "every day" and "always," reflects the Virgin's sense that God exists beyond time, in eternity, and how the manifestation of creation on earth and in human language requires sequence; from the divine perspective, however, the arrangement occurs simultaneously. The last women to enter the city thus reinforce the notion of anachronism as eternity and are a reminder that, as S.H. Rigby writes, "misogyny was ... a philosophical error, not a revealed truth, a matter of fallible human opinion rather than of true faith."[40] Christine's examples of holy women also challenge once more Boccaccio's supposed defense of famous (dead) women in *De claris mulieribus*, which notably includes only pagan women, and compares similarly with Chaucer's *Legend of Good Women*, which he began composing in 1386.[41]

In the conclusion of the *Cité des Dames*, Christine, still conscious of the *ennemis* [enemies] against women, nonetheless implies her development since her original state of despair, for now she can see (*contemplant* [seeing]) the city completed (*CD* 3.19); exile grants her clarity and insight. Christine emphasizes the eternal nature of the city, but also of her vision; she grasps a totalizing perspective of "celles de jadis, celles d'aujourd'hui et celles de demain" [ladies from the past, as well as from the present and future] (*CD* 3.19). Her newfound sense of temporal fluidity facilitates her new status as an authoritative defender of women and a guide to contemporary audiences. The city, like the book itself, is meant to encourage self-reflection, which Christine emphasizes by returning to the symbol of Raison's mirror: "Vous pouvez voir que c'est toute de vertus qu'elle a été construite, matériaux en verité si brillants que vous pouvez toutes vous y mirer, en particulier dans les hautes toitures de l'édifice" ["For you can see that the substance with which it is made is entirely of virtue, so resplendent that you may see yourselves mirrored in it, especially in the roofs"] (*CD* 3.19). Christine thus enacts for the reader the same inward examination Raison fosters in Christine. While the *Consolation* never shows Boethius fulfilling the ethical metamorphosis Lady Philosophy advises, ending instead with the guide's discourse on fate and free will, the *Cité des Dames* shows a subject who sees, transforming her gendered place on the margins into a virtuous central position from which to perceive history as an empowering female-specific temporality, and who, moreover, sees herself as belonging to this eternal time in the way that Dante sees himself fit for Purgatory and, eventually, Paradise.

Like Dante, Christine effectively leverages her exilic position into a distanced perspective and uses the process of historiographical re-creation to re-center herself from the peripheries of the original community. Comparing

---

40 S.H. Rigby, "The Wife of Bath, Christine de Pizan, and the Medieval Case for Women," *The Chaucer Review* 35.2 (2000): 133–165 at 152.

41 Eleni Stecopoulos and Karl D. Uitti discuss how Christine's *Cité des Dames* "constitutes far more profoundly a response to Boccaccio than to Matheolus, whose *Liber lamentationum* ... is merely despicable, a miserable example of 'party-line' late-medieval clerkly misogyny," in "Christine de Pizan's *Livre de la Cité des Dames*: The Reconstruction of Myth," in *Reinterpreting Christine de Pizan*, ed. Earl Jeffrey Richards (Athens: University of Georgia Press, 1992), 48–62 at 49.

the *Commedia* and the *Cité des Dames* reveals the centrality of this lengthened exilic vision to philosophical and emotional self-restoration, but also highlights the flexibility of these metaphors, adaptable to different figurative uses and for varying contexts. For Dante, the *totum simul* of Lady Philosophy's teaching in the *Consolation* translates into the necessary perspective of the political exile, who must rise above oppressive conditions by detaching from the community of origin and identifying with a broader history of exiled figures. Dante's exilic model then becomes a powerful precursor for Christine's defiance of patriarchy and misogyny, as she adapts the form of the vision to rewrite her place within a universal history. While the authors share comparable conditions of solitude, the visions of the *Commedia* and the *Cité des Dames* ultimately emphasize the distinction between solitude and loneliness, imagining the periphery as the place from which the author can radically reconceive of reality and history. Dante and Christine anticipate the pithy notes on exile by the Polish-American writer Czeslaw Milosz: "New eyes, new thought, new distance: that a writer in exile needs all this is obvious, but whether he overcomes his old self depends upon resources which he only dimly perceived before."[42] New eyes, new thought, and new distance are indeed the outcome of exile in the vision narratives of these two medieval authors, whose protagonists ultimately reconcile themselves to their original plights, even if their subject positions appear to shift only in the allegorical space, and who emphasize the power of an ethical perspective and imagination to recover from feelings of alienation and loss. The *Commedia* and *Cité des Dames* theorize about the possibility of countering exile by redefining it according to early discussions of spiritual *peregrinatio*, showing how solitude need not always entail loneliness, longing, or even solipsism, and how it is, rather, a condition in which the individual consciously separates from the original community as a way of better understanding himself or herself and all time.

42 Czeslaw Milosz, "Notes on Exile," *Books Abroad* 50.2 (1976): 281–284 at 281.

CHAPTER 6

A Re-examination of Constance's Exile—Geoffrey Chaucer's *Man of Law's Tale* and Constance's Return Home

Gila Aloni

The various journeys on which Constance, the heroine of Geoffrey Chaucer's *Man of Law's Tale* [hereafter *MoLT*], embarks against her will convey an understanding of exile that goes beyond physical displacement. The tale presents the threat of spiritual exile as a shared religious experience, challenging the Christocentric ideology of medieval Europe and promoting a more nonsectarian view that acknowledges the value of other religious faiths. Chaucer argues that the form of spiritual exile that comes from abjuring personal faith and belief—whether Christian or Muslim—has more dire consequences than being sent abroad or set adrift. The equivalence he draws between Christianity and Islam in this regard sets Chaucer apart from the Christocentric, white, European Middle Ages. It also contrasts with the ideology represented by the Muslim counselors of Constance's future husband, who see the differences between the two religions rather than the similarities: "that ther was swich diversitee / Bitwene hir bothe lawes" (220–221).[1] In *MoLT*, Chaucer uses the threat of spiritual exile as a device to put the Muslim faith on par with Christianity. Chaucer's only reference to the Qur'an and the prophet Mohamed, medieval Christianity's strongest religious rival, takes place in this tale, where he draws an implicit equivalence between the two religions in their shared demand for loyalty to the faith. Rather than extolling the superiority of Christianity, Chaucer promotes a worldview of mutual respect.

Critical interest in *MoLT* has generally focused on the figure of Constance as the constancy of Christian faith and female submission.[2] Though she is sent

1 Geoffrey Chaucer, *The Man of Law's Tale*, in *The Riverside Chaucer*, ed. Larry D. Benson (Boston: Houghton Mifflin, 1987). Line numbers are given in parentheses.

2 David Raybin suggests that Constance "moves unmoving" (69). According to Raybin, "the sea is the symbol of her own holy timelessness" (68). "Custance and History: Woman as Outsider in Chaucer's 'Man of Law's Tale,'" in *Studies in the Age of Chaucer* 12 (1990): 65–84. For a similar view of Constance's extraordinary endurance as an example for the faithful in their time of suffering, see: George R. Keiser, "The Spiritual Heroism of Chaucer's Custance," *Chaucer's Religious Tales*, ed. David Benson and Elizabeth Robertson (Cambridge: D.S. Brewer, 1990),

 | DOI:10.1163/9789004742598_008

on a long sea journey far away from her homeland, Constance never loses her faith. Constance's story begins in Rome, the seat of the Christian Church, and ends in Rome, to which she returns at the end of a life's journey—a return symbolizing the notion that, as John Halbrooks argues, "Rome may be the center of the historical world ... but ... the center of the spiritual world in *The Man of Law's Tale* is the soul of the Christian, which remains constant despite its geographical wanderings."[3] And yet, Constance is not the only figure in the tale who remains "constant" against the threat of spiritual displacement. Constance's mothers-in-law send her away precisely because they fear and feel their sense of spiritual exile. Thus, *MoLT* defines exile as the threat of a psychological, spiritual, and religious expulsion or exclusion rather than a physical one, and as an experience that neither Chaucer's Constance nor either of her mothers-in-law undergo. Moreover, it suggests that Constance's physical location does not function as a condition of her faith because her connection with God is direct and requires no third-party mediation, a key principle of Lollardy, aligning with Chaucer's commentary on religious fidelity through a Lollard lens.

Lollard doctrine rejected the necessity of religious intermediaries, emphasizing direct communication with God rather than reliance on priests or the institutional Church.[4] Rooted in John Wycliffe's teachings, Lollardy asserted that scripture alone is the ultimate authority in religious matters. Wycliffe's influence extended into upper-class circles, and Chaucer, whose patrons included John of Gaunt, may have been sympathetic to certain Lollard ideas.[5] While there is no direct evidence that Chaucer identified as a Lollard, his engagement with Lollard theology is particularly evident in *MoLT* and the Epilogue of *The Canterbury Tales*. Chaucer's most explicit reference to Lollardy appears when the Host reacts to the Parson's refusal to tell a secular or entertaining tale. The Parson rebukes the Host's swearing, adhering to a more moralistic, scripture-centered approach: "What eyleth the man, so synfully

121–36. On female submission, see: Sheila Delany, "Womanliness in the 'Man of Law's Tale'," *Chaucer Review* 9 (1974): 63–72 at 62. See also: Elaine Tuttle Hansen, *Chaucer and the Fiction of Gender* (Berkeley: University of California Press, 1992).

3 John Halbrooks, "The Historiography of Recognition and the Wandering Soul in Chaucer's *Man of Law's Tale*," unpublished, 7. I am grateful to Halbrooks for giving me access to an early version this paper.

4 J. Patrick Hornbeck, *What is a Lollard? Dissent and Belief in Late Medieval England* (Oxford: Oxford Theology and Religion Monographs, 2010).

5 K.B. McFarlane, *Lancastrian Kings and Lollard Knights* (Oxford: Oxford University Press, 1972); Derek Brewer, *Chaucer in his Time* (London: Longman, 1973), 236. See also: David Aers, *Faith, Ethics, and Church: Writing in England, 1360–1409* (Cambridge: D.S. Brewer, 2000).

to swere?" (1171). The Host responds sarcastically: "I smelle a Lollere in the wynd" (1173). By calling the Parson a Lollard, the Host underscores the tension between orthodox religious practices and reformist ideals. His comment implies that Lollardy's rejection of clerical authority and emphasis on direct access to God was widely recognized and, in some circles, controversial. The Host then invites the Parson to preach, saying, "This Lollere heer wil prechen us somewhat" (1177). However, the Shipman immediately objects, arguing that Lollards dangerously undermine religious teaching by interpreting scripture without the aid of priests or explanatory glosses: "He shal no gospel here ne teche" (1180). This exchange reflects Chaucer's awareness of Lollard criticisms of the Catholic Church, particularly their belief that faith should be unmediated and accessible to all, without the hierarchical control of clergy. Lollards were condemned for their insistence on reading and teaching the Bible without a glossary, a practice viewed as heresy by medieval authorities.[6] While Chaucer does not explicitly identify the Parson as a Lollard, the character's emphasis on moral instruction and resistance to embellishing religious teaching with fables and secular entertainment align with Lollard ideals. Thus, while Chaucer's momentary rejection represents orthodox Catholicism, it does not imply that he necessarily agrees.

Chaucer then allocates the space of an entire tale to the Parson. As Karen A. Winstead suggests, "the Parson does not seem concerned about being mistaken for a Lollard when, in his Prologue, he advertises an aversion to 'fables,' an aversion that, like his aversion to swearing, was shared by the Lollards."[7] In his tale, the Parson minimizes the role of priests and confessors in favor of a direct communication between individuals and God. Winstead writes that Chaucer departs from the "the practices of contemporary vernacular penitential tracts" and

> reduces radically both the presence of the priest in the text and the importance of oral confession in the penitential process. … In this respect, he anticipates an approach to vernacular religious literature, as well as strategies for dealing with censorship, that flowered in the generation following his death.[8]

---

6 Karen A. Winstead, "Chaucer's 'Parson's Tale' and the Contours of Orthodoxy," *The Chaucer Review* 43.3 (2009), 239–259 at 240.

7 Winstead, "Chaucer's 'Parson's Tale,'" 240–241.

8 Winstead, "Chaucer's 'Parson's Tale,'" 240–241.

It is fitting that these allusions to pre-Reformation ideas appear after Constance's tale takes her away from and back to Rome. The Lollard approach to religion is that one does not need Church representatives to connect with God; thus, being away from Rome does not entail exile. As Halbrooks explains, "the Papacy and the Emperor receive relatively little attention in the tale, and thus Chaucer removes the exemplum from its institutional context and places the burden of Christian understanding on the individual soul in an often-hostile world."[9] By shifting the focus away from the Church and its representatives, Chaucer underscores the idea that true religious devotion is an internal, individual experience and a self-sustaining force rather than one dictated by physical proximity to Rome or clerical mediation. In doing so, he presents a vision of faith that is resilient and self-sustaining, reinforcing Lollard belief in direct communion with God amid worldly challenges. Constance's unwavering devotion, even in exile, reflects a self-sustaining, personal relationship with God, much like the Lollard vision of religious constancy. Her faith remains intact not because of Rome or the Pope, but because of her individual conviction—a theme that resonates with Wycliffite teachings. Thus, Chaucer's reference to Lollardy in the Epilogue is more than a passing jest; it serves as a commentary on the nature of religious authority and faith. While he does not explicitly align himself with Lollard doctrine, his portrayal of spiritual exile, direct faith, and the questioning of institutional mediation suggest an engagement with Lollard ideas, adding another layer to *MoLT*'s exploration of religious loyalty. Chaucer demonstrates a more freethinking approach to religion in the *MoLT both* by implying some version of the Lollard idea that spirituality resides within, *and* by forging connections between Christianity and Islam that reflect his own cultural curiosity.

MoLT further establishes its focus on the threat of spiritual exile by clarifying that the primary motivation for the journey that Constance's father initiates is an arranged marriage aimed at conversion and religious conquest—not exile in a punitive sense. This particular plotline draws heavily on the genre of crusades romance.[10] As Benjamin Kedar points out, the betrothal agreement between the Sultan and Constance's father "reflects an actual fourteenth-century

9 Halbrooks, "The Historiography of Recognition," 17.

10 For the centrality of religious conversion in this tale see: Carolyn Dinshaw, "Pale Faces: Race, Religion, and Affect in Chaucer's Texts and Their Readers," *Studies in the Age of Chaucer* 23 (2001): 19–42. Celia M. Lewis, "History, Mission, and Crusade in the *Canterbury Tales*," *The Chaucer Review* 42 (2008): 353–382. Lewis explains: "the movements of Custance from Rome to Syria and eventually back to Rome, from bridal missionary to violently expulsed Christian, reflect the failed European impulse to reclaim the Holy Land through conversion, and the crusades that followed" (354).

strategy for converting Muslims. In a 1306 tract, the Frenchman Pierre Dubois wrote that good Catholic girls should be married off to Saracen chiefs so that the Christian brides could encourage their Muslim husbands to seek baptism."[11] However, religious conquest, the motivation for Constance's travel away from Rome, only operates on the surface of the tale. Instead, Chaucer advocates the opposite of forced conversion or conquest, urging adherence to personal beliefs even if they are not Christian because renunciation entails spiritual exile.

Traditionally, the interpretation of Constance's travels after her father sends her away from Rome as exile has its roots in the tradition of stories of exiled queens where the heroine flees an incestuous father or brothers-in-law.[12] In addition, critics have also argued that Chaucer's story is inspired by another trope, that of "a queen exiled for giving birth to a monster,"[13] which also appears in his contemporary John Gower's *Confessio Amantis* and the main source for both, Nicholas Trivet's 1334 *Life of Constance*, in the *Anglo-Norman Chronicle*.[14] The incestuous father trope also appears in the fourteenth-century romance

11 Benjamin Z. Kedar, *Crusade and Mission: European Approaches Toward the Muslims* (Princeton: Princeton University Press, 1988), 210. Kedar refers to Pierre Dubois, *The Recovery of the Holy Land* (*De recuperatione Terrae Sanctae*), trans. Walther I. Brandt. (New York: Columbia University Press, 1956).

12 See: Margaret Schlauch's *Chaucer's Constance and Accused Queens* (1927; repr. New York: New York University Press, 1969). The motif of the incestuous father is also known as the Accused Queen, the Castaway Queen, or the Maiden without Hands. Schlauch uses Chaucer's tale as the basis for her examination of similar themes in folktales and romance in order "to find out what light is shed on such themes by the study of primitive custom and belief and to trace the modifications of these themes in medieval romance" (7). Nancy B. Black identifies "two principal types of fictional narratives, both of which feature a virtuous, noble heroine who, after numerous trials and tribulations [such as rapes and incestuous fathers], returns to royal status at the end of the narrative." See: "Preface," in *Medieval Narratives of Accused Queens* (Gainesville: University Press of Florida, 2003), xi. See also: Elizabeth Archibald, *Incest and the Medieval Imagination* (Oxford: Oxford University Press, 2001), esp. chap. 4, "Fathers and Daughters," 145–91.

13 Benson, *Riverside Chaucer*, 857.

14 Edward A. Block, "Originality, Controlling Purpose, and Craftsmanship: Chaucer's 'Man of Law's Tale'," *PMLA* 68 (1953): 572–616 at 574. See also: Schlauch's *Chaucer's Constance*, esp. 3–8, 35–37, 64–85. The section of Nicholas Trivet's *Les Cronicles* is found in British Library MS Arundel 56 and appears in *Originals and Analogues of Some of Chaucer's Canterbury Tales*, ed. F.J. Furnivall, Edmund Brock, and W.A. Clouston (London: Trubner, 1887), 1–53. The Constance selection from Oxford Magdalen 45, edited by Margaret Schlauch, appears in *Sources and Analogues of Chaucer's Canterbury Tales*, ed. W.F. Bryan and Germaine Dempster (Chicago: University of Chicago Press, 1941), 165–83.

Emaré, which Chaucer knew directly.[15] Thomas Hanks has studied the parallels in diction, phrasing, and plot between Chaucer's tale and *Emaré*, concluding that the major difference between these versions is that "early in the narrative, Emaré's father conceives an incestuous desire for her. Because she refuses him, he casts her adrift."[16] Chaucer alters his sources, shifting the genre and thematic focus of the tale by changing the motivation for Constance's frequent crossings of the sea and long periods spent outside her ancestral territory from incest to arranged marriage and religious conversion.

In the prologue to his tale, Chaucer's Man of Law denounces the incestuous story that prevails in other versions: "Of switch cursed stories I say fey!" (80). More specifically, the Man of Law promises his audience that he will not repeat the incestuous stories told by Gower about Canacee: "But certainly no word ne writeth he/ of thilke wikke ensample of Canacee / That loved hir owene brother synfully" (76–79). Nor will he tell Gower's story of an incestuous father "Tyro Appollonius, / How that the cursed kyng Antiochus / Birafte his daughter of hir maidenhead" (81–83). Scholars generally agree that the Man of Law's comments are meant to mock his contemporaries, that they "are a jibe at Gower's *Confessio Amantis*, where the stories of both Canacee and Apollonius appear."[17] It is far more than a jibe at Gower, however; by prompting his audience with the choice to omit the incestuous element from the tale, Chaucer reveals a fundamental difference between his tale and his sources. In Chaucer's version, Constance's journey overseas is not a punishment for refusing a father's desire.

Chaucer also replaces the idea of Constance's exile as physical punishment for an act of disobedience with her verbal defiance against paternal arranged marriages: "I moste anoon syn it is youre willie" (282). As Yvette Kisor argues, Chaucer "reintroduces the possibility of disobedience through Constance's voiced unwillingness to obey, even as she asserts the inescapable reality of

15 Edith Rickert, "The Romance of Emaré," EETS e.s. 99 (1908; rpt. London: Oxford Univ. Press, 1958), xxviii. *The Middle English Breton Lays*, ed. Anne Laskaya and Eve Salisbury (Kalamazoo: Medieval Institute Publications, 1995). Thomas D. Hanks, "*Emaré*: An Influence on the 'Man of Law's Tale'," *Chaucer Review* 18 (1983):182–8.

16 Hanks, "*Emaré*," 185.

17 Larry Benson, "Incest and Moral Poetry in Gower's *Confessio Amantis*," *The Chaucer Review* 19 (1984):100–109 at 100. For the omission of the incestuous element, see also: Yvette Kisor, "Moments of Silence, Acts of Speech: Uncovering the Incest Motif in the 'Man of Law's Tale'," *The Chaucer Review* 40 (2005): 141–162. Elizabeth Archibald, "The Flight from Incest: Two Late Classical Precursors of the Constance Theme," *The Chaucer Review* 20 (1986): 259–72; Elizabeth Allen, "Chaucer Answers Gower: Constance and the Trouble with Reading," *ELH* (1997): 627–55; and Elizabeth Scala, "Canacee and the Chaucer Canon: Incest and Other Unnarratables," *The Chaucer Review* 30 (1995): 15–39.

her obedience."[18] In other words, Constance's response suggests that she does not experience her travel overseas as an escape or as an exile, but rather as her fate, to which she submits within the medieval structure of exchange of women. She sees her lack of free choice as subjugation dictated by patriarchal, hierarchical, societal structure: "Wommen are born to thraldom and penance, / And to been under mannes governance" (286–288). Her journey is the outcome of an arranged marriage contract. To emphasize the exchange rather than exile, the narrator, a representative of the legal system as a man of law, and Syrian merchants experienced with commodities exchange, facilitate the contract.[19] However, Chaucer satirizes the Man of Law; his underhandedness criticizes the law he represents. Chaucer tells the audience that "Nowher so bisy a man as he ther nas, / And yet he semed bisier than he was" (320–321). This suggests the Man of Law's dishonesty and unreliability, thus questioning the law of exchange he promotes in his tale.

The *MoLT* opens when, with the help of Syrian merchants, the Emperor of Rome and his future son-in-law, the Sultan strike a marriage deal in the market with Constance as a commodity. Then, after being cast adrift, she lands in Northumbria. However, each time Constance arrives in a new place, her mother-in-law takes charge, establishing a new form of exchange. Constance's mothers-in-law reverse the traditional patriarchal structure by becoming players in this exchange. To do so, each one of Constance's mothers-in-law betrays men: one (the Sultana) murders her son, while the other (Alla's mother) lies to her son when she fakes a letter on his behalf to Constance. Breaking the most natural law, mother-child loyalty, allows these mothers to reverse the initial agreement formed by men. Interestingly, the Sultana is also called "Semyrame the secounde" and "Virago" (359), terms with overtones of "manliness," connoting the masculine power she assumes.[20] Structurally speaking, Constance moves from one mother-in-law to the other: the Sultana's banishment of Constance leads her to her second mother-in-law, who, like the first one, removes her son's part in the agreement, sending Constance on another sea voyage that leads her back home. The motivation for each woman is the same: to keep her religious identity and avoid estrangement in her land.

18 Kisor, "Moments of Silence," 143.

19 As Dinshaw points out, Constance's beauty and exemplary character become the commodity merchants bring to the Sultan, and there is a "parallel narration of [the merchants] loading their ships with merchandise and loading their eyes with Constance … 'Thise merchantz han doon fraught hir shippes newe, And whan they han this blisful mayden sayn, Hoom to Surye been they went ful fayn' (II, 171–73)." Carolyn Dinshaw, *Chaucer's Sexual Poetics* (Madison: University of Wisconsin Press, 1989), 88–95.

20 Jill Mann, *Chaucer* (New York: Harvester Wheatsheaf, 1991), 130.

The Sultana who intends to execute Constance by sending her on a sea voyage that she should not survive ends up being executed by the Roman senators, at Constance's father's order:

> For which this Emperour hath sent anon
> His senatour, with roial ordinance,
> And othere lourdes, God woot, many oon,
> On Surryens to taken heigh vengeance
> They brennen, sleen, and brynge hem to meschance. (961–64)

The Sultana is punished for her incestuous desire as much as for her lust for power. Similarly, Donegild, who also intends for Constance to perish on a dangerous sea voyage, ends up being executed by her son, Alla. In the case of both the Sultana and Donegild, execution is the threat to Constance's life, not exile. When Donegild forges the letter that forces Constance to leave as a result of Alla's order, she "… countrefeted lettres in this wyse: / 'the king comandeth his constable anon, / Up peyne of hangyng, and on heigh juyse'" (793–795). Constance is to be placed "… in the same ship as he hire fond, / Hire, and hir yonge sone, and al hir geere, / He sholde putte, and croude hire fro the lond" (799–801). Sending her away saves her life and allows her to eventually return home. According to the Middle English Dictionary, the verb "croude" means "to compel or take by force," but it does not mean exile in Constance's case; for her, the only exile is banishment from her Christian faith.[21] On the one hand, holding true to one's faith transcends religious boundaries; however, on the other, Chaucer elevates Christianity above all other religions when it comes to inter-familial relationships. Whereas either Constance's mothers-in-law murder their son, as in the case of the Sultana, or the son executes his mother in the case of Alla,[22] Constance protects her son Maurice and safely brings him back home to Rome.

The exchange also occurs on the metatextual level of Chaucer with his sources and within the tale itself. Although Chaucer eliminates the incest element in his sources as the motivation for Constance's journey from her father's home, he transfers this element to the Sultan's mother, associating her with Semiramis, a reputed queen of ancient Syria who built Babylon's walls and

---

21 *Middle English Dictionary*, s.v. "Crouden," last modified November 2019, https://quod.lib.umich.edu/m/middle-english-dictionary/dictionary/MED9010.

22 For murder in Chaucer's work, see: Larissa Tracy, "'Mordre wol out': Murder and Justice in Chaucer," in *Medieval and Early Modern Murder: Legal, Literary, and Historical Contexts*, ed. Tracy (Woodbridge: Boydell Press, 2018), 115–36, especially 116.

was renowned for her incest with her son.[23] Yet the marriage contract will not materialize unless it involves the Sultan's christening: "his baronage / And alle his liges sholde ycristned be" (239–40). This request adds another dimension to the tale.

On one level, the condition of conversion to Christianity aims at resolving the apparent "diversitee / Betwene hir bothe lawes" (220–221). However, this seeming diversity dissolves as Christians and Muslims in this tale share loyalty to their respective religions. The advisors who point to this difference may represent the majority of people at the time who saw a "diversitee," but Chaucer, who traveled extensively and met Jews, Christians, and Muslims, understood that in their loyalty to their faiths, they were fundamentally the same.[24] Though they are rivals, it is the similitude between Christianity and Islam—more specifically in their shared understanding of exile as a spiritual act of relinquishing one's belief—that is at the core of this tale. Chaucer equally supports both Muslims and Christians in keeping their belief, emphasizing the common features in the attitude and perception of their respective faiths. The Man of Law comments on the obligation to follow the same law as one requires another: "For swich lawe as a man yeveth another wight, / He sholde hymselven usen it, by right" (43–44). This statement conveys the utmost respect for alterity, whether Christianity towards Islam or Islam towards Christianity. It advances a more nonsectarian worldview that can accept the value of other religious faiths rather than offering a polemic on punitive physical exile as a result of religious differences.

Constance's experience, as well as that of her mothers-in-law, suggests that the state of estrangement and exile is not determined by expulsion from their homeland, and the act of involuntary exit from their native country does not define exile because exile entails a psychological dimension. Therefore, unsurprisingly, the Sultan's mother, who refuses to convert, states, "The lyf shal

23 Johnstone Parr, "Chaucer's Semiramis," *Chaucer* 5 (1970): 57–61.

24 For an analysis of the "transgressive proximity" and the similitude of the Other, see: Susan Schibanoff, "Worlds Apart: Orientalism, Antifeminism, and Heresy in Chaucer's *Man of Law's Tale*," *Exemplaria* 8.1 (1996): 59–96. Reprinted in Kathryn L. Lynch, ed., *Chaucer's Cultural Geography: Basic Readings in Chaucer and His Time* (New York: Routledge, 2002), 248–281. Schibanoff applies Jonathan Dollimore's theory of binary opposition to her analysis of the proximity between Christianity and Islam. See: Jonathan Dollimore, "Augustine: Perversion and Privation," in *Sexual Dissidence: Augustine to Wilde, Freud to Foucault* (Oxford: Clarendon Press, 1991), 131–48. As Schibanoff explains, "in Dollimore's terms, 'similarity' or 'proximity' indicates the intimate relationship that exists between supposedly opposite binaries. Such 'intimacy' ultimately stems from the Christian antidualistic notion of evil as good's privation, not good's opposite, of vice as the perversion rather than antithesis of virtue" (141).

rather *out of* my body sterte / Or Makometes lawe *out of* myn herte" (335–36, my emphasis). The prepositional phrase "out of," which entails movement from within to the outside, repeats twice. The Sultana would rather take life out of her body (exiling from this world) than exclude the prophet Muhammad's law from her heart; she would rather die than exile herself from her own religion and estrange herself within her land. The Sultana refuses to be tied to a new religion, a "newe lawe / But thraldom to oure bodies and penance" (337–338). The impact of the potential conversion, says the Sultana, is on "oure bodies." This perception of the body as the vessel that carries faith, whether Christian or Muslim, establishes yet another parallel between the Sultana and Constance. As Carolyn Dinshaw points out, while Constance travels from place to place, she "holds her faith i*n her body*."[25] More specifically, similarly to the Sultana, she carries it in her heart: "Hir herte is verray chambre of hoolynesse" (167). The word "chambre" here implies one of the four chambers of the heart, but it also suggests a room in one's home. Indeed, the next time the word "chambre" appears, it refers to a room in Constance's home prior to her departure: "Nas herd swich tendre wepyng for pitee/ As in the chambre was for hire departynge" (292–293). Later, when Constance arrives in Northumbria, she falls asleep "in Hermengyldes chambre" (595). The double meaning of the word "chambre" as both a space within her body where she keeps her faith and as a room in her home suggests that Constance carries her home within her. Thus, displacement of her body does not entail exile.

The fourth and last time in which the word "chambre" appears in the tale adds another dimension to this motif of spiritual constancy. It appears when pregnant Constance keeps herself in her room while Alla goes to war in Scotland: "She halt hire chambre, abidyng Cristes wille" (721). If, earlier in the tale, Constance's heart is the "chambre of hoolynesse," now it is in the chambre of the house in which she dwells where she abides Christ's will (167). The physical body and the space of one's home are interchangeable. Furthermore, not only does she keep the faith in her heart, but she can also turn the space she occupies into a chamber of faith. Likewise, Constance's mothers-in-law embody their faith and serve as vessels for it, even if the homeland around them changes.

Despite the image of the Sultana as treacherous and murderous, by operating disloyally to her son, she acts loyally to her faith; unconverted, she remains a faithful Muslim. According to Norman Davis, Islamic law views *jihad* [holy war] as not only a physical war, but a spiritual one, too, which can be waged

25 Carolyn Dinshaw, "Pale Faces," 26. Emphasis in the original. See: Bojana Radovanović's chapter in this volume.

against bad Muslims who no longer deserve the name.[26] According to this view, the Sultana's son is a bad Muslim and should be treated like a traitor; he should be exiled from the world as punishment for his willingness to relinquish his faith. The attitude towards an internal threat forms a fundamental similarity between Christianity and Islam; in the medieval Christian world, heresy was understood as an attack on a religious community from within itself.[27] Susan Schibanoff explains:

> As "outlaws" rather than "inlaws," nonbelievers—pagans or infidels—posed the lesser threat to Christianity. ... By their definition as wayward "insiders," ... the insidious proximity [of the heretics] to the dominant faith created a dangerous instability that demanded resolution, not complacency or tolerance. Typically, that resolution took one of two forms: the heretic was either reassimilated into the fold or altogether driven from it, clearly branded as other through ex-communication or worse fate [i.e. execution].[28]

If, in the Epilogue, Chaucer uses the Lollards to invoke Christian practices of expulsion and exclusion, in the *MoLT* he returns to the same theme via Islam. In doing so, he tacitly (and perhaps ironically) endorses the Lollard-like view that the strength of a faith depends on its adherents' personal, interior spirituality.

Chaucer's *MoLT* written for a predominantly Christian audience largely unfamiliar with Islamic law, highlights similarities between Christianity and Islam by portraying the denial of personal faith as a form of spiritual exile punishable by death. In dramatizing this theme, Chaucer emphasizes the profound consequences of rejecting one's faith, framing it as a universal moral and spiritual crisis. This concept, though articulated within the distinct theological frameworks of Christianity and Islam, carries a shared resonance that bridges the two religions. Indeed, recent scholars illustrate how Christian Iberian literature recast the portrayal of Muslims, presenting them as both potential partners and subordinates rather than solely as enemies.[29] By weaving these parallels into his narrative, Chaucer subtly invites his audience to consider the commonalities between their own beliefs and those of a distant and largely

26 Norman Daniel, *The Arabs and Medieval Europe* (London: Longman, 1979), 265.

27 Bernard, Cullen, "Heresy," *Dictionary of the Middle Ages*, ed. Joseph R. Strayer (New York: Charles Scribner's Sons, 1985) 6:202–4.

28 Schibanoff, "Worlds Apart," 251.

29 Fuentes examines "the alternation between hostile and empathetic view of Muslims in texts written by Iberian Christians" (4). Marcelo E. Fuentes, *Contradictory Muslims in the Literature of Medieval Iberian Christians* (Switzerland: Palgrave Macmillan, 2024).

misunderstood faith tradition, fostering a sense of shared moral and spiritual values.

Chaucer's engagement with Arabic language and Islamic religious concepts was likely indirect but significant, facilitated through Latin translations of major Arabic works.[30] By the fourteenth century, the writings of Islamic philosophers and scientists such as Avicenna (Ibn Sina) (*c.*980–1037), known for *The Canon of Medicine*, and Averroes (Ibn Rushd) (1126–1198), famous for his Aristotelian commentaries, circulated widely in Europe. These texts, translated from Arabic into Latin by scholars like Michael Scot (1175–1236) and Gerard of Cremona (1114–1187), became foundational to medieval intellectual life. As Akbari and Mallette highlight in *A Sea of Languages: Rethinking the Arabic Role in Medieval Literary History*, Chaucer was exposed to Arabic-rooted knowledge, particularly in astronomy, medicine, and religious philosophy.[31] Furthermore, through figures like Maimonides (Musa ibn Maymun) (1138–1204), whose *Guide for the Perplexed* blended Jewish, Islamic, and Aristotelian thought, Chaucer may have indirectly encountered Islamic theological and legal ideas.[32] Additionally, the intense religious polemics between Islam and Christianity during the Middle Ages—manifested in theological disputes, translated texts, and missionary writings—likely shaped Chaucer's awareness of Islamic beliefs. The widespread Latin translations of the Quran and polemical works by Christian scholars such as Ramon Llull and Peter the Venerable engaged with Islamic theology and law, providing a framework through which Chaucer may have encountered Islamic religious discourse. While no direct evidence confirms his fluency in Arabic, the widespread transmission of Arabic scholarship and religious debates in medieval Europe suggests that Chaucer, as a well-traveled courtier and scholar, likely engaged with Arabic-derived terminology and religious concepts in his writings.

Furthermore, Chaucer's engagement with astrology and medicine, as seen in *The Canterbury Tales*, suggests indirect exposure to Arabic terminology and

30 Charles Burnett, *The Introduction of Arabic Learning into Medieval Europe* (Aldershot: Variorum, 1997).

31 Suzanne Conklin Akbari and Karla Mallette, eds., *A Sea of Languages: Rethinking the Arabic Role in Medieval Literary History* (University of Toronto Press, 2013).

32 Shazia Jagot demonstrates that The Ellesmere Manuscript, "preserves an engagement with Arabic learning, specifically judicial astrology or ʿilm al-nujm (the 'science of the stars'), that takes us across geographical space and time, from fourteenth century Canterbury to tenth century Fatimid Cairo: a connection that is not easily discerned at first glance." See, Jagot Shazia, "From Fatimid Cairo to Canterbury: Chaucer and the 'libro Mansor,'" *MEMOS: Medieval and Early Modern Orients*, 6 Dec. 2021: https://journals.openedition.org/remmm/10033?lang=en. Accessed 28 Jan. 2025.

scientific methods, which dominated these fields during the Middle Ages.[33] Arabic contributions to astronomy, such as Al-Zarqali's *Toledo Tables* and the astrological treatises of Al-Farghani, influenced European thinkers and may have reached Chaucer through figures like Roger Bacon or John of Sacrobosco. Specific terms of Arabic origin appearing in Chaucer's works reinforce this influence. For example, in *The Canterbury Tales*, the word *alchemy*—derived from the Arabic *al-kimiya'*—reflects Chaucer's familiarity with the mystical and scientific traditions rooted in Arabic thought. Similarly, the term *zenith*, used in his *Treatise on the Astrolabe*, comes from the Arabic *samt* (meaning "path" or "direction"), a testament to his knowledge of Arabic astronomical concepts. Other Arabic-derived terms such as *azimuth* (from *as-sumut*, meaning "the ways") and *nadir* (from *nazir*, meaning "opposite") further indicate that Chaucer absorbed elements of Arabic language and scientific vocabulary through the intellectual currents of his time.

Chaucer's inclusion of these terms and concepts, while not always explicitly linked to their Arabic origins, reveals his broader engagement with the scientific and philosophical advancements of the Islamic Golden Age, mediated by Latin translations.[34] Arabic linguistic and literary traditions influenced the development of vernacular European literature, challenging the traditional Eurocentric narrative that frames medieval literature as predominantly Latin and Christian in origin.[35] These linguistic traces, combined with his nuanced portrayal of themes like faith and exile in the *MoLT*, suggest that Chaucer not only was aware of Islamic cultural and intellectual traditions but also incorporated their influence into his works in subtle and significant ways. By doing so, he added a layer of universality to his writings that connected Christian Europe with the broader, interconnected world of medieval thought.

---

33 See: Jagot, "From Fatimid Cairo to Canterbury," and Akbari and Mallette, *A Sea of Languages*.

34 The question of Chaucer's exposure to Arabic language and culture has recently gained scholarly attention. Katharine Slater Gittes explores structural parallels between *The Canterbury Tales* and Arabic frame narratives like *One Thousand and One Nights*, suggesting Chaucer may have drawn on the Arabic tradition of embedding stories within a framing tale, highlighting cross-cultural influences in medieval literature. Gittes, "*The Canterbury Tales* and the Arabic Frame Tradition," *The Chaucer Review*, 12.4 (1978): 255–26. See also: Dorothee Metlitzki, *The Matter of Araby in Medieval England* (Yale University Press, 1977). Although I disagree with the book's central claim that Chaucer was hostile toward Islam, it effectively highlights the various ways he uses Islamic religious and political symbols, as well as his perspective on them, while also exploring his depiction of Eastern women.

35 María Rosa Rosa, *The Arabic Role in Medieval Literary History: A Forgotten Heritage* (University of Pennsylvania Press, 1987).

In the Islamic view, religion comprises three main elements: *islam* (submission), *iman* (faith), and *ihan* (doing what is beautiful). The third dimension, doing what is beautiful, means that "the Prophet does not look at the activity itself, but the motivation for the activity."[36] In accordance with this last principle, the motivation for the Sultana's murder of her son—her refusal to spiritually exile herself—categorizes her act as loyalty to one of the main principles of Islam. As Sachiko Murata and William C. Chittick note, "Some of the significance of *iman* can be understood by considering its opposite, *kufr*, a word that is usually translated as 'infidelity' or 'unbelief.'"[37] The Sultana tells her counselors that her son is a rebel, an infidel, a *kufr*: "'Lordes' quod she, 'ye knowen everichon, / How that my sone in point is for to lete / The hooly lawes of our Alkaron, / Yeven by Goddes message Makomete'" (330–33). In using religion as a pretext for murder, the Sultana relies on one of the principles of Islam which supports the law of *jihad*.[38] Furthermore, as Murata and Chittick explain, "behind all the stress on practice is the recognition that the Koran must become flesh and blood. It is not enough for people to read the Koran or learn what it says. They must embody the Book. It must become the determining reality of what they do (*islam*), what they think (*iman*) and what they intend (*ihsan*)."[39] From a Muslim viewpoint, in rejecting Islam and converting to Christianity, the Sultan deserves death for disobeying *iman*. While the Sultana acts in a way that seems to be utterly opposed to maternal instinct, she acts in full compliance with principles at the heart of her religion, principles shared by the dominant medieval Christian ideology. Therefore, in the act of violence against the Sultan, the Sultana "embodies the book," punishing him for abandoning his commitment to Islam and not being as constant as Constance in keeping her faith.

The Man of Law declares the importance of commitment to one's word in the prologue to his tale. When the Host invites the Man of Law to keep his promise to tell his tale, the Man of Law answers, "Biheste is dette" (41). In other

36 Sachiko Murata and William C. Chittick, *The Vision of Islam* (New York: Paragon House, 1994), xxix.

37 Murata and Chittick, *The Vision of Islam*, 40.

38 See also: Gila Aloni, "M(ons)ters in laws: Maternal Models in the 'Man of Law's Tale,'" in *Mélanges de Langue, Littérature et Civilisation Offerts à André Crépin à l'Occasion de Son Quatre-Vingtième Anniversaire*, ed. Danielle Buschinger and Arlette Sancery, *Medievales* 44 (2008): 1–10. Some aspects of the above discussion appear in my chapter, co-authored with Shirley Zisser, "Geoffrey Chaucer's 'Lyne Oriental': Mediterranean and Oriental Languages in the 'Treatise on the Astrolabe,'" *Mediterranean Historical Review* 16.2 (2002): 69–77.

39 Murata and Chittick, *The Vision of Islam*, 9.

words, a promise is a debt. He must keep his promise, although, as the Man of Law says, he cannot rhyme as well as Chaucer does in *The Legend of Good Women,* also known by the title *The Legend of Cupid's Saints.*[40] The allusion to *The Legend of Good Women* connects the *MoLT* to another Chaucerian text centered on the theme of fidelity to the God of Love. Whether to Cupid, Allah, or the Christian God, fidelity to a god is the common denominator among all the women in the collection. Thus, when the host prompts the Man of Law to keep his promise to tell his story, and the latter replies, "Hooste, ... *depardieux,* ich assente; / To breke forward is nat myn entente," (my emphasis, 40–41) the Man of Law also invokes the idea of not breaking an agreement with God. He swears in God's name to agree: "depardieux, ich assente" (40). The semantics of this particular oath, "depardieux," adds another dimension to the text that follows the Prologue in suggesting that he will not "depart" from dieux (God). The double entendre connects spiritual betrayal to a spatialized metaphor of departure. The stanza that opens with a spiritual departure ends with a reference to an involuntary physical departure from one's homeland and the allusion to Ovid and his letters: "or he hath toold of loveris up and doun / Mo than Ovide made of mencioun / In his Episteles, that been ful olde. / What sholde I tellen hem, syn they been tolde?" (53–56). Ovid's *Episteles,* known as *Epistulae ex Ponto* (*Letters from the Black Sea*), in which he expresses to his wife and friends the grimness of his exile, contrasts with Constance's experience; unlike Ovid, she does not express feelings of homesickness, frustration, and anger. Indeed, Chaucer declares that there is no need to tell of such experience "syn they have been tolde" (56). In other words, Chaucer brings up the allusion only to negate it and to refocus on another form of exile that has not yet been described.

Throughout the tale, the word "exile" appears only once—and not in relation to Constance, but within the context of the people of Northumbria—the land where Constance arrives after she leaves Syria.[41] The narrator explains

40 According to Spearing, "Several scholars have noted the resemblance of the 'Man of Law's Tale' to the vitae of saints, and especially of female saints, that were so popular in the Middle Ages." See: A.C. Spearing, "Narrative Voice: The Case of Chaucer's 'Man of Law's Tale,'" *New Literary History: Voice and Human Experience* 32.3 (2001): 715–46 at 738.

41 Upon Constance's arrival to Alla's kingdom, Northumbria, she meets the constable and his wife "Hermengyld [who] loved hire right as hir lyf" (535). Hermengyld's adoration for Constance leads her to convert. Unlike Constance's mothers-in-law who are united in their rejection of the idea of conversion embodied by Constance, Hermengyld is the only one who welcomes Constance and her Christian faith. However, she ends up being murdered by "aknight who kitte the throte of Hermengyld atwo" (600) and places the knife next to Constance's bed as retaliation for her refusing his advances. Although the pretext

that most of the Christians who used to live in Northumbria had to escape: "Because of pagans, that conquered all about" (542) and "... To Walys fledde the Cristyanytee ... / Ther was hir refut for the meene while" (544, 546). The circumstances of conquest that force those Christians to leave their land do not turn them into exiles; in Chaucer's view of this experience, they "fledde" their homes but maintain their faith. The word exile refers to this small group of people: "But yet nere Cristene *Britons so exiled* / That ther nere somme that in hir privetee / Honoured Crist and hethen folk bigiled" (547–49, my emphasis). The assertion, "... nere ... *so* exiled" (my emphasis) suggests that the ability to practice Christianity secretly is only a partial exile; complete exile would mean not being able to practice their faith in any way.[42]

This is the fear that Constance's second mother-in-law, Donegild, expresses when Constance and her son, Alla, are about to marry: "Hir thoughte hir cursed herte brast atwo/ She wolde noght hir sone had do so; / Hir thoughte a despit that he sholde take/ So strange a creature unto his make" (698–700). The idea of Constance as a stranger who can rule the land together with her son leads Donegild to cast Constance away. Unlike the Sultana, Donegild does not perceive the conversion to Christianity as a form of exile but rather as subordination to a foreign daughter-in-law that threatens her political power.[43] Constance's departure, which ultimately results in her return home, is not cast as exile; in contrast, Donegild refuses to endure exile within her own land under foreign dominion. Thus, *MoLT* establishes exile not as physical removal but as a psychological and spiritual threat.

The tale also flirts with the idea of exile as a linguistic phenomenon, similar to what Catherine Keen, in her analysis of Dante's *De vulgari*, has called "linguistic alienation":

> It is a commonplace of Roman writing on exile to emphasize the linguistic alienation experienced by the cultivated Latin citizen in his banishment, where he finds himself surrounded by speakers of cacophonously

---

for the killing is lust, in the context of Constance's voyages of conversion, it may also be retaliation for renouncing personal belief.

42 This passage alludes to the Saxon settlement *c.*480 CE. When the Romans pulled out of Britain *c.*420, they took Christianity with them, but some Britons remained Christian. When the Saxons (Danes, Jutes, Frisians, Geats, and Angles) arrived, they pushed the Britons further west into Wales.

43 For the view of non-Christian parallels to Christianity, see: Larissa Tracy, "Knight of God or the Goddess?: Rethinking Religious Syncretism in *Sir Gawain and the Green Knight*," *Arthuriana* 17.3 (2007): 31–55. More specifically, Tracy reexamines "modern assumptions about the nature of Christianity and pagan suppression in the Middle Ages" (8).

> barbaric tongues. ... At times, the exiles express the fear that their own mastery of Latin will be undermined through lack of practice, deracinating them from the language as well as the site of their patria; ... Dante, ... seems to experience exile in the *De vulgari* as an exposure to linguistic chaos.[44]

However, Constance does not experience such "linguistic alienation." When she arrives in Northumbria, the locals understand her mother tongue: "A maner Latyn corrupt was hir speche, / But algates thereby was she understonde" (519–520). Chaucer differs from his sources, specifically Trivet, with this linguistic aspect of exile. As Christine F. Cooper points out, "rather than being learned in many languages and able to speak Saxon to the constable, Custance speaks only her own language, which is nevertheless understood by the Northumbrian."[45] Cooper explains this linguistic situation as part of the tale's reliance on hagiography, where medieval saints usually experience "the gift of xenoglossia, or the miraculous ability to speak, understand, or be understood in a foreign language that the recipient has never learnt formally."[46] In adapting Trivet's chronicle, Chaucer might have suggested her "xenoglossic gifts,"[47] but he implies that Constance never undergoes a "linguistic chaos" such as the one Dante's experiences, which provokes a feeling of alienation. Chaucer adapts his sources with other linguistic choices, clarifying the exilic threat facing Constance.

Among the five names that Chaucer chooses to adopt from Nicholas Trivet's *Anglo-Norman Chronicle* and his *Life of Constance*, he picks Alla.[48] Trivet's version names the Emperor of Rome Tiberius Constantinus, his wife Italia, the constable Elda, the bishop Lucius (mentioned by Chaucer only in line 716), the senator Arsemilus, his wife Helen, and the Pope Pelagius. Chaucer retains only the names of Constance, Alla, Hermengyld, Donegild, and Maurice, accentuating their significance, especially concerning religion. Dropping the emperor's wife's name, "Italia," and retaining the name "Alla" suggests that his focus in this displacement tale is not geographical but spiritual. It is a tale about the

44 Catherine Keen, "The Language of Exile in Dante," in *Reading Medieval Studies: Dante, Current Trends in Dante Studies* 27, ed. Claire E. Honess (Reading: University of Reading, 2001), 90–91.

45 Christine F. Cooper, "'But algates therby was she understonde': Translating Custance in Chaucer's 'Man of Law's Tale'," *The Yearbook of English Studies* 36.1 (2006): 27–38 at 29.

46 Cooper, "'But algates therby was she understonde,'" 28.

47 Cooper, "'But algates therby was she understonde,'" 31.

48 Edward A. Block, "Originality, Controlling Purpose, and Craftsmanship: Chaucer's 'Man of Law's Tale,'" *PMLA* 68 (1953): 572–616 at 574.

religious identity to which Constance and her mothers-in-law are equally loyal regardless of their divergent religions.

Chaucer summarizes Constance's journey with: "Now is she scaped al hire aventure" (1151). Constance's voyages are an "aventure"—a misfortune or adventure. Likewise, earlier in the tale, as Constance leaves Syria due to the Sultana's scheme, the narrator explains that "Yeres and dayes fleet this creature / the See of Grece unto the Strayt / Of Marrok, as it was hire *aventure*" (463–465, my emphasis). The repetition of the word "aventure" underscores the idea that Chaucer's Constance's traveling experience should not be confused with exile. Instead of exile, *MoLT* advocates for an inner home sustained by the faithful despite all misfortunes—an unmediated connection with God and steadfast devotion to one's faith free from the intervention of church representatives, as seen in Constance's home in Rome. Constance's unmediated spirituality, her individual psychological experience, deemphasizes religious differences and draws an implicit equivalence between Christianity and Islam, underscoring the existential destructiveness of spiritual exile.

CHAPTER 7

"There the Earl Had Their Heads Cut Off": Executions and Political Murders in Medieval Scandinavia

Kim Bergqvist

In thirteenth-century Sweden, kings began referring to Roman law and its concept of treason to legitimize their use of political violence in executing magnates who rebelled against them or otherwise became their political enemies.[1] Kings implemented a strategy of executions to deter powerful noblemen from reaching too high and challenging the king's position, or from encroaching on monarchical authority. Public executions and political murders of noblemen in the Scandinavian kingdoms (Sweden and Norway) during the Middle Ages, particularly in the context of civil wars and rebellions, suggest that these events were closely connected to larger political and legal developments in the Scandinavian realms. These were the consolidation of monarchical authority, the centralization and institutionalization of the monarchy—i.e. state formative tendencies—in close collaboration with the Church, and the introduction of new legal stipulations.[2] However, parallel to this, narratives surrounding these executions imply resistance to those trends and justification of such resistance using different models of defiance. The author of a verse chronicle

1 Erland Hjärne, *Fornsvenska lagstadganden*, vols. 1–3 (Uppsala: Almqvist & Wiksell, 1951), 31–176; Hugo Yrwing, *Maktkampen mellan Valdemar och Magnus Birgersson, 1275–1281* (Lund: Vetenskaps-Societeten i Lund, 1952), 55–57; Gösta Åqvist, *Kungen och rätten: Studier till uppkomsten och den tidigare utvecklingen av kungens lagstiftningsmakt och domsrätt under medeltiden* (Lund: Institutet för rättshistorisk forskning, 1989); Fredrik Charpentier Ljunqvist, "Kungamakten och lagen: En jämförelse mellan Danmark, Norge och Sverige under högmedeltiden" (PhD dissertation, Stockholm University, 2014), 63–66.

2 Olle Ferm, "Transformations sociales et émergence de nouvelles élites dans le royaume de Suède, 1220–1350," in *Les élites nordiques et l'Europe occidentale (XIIe–XVe siècle)*, ed. Tuomas M.S. Lehtonen and Élisabeth Mornet, 53–65 (Paris: Publications de la Sorbonne, 2007); Knut Helle, "Towards Nationally Organised Systems of Government," in *The Cambridge History of Scandinavia*, ed. Knut Helle (Cambridge: Cambridge University Press, 2003), 1:345–52; Philip Line, *Kingship and State Formation in Sweden, 1130–1290* (Leiden: Brill, 2007); Herman Schück, "Sweden under the Dynasty of the Folkungs," in *The Cambridge History of Scandinavia*, 1:392–410 and idem, "The Political System," in *The Cambridge History of Scandinavia*, 1:679–709.

 | DOI:10.1163/9789004742598_009

in Old Swedish from around 1320, *Erikskrönikan* (*The Chronicle of Duke Erik*), attempted to demonstrate the injustice of royal executions and the validity of resistance to unjust kings by siding with the executed rebels or magnates who fell from grace. The chronicler criticizes royal abuse of power and legitimates the concept of resistance by engaging with the notion of rebel martyrs and creating sympathy for the defeated party. Essentially, the chronicler condemns the ruling factions' abuse of political power by portraying these executions as nothing more than illicit and illegal political murders.

The strategic use of executions by the monarchy demonstrates essential aspects of the self-image, relative strength, and perceived legitimacy of the monarchy. Differences in strategy over time when it comes to how public executions were used or staged thus reveal more about political changes in a wider sense—yet, due to dissenting voices, they cannot be expected to tell a linear story.[3] The evidence of executions in Sweden and Norway over the course of the thirteenth and fourteenth centuries demonstrates the importance of pragmatism and political necessity in this context. The contested nature of the political utility of execution also reveals the complexity of treason and execution.

Evidence that executions were used to get rid of political enemies survives in the Old Swedish rhymed chronicle *Erikskrönikan* alongside annalistic accounts and contemporaneous documentary sources.[4] The rhymed chronicle, composed by an anonymous author, narrating major events in Swedish history between *c.*1220 and 1319 (with an emphasis on the final few decades), details recurring insurrections against the king by a faction known as the *Folkungar*,[5] and of the fratricidal conflicts of the royal Bjälbo dynasty through the 1270s and early 1300s, practically up until the time of composition. In the chronicle, the accounts of opposition to the king repeatedly end with some or all of the revolt leaders executed by decapitation, by order of the Swedish king or *jarl* [earl]. The chronicle mentions several such beheadings, which occurred in 1248, in 1251, and again in 1280. Additionally, it records several executions

---

3 Katherine Royer, "Reading the Execution Ritual in Late Medieval England," *Historical Reflections/Réflexions Historiques* 29.2 (2003): 338–39.

4 All original quotations are from *Erikskrönikan enligt Cod. Holm. D2 jämte avvikande läsarter ur andra handskrifter*, ed. Rolf Pipping (Uppsala: Svenska fornskriftsällskapet, 1963). Line numbers are given in parentheses. English translations are from *The Chronicle of Duke Erik: A Verse Epic from Medieval Sweden*, trans. Erik Carlquist and Peter C. Hogg (Lund: Nordic Academic Press, 2012). Page numbers are given in parentheses.

5 On the term *Folkung* and its employment by the author of *Erikskrönikan*, see: Rolf Pipping, *Kommentar till Erikskrönikan* (Helsinki: Svenska litteratursällskapet i Finland, 1926), 43–50 (art. 37).

in the civil war of the first two decades of the fourteenth century, when King Birger Magnusson (r. 1290–1318) and his two younger brothers were involved in a fratricidal conflict.

The executions are a form of ritualized performance meant to inspire fear and obedience in the audience, as were the writings produced around them. Executions also had political utility as narratives—in eyewitness reports, in ballads, and in chronicle accounts—but they served different ends, and the narratives of executions were appropriated by differing actors. While the monarchy commonly used them as deterrent and propaganda, opposing forces could highlight the sanctity of executed rebels, thus legitimizing their purpose. The importance of executions to the political community is visible in the historiographical works produced in the medieval period, and in literary texts that reinterpret these judicial phenomena, recasting them with various ideological slants. Arguably, it was the potential to shock and inspire fear and awe that made execution a useful tool, because it alerted some actors to the dangers of politics.[6] Kings used executions to deter unruly magnates from violent resistance, and the mounting risks increasingly came to affect magnates' decisions about whether and how they resisted the king.[7]

Concomitant with the strengthening of monarchical authority in the thirteenth-century is the use of capital punishment against the king's enemies, partly because of the reintroduction of precepts from Roman law.[8] This process has often been described as leading to a conflict between the king and the magnates of his kingdom, but this represents a simplified view of things. Members of the nobility also stood to gain from the expansion of royal government, insofar as they participated in it as holders of crucial offices, fiefs, etc., and as benefactors of royal grace and munificence.[9] There can be no doubt, however, that the strengthening of royal rule which came about through the legitimacy granted by the support of the Church, alongside new legal stipulations of royal authority, created new ways in which the king could deal

6 John Gillingham, "French Chivalry in Twelfth-Century Britain?," *Historian* 122 (2014): 10.

7 Adrian Jobson, "The Rebel's Four Dilemmas in the Long Thirteenth Century," *Thirteenth Century England XVI: Proceedings of the Cambridge Conference, 2015*, ed. Andrew M. Spencer and Carl Watkins, 89–112 (Woodbridge: Boydell Press, 2017).

8 Fredrik Charpentier Ljungqvist, "Legitimising Royal Power in Medieval Scandinavian Laws," in *Nordic Elites in Transformation, c. 1050–1250, Vol. III: Legitimacy and Glory*, ed. Wojtek Jezierski et al. (London: Routledge, 2020), 118.

9 John Watts, *The Making of Polities: Europe, 1300–1500* (Cambridge: Cambridge University Press, 2009), 213; Justine Firnhaber-Baker, "Introduction: Medieval Revolt in Context," in *The Routledge History Handbook of Medieval Revolt*, ed. Justine Firnhaber-Baker (with Dirk Schoenaers) (New York: Routledge, 2017), 1–15.

with political opponents, be they defined as usurpers, pretenders, rebels, or enemies.[10]

Jarl Birger Magnusson (*c.*1210–1266) introduced many of these legal changes into Swedish society in the thirteenth century, followed later by select rulers of the dynasty he engendered. Some of the earliest legal stipulations recorded in written form stem from the period when Birger's influence was most acutely felt, during his eldest son's reign as a minor king (from 1250 onward). Birger was responsible for the introduction of peace laws and stipulations about female hereditary rights.[11] According to Erland Hjärne, the evidence surrounding Birger's harsh retaliation against the rebels of the Folkung faction demonstrates that certain principles regarding high treason (*crimen læsæ maiestatis*) derived from Roman law appear in Sweden around the middle of the thirteenth century.[12]

The rhymed chronicle says:

> Een aff th*e*m heet junker karl/ ha*n* satte sik a moth birge järl
> birge jerl ville ok ha*n* fordriffua/ ok alla the ner ho*n*om ville bliffua
> Folku*n*ga sampnado sik ath*e*r tha/ ok toko folk huar the ku*n*no faa
> vplenzska danska oc nordme*n* soma / ok thydiska me*n* so*m* vidh*e*rla koma
> The wordo tha swikne i r*e*tte tro/ jnnan vesma*n*na lande vid herwadz bro
> Birge jerl ok biscop koll/ var h*er*ra gaff th*er* til eth tool
> The loffuado th*e*m tro oc sworo th*e*m edha/ oc villo th*e*m felugha til sik ledha
> Ok talado for th*e*m yffrid slät/ ok sagdo at the villo haffuat til säät
> Swa at folku*n*ga lagdo thera vapn nid/ thy at biscop koll haffde swor*e*t them frid
> Ok gingo til thera ou*er* ena aa/ th*er* loth th*e*m jerlin hoffwod aff slaa.
>
> *Erikskrönikan*, ed. Pipping, vv. 242–61

[For his part, Earl Birger wanted to banish him [Lord Karl] and all who supported him. Then the Folkungs gathered again and collected people wherever they could get them—Swedes, Danes and some Norwegians,

---

10 Still the most detailed study of the earliest cases is Hjärne, *Fornsvenska lagstadganden*; Elsa Sjöholm, *Sveriges medeltidslagar. Europeisk rättstradition i politisk omvandling* (Stockholm: Institutet för rättshistorisk forskning, 1988) was an early proponent in Swedish scholarship for viewing the Swedish medieval laws as European thirteenth- and fourteenth-century innovations rather than Nordic customary law, and for interpreting laws in a context of politics and power rather than legal genealogy.

11 Åqvist, *Kungen och rätten*, 14–52.

12 Hjärne, *Fornsvenska lagstadganden*, esp. 91ff.

> and Germans who came from far and wide. They were then deceived in Västmanland at Herrevadsbro. Earl Birger and Bishop Kol—Our Lord gave His permission for it—promised them good faith, and swore an oath with them and wanted to bring them trustingly to their side, and spoke very pleasantly to them and said that they wanted to come to terms with them, so the Folkungs laid down their arms, as Bishop Kol had promised them peace, and went to them across a small river. There the earl had them beheaded.] (42–43)

The chronicler indirectly criticizes Birger jarl here. For one, his actions against the Folkungs in 1251 breached the peace agreement, so the beheading of their leaders can hardly be considered the outcome of a judicial procedure. He vowed to allow them safe passage for the negotiations, and then took the opportunity to execute them when they were unarmed. Secondly, the chronicle reports the rumour that Birger wished to poison Karl, vanquishing the last of the Folkungs by a final murder (vv. 278–79). Executions of political antagonists appear to increase in frequency in thirteenth-century Sweden. *Erikskrönikan* portrays the executed rebels sympathetically, suggesting its author deliberately defended the right to resistance. The chronicler repeatedly mentions their saintliness or expresses hope that their souls are now with God. Referring to young Lord Karl (Ulfsson, d. 1260), the chronicle states: "nw er ha*n* i hy*m*merike thz er my*n* tro" [Now he is in heaven, that is my belief].[13] This could be partly because contemporaries saw *jarl* Birger's actions as unconventional and in breach of social norms. Their ability to inspire astonishment had not lessened even seventy years later:

> Jwnker karl war ekke thär/ the*r* varo tha yffrid marge när
> Tha gik folku*n*ga äät/ wald oue*r* ok mykin ore*t*h
> folku*n*ga ok thera frender/ dogho tha marge alle i sände*r*
> Ok fingo tha swa ilt affslagh/ the koffrado sik ey än i dagh
> Sidha*n* thorde enge*n* a mot jerli*n* standa/ ä huat ha*n* ville haffua til ha*n*da.
>
> *Erikskrönikan*, ed. Pipping, vv. 262–71

> [Young Lord Karl was not there, but many others were. The Folkung clan was then subjected to violence and much injustice. Many of the Folkungs and their kinsmen died there, all at the same time, and suffered such

13 *Erikskrönikan*, ed. Pipping, v. 353; trans. in *The Chronicle of Duke Erik*, 47.

> serious losses that they have still not recovered to this day. Then no one dared set himself up against the earl, whatever he decided to do.] (42–43)

In 1278, another revolt broke out, again led by a group called the Folkungs. This faction was portrayed as a reiteration of the previous ones, but whether they were connected by kinship or other forms of alliance remains uncertain, due to the scarcity of available sources. In 1280, this revolt ended similarly, with King Magnus Birgersson (r. 1275–1290) deceiving the rebel leaders to gain control of the situation and beheading the leaders, those *erlike riddara*, "honest knights," effectively ending the challenges to the ruling dynasty from the Folkungs. The chronicle emphasizes negotiations between the parties; dissent among the mighty had been the normal order of things, but now kings could get rid of political rivals and enemies by accusing them of treason and condemning them "in legem Juliam Majestatis," according to the Julian Law of Majesty, the Roman legislation on treason attributed to Julius Caesar.[14] This signified a change both in the status of kingship and in the interpretation of challenges to the king's authority, since the king's use of the notion of *crimen læsæ maiestatis* (crimes injuring or offending majesty or sovereignty, i.e. high treason) undermined the right of resistance. By this time, the prospect of executing political enemies accused of treason created the possibility of ultimately eradicating a challenger for the throne which assisted *jarl* Birger's descendants in firmly securing royal power within their family for more than a hundred years.

In general, the development of further legal stipulations against crimes like regicide, treason, and clandestine conjurations or secret coalitions (*lønlek samband*) among the magnates, during the second half of the thirteenth century, clearly points to a strengthening of the king's legal possibilities for punishing rebels and rooting out treachery and disloyalty by harsh means.[15] The statutes of the National Church Assembly, the provincial council, in Telge in October of 1279 (*Statuta concilii Telghiensis*) clarifies the Church's view regarding the inviolability of the king's person. In the final section, titled *De captiuitate regis* (*On the Imprisonment of the King*), they proclaim a prohibition against the imprisonment, banishment, and killing of the king.[16] It is likely that these

---

14 Diplomatarium Suecanum (Stockholm 1829–), [hereafter DS], 753 (Svenskt Diplomatariums huvudkartotek över medeltidsbreven, accessible at riksarkivet.se/sdhk, herafter SDHK, no. 1217); Erland Hjärne, "Holmger, Filip och Helena. Ett personhistoriskt bidrag till belysning av rättsåskådning och politik i Sverige omkring 1280," *Kungl. Humanistiska Vetenskaps-Samfundet i Uppsala Årsbok* (1951): 55.

15 DS 813, the statute of Skänninge 1284 (*Skänninge stadga*) (SDHK no. 1316); DS 692, "De captiuitate regis" 1279 (possibly 1275) (SDHK no. 1070).

16 DS 692.

are the result of the conflict between King Valdemar and his younger brother Magnus, who deposed the king in 1275 after the battle at Hova.[17] Similar ordinances were passed in Denmark, such as the 1252 Ordinance of Abel, which greatly expanded the number of *crimen læsæ maiestatis* and allowed the king's men to imprison suspected traitors on mere suspicion.[18] Hence, the conflict involved increased control on the part of the king and lesser legal certainty for noblemen, on whose actions aspersions were cast.

The statutes of 1279 and the 1284 Statute of Skänninge relate to two different crimes pre-dating the influence of Roman Law: *rættæn hærræ dræpær* [to kill one's rightful lord] and *awghæn skiold* [high treason]. While the oldest Swedish provincial laws regarded the crime of high treason as a crime against the population at large, later laws came to define it as a crime against the king.[19] In Norway, the twelfth-century regional laws contained the concept of treason against the country (*landráð*), albeit vaguely defined, but the later National Law (1274) and other thirteenth-century sources put more emphasis on the person of the king. Sverre Bagge nonetheless cautions against drawing too sharp a distinction between loyalty to the king versus to the "nation."[20]

However, the chronicler does not agree with the rulers regarding the legality or justification of these aforementioned executions. He considers them illicit political murders, and they are depicted not as legal cases carried out with all propriety, but rather as sly political maneuvers, wherein cunning and ill intent are regularly needed to combat political enemies. Regarding the events of 1278–1280, the chronicler reports:

> Th*er* ept*er* loot konu*n*ge*n* sc*ri*wa breff / ok säthia vti sköön ord ok gaff
> Ok badh the he*rr*ana til sik fara / ok möta sik jnnan skara [...]
> Thaghar the komo oc ha*n* them saa / tha loot ha*n* them genast faa
> Ok loot th*em* gensta*n* til stokholm sända / thera liiff fik th*er* een ända

17 Cf. Yrwing, *Maktkampen mellan Valdemar och Magnus Birgersson, 1275–1281*, 57–62; Yngve Brilioth, *Svenska kyrkans historia, vol. 2: Den senare medeltiden, 1274–1521* (Stockholm: Svenska kyrkans diakonistyrelses bokförlag, 1941), 28.

18 Helle Vogt, "The King's Power to Legislate in Twelfth and Thirteenth Century Denmark," in *Law and Power in the Middle Ages: Proceedings from the Fourth Carlsberg Academy Conference on Medieval Legal History*, ed. Per Andersen, Mia Münster-Swendsen, and Helle Vogt, 2nd ed. (Copenhagen: DJØF Publishing, 2012), 12.

19 Ljungqvist, "Legitimising Royal Power in Medieval Scandinavian Laws," 118. In the Swedish Law of the Realm (Magnus Erikssons Landslag, *c.*1350), crimes regarded as *crimen læsæ maiestatis* are collected in a separate section (*balk*) divided into two parts, regulating treason and rebellion against the king and high treason respectively.

20 Sverre Bagge, *From Viking Stronghold to Christian Kingdom: State Formation in Norway, c. 900–1350* (Copenhagen: Museum Tusculanum Press, 2010), 176.

> jnna*n* eth torn wid norr*e* broo / th*er* tror iak at h*er*ra jon philp*usson* doo
> Ok h*er*ra jon karss*on* the twe / huilke erlike riddara varo the
> The wordo th*er* halshugne bade / var h*er*ra giffue thera siäl roo oc nade
> H*er*ra philpuss aff rwmby / ha*n* bötte en stoor deel aff thy
> th*er* ha*n* jnna*n* swerike atte / fför än konu*ng*e*n* ok ha*n* the wordho satte.
>
> *Erikskrönikan*, ed. Pipping, vv. 1074–77, 1080–93

> [After that the king dictated a letter, formulated in ornate and well-chosen terms, to come and meet him near Skara [...] When they arrived there, and he saw them, he at once had them arrested and sent them straight to Stockholm. There they ended their lives in a tower near the North Bridge. There I believe that Sir Johan Filipsson and Sir Johan Karlsson died; those two—what honest knights they were! Both were beheaded there. May Our Lord grant their souls peace and grace! Sir Filip of Rumby had to pay a large part of what he owned in Sweden as a fine before he and the king could be reconciled.] (80–81)

These narratives oppose the idea that courtly ideals worked in a civilizing manner to deter rulers and nobles from using extreme forms of violence against other nobles.[21] Iain MacInnes makes a similar case regarding medieval Scottish monarchs and how they treated manifest rebels through either summary execution or public spectacle.[22] Some scholars argue that there was not much choice for the king, since non-violent responses could be perceived as a sign of weakness, similar to how the failure to execute capital punishments could lead to criticism or ridicule against the monarch in medieval Poland, as Radosław Kotecki explains.[23] MacInnes, however, argues against the "violent" paradigm, which depicts the Scottish monarchs as particularly ruthless types whose authority and grasp of power were dependent on their swift and bloody response to challenges from rebels. This perspective ignores other non-violent means of retribution and reconciliation—e.g. imprisonment, fines, and ritual submission—which were all, according to MacInnes, more frequently used than capital punishment, typically considered "a final resort rather than a

21 Cf. John Gillingham, *The English in the Twelfth Century: Imperialism, National Identity, and Political Values* (Woodbridge: Boydell Press, 2000).

22 Iain A. MacInnes, "'A somewhat too cruel vengeance was taken for the blood of the slain': Royal Punishment of Rebels, Traitors, and Political Enemies in Medieval Scotland, c. 1100–c. 1250," in *Treason: Medieval and Early Modern Adultery, Betrayal, and Shame*, ed. Larissa Tracy (Leiden: Brill, 2019), 119–46.

23 See: Kotecki, "To Kill, Banish, or Save?: Performing End-Game Punishment and the Ruler's Authority in Piast Poland," in this volume.

principal weapon."[24] With Magnus Birgersson, both possibilities were available to, and used by, the king: certain leaders were beheaded, while at least one was able to avoid a death sentence through a negotiated estate seizure.

Additionally, apart from the categorization of the monarchy's strategies, there is the question of the contemporary response to the punishments. These changes and the royal initiatives did not quench the need for—nor the possibilities of—resistance.[25] It is especially thought-provoking how the very act of executing someone for treason is what might enable their transformation into a perceived saint in other circles. As Claire Valente argues, the sanctification of an executed rebel was an effective way to justify or legitimize the continuation of a rebellion or to create sympathy for the defeated party.[26] Clearly, the cult surrounding the murdered Swedish king, Saint Erik (Jedvardsson), and the executed pretender Holmger Knutsson, display how the act of killing a political enemy, whether on the battlefield, in an ambush, or by executing them, could turn their death into a symbol that cast their lives in a new light.[27]

In *Erikskrönikan*, the magnates executed (or murdered) by order of kings or other representatives of monarchical authority are portrayed as martyrs or at least quasi-martyrs. In several cases, a saintly cult of these men sprang up and could carry on for centuries. One example is Holmger Knutsson (d. 1248), the son of Knut Långe, who drove King Erik Eriksson into exile and was elected king to replace him. But after Knut's death, Erik returned from his Danish exile and fought a new battle:

> Ok sidha*n* wart ath*e*r en a*n*nor strid
> Erik konu*n*g war tha ey seen / ok kom tha i rikit ath*e*r i geen
> Folku*n*ga sampnado sik ok tha / ok wildo konu*n*geno*m* a*n*nan tiid besta
> Erik konu*n*ge lykkadis tha bäth*e*r / ok wan tha sigh*e*r i sparsäth*e*r
> folku*n*ga flyddo ok haffdo tapat / th*e*n bleff död*e*r som thz war skapat
> Til gestringa land flydde holmger tha / Th*e*r loot konu*n*g *e*rik han faa

24 MacInnes, "'A somewhat too cruel vengeance …,'" 142–43. MacInnes argues that the "violent" paradigm of medieval Scotland has been stressed by its stark contrast to the perceived "Golden Age" of English political life, notably manifested in the works of Gillingham.

25 On the right of resistance in medieval Scandinavia, see: Lars Hamre, "Oprørsret," *Kulturhistoriskt lexikon för nordisk medeltid* (1967), vol. 12: cols. 629–31.

26 Claire Valente, "Simon de Montfort, Earl of Leicester, and the Utility of Sanctity in Thirteenth-Century England," *Journal of Medieval History* 21.1 (1995): 27–49.

27 Rolf Sjöberg, "Rex Upsalie och vicarius—Erik den helige och hans ställföreträdare: Något om Erikskulten och de äkta folkungarnas uppror på 1200-talet," *Fornvännen* 81 (1986): 1–13.

Ok loot sidha*n* hugga ho*no*m howodit aff / ok loth ho*no*m fylgia vänlika til graff
loot ha*n* erligha beganga / mz klerka the ha*n* ku*n*ne fanga
Jnna*n* eth klost*er* thz heyt*er* skoo / th*er* badh ha*n* sik i leggia för än ha*n* doo
gud gaff ho*no*m nad*er* oc giorden hälagh / huar gudi tiänar ha*n* er sälig*h*.

Erikskrönikan, ed. Pipping, vv. 48–66

[Then a new conflict arose again. King Erik did not tarry long then but returned to the realm again. The Folkungs then gathered and wanted to fight the king yet again. King Erik then had better success and won a victory at Sparrsätra. The Folkungs fled, having lost; whoever, for whom fate had so decided, died. Then Holmger fled to Gästrikland. There King Erik had him captured and subsequently had him beheaded but allowed him a splendid funeral; he let him be buried honourably by the priests that he could find. Before Holmger died, he asked to be buried at a monastery called Sko. God gave him grace and made him holy—he who serves God is blessed.] (32–33)

Holmger was captured and beheaded; not discourteously dispatched but honored, both by the king and by the clergy, according to the chronicler. Clearly royal authorities could not silence the growing posthumous popularity of rebels like Holmger. A notice about Holmger in a miracle collection mainly concerning the Danish King Erik IV Plovpenning (d. 1250), says that Holmger was also renowned for his miracles, and he was still venerated locally in the fifteenth century. The costly and intricately embroidered fifteenth-century covering produced for his grave in the church at Sko monastery demonstrates the longevity of his cult, and perpetuates the view of this executed pretender cultivated even centuries after his death. The border of the covering bears the following legend:[28]

Datum prec/lara regali stirpe sueorum Holmgerum moru[m] speculu[m] mors st/auit amara hicque cubat c/apite plexus s[ed] mors preciosa monstratur rite multis sigis/speciosa.

28 Hanna Källström, "Holmger Knutsson—en långlivad lokal helgonkult i Uppland," *Fornvännen: Journal of Swedish Antiquarian Research* 107.3 (2012): 179–88; Jan Svanberg, *Furstebilder från Folkungatid*, 2nd ed. (Fornbyn: Västergötlands Museum, 2012), 92.

> [Holmger, born of the glowing royal line of the Swedes, a mirror of good manners, struck by bitter death, lies here decapitated. His precious death demonstrates his glory by many signs.]

Some evidence suggests that the clergy quite quickly opted to control the cult of Holmger, which points to ecclesiastical interests directing local cults in competition with those of other saints.[29] The rebels could also be attempting to plug into religious authority. The manner in which they met their end must have been of utmost importance for the posthumous reputation of these men, since a good death was necessary to make a claim to sanctity.[30] The English Benedictine monk and annalist William Rishanger, at St. Albans, the so-called "Chronigraphus," depicts the rebel Simon de Montfort in his chronicle as a model of virtue—chivalric, learned, moderate, and pious—and thus connected his oppositional political actions to a virtuous life in service of the Church. The supposed miracles surrounding his death in battle and subsequent mutilation by royal forces, and the appearance of heavenly signs at the place of his death, stimulated a cult around his remains, buried in Evesham Abbey church.[31] Thomas of Lancaster, similarly, was depicted upon his death as a virtuous man who worked determinedly to make the king observe the ordinances his magnates had imposed upon him, but this was surely dependent upon the manner of his death, which was essential in sanctifying him, for re-evaluating his life and deeds, and for giving his political actions a different quality.[32]

Executing political enemies could work as a political weapon for kings, but it could sometimes backfire, legitimating rebels against these kings, and contribute to sanctifying opposition. The flourishing cult of Holmger Knutsson, whose death in 1248 put an end to one attempt at opposing the Swedish king, was quite quickly followed by another attempt, the one so brutally and cunningly ended by Birger jarl in 1251. The cult potentially fostered opposition and resistance. At the same time, it was the very development of kingship, monarchical authority, and treason laws that led to the possibility of rebel martyrs. If these men had been considered part of a feud or mere enemies of a political rival, they would most likely not have become objects of devotion; because the king labelled them traitors, they could be presented by the opposing side

29 Källström, "Holmger Knutsson," 186; Valente, "Simon de Montfort, Earl of Leicester," 48.

30 Klaus P. Jankofsky, "Public Executions in England in the Late Middle Ages: The Indignity and Dignity of Death," *OMEGA—Journal of Death and Dying* 10.1 (1980): 43–57.

31 Carl Watkins, "Saints and Martyrs in Late Medieval Religious Culture," in *The Medieval World*, ed. Peter Linehan, Janet L. Nelson, and Marios Costambeys (London: Routledge, 2018), 385–402 at 391.

32 Watkins, "Saints and Martyrs in Late Medieval Religious Culture," 391.

as legitimate rebels who resisted a tyrant or opposed an unlawful king. It was the fight against oppression by a "tyrannical" ruler that created the potential for veneration.

Not all those executed on political grounds were parties to revolts or pretenders to kingship. On February 10, 1306, Tyrgils Knutsson, a long-standing advisor to King Birger Magnusson of Sweden, the kingdom's *de facto* ruler during the king's minority as the head of the regency council, and one of the leading men of the realm, was executed.[33] He was beheaded and his body brought to the monastery of the Franciscan Order in Stockholm, where he was eventually buried. Sources reveal surprisingly little about why Tyrgils was executed, the nature of his crimes, and if the decision to execute him was brought about by the king's ducal brothers (the youngest of whom was Tyrgils's son-in-law), with whom the king had recently been reconciled.

Birger was ten years old at his accession and should have reached majority well before his coronation in 1302. Tyrgils Knutsson's powerful position stemmed in part from his close familial ties to the royal dynasty, symbolically strengthened by his sponsorship of the youngest son of King Magnus Birgersson. He formed part of the circle around the king as early as 1285 and became a member of the royal council in 1288. When King Magnus was on his deathbed in 1290, the *Erikskrönika* indicates he appointed Tyrgils regent for his young son and as the temporary ruler of the kingdom, though this claim is uncorroborated. His position was strengthened by the successful eastern crusading endeavors and shored up by the powerful provincial magnates.[34]

According to the chronicle, Tyrgils was critical of the liberties and tax exemptions enjoyed by the Church, insofar as they placed a heavier burden on the other estates in times of financial strain for the crown. In 1305, an ongoing conflict between King Birger and his younger brothers was temporarily laid to rest, and perhaps in conjunction with important members of the church hierarchy, this led to the decision to imprison and prosecute Tyrgils. His daughter's marriage to the king's youngest brother was dissolved due to spiritual kinship, because Tyrgils had carried Valdemar to his baptism. For Tyrgils, the condemnation meant the complete forfeiture of all lands and goods, which were seized by the crown.[35] He was sentenced to death and executed in Stockholm.

Apart from the king's or even the dukes' motivations behind getting rid of Tyrgils Knutsson, the conflictual relationship between Tyrgils and the

33 *The Chronicle of Duke Erik*, 140–44.

34 Seppo Suvanto, "Tyrgils Knutsson," in *Biografiskt lexikon för Finland, vol. 1: Svenska tiden* (Helsinki: Svenska litteratursällskapet i Finland, 2008), 701–03.

35 Hjärne, *Fornsvenska lagstadganden*, 102.

Church in Sweden, led at this time by the Archbishop Nils Allesson (Nicolaus Allonis), was instrumental in his downfall. During this period in Swedish history, the monarchy strongly favored the Church in the form of increased privileges, and some sectors of the secular aristocracy appear to have resisted this development.[36] Both the spiritual and secular aristocracy were granted major privileges during the second half of the thirteenth century (notably the statutes of Alsnö 1279/1280 and Söderköping 1281). Some may have considered the privileges granted to the Church by Magnus Birgersson (Ladulås) recompense for backing his pretentions to the throne, when he could easily have been labelled a usurper after deposing his elder brother Valdemar in 1275. The general exemption of the Church from royal tax had tellingly been promised at Magnus' coronation in 1276.

An annal entry from year 1303 notes:

> Incepit dissidium inter ecclesiasticos et proceres prophanos regni Seciæ subjeceruntqve vniversum clerum tributis et exactationibus, qvi antea gavisus erat ecclesiastica libertate. Eodem anno conatus est rex Birgerus ad suggestionem domini Trugilli marscalci captivare reverendum dominum archiepiscopum cum cæteris regni Svetiæ episcopis circa festum Magdalenæ.[37]
>
> [Discord began between the men of the church and the secular magnates in the kingdom of Sweden, and this burdened the priesthood—which before had rejoiced in the liberty of the church—with taxes and duties. In the same year the king attempted, at the instigation of the constable Lord Tyrgils, to capture the venerable Archbishop along with the other bishops of Sweden around the feast day of St. Mary Magdalen [July 22].]

The Archbisop Nils Kettilsson (Nicolaus Catilli, 1308–1314, the successor of Nils Allesson) was responsible for refusing Tyrgils' burial in consecrated ground upon his execution, though his remains were later moved by the Franciscans of the Greyfriars monastery.[38] Kettilsson was involved in political intrigue and conflict at the very highest level, even on an international scale, for at least a

---

36 Brilioth, *Svenska kyrkans historia, vol. 2*, 46–51.

37 "Annales 826–1415," in *Annales suecici medii aevi*, ed. Göte Paulsson (Lund: Gleerup, 1974), 386.

38 Sven-Erik Pernler, "Nicolaus Catilli," in *Svenskt biografiskt lexikon* (1987–1989), 26:598. In this regard, it is reminiscent of the cult of Simon de Montfort, targeted by King Henry III, who had Simon's remains reburied in a secret location, since he did not deserve to rest in holy ground: Watkins, "Saints and Martyrs in Late Medieval Religious Culture," 391.

decade, and had to handle the conflict between the three royal brothers. His must have been an important voice in the royal council, demonstrating the difficulty of distinguishing between secular and clerical voices and political actors in the period.[39] Sometimes legal justification could be created after the fact, legitimating what was by all accounts a political murder, by referring to treason laws. The king's enemies were enemies of the state, blurring the line between those executed for treason after prosecution and sentencing, and those killed in the heat of the moment by order of the king, in the context of outright confrontations between the king and his opponents.[40]

Nonetheless, political murders masked as judicial executions could shock and launch people into action. Thus, in 1318, the untimely and horrendous deaths of the two dukes Erik and Valdemar, younger brothers of King Birger Magnusson, lent them an air of sanctity.[41] Their deaths, vividly depicted in *Erikskrönikan*, were not by execution, but were acts of political murder. Their older brother saw his position threatened, and the conflict between the brothers escalated at times to what amounts to civil war. Imprisoning the dukes—at a gathering under the guise of peace-brokering—was designed to get rid of the challengers once and for all:

> Ok loot th*e*m jnna*n* thz nidarsta rwm / th*e*r war konu*n*geno*m* litit wm
> at the haffdo ilt bade nat ok dagh / th*e*n stook ha*n* fik mangt eth slagh
> th*e*r h*er*tugh erik jnnan sat / ok gaffwo hono*m* th*e*r til litin maat [...]
> th*e*ra pina war ill ok owarkwnsam
> wm nokor me*n*niskia haffdit seet / thz war*e* wäl eno*m* hedni*n*gia leet
> hertogh eriks stook slo ma*n* swa fast / at th*e*r eth stykke wt aff brast
> Ok took hertoghin widh sith ögha / Awi th*e*n last of then ofögha
> The begingo a hono*m* thz sin / blodit flöt nidh ath hans kin
> Ok swa nidh vthi hans barm / awi th*e*n kwmber ok th*e*n harm
> the tha a sik siellfue sagho / ok swa jammerlika lagho
> fangne jnna*n* dötzsins bandom / th*e*n död th*e*m stodh tha for handom
> ha*n* war bätre a ath gaa / än the pina the tholdo tha [...]
> thz lyste konu*n*geno*m* wäl ath see
> Th*e*ra pina ok thera nödh / ha*n* war orädder wm thera dödh [...]

39 Pernler, "Nicolaus Catilli."

40 This occurred, for instance, in the 1288 killing in Alfaro of Diego López de Haro by King Sancho IV of Castile-León and his followers, and in sixteenth-century Sweden, when King Erik XIV decided to take matters into his own hands when confronted with the supposedly treasonous members of the Sture family.

41 Christian Lovén and Herman Bengtsson, "De heliga hertigarna Erik och Valdemar," *Historisk tidskrift* 131.2 (2011): 227–49.

then gud som alt forma
giffue them hy*m*meri*kis* ära/ for then pino the tholdo thäre
Erikskrönikan, ed. Pipping, vv. 3936–41, 3949–65, 3969–71, 3975–77

[Then the king took the step of moving both his brothers and placing them in the lowest dungeon. It concerned the king little that they suffered both night and day. The stock in which Duke Erik sat received many blows, and in addition they gave him very little food. [...] Their torment was harsh and pitiless. If anyone had seen it, it would have seemed repugnant even to a pagan. They hit Duke Erik's stock so hard that a piece of it flew off and hit the duke by one of his eyes. Alas, what a crime and an offence they committed against him at that time! The blood flowed down along his cheek and onto his chest. Alack, the distress and the injustice that they then saw inflicted on themselves, lying so lamentably trapped in the snares of death! To undergo the death that faced them at that point was preferable to the torment that they suffered then. [...] It pleased the king well to see their torment and their distress; he was not concerned that they might die. [...] May the God who is omnipotent grant them honour in heaven for the torment that they suffered there!]. (206–7)

The descriptions of the dukes' torment are much more physical and explicit than the chronicle's earlier descriptions of executions and have been compared with poetic depictions of the suffering of Jesus Christ.[42] Aware of their fate, they made the necessary arrangements by writing their last wills and testaments (dated January 18, 1318) while in captivity, where they were starved to death.[43]

Tha läste ha*n* tornit ful fast / ok giorde sik siälffwm mykin last
ok kastade nykelin wt i the aa / swa at ha*n* wart ey gode*r* athe*r* faa
Til stekaborgh ha*n* tha foor / the*n* gud the*r* i hy*m*merike boor
bätre hwariom sin skadha ha*n* fik / ok hempnis thz ha*n* a them begik
[T]ha haffde hertogh Erik / nyo dagha sw sagde ma*n* mik
vta*n* drik ok vtan math / thz war wnde*r* at ha*n* swa gaat
Ok ällowo dagha h*er*togh Waldemar / Jak tror at thz for the*n* skuld war
at h*er*tugh eriks pyna war mer*e* / thy wordo ha*n*s dagha eke flere

42 Sven-Bertil Jansson, "Medeltidens rimkrönikor: Studier i funktion, stoff, form" (PhD dissertation, Uppsala University, 1971), 172–76.
43 DS 2132 (SDHK no. 2850).

Tessalu*n*d swälte ha*n* them i hall / thz sighia faa me*n* at ha*n* giorde well
war he*rr*a giffue them hy*m*merik / fore then harda dödh the tholdo a sik.

Erikskrönikan, ed. Pipping, vv. 4052–71

[Then he shut up the tower completely and incurred great shame by throwing the key out into the river, so that it would not be easy to find it again. [...] May the God who dwells in heaven redress the harm done to each of them and avenge that which he perpetrated against them. Then Duke Erik, I am told, was deprived of drink and food for nine days—it was a wonder that he endured it—and Duke Valdemar for eleven days. I believe it was because Duke Erik's torment was greater that his days were fewer. In that way he starved them to death. Few are those men who say he acted rightly. May Our Lord grant them heaven for the hard death they suffered!]. (210–11)

King Birger's treatment of his brothers aroused a great degree of displeasure among both the magnates in the council and the populace at large, leading to a general uprising against the king, who was forced into exile. King Birger's treatment of his younger brothers was clearly perceived as a vengeful and murderous act. They were imprisoned through an ambush and starved to death without due process and without a conviction. Their suffering is not glossed over, rather the chronicler depicts both their pain and the king's neglect. Accounts of the murders played a crucial role in legitimizing those acts of defiance.[44] First, when they sparked the uprising resulting in Birger's deposition, and later, when the chronicle narrative presents its views of the past, as an act of remembrance but also to glorify the actions of the current regime in the 1320s.

Of course, there are examples where the line between execution and murder in the name of political expedience becomes blurred. In 1320, the council of the realm had the son and heir of the deposed King Birger executed. Magnus Birgersson was without doubt executed to get rid of a potential pretender to the throne. Even in a principally electoral monarchy, his claim to kingship as the eldest son of King Birger Magnusson was so strong it would have been problematic—after his father's deposition and the election of Magnus' cousin, bearing the same name—for the boy-king Magnus Eriksson and his regents to keep young master Magnus around.

44 Jerker Rosén, "Striden mellan Birger Magnusson och hans bröder: Studier i nordisk politisk historia 1302–1319" (PhD dissertation, Lund University, 1939), 282–343.

The *Erikskrönika* also suggests that it was a political murder or a quasi-legal act by claiming Magnus' death occurred to pay for his father's crimes, rather than for any action of his own.[45] Some legal historians, notably Erland Hjärne, have discussed the possibility that Magnus was sentenced to death for high treason.[46] Partly because, as Hjärne argues, his death sentence could not lawfully have been passed on account of his father's actions.[47] Magnus' actions in support of his father against the united front of the ducal party would thus have been considered an attack upon the realm, and this could have been justification enough for the death sentence. Nevertheless, the chronicle does not mention this. Later sources, such as Olaus Petri's (1493–1552) *En Swensk Cröneka*, explain that King Birger's opponents, including the ducal party and prior supporters of the exiled king, were outraged, and so his father's crimes were the reason for his killing.[48] The absence of outright legal justification may be due to a lack of interest or a choice of perspective by the author of the *Erikskrönika*, yet this account may also indicate wider trends in the political culture at the time. If the killing of defeated enemies or the murder of political opponents or potential rivals were not perceived as legally defensible, it makes sense that the potentially feeble explanations offered to present them as justified executions left the chronicler unconvinced.

Another captivating aspect of the killing of *junker* Magnus is that it was carried out by the council or the leaders of the ducal party, not by order of the king. This is not an enemy killed in battle in the heat of civil war, nor a murder done in secret. The leaders of the rebellion against King Birger considered him deposed, and they now represented the realm. In the chronicle, the execution occurs before the election of Magnus Eriksson as king, contrary to evidence from other sources; this is most likely because its author wished to conclude the chronicle with the election, and for this act to be untainted by innocent blood. However, disregarding the chronological distortion presented by the *Erikskrönika*, the regency council for the young king made the decision to execute a traitor to the realm.[49]

---

45 Cf. Kim Bergqvist, "Debating the Limitations of Kingship in Fourteenth-Century Sweden: Political Language and Norms in Romance and Chronicle," in *The* Eufemiavisor *and Courtly Culture: Time, Texts and Cultural Transfer*, ed. Olle Ferm et al. (Stockholm: KVHAA, 2015), 67–85, esp. 79.

46 Hjärne, *Fornsvenska lagstadganden*, 122–48.

47 Hjärne, *Fornsvenska lagstadganden*, 139ff.

48 Olaus Petri, *En swensk cröneka*, ed. Jöran Sahlgren (Uppsala: Sveriges kristliga studenträrelses förl., 1917), 108.

49 Cf. Gisela Vilhelmsdotter, "Riddare, bonde och biskop: Studier kring tre fornsvenska dikter jämte två nyeditioner" (PhD dissertation, Stockholm University, 1999), 74–78.

Two years prior to *junker* Magnus' execution, a one-time favorite of King Birger—Johan Brunkow—was executed by being broken on the wheel.[50] Traditionally identified as the man responsible for carrying out the imprisonment of the dukes in Nyköping in 1317, which led to their eventual starvation and death, Johan Brunkow may have only acted on direct orders from the king or he might have been responsible for the plan itself. Either way, the dukes' faction blamed him enough to make sure he paid with his life.[51] Again, actors other than kings may have organized executions within the highest political sphere; their legal justifications and rhetoric would have focused not on the king's person, but on the realm.

From the final decades of the thirteenth century and just after the turn of the fourteenth century, there are several examples of Norwegian noblemen who rose to great national and international prominence and then fell from grace. A parallel career and ignominious end to that of Tyrgils Knutsson can be found in that of the Norwegian baron Audun Hugleiksson ("Hestakorn"), who was hanged in Bergen about three years prior to Tyrgils's execution. According to the Icelandic annals, his execution occurred on December 2, 1302.[52] Like Tyrgils, Audun had a long and prominent political career, bolstered by his close connections to royalty, and he spent several decades in service to king and crown. Like his Swedish counterpart, he reached the highest position during the minority of a king, Eirik Magnusson (r. 1280–1299). In 1281, he was already considered the foremost of the council according to the contemporary *Árna saga biskups*, the saga of Icelandic bishop Árni Þorláksson (d. 1298).[53] Like Tyrgils, Audun fell far and hard from his position atop the hierarchy, but he also suffered the ignominy of being executed by hanging. This method of execution stands in sharp contrast to beheading, which was usually reserved for nobility as a swifter and less gruesome form of punishment. The hanging was likely an attempt to dishonor the baron, to warn others, and potentially act as an indicator of his specific crime.

---

50 Rolf Pipping, "Johan Brunkow," *Svenskt biografiskt lexikon* (1926), 6: 527; Hjärne, *Fornsvenska lagstadganden*, 114–22.

51 Pipping, "Johan Brunkow."

52 Knut Helle, "Audun Hugleiksson 'Hestakorn'," *Norsk biografisk leksikon*, available at https://nbl.snl.no/Audun_Hugleiksson_"Hestakorn," accessed June 7, 2022; "Lögmannsannáll," entry for 1302, in *Islandske Annaler indtil 1578*, ed. Gustav Storm (Christiania: Det norske historiske Kildeskriftfond, 1888), 263.

53 *Biskupa sögur* 3, ed. Guðrún Ása Grímsdóttir (Reykjavik: Hið íslenzka fornritafélag, 2008), 3–212. See also Haki Antonsson, "*Árna saga biskups* as Literature and History," *Journal of English and Germanic Philology* 116.3 (2017): 261–85.

Another example is the baron Alv Erlingsson (d. 1290). According to narratives of his execution at the hands of local representatives of the Danish king, he was broken on the wheel.[54] The medieval Norwegian laws did not incorporate principles of *crimen læsæ maiestatis* as clearly as did Danish and Swedish law. Nonetheless, crimes of treason against king or realm were considered dishonorable in the highest degree and were counted among the so-called *niddingsværk*—crimes which implied a complete loss of honor—requiring this ignominious method of execution.[55]

Contrary to the parallel Swedish cases where magnates were executed by the sword, the Norwegian monarchy in the thirteenth century resorted to other methods of execution for rebellious noblemen. Punishing rebellion against the king by shameful methods of capital punishment was meant to inspire fear, repulsion, and shock among the audience as a deterrent from acting against the king's wishes, deviating from his policies, taking his castles, or killing any of his officers. Execution methods say a lot about the connection between crimes and their perception in society.[56] Part of the reasoning was that the punishment should be appropriate in relation to the gravity of the offense; the worse the transgression, the harsher the punishment.[57] Executions were used to deter others from repeating the crimes of the delinquents, but were also pragmatic actions undertaken to remove what was perceived as real or potential threats.

Sverre Bagge points to the fact that the careers of both Audun Hugleiksson and his contemporary Bjarne Lodinsson climaxed during the reign of King Eirik Magnusson, and they both fell from grace under Haakon v Magnusson (r. 1299–1319).[58] Alv Erlingsson also rose to prominence during the regency for Eirik Magnusson. In the year of Audun's execution, Bjarne Lodinson was imprisoned. The rise and fall of these men were connected with the possibilities the regency for a minor king created for leading aristocrats, and with

54 Tore Skeie, *Alv Erlingsson: fortellingen om en adelsmanns undergang* (Oslo: Spartacus, 2009). Both dishonorably executed Norwegian barons, Audun Hugleiksson and Alv Erlingsson, would become the subjects of popular songs. That is not to say they were revered as saints, but their deaths inspired a popular "afterlife" for the executed noblemen, similar to Simon de Montfort and other political saints, one may surmise.

55 Per-Edwin Wallén, "Högmålsbrott," *Kulturhistoriskt lexikon för nordisk medeltid* (1962), vol. 7: cols. 288–289; Per-Edwin Wallén and Lars Hamre, "Majestätsförbrytelse," *Kulturhistoriskt lexikon för nordisk medeltid* (1966), vol. 11: cols. 243–249; Poul Meyer, "Dødsstraf," *Kulturhistoriskt lexikon för nordisk medeltid* (1980), vol. 3: cols. 455–59; Ljungqvist, "Legitimising Royal Power in Medieval Scandinavian Laws," 117.

56 J.S. Bothwell, *Falling from Grace: Reversal of Fortune and the English Nobility, 1075–1455* (Manchester: Manchester University Press, 2008), 58–71, 78–79; Meyer, "Dødsstraf."

57 Royer, "Reading the Execution Ritual in Late Medieval England," 328–29.

58 Bagge, *From Viking Stronghold to Christian Kingdom*, 340–41.

King Haakon's displeasure with a number of political measures (in foreign policy and finance) that had been taken during the preceding regime. Bagge argues that King Haakon decided to punish certain individuals for decisions he believed to be detrimental to the realm.

King Haakon also removed certain figures from power, replacing them with aristocratic men who would be indebted to him for their positions.[59] This is very similar not only to Tyrgils Knutsson's situation, but also to the negative view King Magnus Eriksson of Sweden and Norway (r. 1319–1364) held of the regency council's actions during his minority.[60] He complained in a statute from 1335 of the many harmful customs that evolved during his childhood. He sought to quench these by prohibiting magnates from riding across the land with full weaponry or great hosts.[61] According to Steinar Imsen, both Alv Erlingsson and Audun Hugleiksson were favorites of Duke Erik Magnusson's widow, Ingebjørg, mother of King Magnus Eriksson.[62] This is likely one of the reasons their situation was precarious, because her position was itself challenged by the councils of both the Scandinavian kingdoms. So, rather than being due to a young king coming of age and coming to terms with the events of the regency, the sudden shifts in the fate of these noblemen had more to do with a regime shift when Eirik died and his younger brother Haakon received the crown.

In mid-fourteenth-century Sweden and Norway, there were uprisings against Magnus Eriksson (prior to his eventual deposition) that might have led to a number of executions in the political culture of the previous century. According to the limited accounts in the sources, several leading Swedish magnates who colluded with King Magnus' eldest son Erik in his rebellion went into exile after the uprising failed, due in no small part to the premature passing of Erik, possibly from bubonic plague.[63] To some extent, the actions of these exiled magnates brought about the deposition of Magnus Eriksson in

59 Bagge, *From Viking Stronghold to Christian Kingdom*, 341, 356–58.

60 Hans Torben Gilkær, *The Political Ideas of St. Birgitta and her Spanish Confessor, Alfonso Pecha: Liber Celestis Imperatoris ad Reges: A Mirror of Princes*, trans. Michael Cain (Odense: Odense University Press, 1993), esp. 185–86; Kim Bergqvist, "Kings and Nobles on the Fringes of Christendom: A Comparative Perspective on Monarchy and Aristocracy in the European Middle Ages," in *The Routledge History of Monarchy*, ed. Elena Woodacre et al. (Abingdon: Routledge, 2019), 627–28.

61 DS 3175, November 30, 1335, Skänninge (SDHK no. 4197).

62 Gilkær, *The Political Ideas of St. Birgitta and her Spanish Confessor*, 182ff; Steinar Imsen, "Dronningmakt i Norge," in *Dronningemagt i Middelalderen: Festskrift til Anders Bøgh*, ed. Kasper H. Andersen and Jeppe Büchert Netterstrøm (Aarhus: Aarhus Universitetsforlag, 2018), 259; Bagge, *From Viking Stronghold to Christian Kingdom*, 357–58.

63 Sten Engström, "Landsförvisningen av de svenska oppositionsledarna 1362–63," *Historisk tidskrift* 49 (1929): 310–26.

1364 and the election of his nephew Albrecht, son of the Duke of Mecklenburg, as Swedish king.

An intriguing episode in this period is the murder of Bengt Algotsson, a favorite of King Magnus Eriksson, whose position at court in proximity to the king caused a lot of ill will among the high aristocracy.[64] Rumors abounded about King Magnus and his favorite—notably, he was the only non-royal recipient of the ducal title in the Swedish Middle Ages. St. Birgitta disseminated a rumor that the king and Duke Bengt were engaged in an illicit sexual affair.[65] In any case, the notion that the magnates took it upon themselves to murder the king's favorite—or to punish him for treason against the realm—suggests that the magnates appropriated certain ideas about treason and that political murders of this sort were clearly not exclusive to the monarch.

In 1358, or possibly in 1360, the Norwegian magnate Orm Øysteinsson was executed by order of King Magnus and his son, King Haakon of Norway, after accusations of his financial misbehavior as high steward and political disloyalty during the conflict in Sweden. Orm's lands, primarily located in Bohuslän, were confiscated by the crown.[66] Magnus Eriksson, as king of both Sweden and Norway, had to contend not only with rebellious Swedish noblemen and with the challenges posed by his son Erik's moves to secure a position of power for himself, but also with the resistance of some of his powerful Norwegian subjects. Remarkably, he mostly chose to forgive defiant noblemen and let them resume their service to the crown rather than having them executed or exiled.[67]

The later Middle Ages in Northern Europe were heavily affected by the establishment of the Kalmar Union and the developments within the Union or, rather, the political struggles and intermittent crises suffered by its constituent kingdoms and groups within these. Dick Harrison's notion of the possibility of "[g]etting away with treason" in this context is a valid point, but one

64 Gilkær, *The Political Ideas of St. Birgitta and her Spanish Confessor*, 198ff.

65 Michael Nordberg, *I kung Magnus tid: Norden under Magnus Eriksson, 1317–1374* (Stockholm: Norstedts, 1995), 240. A very late observation claims that Karl Ulfsson, whose daughter had been set aside by Bengt Algotsson, was responsible for his murder.

66 Erik Opsahl, "Orm Øysteinsson," *Norsk biografisk leksikon*. Available at https://nbl.snl.no/Orm_%C3%98ysteinsson. Accessed June 8, 2022.

67 Grethe Authén Blom, *Norge i union på 1300-tallet* (Trondheim: Tapir, 1992), 1:126–32; Kim Bergqvist, "Osämja och fiendskap mellan kungar och stormän: Lojalitetskonflikter och politiska värden i Norge och Sverige, c. 1250–1370," *Collegium Medievale* 32.2 (2019): 171–91, esp. 176.

that is not exclusive to the fifteenth century in Scandinavia.[68] Major changes already occurred along those lines in the 1330s, during the reign of Magnus Eriksson, who resorted to (temporary) exile rather than execution to punish the worst dissensions of the magnates.[69]

This use of execution and political murder by royal authorities is not specific or unique to medieval Scandinavia. In an Iberian context, François Foronda argues that the Castilian monarchy's increasing reliance upon murders and executions in the thirteenth and fourteenth centuries signified the strategic employment of a reign of terror.[70] Fernando Arias Guillén recently challenged this view by pointing out that seven magnates murdered by the monarchs between 1277 and 1340 was hardly enough to characterize their reigns as employing a policy of terror.[71] For Sweden and Norway, such a proposition is similarly improbable. Katherine Royer argues that executions were meant to display and enforce the authority of the monarchy.[72] She makes the cogent point that the specific political circumstances of each execution must be considered; though ideologically connected through the nexus of treason and the maintenance of monarchic authority, each execution responded to contingent causes and was connected to specific motivations and intended effects. This also explains the differences in the method of execution. Furthermore, pragmatic considerations by the king and his representatives would have played an essential part in each case.

In this context, it is still possible and valuable to uphold a distinction between executions and political murders. For some of the thirteenth- and early fourteenth-century events studied here, the condemnation of those executed was justification in hindsight, and the "legality" of the executions based on contested or newly imported legal innovations, as much as on established and generally accepted legal principles. The execution of political enemies was a tool which was invested with legitimating discourses to harness its potential in dissolving political conflicts that threatened the king's position. The legal framework and juridical motivations of such actions became increasingly

68 Dick Harrison, "Murder and Execution within the Political Sphere in Fifteenth-century Scandinavia," *Scandia* 63.2 (1997): 259–79.

69 Engström, "Landsförvisningen av de svenska oppositionsledarna 1362–63."

70 François Foronda, *El espanto y el miedo: golpismo, emociones políticas y constitucionalismo en la Edad Media* (Madrid: Dykinson, 2013); idem, "El miedo al rey: Fuentes y primeras reflexiones acerca de una emoción aristocrática en la Castilla del siglo XIV," *e-Spania* 4 (2007), http://e-spania.revues.org/2273. Accessed June 5, 2022.

71 Fernando Arias Guillén, *The Triumph of an Accursed Lineage: Kingship in Castile from Alfonso X to Alfonso XI (1252–1350)* (Abingdon: Routledge, 2021), 143.

72 Royer, "Reading the Execution Ritual in Late Medieval England."

important. Kings were interested in not appearing weak, in dealing swiftly and harshly with rebels and other political enemies, but they were also concerned with not alienating entire aristocratic families—a tenet that perhaps became more important in the fourteenth century.[73] Earlier research suggests only a strong, legitimate, and stable regime could afford to pardon perceived traitors while "weak" regimes were more prone to execute or murder political opponents. Mia Korpiola has argued that the Swedish king acquired this power to pardon by the thirteenth century.[74] Other evidence suggests a particularly weak king in a precarious political situation like that of Magnus Eriksson could not risk provoking the magnates by resorting to capital punishment, demonstrating that no single explanation for a political strategy can be ubiquitously valid; political circumstances change and explanations are necessarily contingent on these.

Meanwhile, however, actors in opposition to the king used different discursive strategies to contest the meaning of these deaths—be they political murders or (legal) executions. Deaths could be symbolically potent for the supporters of a rebel. These deaths seldom played out as the king hoped—as evidence of his forceful but rightful rule, with swift justice meted out to opponents—but rather came to signify the arbitrariness of royal decision-making, the fear of unjust punishment, and the risk of falling from grace without cause. Narratives feeding into these ideas could survive for many decades in oral form and eventually find written expression, as seen in the example of the *Erikskrönika*. Thus, the political utility of executions was nebulous and hard to grasp, contested and impossible to lock down.

---

73 I explore the ramifications of rebellions and punishment for treason for the families of rebels in a forthcoming publication, entitled "Traitors' Kin," forthcoming in *Noble Rebellion in Medieval Europe, c.1150–1350*, ed. Adrian Jobson and Fernando Arias Guillén (Leiden: Brill).

74 Mia Korpiola, "'The People of Sweden shall have Peace': Peace Legislation and Royal Power in Later Medieval Sweden," in *Expectations of the Law in the Middle Ages*, ed. Anthony Musson (Woodbridge: Boydell Press, 2001), 35–51.

CHAPTER 8

To Kill, Banish, or Save?: Performing End-Game Punishment and the Ruler's Authority in Piast Poland

Radosław Kotecki

The history of the death penalty in medieval Poland divides into two stages: a phase defined by the domination of the royal judiciary and a phase in which the prerogative to mete out capital punishment was widely enjoyed by domain, especially municipal, courts.[1] In the latter phase, in the fourteenth and fifteenth centuries, the death penalty gradually became the realm of German Law, which spread in Poland from the thirteenth century onward. It was under the influence of this law that professional institutions of bloody justice, so characteristic of the late medieval and early modern periods, developed in Poland with the institution of the municipal hangman at the forefront, while execution turned into a legally fortified spectacle conducted in specially marked out places in the town.[2]

However, before municipal and other domain courts gained significance as venues for adjudication and execution of the death penalty in the later fourteenth century, the *iurisdictio* or *ius gladii* [jurisdiction or right of the sword], i.e. the right to take life in the name of justice, was a natural prerogative of the rulers—the princes, dukes, and kings of the first Polish dynasty of the Piasts, who ruled in Poland from the tenth century to 1370. Contrary to the now well-studied later phase, the image of the earlier rulers' dominance in the field

1 The second phase, mainly due to the abundance of legal sources and those of judicial provenance, remains better studied. See especially: Witold Maisel, *Poznańskie prawo karne do końca XVI wieku* (Poznań: Uniwersytet im. Adama Mickiewicza, 1963); Hanna Zaremska, *Niegodne rzemiosło. Kat w społeczeństwie Polski XIV–XVI wieku* (Warsaw: Państwowe Wydawnictwo Naukowe, 1986). Henryk Grajewski's book, although conceptually and methodologically outdated, still remains the best source for the earlier period. Henryk Grajewski, *Kara śmierci w prawie polskim do połowy XIV wieku* (Warsaw: Wydawnictwo Prawnicze, 1956).

2 The growing significance of towns as an arena for the administration and execution of the death penalty in late medieval Poland even caused the municipal courts to be involved in the adjudication of criminal cases reserved for other courts, including those under the jurisdiction of *starosta*'s [royal officer] courts. As a rule, executions ordered by domain, ecclesiastical, and monarch's courts were carried out by the municipal executioner in late fourteenth and fifteenth centuries. See: Zaremska, *Niegodne rzemiosło*, 20.

 | DOI:10.1163/9789004742598_010

of bloody justice appears at many points unclear. This ambiguity can be attributed, in part, to the fragmentation of the available source material, particularly with regard to Poland's early history. Yet, it is also a consequence of the progressive evolution of monarchical prerogatives within the sphere of criminal jurisdiction. This evolution, solidifying over time, only found firmer footing in legal norms during the twelfth century, as exemplified by the so-called *ius ducale*, or ducal law, primarily preserved within thirteenth-century charters. At this time, the Piasts used the death penalty to exercise their authority and navigate their power over their subjects. Consequently, an exploration of executions and banishments within the context of Piast rule transcends the boundaries of a mere legal inquiry. It concurrently unveils the intricacies of political strategy, shedding light on the roles played by these ultimate sanctions in the preservation of power.

Socio-political changes that took place during the period of Piast rule had a large impact on rulers' ability to administer capital punishment. They resulted in the shifting position of the rulers who, at times, reached for a royal title (as in the years 1025, 1076, 1295, 1320, 1333) and, at other times, had to share their rule with other, often numerous, representatives of a fragmented dynasty, keeping only certain duchies and lands under their lordship. These transformations, as a rule, did not deprive Piast rulers of their prerogatives to apply bloody jurisdiction within their domains because all members of the dynasty elevated to power retained the full and sovereign rights in their duchies as a result of holding ducal dignity—the *honor ducis*. However, these changes affected the authority of individual dynasts, consequently influencing the practical ability to carry out the punishments. Equally significant was the impact on the broader public's perception of the monarchs' authority. This is a logical consequence since, under Piast rule, justice often bore a distinct and personal dimension. After all, the power of the monarch's rulings was based not only on the provisions of the law but also on the power of the personal authority and *honor* which sanctioned all the ruler's decisions, including those condemning individuals to death or exile from the duchy or kingdom.[3]

3 Compare Stanisław Borowski, *Ściganie przestępstw z urzędu w średniowiecznem prawie polskiem* (Warsaw: Uniwersytet Warszawski, 1933), 38–40 and Grajewski, *Kara śmierci*, 38. On the idea of ducal power in Poland and the concept of *honor ducis* as a central category of ruling, see: Marcin R. Pauk, "'Regnum in se divisum'. Ku syntezie kultury politycznej Piastów doby dzielnicowej," in *Oryginalność czy wtórność? Studia poświęcone polskiej kulturze politycznej i religijnej (X–XIII wiek)*, ed. Roman Michałowski and Grzegorz Pac (Warsaw: Wydawnictwa Uniwersytetu Warszawskiego, 2020), 76–163 at 92–100; as well as idem, "Language of Power and Communication in the Piast Dynasty: Toward a Reappraisal of Polish Political Culture of the 12th–13th Century," in *Rulership in Medieval East Central Europe: Power, Rituals and*

The scant body of published research addressing the topic of monarchical punishment in Piast Poland has predominantly concentrated on delineating the categories of offenses that incurred the severest penalties. These studies have shown limited inclination towards exploring extralegal influences or delving into the ideological and societal context surrounding the judiciary.[4] Meanwhile, the Piast ruler's capacity to mete out the punishment was contingent upon both practical application and public perception. This was not solely governed by established legal frameworks but was also significantly influenced by the prevailing social and political factors that shaped the force of the monarch's authority. Available sources not only elucidate the intricate interplay between the ruler's authority and their ability to administer punishment, but they also illuminate a noteworthy incongruity. This disjunction becomes apparent during the reign of the Piast dynasty, particularly from the beginning of the twelfth century when informative sources come to the fore. They reveal a dissonance between the prevailing archetype of a severe ruler vested with formidable authority and the actual realities of governance. Closer examination of specific accounts reveal that the idealized image, often presented as laudatory depictions of the ruler, did not invariably align with actual circumstances. This applies not only to rulers who lacked great authority, but also to those monarchs who already held an unquestionable position within society, vis-à-vis knighthood and nobles. According to these sources, the public usually perceived the lack of sufficient severity or ruler's firmness in administering the death penalty negatively, as a manifestation of weakness. The same sources also show, however, that sentencing someone to death was not always beneficial for the rulers, especially when the punishment was issued against knights and nobles. With these groups, the Piasts preferred to demonstrate their authority through the threat of execution rather than seeking final solutions instantly, partly because they feared the influence of the high-born if that threat did not materialize. In such situations, the rulers had to look for other means of keeping up the image of their power and authority. The available evidence highlights two particularly useful means of maintaining that impression: the Piasts' wives could release the convicts from the threat

---

Legitimacy in Bohemia, Hungary and Poland, ed. Grischa Vercamer and Dušan Zupka (Leiden: Brill, 2021), 178–97.

4 I omit the book by Henryk Grajewski (n. 2 above), as he approaches the problem from the extreme viewpoint of Marxist ideology. For other works, see: Marceli Handelsman, "Die Strafe im polnisch-schlesischen Rechte im XII u. XIII Jahrhundert," *Zeitschrift für vergleichende Rechtswissenschaft* 18 (1905): 209–65; idem, *Kara w najdawniejszym prawie polskim* (Warsaw: Wende i S-ka, 1908).

of death, or they might sentence the convict to banishment from a duchy or kingdom, denoting a temporal state of social death for the convict but leaving the door open for a future return to the monarch's grace through the intercession of mighty friends.

In Poland, the nexus between the monarch's authority and the execution of punishment had its source in the practice of exercising power. The notion that the monarch's prerogative to impose penalties of death or exile was unequivocally solidified by the first historical Piasts and builders of Polish statehood at the turn of the tenth and eleventh centuries no longer seems valid. The available sources rather indicate that, in the early period of Poland's history, rulers—including those who vigorously introduced a new religion and monarchical model, such as Bolesław the Brave (r. 992–1025)—avoided punishing their subjects with death, preferring corporal, disciplinary, or penitential punishments.[5] Two factors were likely responsible for this tendency: the great influence of Church norms in the early East Central European monarchies and that of the Carolingian-Ottonian model of the ruler as a good shepherd who guides his sheep in the right path and is responsible for his people's salvation.[6]

The Piast rulers monopolized the judicial power in their hands, which gave them their criminal prerogatives as well as other powers akin to those found

5 Compare Radosław Kotecki, "'Aeternum Dei servitium ad sanctum locum': Pokuta zabójców Pięciu Braci Męczenników w relacji Brunona z Kwerfurtu," *Kwartalnik Historyczny* 121.1 (2014): 41–71; and Zbigniew Dalewski, "Pokuta Bolesława Chrobrego," in *Księga. Teksty o świecie średniowiecznym ofiarowane Hannie Zaremskiej*, ed. Halina Manikowska (Warsaw: Instytut Historii PAN, 2018), 73–101 at 96–97.

6 For more see: Kotecki, "'Aeternum Dei servitium ad sanctum locum'"; Marcin R. Pauk, "'Ergo meum maximum et primum sit decretum'—Prawo kanoniczne i sądownictwo kościelne w tzw. 'Dekretach' księcia Brzetysława I," in *Právní kultura středověku*, ed. Piotr Węcowski and Martin Nodl (Prague: Filosofia, 2016), 27–44. This model can be also observed in other Slavic countries as well. Compare tenth- through twelfth-century accounts of Bohemian duke St. Wenceslas (d. 935), who is said to have abolished the gallows in his country, preferring corporal and penitential punishments to capital punishment. On this model, see: Joanna Nastalska-Wiśnicka, *'Rex martyr'. Studium źródłoznawcze nad legendą hagiograficzną św. Wacława (X–XIV w.)* (Lublin: Werset, 2010), 267–70. Also, the early twelfth-century *Povest vremennykh let* provides an account of Vladimir the Great (r. 980–1015), who did not want to punish criminals with death for fear of falling into deadly sin until the bishops intervened and taught the ruler about his power to punish in God's name. On the account, see: Walter K. Hanak, *The Nature and the Image of Princely Power in Kievan Rus', 980–1054: A Study of Sources* (Leiden: Brill, 2014), 45–46; Marcin R. Pauk, "'Washing Hands in a Sinner's Blood': Ducal Power, Law and Religious Zeal in the Process of Central European Christianization—Preliminary Remarks," in *Leben zwischen und mit den Kulturen. Studien zu Recht, Bildung und Herrschaft in Mitteleuropa*, ed. Renata Skowrońska-Kamińska and Helmut Flachenecker (Toruń: Wydawnictwo Naukowe Uniwersytetu Mikołaja Kopernika, 2015), 23–34 at 30–31.

in Western, particularly German, *Territorialmacht* models. Recent research, specifically that of Sławomir Gawlas, suggests that those ducal prerogatives underwent a process of evolution over the course of the late-eleventh and, especially, twelfth centuries. These prerogatives only gradually gained institutional character as Poland assimilated Western patterns of state modernization, particularly those influenced by Ottonian, Salian, and Staufen Germany, and embraced the concept of monarch's *regalia*.[7] As a consequence, only in the twelfth century did the dukes enjoy the most important judicial prerogatives, which had not previously been reserved exclusively for them, in a society that traditionally claimed some right to collective punishment for public wrongs.[8] Among new ducal prerogatives, the *iudicium magnum* or *supremum* [higher courts of the ruler] played an especially significant role. These courts focused on crimes described as *causae maiores*—crimes which are particularly grave and, as a rule, punishable by the death penalty or banishment.[9] These included, first and foremost, all crimes against the essential interests of the monarchy, particularly the betrayal of the ruler and the country, surrendering castles, sending foreign troops on the country, or endangering the ruler's life. At the same time, this category included all violent acts that posed a threat to public order, such as killing another person, severe bodily harm, and, above all, organized robbery and plunder (*spolium publicum, latrocinium, violentia*). The most telling examples of the importance of this form of justice are the thirteenth-century dukes who jealously guarded it as reserved ducal prerogative and only occasionally granted exceptions to this jurisdiction for the benefit of domain courts as a judicial immunity.[10] This suggests that the Piast rulers,

---

7 Sławomir Gawlas, *O kształt zjednoczonego królestwa. Niemieckie władztwo terytorialne a geneza społeczno-ustrojowej odrębności Polski* (Warsaw: DiG, 2000), 78–80; Andrzej Marzec, "Królewskie sądownictwo prawa polskiego za panowania Władysława Łokietka i Kazimierza Wielkiego," in *Právní kultura středověku*, ed. Piotr Węcowski and Martin Nodl (Prague: Filosofia, 2016), 81–104 at 83. For an overview of the concept of princely power and prerogatives in the Empire, see: Jörg Rogge, "The Growth of Princely Authority: Themes and Problems," in *The Origins of the German Principalities, 1100–1350: Essays by German Historians*, ed. Graham A. Loud and Jochen Schenk (Abingdon: Routledge, 2017), 23–36.

8 Some twelfth- and thirteenth-century sources refer to holdovers of the old collective punishments of tearing and stoning to death. On this, see: Paweł Gołdyn, "Ukamienowanie i rozszarpanie w polskiej wczesnośredniowiecznej praktyce karnej," *Czasopismo Prawno-Historyczne* 58.2 (2006): 127–133. On stoning as a characteristic collective punishment of early medieval legal culture, see also: Abel de Lorenzo Rodríguez's essay in this volume.

9 In sources, these crimes are referred to by different names: "causae magnae," "graves," "capitales," "capitis," "sanguinis," "reservatae," "enormes," or "iudicium capitis," "poenae sanguinis," "his ducale," etc. Some of them clearly point to the ultimate penalty in the criminal justice system.

10 Juliusz Bardach, *Historia państwa i prawa Polski. Do połowy XV wieku* (Warsaw: Państwowe Wydawnictwo Naukowe, 1965), 325–37.

reserving the right to impose the death penalty or banishment for such crimes, sought to strengthen their authority by seeking to appear both as individuals endowed with an exceptional position and as superiors with special privileges to care for public safety and order. The exclusive prerogative to impose sentences of execution and exile was, therefore, a means of modelling the image of the monarch's authority in the eyes of his subjects.

In the court and church circles of Piast Poland, narrative sources fully confirm the image of the ruler who would severely and decisively use his power to execute the highest justice. The annals written in Poznań, the capital of the Duchy of Greater Poland, during the reign of the Piasts who came from Silesia include a typical example. Henry of Głogów (r. 1274–1309) was a stranger, and, therefore, he was not very popular in Poznań. The local annalist, despite condemning the duke for exploiting his subjects and favoring the Germans over the Poles, decided not to forget to praise Duke Henry, who "fuit rigidus valde furibus et predonibus ac violentis" [was very strict towards plunderers, robbers and the violent], which is why "temporibus suis pax maxima fuit in Polonia et in omnibus terris suis" [during his time there was a great peace in [Greater] Poland and in all of his lands].[11] The author apparently remembered well the harshness of the ruler and his severe suppression and punishment of bandits and robbers even though he had no reason to support him in political terms. Similarly, the contemporaneous epitaph, analogous to other fourteenth-century epitaphs of other Piast rulers, praises Duke Henry, suggesting that the then-cultivated ideal of the ruler centered on him being a harsh avenger of rapes, villainies, and other crimes against public order: "Pace quievisti, Polonia, tuta fuisti / Sub ducis Henrici clypeo, tu nunc benedici / Patria tranquilla poteras, quod nullus in illa / Fur fuit aut praedo" [You stayed in peace, [Greater] Poland, you were safe / Under Duke Henry's shield, blessings then / You could enjoy, peaceful homeland, that there was none in you / Thief or robber].[12]

11 *Annales capituli* Posnanensis, in *Annales Poloniae Maioris*, ed. Brygida Kürbis, Monumenta Poloniae Historica, Nova series 6 (Warsaw: Państwowe Wydawnictwo Naukowe, 1962), 54, and editorial comment 78 n. 425. Compare with the opinion of *Chronica Polonorum* on that ruler: "fuit seriosus et timorosus." *Chronica principum Poloniae*, Monumenta Poloniae Historica 3 (Lviv: Akademia Umiejętności, 1878), 537. On the real basis for such opinions about Duke Henry, see: Antoni Gąsiorowski, "'Districtus' w Wielkopolsce początków XIV wieku," *Roczniki Historyczne* 32 (1966): 173–93 at 189–90; Tomasz Jurek, *Dziedzic Królestwa Polskiego. Książę głogowski Henryk (1272–1309)* (Poznań: Wydawnictwo Poznańskiego Towarzystwa Przyjaciół Nauk, 1993), 76, 95.

12 Edition in Tomasz Jurek and Michał Rzepiela, "Lubiąskie epitafium księcia Henryka głogowskiego. Nowo odkryty zabytek poezji łacińskiej z początków XIV wieku," *Roczniki Historyczne* 71 (2005): 185–99 at 190–91.

So significant was this ideal that annalists and chroniclers include the effectiveness of the rulers' execution of justice in evaluating the success of their respective reigns. Casimir III the Great (r. 1333–1370) for example, the last Piast who reigned over the reunited Kingdom of Poland in the fourteenth century, is described as eagerly and freely using capital punishment. The author of the *Kraków Cathedral Chronicle*, written only a few years after Casimir's death, effusively praises the king for his effective use of the death penalty:

> Regio diademate insignitus regnum populumque a Deo sibi traditum viriliter ac utiliter gubernabat. Nam secundum prophetam pacem et veritatem atque iusticiam dilexit. Erat enim bonorum et iustorum piissimus tutor et defensor, malorum vero, predonum, violentorum, calumpniatorum sevissimus persecutor. Nam quicunque latrocinia sive furta faciebant, quantumcumque fuerant nobiles, ipsos mandabat decollari, submergi et fame mortificari, cum fratribus eorum et cognatis comedens et bibens pariter et dormiens; Deum habens adjutorem, non timebat, quid faciat sibi homo. Calumpniatores vero, quos reperit, ipsos ferro ignito in facie aduri mandabat. Ipsius temporibus nullus autem nobilis pauperi audebat facere violenciam, sed in statera equitatis omnia dirigebantur.
>
> [Bravely and to everyone's advantage he ruled, crowned with a royal crown, over a state and nation entrusted to him by God. For, according to the prophet, he loved peace, truth and justice: he was the most ardent guardian and defender of the good and the righteous, and the most severe persecutor of the wicked, the robbers, the ruffians and the slanderers. Whosoever committed villainy or theft, even if it were the noblemen, he had them decapitated, drowned and starved to death, yet not ceasing to eat, drink and sleep with their brethren and relatives, for having God as his assistant, he was not afraid of what man would do to him. When he found them, he had the slanderers stigmatized on their faces with a burning iron. In his day none of the nobles dared to persecute the poor, and everything was judged according to the scales of justice.][13]

For the chronicler, the monarch's passion in imposing the death penalty is an essential component of constructing the image of a strict and powerful ruler, one who enjoys the grace and protection of God and the universal respect of his subjects. In this context, the statement that King Casimir decapitated,

13 *Cronica 1202–1377*, ed. Wojciech Kętrzyński, in "O rocznikach polskich," *Rozprawy Wydziału Historyczno-Filozoficznego Akademii Umiejętności w Krakowie* 34 (1896): 166–90 at 187.

drowned, and starved not only commoners but also representatives of the nobility, underscores the magnificence of Casimir's power, authority, and personal charisma. For the same reason, the author emphasizes that the king continued to maintain close, even intimate contact with the relatives of the nobles sentenced to death upon his orders, without any fear of reprisals. The *Kraków Cathedral Chronicle* is an apologetic text, but it still has value. On the one hand, its content illustrates the high expectations which arose for Casimir III's successors after his death;[14] simultaneously, it conveys the advancements made during his reign in the realm of enforcing royal justice.[15]

Another contemporary description of the king's rule survives in the so-called *Annals of Traska*, composed during Casimir's reign. This source, in part, aligns with the narrative presented in the *Kraków Cathedral Chronicle*, while also introducing some variations in Casimir's portrayal:

> Coronatus autem statim in maleficos in tantum desevit ut in modico tempore multos eorum delevit, dans metum pluribus, ut se a furtis et latrociniis cohiberent. Ut de factum est quod omnes qui vero furtis et latrociniis inserviebant aut intercessione baronum ad mansuetudinem sunt reducti aut perpetuo exilio fuerunt sine mora ad mortem dampnati.
>
> [Immediately after the coronation, [Casimir] went so far against the evildoers that he soon exterminated many of them, driving many to such a fear that they would refrain from stealing and robbery. Thus all who were actually committed to theft and robbery, either were pardoned through the intercession of the lords, or were immediately sentenced to eternal exile [or] to death.][16]

A notable disparity emerges between the ideal of the uncompromising monarch depicted in the *Kraków Cathedral Chronicle* and the reality presented

14 *The Kraków Cathedral Chronicle* was written during the reign of Casimir's successor Louis I the Great of Hungary. Another contemporary chronicler, Jan of Czarnków, made it clear that under the rule of Louis (1370–1384) and the regency of his mother Elizabeth, the public order that had previously prevailed was not properly secured. *Joannis de Czarnkow Chronicon Polonorum*, ed. Jan Szlachtowski, Monumenta Poloniae Historica 2 (Lviv: Akademia Umiejętności, 1872), 651, 721.

15 Among others, see: Borowski, *Ściganie przestępstw*, 48–49; Józef Matuszewski, "'Ręka pańska'. Ze studiów nad najstarszym zwodem prawa polskiego," *Przegląd Zachodni* 11.3–4 (1955): 598–612 at 611–12.

16 *Annales Polonorum vel Trascae dicti*, ed. August Bielowski, Monumenta Poloniae Historica 2 (Lviv: Akademia Umiejętności, 1872), 859–60.

perhaps more faithfully in the *Annals of Traska*. In the *Annals*, the death penalty, while still imposed passionately by the king contrary to what the Kraków chronicler suggests, turns out to be less of a self-evident *solution* against all criminals. The guilty representatives of the knighthood could escape death if other nobles were willing to intercede on their behalf. The range of punishments imposed by Casimir also turns out to be wider than those outlined in the *Kraków Cathedral Chronicle*. Not only is the king said to adjudicate capital punishment; according to the author of *Annals of Traska*, he also punished the perpetrators of crimes more gently by banishing them from the kingdom. No less significant is the message that the ruler was particularly zealous in exercising his prerogatives shortly after his coronation, as it shows Casimir's intention to consolidate his authority from the outset of his reign. There is no reason not to trust the annalist in this regard since he was connected with the royal court in the 1330s and 1340s, and, as a result, he was well informed about the young king's strategy of establishing his own authority. Consequently, the text suggests that Casimir's rule was marked not only by unwavering severity or a predilection for death sentences but also by the availability of alternative punitive measures, including exile.

The depiction of Casimir in the *Annals of Traska* finds its counterpoint in the portrait of his father, Władysław the Elbow (duke from 1275, King of Poland 1320–1333). The following excerpt presents an unexpected contradiction to the ideal of a stringent ruler, without criticizing the monarch:

> Hic inter virtutum karismata tribus ultra humanum estimacionem effloruit luculenter. Videlicet insigni pietate, quia nisi coactus aliquem morti tradi iussit, inestimabili humilitate, ut quid esset fastus aut superbia penitus ignoraret, indicibili paciencia, nam vindex iniurie nullatenus esse potuit, ymo se iniuriantibus humanissimum exhibuit, placidum vultum in omnibus illis ostendens. Quapropter inspector omnium actuum Deus tantum decorem suo corpori in morte contulit, ut quamvis diebus pluribus sua sepultura fuerit protelata, semper firmus in suo decore placabili seu amicabili ad magnam omnium admiracionem et stuporem permansit.
>
> [Among the spiritual gifts of the virtues, three of them shone brilliantly beyond human comprehension, namely extraordinary goodness, because he did not have anyone executed, except out of necessity; invaluable humility, so that he knew not what haughtiness and pride were; unspeakable patience, for he could not in any way avenge the harm suffered, but rather was very human in relation to the wrong-doers, always turning a gentle face to them. Therefore God, examining all the deeds, gave his

> body such a beautiful appearance after death that, although his funeral was postponed for several days, he still kept his beautiful appearance with a gentle or friendly expression, which aroused general admiration and astonishment.][17]

Compared to the portrayal of Casimir and the ideal of a strict ruler, his father's image is composed in a way that seems to cover the limitations of Władysław's rule and the lack of sufficiently strong authority remembered by his contemporaries. What was a manifestation of the ideal of grace and humanity towards wrong-doers for the annalist, other chroniclers more bluntly called out as ineptitude and indecisiveness against criminals.[18] Such opinions appear to have been widely shared by the public under the reign of the last Piasts on the Polish throne. For example, the bishop of Poznań, John IV of Kępa (d. 1346), spoke about the deficiencies of Władysław's rule, revealing, at the Polish-Teutonic trial only six years after the king's death, that he

> non erat bonus iusticiarius et multa dampna, iniurie et spolia et oppressions fiebant in dicta terra Pomoranie, taliter quod fere fuit deserta in totum, quia dictus dominus Wladislaus dominus dicte terre Pomoranie et rex Polonie nolebat dictos excessus corrigere nec iusticiam facere de malefactoribus in eadem.
>
> [was not a good justiciar and a lot of wrongdoing, injustice, villainies and rapes took place in the Pomeranian land, so that the land was completely desolate, because Władysław, the owner of the Pomeranian land and the King of Poland [*recte* duke in some Polish lands at the time] did not want to punish the aforementioned crimes, nor to administer justice to the criminals.][19]

According to the bishop, Władysław's inability even pushed the magnates and subjects to depose him from both Pomerania and his Polish lands and replace him with a ruler who wielded greater authority, King Wenceslas II of Bohemia (King of Poland 1300–1305).[20] Moreover, the sources record Władysław's difficulty with imposing the death penalty. For example, according to the account

17 *Annales Polonorum vel Trascae dicti*, 859.

18 The negative opinions of Władysław have been summarized in Gerard Labuda, "Zapiska o zaburzeniach chłopskich w dobrach klasztoru przemęckiego w roku 1309," *Roczniki Historyczne* 20 (1952): 121–38.

19 *Lites ac res gestae inter Polonos Ordinemque Cruciferorum*, ed. Ignacy Zakrzewski and Jadwiga Karwasińska, 2 vols. (Poznań: Biblioteka Kórnicka, 1890–1935), 1:150.

20 *Lites ac res gestae*, 1:150.

in *Annales S. Crucis*, Władysław sentenced certain nobles to death by being dragged by horses and hanged for surrendering Polish castles to the Teutonic Knights. Although it was the most serious crime according to the law, the sentence was not executed because the royal council opposed the king's will and mitigated the original sentence to one year of imprisonment in a tower.[21] This narrative peculiarly underscores the passivity of the king, and even his indolence. Additionally, this event reflected poorly on Władysław because it took place shortly after his coronation, whereas his son, Casimir, was remembered as particularly harsh and eager to impose sentences of death and exile at the inauguration of his reign. Władysław clearly preferred not to cross the knighthood that gave him power.

This does not mean, however, that Władysław the Elbow was never relentless in his exercise of judicial power. A significant display of his resolve came after the downfall of the Přemyslids' rule in Poland, during the conspiracy led by the mayor of Kraków, Albert. This conspiracy, designed to wrest away Władysław's rule in Lesser Poland and endorse John of Bohemia in 1311–1312, faced the full force of his wrath. According to available accounts, after suppressing this rebellion, the duke ordered that the most active conspirators be captured, dragged by horses around the city until weary, and then hanged on gallows outside the walls of Kraków, where their bodies were to remain in public view until they decayed completely.[22] Albert himself did not share this fate, but it was only because he was captured and taken from Kraków by the

21 *Annales S. Crucis*, ed. Anna Rutkowska-Płachcińska, Monumenta Poloniae Historica, Nova series 12 (Warsaw: Polska Akademia Umiejętności, 1996), 65: "Item post coronacionem Wladislai regis predicti et ipse rex dans treugas predictis fraudulentis nobilibus, visis personis ipsorum voluit suspendi et equis trahi. Tamen consilium ipsius non permisit sed ipsos incarceravit, ad turrim in castro Tanczin reposuit infra integrum annum. Anno elapso ipsos ad fideiussoriam caucionem dedit, videlicet quod duo milia marcarum Cruciferis restituere debuerunt et terram Pomeranie exemere et exbrigare ab eisdem."

22 *Annales capituli Cracoviensis*, in *Annales Cracovienses priores cum kalendario*, ed. Zofia Kozłowska-Budkowa, Monumenta Poloniae Historica, Nova series 5 (Warsaw: Państwowe Wydawnictwo Naukowe, 1978), 19–105 at 104: "Et tunc imediate illustrissimus princeps Wladyzlaus civitatem predictam subintrans denuo civium aliquos captivavit carceralique custodie reclusit. Hos captivatos seviter per totam civitatem equis traxit tractosque patibulo extra civitatem miserabiliter suspendit, ibidemque funera tamdiu pendere fecit, quoadusque nervi putrefacti ossium compaginem dissolverunt." See also: *Rocznik kujawski*, ed. August Bielowski, Monumenta Poloniae Historica 3 (Lviv: Akademia Umiejętności, 1878), 204–12 at 209: "… cives autem quosdam, qui culpabiliores huis criminis erant, equis trahi et extra civitatem suspendi precepit." As most of the rioters were Germans, *Krasińskis' Annals* claims that those who could not pronounce the Polish words *soczovycza* (lentil), *koło* (wheel), *mieyle* (grinds) and *młyn* (mill) were beheaded: *Rocznik Krasińskich*, Monumenta Poloniae Historica 3 (Lviv: Akademia Umiejętności, 1878), 127–35 at 133.

Duke Bolko of Opole. As recounted in the fourteenth-century *Song about the Mayor Albert*, as a result of his actions, the rebel was denied access to the Polish borders and forced to go to Bohemia, where he remained in exile and died a beggar.[23] His house in Kraków was demolished, and Władysław built a fortification in its place to enhance his power over the growing municipal town.[24]

Although the chronicles illustrate certain general tendencies and reflect the feelings of the authors and their circles, their opinions about the last two Piasts—Władysław the Elbow and Casimir the Great—do not fully reflect the complicated reality of punishment in this period. This applies to both the account about Władysław, who sometimes made use of his prerogatives sturdily, and to his more powerful and undoubtedly more effective son, Casimir. Sławomir Gawlas recently noted that Casimir the Great was eager to threaten those who opposed his decisions with the death penalty, but in practice he did not necessarily carry out these threats.[25] For example, when merchants and city councilors in Kraków refused to use the coin at the rate imposed by the king, they faced the threat of sharing the fate of rebels in 1312, i.e. the loss of property and life, demolition of houses, and exile of wives and children. In the end, however, the king did not carry out these threats but turned to symbolic violence: he ordered that the market hat in the square in Kraków, representing the trade immunity of the municipal council, be overturned and destroyed. Therefore, the king capitulated rather than scoring a victory. There are also examples from the reign of Casimir that cast doubt on the claim of the *Kraków Cathedral Chronicle* that the king was as zealous in imposing the death penalty on the common people as on the nobility. The story of the palatine, Peter Nieorza, who violated the royal monopoly by forcing hospitality on the royal mine administrators in Wieliczka, confirms it. According to the mine statute,

23 Henryk Kowalewicz, "Pieśń o wójcie krakowskim Albercie," *Pamiętnik Literacki* 56.3 (1965): 125–38 at 134–35. The credibility of the information is advocated by Wojciech Mrozowicz, "Pieśń o wójcie krakowskim Albercie—przekaz historyczny w poetyckim sztafażu," *Annales Universitatis Paedagogicae Cracoviensis. Studia Historica* 13 (2013): 32–42.

24 Jan Długosz adds that some of the rioters were punished with breaking on the wheel. See: *Ioannis Dlugossii Annales seu cronicae incliti Regni Poloniae*, liber V–VI (Warsaw: Państwowe Wydawnictwo Naukowe, 1973), 83–84: "Aliquos autem cives Cracovienses sedicionis prefate auctores in horrorem patrati sceleris, ut essent pro exemplari et cautelae futurorum, comprehendit et equis per vicos tractos in patibulum aut rotam egit. Ex domo autem advocati arcem erigit et in valva sancti Nicolai turrim extollit atque illic militum collocat presidium, vacillantem ceterorum Cracowiensium civium fidem arce illa et presidio fidam sibi de cetero effecturus."

25 Sławomir Gawlas, "Kazimierz Wielki—jaki był?" in *Świat średniowiecza. Studia ofiarowane Profesorowi Henrykowi Samsonowiczowi*, ed. Agnieszka Bartoszewicz et al. (Warsaw: Wydawnictwa Uniwersytetu Warszawskiego, 2010), 761–87 at 780–82.

despite Peter Nieorza falling out of royal favor due to his actions, no severe punishments were meted out. Instead, it is recorded that after a period of two months in royal disfavor, he was reinstated into the king's good graces through the intercession of his mighty friends. The issuance of an order following this incident, which threatened the penalty of beheading and the confiscation of property (*poena colli ac bonorum*), seems to be intended more as a deterrent than an actual punitive measure.[26]

According to Gawlas, these examples do not change the general perception of the reign of Casimir the Great, whose authority was so profound that he solved problems by demonstrating royal anger as an instrument of power.[27] However, they do not fully confirm such a view either but rather point to some discrepancies between the king's threats and his actions. One of his legislative statutes exemplifies such discrepancy. While it was designed to enhance the monarch's prestige, the king himself admitted that many knights (*de militali prosapia procedentes*) who indulged in villainies went unpunished. Instead, they opted to leave the country voluntarily, later returning to regain royal favor, thanks to the intercession of their friends and their own expressions of humility.[28] This example suggests a disjunction between the constructed image of the monarch as a fierce judge against all villains and the real reach of his royal jurisdiction.

Undoubtedly, the period of Casimir III's reign was when the monarch's authority experienced moments of spectacular growth, especially compared with the thirteenth-century period of fragmentation in which the hitherto united Piast domain disintegrated into many independent duchies ruled by the Piasts of various branches. Even the reign of Władysław Jagiełło (r. 1386–1434), however, exhibited this expansion of power. He is said to have shown his

26 *Ustawa urządzenia żup Krakowskich soli wydana przez Kazimierza Wielkiego roku 1368*, ed. Zygmunt Antoni Helcel, Starodawne Prawa Polskiego Pomniki 1 (Warsaw: Księgarnia Sennewalda, 1856), 217–24 at 218–19.

27 Gawlas, "Kazimierz Wielki," 780.

28 *Prawodawstwo wiślickie Kazimierza Wielkiego*, ed. Zygmunt Antoni Helcel, Starodawne Prawa Polskiego Pomniki 1 (Warsaw: Księgarnia Sennewalda, 1856), 191–206 at 206 (c. 15.34): "Saepius contingit, ut quidam de militali prosapia procedentes, veluti prodigi honoris et famae ipsorum, furta seu latrocinia committentes, sint profugi nostri regni spontanea voluntate ipsorum, et sic occasionem habentes, plura mala committere non formidant, pro quibus incidunt in iram nostrae indignationis. Tandem do commissis furtis et ceteris actibus malis poenitentia ducti, amicorum suorum intercessione mediante, nostram clementiam implorare consueverunt, et sic nostrae gratiae de novo restaurantur." Compare with Grajewski, *Kara śmierci*, 230.

disapproval simply by not shaking hands.[29] It is doubtful, however, that in the case of Casimir this growth would so greatly enhance the effectiveness of his royal power to punish by death the representatives of nobility as presented in the *Kraków Cathedral Chronicle*. Against the background of individual cases, it is even clearer that this text shows a postulated ideal rather than reality; an ideal that in Poland had a tradition dating back much earlier than the reign of the last Piasts on the Polish throne.

The oldest narrative of Polish history, the chronicle of Gallus Anonymus from the middle of the second decade of the twelfth century, mirrors a similar idea of monarchical authority. It also highlights challenges that monarchs faced when it came to administering ultimate punishments to individuals from the upper echelons of society. The chronicler draws a strongly idealized portrait of Bolesław the Brave, a ruler who is said to have been a model for all his successors.[30] From the beginning of this story, Gallus emphasizes the king's relationship with the nobles as one based on the principle of the royal love and benevolence towards his barons:

> Duces vero suosque comites ac principes acsi fratres vel filios diligebat, eosque salva reverentia sicut sapiens dominus honorabat. Conquerentibus enim super illis inconsulte non credebat, contra lege condempnatis iudicium misericordia temperabat.
>
> [The king loved his dukes, *comites*, and princes as if they were his brothers or his sons, and as far his dignity permitted he honored them as a wise master would. If any complaint was made against them, he never would rashly believe it; while for those who had been sentenced [to capital punishment] he would temper judgement with mercy.][31]

According to Gallus, however, the principle of the king's concern for his nobles is clearly limited by Bolesław's right to punish them with death as befits a

29 Maria Koczerska, "Łaska królewska, czyli kontakty władcy z poddanymi w Polsce późnośredniowiecznej," in *Człowiek w społeczeństwie średniowiecznym*, ed. Roman Michałowski and Ewa Biernacka (Warsaw: DiG, 1997), 437–51.

30 For the Bolesław's portrait as an *exemplum*, see: Przemysław Wiszewski, *'Domus Bolezlai': Values and Social Identity in Dynastic Traditions of Medieval Poland (c.966–1138)* (Leiden: Brill, 2010), 173–215.

31 Gallus Anonymus, *Gesta principum Polonorum*, 1.13, ed. and trans. Paul W. Knoll and Frank Schaer (Budapest: Central European University Press, 2003), 58, 60 (Latin), 59, 61 (English). Hereafter volume, chapter, and page numbers for the Latin and page numbers for the English are given parentheses.

powerful ruler. The relationship between the king and his nobles is therefore hidden by an internal contradiction. When one of the powerful commits a crime worthy of the death penalty, this contradiction tests Bolesław's authority, requiring extraordinary measures in the process of re-connecting the guilty to the state of royal love.

Thus, according to Gallus, proper relations can be rebuilt only thanks to the royal wife and her exceptional wisdom and special position with the king:

> Sepe namque uxor eius regina, prudens mulier et discreta, plures pro culpa morti deditos de manibus lictorum eripuit et ab imminenti mortis periculo liberavit, eosque in carcere, quandoque rege nesciente quandoque vero dissimulante, sub custodia vite misericorditer reservavit. (1.13.60)
>
> [For often his wife the queen, a wise and discrete woman, would rescue those condemned to death for some crime from the hands of the executioners and save them at the last minute from the threat of death. She would leave them under guard in the prison, their lives preserved through her mercy. At times the king did not know of this, and at times he would pretend not to.] (61)

Next, Gallus explains that during court feasts, whenever the king recollected knights and barons he had lost,

> [t]unc regina venerabilis pium pectus regis blanda manu demulcens, sciscitabatur ab eo, si carum ei fieret, si quis eos sanctus a morte forsitan suscitaret. Cui rex respondebat, se nichil tam preciosum possidere. ... Hec audiens regina sapiens et fidelis pii furti se ream et consciam accusabat et cum amicis XII et uxoribus eorum ad pedes regis pro sui dampnatorumque venia se prosternebat. Quam rex benigne complexans cum osculo de terra manibus sublevabat, eiusque fidele furtum, ymmo pietatis opera collaudabat. Eadem igitur hora pro captivis illis, per mulieris prudenciam vite reservatis cum equis plurimis mittebatur et euntibus redeundi terminus ponebatur. ... Tunc vero letitia multiplex illis residentibus accrescebat, cum regina regis honorem ac regni utilitatem sic sapienter observabat et rex eam cum amicorum consilio de suis petitionibus audiebat. Illi autem, pro quibus missum fuerat, venientes, non statim regi sed regine presentabantur, qui ab ea verbis asperis et lenibus castigati ad regis balneum ducebantur. (1.13.60, 62)

> [[t]he venerable queen, stroking the king's merciful breast with a gentle hand, would ask him if it would please him if some saint should raise them from the dead. To which the king would reply that he possessed nothing so precious. … Hearing this, his wise and faithful queen would admit her guilt and her well-intentioned trickery, and then she and the twelve friends and their wives would all throw themselves at the king's feet and plead pardon for themselves and the condemned. The king would embrace her fondly and kiss her and take her hands and raise her from the ground and speak in warm terms of her true-hearted trickery—indeed, of her works of mercy. … Then the guests at the banquet would burst into joy and delight that the queen had shown such wisdom in guarding the interests of the country while respecting the king's honor, and that the king had taken the advice of his friends and listened to her and her petitions. When those [criminals] who had been sent for arrived, they were not presented to the king first but to the queen. She would rebuke them with both sharp and mild words, and then have them taken to the king's bath.] (61, 63)

It is clear from the account that, although the king gave criminals their lives through the intercession of his beloved queen, restoring them to the state of royal love could not violate the authority of the ruler—the king's *honor*. In such situations, at least a symbolic punishment was necessary, which, according to Gallus, took place in the royal bath.

> Quos rex Bolezlauus, sicut pater filios secum balneantes corrigebat, eorumque progeniem memorando collaudabat. Vos, inquit, tanta, vos tali prosapia exortos, talia committere non decebat. Etate quidem provecciores verbis tantum tam per se, quam per alios castigabat, minoribus vero verbera cum verbis adhibebat. Sicque paterne commonitos ac indumentis regalibus adornatos, datis muneribus collatisque honoribus, ire domum cum gaudio dimittebat. Talem igitur sese rex Bolezlaus erga populum et principes exhibebat, sic sapienter et timeri et amari se a cunctis sibi subditis faciebat. (1.13.60, 62)

> [There King Bolesław would bathe with them as a father would with his children, berating them and dwelling on the praises of their forebears. "It was unworthy of you, who are descended from such a distinguished family, to stoop to such things." The older ones he would merely rebuke either personally or through others, while for the younger ones the words would

> be accompanied by the switch. After this paternal reprimand he would dress them in royal garments, give them presents and honors, and send them home with joy. Such was King Bolesław's way of treating the people and the princes, and thus through his wise ways he caused himself to be both feared and loved by all who were subject to him.] (61, 63)

This chronicle account raises many questions. As Jacek Banaszkiewicz points out, there are a few cracks in this portrayal of the king, resulting from idealizing the figure of the ruler himself and the situation.[32] The chronicler struggles internally between presenting the king as harsh and powerful, while at the same time emphasizing his gentleness towards the representatives of the state elite. The result is a form of intrigue, the "well-intentioned trickery" of the queen, which allowed the convicts to be saved without costing the king his authority—while even strengthening it, according to the chronicler in the final paragraph: "he caused himself to be both feared and loved by all who were subject to him" (1.13. 61, 63). Thus, Gallus undoubtedly takes into account the social expectations that rulers be cautious in imposing the death penalty and, in particular, not impose it recklessly, especially on the high-born, for whom the king should be a loving and kind father or brother rather than a severe judge.

Unfortunately, it is impossible to verify unambiguously the role of the king's wife in releasing convicts because of the lack of other contemporary sources, but as the comparative research on the role of the Piast wives suggests, such a scenario seems possible. What is more, it could have taken place with the consent of the ruler himself.[33] According to Gallus, this was not an isolated incident; it was almost routine practice that took place whenever there was a need to rescue someone. Moreover, at one point Gallus explicitly states that Bolesław knew nothing about his wife's merciful deeds; however, at other times he says Bolesław merely pretended not to know. The description of the king's actions following the disclosure of the queen's "well-intentioned trickery" suggests that, in the chronicler's eyes, the practice of giving criminals the opportunity to return to royal grace was both customary and institutionalized.

32 Jacek Banaszkiewicz, "Król i łaźnia, Bóg i łaźnia (Gall Anonim o Bolesławie Chrobrym; 'Provest' vremennych let' o stworzeniu Pierwszego Człowieka)," in *Wyobraźnia średniowieczna*, ed. Teresa Michałowska (Warsaw: Wydawnictwo Instytutu Badań Literackich, 1996), 205–22 at 207.

33 Grajewski, *Kara śmierci*, 228–29. On the idea of rulers' wives seeking mercy from their spouses, see: Grzegorz Pac, *Kobiety w dynastii Piastów. Rola społeczna piastowskich żon i córek do połowy XII wieku—studium porównawcze* (Toruń: Wydawnictwo Naukowe Uniwersytetu Mikołaja Kopernika, 2013), 117–50.

Such mercy would not occur, however, without reminding the convicted that they can enjoy true life only by remaining in the king's favor.[34]

Not accidentally, Gallus uses similar language to describe banishment by the king, a substitute for the death penalty that causes the social annihilation of the evildoer:

> Talem etiam gratiam ei Deus contulerat et ita visu desiderabilis cunctis erat, quod si forte quemlibet a conspectu suo pro culpa veniali momentaneo removebat, quamvis ille rerum suique libertate frueretur, donec benivolencie eius ac conspectui redderetur, non se vivere, sed mori, nec se liberum, sed trusum carceri reputabat. (1.12.56, 58)
>
> [Moreover, God endowed Bolesław with such charm, and all were so attracted to the sight of him, that if ever he banished anyone from his presence even for a short time because of a minor transgression, even if the person continued to enjoy his possessions and liberty, he would feel as though he was dying rather than alive, and not free but cast into a dungeon until he was readmitted to the king's grace and presence.] (57, 59)

In this account, Gallus appears to refer to real solutions applied by the Piasts, whose aim was to maintain the authority of the monarch while also refraining from imposing a final and irreversible penalty. As Grischa Vercamer suggests, the approach in the Gallus text reflects the reality of the turn of the eleventh and twelfth centuries and the position of the nobility themselves, who were in favor of the more conciliatory model of monarchical justice, reminiscent of the approach used during the reign of Bolesław III the Wrymouth's father, Władysław Herman (r. 1079–1102). Consequently, the text conceals underlying criticism against Bolesław (r. 1102–1138), the ruler during whose rule Gallus composed his work. The latter preferred a more rigid approach towards the noblemen, being aware of the dangers of increasing their power.[35]

The administration of the death penalty in Poland was a concern not only for rulers like Bolesław III the Wrymouth or the last Piasts on the Polish throne, who held sway over most of the Polish territories, but also for the dukes of

34 Especially in view of the well-known function of baths as a means of social and spiritual reintegration in Slavic culture. See: Banaszkiewicz, "Król i łaźnia," 208. Compare with Pac, *Kobiety w dynastii Piastów*, especially 143–48.

35 Grischa Vercamer, "Das Bad des Königs—beschreibt Gallus Anonymus ein genuin piastisches/polnisches Ritual?" *Frühmittelalterliche Studien* 43.1 (2009): 349–72 at 368–69. Compare with Grajewski, *Kara śmierci*, 228.

the thirteenth century, when the Polish sovereignty ultimately disintegrated, resulting in many smaller principalities. Ruling over increasingly shrinking resources, the Piasts experienced various challenges during this period, which frequently led to a decline in their status and authority, at times necessitating competition with increasingly influential towns, knights, or bishops. Under such conditions, exercising monarchical judicial powers was not always easy, nor was it always politically viable or even possible. Some of the most illustrative examples of the obstacles encountered by the dukes to impose punishments can be found in accounts of those who ruled over the Silesian duchies.

Such examples survive in accounts of Bolesław III's great-grandson, Henry the Bearded (r. 1201–1238), a representative of the early generation of dukes in divided Poland. Henry was known for his efforts to strengthen the foundations of his power both by vigilantly preventing the dominance of knightly families and by enforcing the jurisdictions resulting from the *regalia*.[36] The sources that shed light on his rule reveal the limitations on his ability to carry out capital punishment, although they sometimes highlight his firm attitude towards criminals.[37] For example, the *vita* of his wife, St. Hedwig of Andechs (d. 1243), suggests that she cultivated the "institution" noted already by Gallus that bestowed the grace of the monarch through the intercession of his wife. *Vita S. Hedvigis* describes this in a manner consistent with the convention of hagiographic sources, emphasizing the image of Hedwig as a merciful guardian of the weak in the story of a priest accused of sacrilege and saved from death, and that of a thief guilty of petty theft.[38] In this source, however, there is a much more interesting story about a noble or knight called "facinorosus" [criminal] and "publicus hostis ducis et terre adversarius" [the public enemy of the duke and homeland's adversary], meaning that he must have committed serious treason or a crime against public order. The similarity of the situation to that noted by Gallus is conspicuous, as is the similar lack of internal

36 Gawlas, *O kształt*, 81–83.

37 Following lost evidence, late medieval sources attribute obstinacy against criminals to him: *Ioannis Dlugossii Annales*, 280–81: "rem publicam provide ordinavit, leges, quibus humana audacia coherceretur, instituit et conscripsit, ... pestiferum genus hominum, videlicet maleficos et calumniators exterminavit"; *Annales Silesiaci compilati*, ed. Mieczysław Błażowski, Monumenta Poloniae Historica 3 (Lviv: Akademia Umiejętności, 1878), 677.

38 *Vita sanctae Hedwigis ducissae Silesiae*, ed. Aleksander Semkowicz, Monumenta Poloniae Historica 4 (Lviv: Akademia Umiejętności, 1885), 501–655 at 548 and 555. See also: Maciej Michalski, *Kobiety i świętość w żywotach trzynastowiecznych księżnych polskich* (Poznań: Wydawnictwo Poznańskie, 2004), 220.

consistency resulting from excessive idealization—albeit this time of the duke's wife, rather than the duke himself.

On the one hand, this account of the *Vita*, also known from the middle fourteenth-century illuminated version in *Codex of Lubin* [**Figures 8.1–8.2**], illustrates the ruler passing the sentence quickly and clandestinely carrying it out, highlighting his resolute determination to execute the offender. On the other hand, the duchess, without any fear, dares to release the villain, who, taken off the gallows, turns out to be alive despite the hours he spent with the loop tightened around his neck. However, it is important to note that the narrative does not provide any counterbalance to the potential loss of the duke's authority resulting from nullifying the ducal sentence. It does not underline Duke Henry's greatness, magnanimity, or prudence, as Gallus Anonymus does by emphasizing the advantages of Bolesław the Brave pardoning noble prisoners condemned to death. In this case, everything is explained by the holiness of St. Hedwig, who commutes a sentence against the ducal will. In the whole scenario, the duke has nothing to say, but he must acknowledge his holy wife's wish and hand the condemned over to her. Moreover, the source stresses the customary nature of that action in passing words spoken by the duke to his wife: "istum ut aliud tibi dono" ["I give him to you, as I have given others"].[39]

The *Henryków Book* is another source that illustrates the various challenges the Silesian duke encountered when attempting to administer ultimate justice.[40] Despite holding Duke Henry in high regard as both a benefactor of the monastery and a ruler, the author of the chronicle's first book, Abbot Peter, depicts a reality in which royal justice did not play a major role. Abbot Peter makes it clear that the ruler's authority was of little importance to the inhabitants of the Henryków region and this part of Polish–Bohemian borderland. This is evident not only in the fact that everyone was competing, but also in the omnipresent violence manifested by countless acts of rape, theft, seizure of goods, and fights, as well as aspirations among the stronger knights to subjugate the weaker ones, forcing their service and loyalty.[41] The story of the knights from Piotrowice illustrates the duke's powerlessness to enforce justice: "De istorum violentia et malignitate" [Of their violence, and malice], writes

39 *Vita sanctae Hedwigis*, 555–56.

40 On this source, see in particular Piotr Górecki, *The Text and the World: The 'Henryków Book', Its Authors, and Their Region, 1160–1310* (Oxford: Oxford University Press, 2015).

41 The problem of violence in the Henryków region is discussed in more detail by Piotr Górecki, "Violence and the Social Order in a Medieval Society: The Evidence from the Henryków Region, ca.1150–ca.1300," in *'The man of many devices, who wandered full many ways': Festschrift in Honour of János M. Bak*, ed. Balazs Nagy and Marcell Sebők (Budapest: Central European University Press, 1999), 91–104.

FIGURE 8.1 Leaf from illuminated *Vitae beatae Hedwigis, Codex of Lubin* (1353), Getty Library, Ms. Ludwig XI 7 (83.MN.126), fol. 64v. Saint Hedwig asking for the life of a man condemned to be hanged
DIGITAL IMAGE COURTESY OF THE GETTY'S OPEN CONTENT PROGRAM

FIGURE 8.2 Leaf from illuminated *Vitae beatae Hedwigis, Codex of Lubin* (1353), Getty Library, Ms. Ludwig XI 7 (83.MN.126). Saint Hedwig rescuing a man from hanging
DIGITAL IMAGE COURTESY OF THE GETTY'S OPEN CONTENT PROGRAM

Abbot Peter, "esset multum dicendum" [one would have a lot to say]. They, he continues,

> in nemore illo latitabant quasi quidam latrunculi et rarissime vel nunquam coram antiquis ducibus apparebant. Unde exercuerunt in pauperes circumsedentes pro placito suo violentiam sicut voluerunt. Et sciendum, quod dux antiquus cognomine Barbatus non poterat in illis silvis diebus suis propter eorum violentiam aliquam villam locare.
>
> [hid in the wilderness as if some scoundrels, and very rarely or never did they show up in front of the old dukes. So they robbed and looted the poor people in the neighborhood as much as they wanted. And one should know that the late Duke [Henry] with the nickname Bearded could not establish any village in these forests in his days because of their violence.][42]

This description is a classic example of what the sources name *latrocinium*, *spolium*, and *violentia*, i.e. public crimes that demanded a severe judgment by the monarch. Yet, according to the accounts, none of these acts were punished in any way because the prince proved helpless against the knights.

This situation in the area of Henryków seems to have been norm in the first half of the thirteenth century and did not change quickly. The *Henryków Book* explains that in the following years knights did not even respect the *regalia* of dukes; after the 1241 Mongol invasion, under the reign of Henry the Bearded's grandson, Bolesław II Rogatka (r. 1241–1278), it was social practice or custom, not the will of the ruler, that determined the justice system. If the duke wanted to establish order, he did it reluctantly and without imposing any penalties, let alone ultimate ones. He also relied on mediation between the parties and was forced to tolerate a state in which the intermediary agreements remained the letter of the law. This reality only began to change in the late thirteenth century. Starting in the 1270s, the author of the second book, also named Peter, registers the slow but steady progress in establishing the duke's justice system in these regions. This chronicle attributes more information about the death and exile sentences to Henry IV Probus (r. 1270–1290), also known from other sources for building his authority by executing harsh punishments.[43] The author of the

42 *'Liber fundationis Claustri Sancte Marie Virginis in Heinrichow' czyli Księga Henrykowska*, ed. Roman Grodecki, 2nd ed. (Wrocław: Muzeum Archidiecezjalne, 1991), 139, 144–45.

43 See, e.g.: *Schlesisches Urkundenbuch V: 1282–1290*, ed. Winfried Irgang (Cologne: Böhlau, 1993), no. 183.150 and 151, no. 192.158, and no. 287.226.

second book asserts that Bolko I the Strict (r. 1291–1301) willingly reached for the death penalty—and celebrates him as *dux christianissimus* for doing so.[44]

In the *Henryków Book*, the antithesis of rulers like Bolko I is represented by the portrayal of Bolesław Rogatka, characterized as an ineffectual ruler lacking authority. The text describes him as a ruler who engaged in frivolous and foolish tricks, displaying a greater inclination for games and tournament participation than for the responsibilities of governing and dispensing justice.[45] The chronicler's critical view aligns with the popular opinion of his contemporaries. Peter of Byczyna, the author of the fourteenth-century *Chronica principum Poloniae,* offers different information with a similar general message.[46] He supplements this widely held notion with an intriguing, albeit circumstantial story, of Bolesław's inefficient administration of death sentence. According to chronicler, one day in Legnica, Bolesław was to sentence someone accused of some "evil deed" (*flagitium*) to death by beheading. The duke's justiciars, however, secretly arrange for his release nullifying the ducal sentence. But destiny wants the duke, who later visited Złotoryja (Goldberg), to notice the one he thought had been beheaded, mining gold and busy carrying the excavated material. Baffled, he asks his officials if this was indeed the same man he had ordered to be executed. According to Peter, these officials, seemingly unfazed, explained that the man must have miraculously risen from the dead. To add a touch of humor, the chronicler continues that the duke indeed took this explanation seriously. However, the duke's subjects, finding the entire situation rather absurd, coined a saying "si quisquam foret decollandus sibi in nullo nocere, cum et ipse, qui decollatur, in Aureo Monte possit thynam portare" [if someone was sentenced to be beheaded but wanted to avoid any harm, he should carry buckets in Złotoryja together with the decapitated man] (498). Although this story is an anecdote, the monarch's subjects perceived the inappropriate execution of the death sentence as an assessment of the monarch who they joked about as an ineffective justiciar. This tale offers a unique

44 See: Górecki, "Violence and Social Order," 98; Marek Cetwiński, "Przestępcy i sprawiedliwość w 'Księdze Henrykowskiej,'" in *Kultura prawna w Europie Środkowej*, ed. Antoni Barciak (Katowice: Instytut Górnośląski, 2006), 300–7.

45 *'Liber fundationis'*, 129–30, 142.

46 *Chronica principum Poloniae*, ed. Zygmunt Węclewski, Monumenta Poloniae Historica 3 (Lviv: Akademia Umiejętności, 1878), 491. Hereafter page numbers are given in parentheses. For more on this author's view, see: Roman Heck, "Akcenty społeczne i moralizatorskie w 'Kronice książąt polskich,'" in *'Cultus et cognitio'. Studia z dziejów średniowiecznej kultury*, ed. Stefan K. Kuczyński (Warsaw: Państwowe Wydawnictwo Naukowe, 1976), 181–92 at 186–87.

opportunity to witness the socially negative perception of a ruler who was unable to competently oversee and execute the process of capital punishment.

The *Chronica principum Poloniae* by Peter of Byczyna tells yet another noteworthy story, shedding light on the perception of exercising ultimate judiciary in the context of ducal authority. While largely a fictional story, it is much more substantive than the previous one, referring to specific events and, as Marek Cetwiński emphasizes, showing the complicated world of the ruler's relations with his subjects from the viewpoint of psychological and sociological truth.[47] The central character in this account is Henry V the Fat (r. 1273–1296), the son of Bolesław Rogatka and the brother of Bolko I the Strict, who belonged to the generation of the Silesian Piasts that adopted a more resolute approach to dealing with criminals and did not shy away from imposing sentences of death or banishment combined with confiscating property.

Peter of Byczyna describes the events as follows. Duke Henry has a mighty advisor, Pakosław, whose counsel he greatly values. One day, Pakosław kills another nobleman who has many friends. These friends swiftly appear at the ducal court, demanding justice for the murder. Having listened to their demands, the duke becomes "very confused and sad" (*valde territus et turbatus*), and yet, pressured, he promises justice (503). However, the story indicates that the duke does not want to punish his knight with severity. Instead, he makes an effort to save him, urging Pakosław to try to reconcile with his enemies. But Pakosław does not want to hear anything like that and

> [i]lle autem, de deviciis et amicis confisus presumensque de ducis gracia, ampullose respondit: bene audio, nolo negare, quod feci. Dux autem dixit: vade, interloquaris cum tuis amicis et aliter respondeas; nisi enim aliter responderis, faciam iusticiam, quam oportet. Receptis itaque amicis, ad partem cum eis consiliatus est, quid respondeat adversariis pro fienda iusticia clamantibus ex adverso. (503)
>
> [thanks to his riches and friends, he trusted in the duke's support, so he answered harshly: "You heard well, I do not deny what happened." The duke replied: "Go, talk to your friends, and answer differently, for if you give no other answer, there will be justice as usual." Coming to his friends, he partly listened to their counsel as to what he ought to say to the opponents who had filed a complaint for justice against him.]

---

47 Marek Cetwiński, "Porwanie Henryka Grubego. Próba interpretacji," in *Genealogia—władza i społeczeństwo w Polsce średniowiecznej*, ed. Andrzej Radzimiński (Toruń: Wydawnictwo Uniwersytetu Mikołaja Kopernika, 1999), 276–89 at 278.

However, when Pakosław returns to the duke,

> maioru quam prius arrogancia respondebat, se fecisse homicidium, publice confitendo. Dux igitur magis turbatus dixit: valde stulte respondes; habeas adhuc tercio bonam interlocutoriam et melius deliberes ...; sagaciter ergo tibi provideas sapienciusque respondeas, quod si neglexeris, faciam quod oportet. Propter quo habito consilio cum amicis, non negando sed confitendo crimen, sicut prius arroganter respondit, non metuens ducis sentenciam. (503)
>
> [with even greater insolence than before, he replied that he had committed homicide, admitting this publicly. The duke, very agitated, said: "Go, prepare the answer; talk for the third time and think about it ...; find with patience the correct answer against the complainants." Then again [Pakosław] advised his friends, not denying, but confessing the crime, and as before he responded boldly, not fearing the duke's sentence.]

Peter of Byczyna reveals the behind-the-scenes actions meant to prevent the noble and powerful knight from being sentenced to death by the duke. Therefore, the duke demands Pakosław mitigate his attitude and pays appropriate compensation to the victim's relatives. Thus, Duke Henry chooses a method, which, according to the *Henryków Book*, his father used earlier. He does not administer justice out of hand, but prefers the way of customary law and compromise. Yet, the duke cannot indefinitely test his own authority. When Pakosław rejects the duke's advice for the third time, Henry finally decides to sentence him. Peter constantly stresses that Pakosław's cocky attitude leaves the ruler no choice:

> Pronunciavit enim dux et dixit in hunc modum sentenciam: ex quo te hoc crimen fecisse fateris post tantam deliberacionem, iusticiam facere me oportet. Mandavit igitur eum duci de gradu et in castri medio omnibus decollari. (503–4)
>
> [The duke proclaimed it to him and thus announced the sentence: "For the fact that you do not deny committing the crime even after reflection, I administer justice as it should be." Therefore [the duke] ordered that [Pakosław] be placed on the step and beheaded in the middle of the castle [courtyard] in front of all [gathered people].][48]

48 The term *gradus*, which in the story denotes a step or stair situated "in the middle of the castle," can plausibly be interpreted as an elevated platform designed for executions—a

However, this is not the end of the story. Peter of Byczyna goes on immediately to the matters initiated by the beheading of Pakosław. The convict's son Lutko, about eighteen or twenty years old who also served the duke, witnessed all these events and is in great pain over his father's fate. He immediately becomes a matter of concern for the duke's advisors, who attempt to persuade Henry to expel him from service to prevent him from avenging his father. The duke decides not to take their advice, but in the presence of his counselors and other prominent figures of his duchy, he addresses the young man, saying:

> tu scis, vidisti et audisti, quomodo pater tuus vitam suam perdidit sua sponte propter magnam eius arroganciam, quoque me facere ideo iusticiam oportebat, nunc elige tibi quod vis, aut patris mortem patienter transeas, sic eciam quod nec aliquid rancoris in corde contineas, aut recedas a nobis. (504)
>
> [You know, and you saw, and you heard how your father lost his life voluntarily because of his great arrogance, how I had to do justice to him. I am now giving it to you under consideration, patiently endure your father's death, not holding any grudge against me in your heart, or leave us.]

According to Peter of Byczyna, it turns out that Duke Henry and his courtiers considered banishing Lutko as a man closely associated with the condemned Pakosław. But Duke Henry, giving priority to the rules of love, is said to have ultimately decided to keep his knight at his side. We are told, he achieves this goal when, after being given some time for reflection, Lutko and his friends come to the duke, bent in half, weeping, and giving a guarantee that Lutko will not grieve for his father in word or deed. He solemnly promises the duke that he will serve him faithfully. Seeing this, in tears, the duke announces to Lutko:

> nunc ego ero pater tuus et benefaciam tibi, ut omnes amici tui habeant mihi referre graciarum merito acciones. Suscipiens igitur ipsum, eum in specialem ministrum ad summum eius consilium evocavit, dans sibi plurima et ceteris eum preferens quibuscunque, et pluribus annis fuit in ducis obsequio, tanquam ille, de quo peramplius presumebat. (504)

---

stepped podium or gallows, where sentences of death were carried out. On such stepped structures used for capital or corporeal punishment, usually situated in the center of public spaces like assembly places, squares, or markets, in Slavic countries, see: Jacek Banaszkiewicz, "'Pons mercati', 'gradus lignei', 'stepen' i inne. Uwagi o znaku władzy i prawa słowiańskich miejsc wiecowych," *Annales Universitatis Mariae Curie-Skłodowska. Sectio F* 45 (1990): 79–89, rprt. in Jacek Banaszkiewicz, *W stronę rytuałów i Galla Anonima* (Kraków: Avalon, 2018), 13–27.

> ["from now on I am your father and your benefactor, and all your friends will be able to speak of my goodness." He elevated him, called him as a special servant to his main council and, preferring him before many others. [This way] Lutko served the duke for many years as the one about whom the duke was especially concerned.]

In the long run, however, the duke's decision to keep Pakosław's son at court leads to Henry's personal tragedy, which Peter meticulously describes in his chronicle. The aforementioned Duke of Głogów, Henry III, who competed with Henry V the Fat, ultimately succeeds in winning Lutko to his side. As a result, Lutko betrays his master and not only leaves his court but, bribed and incited by his new master to take vengeance, dares to kidnap Henry and hands him over to the Duke of Głogów as a prisoner. In this way, Lutko brings tragedy to his former master for taking his father's life because, according to the chronicler, Henry spends the next six months in a terrible prison. Allegedly, the duke was locked in a special chest, with an iron grate through which he could breathe and receive food, while another, similarly well-protected opening, was left for him to defecate through. Also, a mass of vermin was said to have crawled around his thighs and back, especially since he could not stand, sit, or even lie down in such a confined space (505–6).

Regardless of the credibility of all details of the chronicle account, this example shows like no other that there was a great deal of risk involved to the Piasts in enforcing death sentences on high-born knights who had political influence; after their death they had relatives and friends who were ready to challenge the ruler's authority in the name of the honor of the family and group. As a result, it is easier to understand the *Kraków Cathedral Chronicle*'s message praising the greatness of Casimir the Great by saying that the king, despite sentencing many noble and wealthy people to death for committed crimes, was not afraid to eat, drink, and even sleep with their relatives. However, that such a motif appears in the apologetic description of the king written down by a well-informed observer, suggests that even the royal court of the most powerful Piast was not entirely free from the fears of the lesser Silesian duke's court.

In this context, the relationship between carrying out the death penalty and the monarch's authority in Piast Poland are at least ambiguous and certainly complex. On the one hand, it was important for a monarch to create the picture of a strict and powerful ruler who makes use of his prerogatives of the *regalia* and shows criminals no mercy, even those of knightly and noble origin. Such a picture became increasingly popular in the thirteenth century, reaching its climax in the fourteenth century, especially during the reign of Casimir the

Great. It may be assumed that this process proceeded in line with the institutionalization of ducal power as the rules of *Territorialmacht* were assimilated from Germany and the West along with the principles of Roman Law. However, early manifestations of this phenomenon may already be seen in Gallus's portrait of Bolesław the Brave sentencing barons and *comites* to death for various crimes. It should be noted, however, that in his narrative Gallus still favors penance over the death penalty as an appropriate ruler's punishment for criminals, typical of the early medieval model of a ruler responsible for the salvation of his subjects' souls. Only later sources ignore this problem with symptomatic silence, exposing instead the ideal of a ruler severe in punishing, and testifying to the changes in the perception of a ruler's power and position.

There is no doubt that the model of a strict ruler influenced public opinion so strongly that the quality of the rule and authority of individual Piasts were assessed from this viewpoint. This ideal also influenced the rulers themselves, who made efforts to meet social expectations and thus strengthen the foundations of their authority in practical terms. At the same time, however, the analyzed sources show that the imposition of the death penalty caused many difficulties, which constituted a kind of test of the ruler and his authority. The sources clarify the problems with levying the death penalty against knighthood, especially the representatives of politically engaged nobility. This challenge does not seem to have been overcome until the end of the Piast era, because even the reign of Casimir the Great, a ruler of exceptional authority compared to his predecessors, faced similar obstacles. Apart from the model ruler who severely punished the villains, there was still another model that built the monarch's relationship with the knighthood on the partnership principle. The latter should potentially be dated to the period until the early twelfth century, the times before the modernization of power according to patterns of *Territorialmacht*, when the ruler's position was to a great degree based on mutual care, love, and brotherhood with his warrior retinue.[49] The *Chronica principum Poloniae*, illustrates the continuity of this social norm in its depiction of the relationship between Henry V and Pakosław as similar to the

49 On mutual friendship as a central idea of the relationship between a ruler and his warriors in early medieval Slavic countries, see: Paweł Żmudzki, *Władca i wojownicy. Narracje o wodzach, drużynie i wojnach w najdawniejszej historiografii Polski i Rusi* (Wrocław: Wydawnictwo Uniwersytetu Wrocławskiego, 2009), 159–60, 330–81, 400. For broader northern European perspective, compare with Lars Hermanson, *Friendship, Love, and Brotherhood in Medieval Northern Europe, c. 1000–1200* (Leiden: Brill, 2019), 78–79, 150–63. There is no consensus on when the institution of the ruler's *druzhina* disappeared in Poland. It can be assumed that it still existed, at least in a rudimentary form, under Bolesław III in the early twelfth century.

relationship between the monarch and wealthy knights two and a half centuries earlier by Gallus Anonymus, who expected the monarch to correct the nobles in his goodness, as is appropriate for a merciful father. In Peter of Byczyna's account, this is exactly how Henry v treats Pakosław by trying to do everything to avoid execution. There is a relationship between the duke and the noble, best reflected in the alleged duke's words addressed to Pakosław's son, Lutko, when he prostrates himself in front of the duke: "nunc ego ero pater tuus et benefaciam tibi" [from now on, I am your father and your benefactor] (504).

However, this relation was not solely shaped by ideological factors. Knighthood and nobility, especially when Poland was divided into numerous principalities, was a social group with its own political agenda, which every ruler had to take into account. In such conditions, the death sentence against a nobleman did not seem obvious, it was rather the last possible option. The ruler, caring for his authority, often had to face the dilemma of whether he would gain more by raising fear, creating a harsh image or by arousing love, by presenting a gentle face. Under such conditions, performing end-game punishment required from rulers a great deal of caution and prudence.

These surviving sources shed light on a tool that may have eased the monarchs' predicaments in this context: banishment. They reveal that exile emerged as an alternative to the death penalty, providing a less severe form of punishment that allowed rulers to preserve their authority without resorting to irreversible measures. As revealed by Gallus, this punishment equaled death for the wrongdoer, because it banished them from the community in which they resided and from the monarch's favor and love. However, the use of exile signaled a shift towards a more lenient approach to justice.

It is plausible that weaker rulers opted for exile instead of the death penalty more frequently than the mighty ones. However, the strength of the ruler was not the sole determining factor in choosing between these two options. Paradoxically, during the reign of Casimir the Great, a ruler of exceptional authority, knights actively avoided the monarch's justice by voluntarily undergoing exile, with the possibility of reintegration into royal favor through the mediation of friends. Exile, therefore, was a tool that had a tendency to evolve into a social custom over which the ruler did not have complete control, potentially undermining the monarch's authority.

CHAPTER 9

Nostalgia in Medieval English Narratives of Outlaws, Exiles, and Execution

Larissa Tracy

In medieval society, especially England, exile, execution, and outlawry were closely connected. Exile could be a product of law, as with formal banishment, or a function of extra-judicial coercion, with or without actual threats, where individuals were sent away against their will.[1] Some went into exile of their own volition, choosing absence rather than confronting political or social difficulties at home.[2] Some were lawless; others were victims of the law—as the variety of medieval exile and outlaw narratives attests. Exile could result from a sentence of outlawry; outlawry could become a form of exile. Both could result in execution, either within the legal apparatus or outside it.

Later medieval outlawry echoed older traditions of exile in pre-Conquest England, when banishment was a mode of adjudicating and punishing participants in blood feuds as an alternative to capital punishment. However, as with earlier forms of exile, outlawry in the fourteenth century left the subject vulnerable to vigilante violence; he could be killed with impunity—extra-judicial execution—without his murderers ever facing legal consequences. According to Timothy Jones, "Without access to the king's justice, his property, his legal contracts, his friends and relatives, or feudal associations, the outlawed man was at the mercy of enemies who had every incentive to kill him."[3] While Jones sees exile and outlawry as separate concepts, they share the same severance from society and community and the same threat of execution if the exile or outlaw returns. They are intimately connected. Narratives of valiant exiles and stalwart outlaws, especially those set in a murky past or a vaguely identifiable present like the *Gest of Robyn Hode* (*c.*1450?) and *Robin Hood and Guy of Gisborne*, were exceptionally popular. They evoke a sense of nostalgia—a longing for a simpler, more idealistic past or place, often rooted in criticism of the present. In each text, the exile employs execution—killing for the love of

1 C.P. Lewis, "Gruffudd ap Cynan and the Reality and Representation of Exile," in *Exile in the Middle Ages* (Turnhout: Brepols, 2004), 39–51.

2 Lewis, "Gruffudd ap Cynan," 39.

3 Timothy S. Jones, *Outlawry in Medieval Literature* (New York: Palgrave, 2010), 39.

 | DOI:10.1163/9789004742598_011

justice—as a means of restoring orthodox authority structures and enacting sanctioned violence against their enemies. By expressing the need for outlaws to literally take the law into their own hands by executing corrupt officials, these narratives criticize the failure of the medieval English political system to enact justice fairly, disrupting the nostalgia the exile should have for their home.

The Gest of Robyn Hode [hereafter *Gest*] and *Robin Hood and Guy of Gisborne* [hereafter *Guy of Gisborne*] nostalgically recall a time when the outlaw Robin Hood—an exile from lawful society with a traditional sense of justice and loyalty—could prevail. In the *Gest* and *Guy of Gisborne*, the exiled outlaw does not experience nostalgia himself but rather inspires the audience to reflect on this time and space as simpler or more ideal by evoking legal structures that have been overturned by corruption. The poet expresses nostalgia for a fictional past governed by a sense of law, order, and justice where the outlaw can remain a loyal subject of the king but fall outside the purview of royal justice because of lower-level internal corruption. Nostalgia restores a sense of community and criticizes instances when the present nation does not live up to its past. As Renée Trilling explains in relation to Old English poetry, "Nostalgia, which paradoxically affirms the past (and very often a fictional past at that) by reconstituting the story of its passing, is primarily concerned with the present."[4] In the ballads, too, the authors pick at contemporary discontent by portraying past heroic figures as living in or representing a better time.

The *Gest* is the longest and most intricate of these ballads, separated into eight fittes; it is either a compilation of extant ballads or a reworking of the known materials of the tradition.[5] Thomas Ohlgren writes that the *Gest* was very likely composed or compiled during the reigns of Henry V (r. 1413–1422) or Henry VI (r. 1422–1461/1470–1471), but he convincingly argues that the "historical time of the various social, cultural, and economic practices—bastard feudalism, livery and maintenance, archery and forest law, and the emergence of mercantilism—belongs instead to the early decades of the reign of Edward III."[6] Stephen Knight writes that the *Gest* projects the myth of Robin Hood onto a "larger screen, linking together in one sequence the forces of authority that are held to be oppressive: church, local government, towns and,

---

4 Renée Trilling, *The Aesthetics of Nostalgia: Historical Representation in Old English Verse* (Toronto: University of Toronto Press, 2009), 4.

5 Stephen Knight, *Robin Hood: A Complete Study of the English Outlaw* (Oxford: Blackwell, 1994), 75.

6 Thomas H. Ohlgren, "Edwardus redivivus in *A Gest of Robyn Hode*," *The Journal of English and Germanic Philology* 99:1 (Jan. 2000): 1–28 at 2.

here at least, their national focus at the royal level in city and court, though not precisely in the person of the king."[7] The tale merges "the social ranks of knights with sturdy yeoman and places issues of law and justice firmly in the foreground."[8] In these texts, the law plays a central role in the sentence of exile or execution, just or unjust, and in the community to which the exile longs to return or wishes to establish. The *Gest* envisions an England governed by good laws before the current climate of corruption or usurpation. *Guy of Gisborne* captures one moment of Robin's exile and the extrajudicial execution of the corrupt officials who hunt the outlaws, where Robin and Little John act in self-defense. In the *Gest*, the good king (Edward, probably Edward III) is on the throne, and it is the Church and petty civil administrators who exploit the people. Robin, in his forest exile, seeks to redress the wrongs done to members of the fighting class by nefarious members of the praying class, who *prey* on those whose fortunes have fallen. Here an honorable knight, Sir Richard Lee, seeks to free his son who has been unjustly judged for unintentionally killing his opponent and his opponent's squire in a tournament (*Gest* 209–212).[9] He is being held for ransom by the Abbot of St. Mary's, whose only interest is taking Sir Richard's land in collusion with the chief justice of England and the Sheriff of Nottingham (*Gest* 213–216). Secular law and canon law conspire to deprive the nobility of their rights, but the outlaw restores them and exacts a fitting punishment.

In a sense, however, the outlaw usurps the king's authority to restore justice to his realm that, ironically, manifests in public displays of legitimate execution. *On the Laws and Customs of England* [hereafter *Bracton*] (*c*.1240s–1250s), attributed to Henry Bracton, outlines the validity of killing when "proper legal procedures" have been observed or when the killing is "unavoidable" (2:340.25–34; 2:341.1–2).[10] Exile narratives frequently feature violent justice that must be enacted outside the regular avenues of law because the agents

7 Knight, *Robin Hood: A Complete Study*, 80.

8 Richard Kaeuper, *Chivalry and Violence in Medieval Europe* (Oxford: Oxford University Press, 1999), 113.

9 *Gest of Robyn Hode*, in *Robin Hood and Other Outlaw Tales*, ed. Stephen Knight and Thomas Ohlgren, *TEAMS Middle English Texts Series* (Kalamazoo, MI: Western Michigan University Press, 2000), 80–168. All quotations from the Robin Hood ballads are from this edition. Line numbers are given in parentheses.

10 The Latin text and English translation of *Bracton* are from Bracton Online: *Bracton: De Legibus Et Consuetudinibus Angliæ* (*Bracton on the Laws and Customs of England attributed to Henry of Bratton, c. 1210–1268*), reproduced from the dual language critical edition by Samuel Thorne, with the Latin text of George Woodbine, 4 vols (Cambridge: Harvard University Press, 1977): http://bracton.law.harvard.edu/Framed/mframe.htm, 2:378. Accessed: 20 May 2016. Hereafter, page and line numbers are given parentheses.

of the legal system itself are corrupt. The need for cruel executions performed by the outlawed hero problematizes the idea of this time as one that is *better* than the present, offering a mirror image against which medieval audiences could evaluate the current moment. Exile and execution operate in tandem in these narratives, much as they did in later medieval English society, by creating a troubling contradiction between heroism and the law. Heroes exiled by corrupt legal authorities must engage in unheroically brutal—even lawless—violence to reinstate or correct the legal structures.

In the *Gest*, Robin and his men detain the impoverished Sir Richard and aid him in recovering his fortune. Thinking the knight is away at war (possibly on the Continent in one of Edward III's campaigns), the abbot calls in the debt a few hours early. Robin stands surety for Sir Richard, is not only repaid, but makes a profit, teaching the over-worldly abbot a serious lesson in piety and poverty. The king gets involved personally—even joining the outlaw band for a raucous outing in Nottingham, and after a series of disguises and subterfuges, which leave the Sheriff dead, the king asks Robin to come to court. Robin agrees, but only for as long as it pleases him; after that time, he tells the king he will come back to the forest to shoot deer, as has been his custom. The king only grants him leave to be gone seven days to visit the chapel of Mary Magdalene that he claims he keeps in the wood, but instead Robin stays in the forest for twenty-two years in self-imposed exile before being treacherously slain by the false Prioress of Kirklees, an abrupt ending to the tale. The last comment the *Gest* makes is that Robin is a "good outlawe, / And dyde pore men moch god" (1823–4). In the nostalgic world of the *Gest*, the king recognizes Robin's qualities and exonerates him, despite wanting to execute him early on. Here, the outlaw receives justice at the hands of the king, after suffering the injustice of his corrupt officials, and ultimately regains freedom in defying the king's orders. The exilic space of the forest becomes Robin's home, and in it, he can enact the idealistic qualities missing from the royal court.

Despite existing outside the law, Robin still operates within a specific royal jurisdiction. For Robin Hood, the forest is clearly that space envisioned by medieval law "in which the hunting of game was reserved for the king, so that forest could include woodland, open heaths, farmland and even villages."[11] The forest was a "gathering place for masterless men seeking a meager subsistence,

11 Fiona Beglane, "Deer in Medieval Ireland: Preliminary evidence from Kilteasheen, Co. Roscommon," in *Medieval Lough Cé: History, Archaeology, and Landscape*, ed. Thomas Finan (Dublin: Four Courts Press, 2010) 145–58 at 148–9. For more on the forest and early modern literature, see: Jeffery S. Theis, *Writing the Forest in Early Modern England: A Sylvan Pastoral Nation* (Pittsburgh, PA: Duquesne University Press, 2010).

for cottagers and squatters who sometimes enjoyed freedom of tenure as well as for outlaws and religious dissenters," but the distinction between "the lawless and lawful forest dweller was usually hard to draw."[12] The forest was securely the property and provenance of the king, but in the *Gest* the king must enter the forest on Robin's terms in order to find him and, having done so, embrace the outlaw life for at least a short time. Arguably, Robin Hood creates an exile court in the "grene wode tre" (*Gest* 1506) where he and his men, "yemen of this foreste" (*Gest* 1505) live "by our kyngesdere" (*Gest* 1507); however, Robin cannot abide the inherent corruption that dwells within the stone walls of castle and court, and consequentially places himself at risk of capture and execution. That possibility hangs over every one of the Robin Hood ballads, even the *Gest* with its jovial tone.

The *Gest* criticizes not only those who engage in malfeasance, but also the system that allows such corruption to fester, and the ways in which the processes of the law—including execution and exile as punishments—are abused by secular and religious officials who prey on good and honest people of all classes (particularly the gentry in the earlier ballads). Robin's outlaw status reinforces social hierarchies by maintaining the primacy of royal authority and elevating it above the mid-level corruption that seems to run rampant, especially in the *Gest* with the justices who are in the abbot's pocket and plot with him to disinherit Sir Richard (*Gest* 377–8). The Prior, a monk who ranks beneath him, rebukes the abbot: "'And ye be so light of your consyence, / Ye do to hym mochwronge'" (*Gest* 359–60). The abbot suggests that Sir Richard will be executed for failing to pay what he owes (365–368), implying that he can fix a trial to find this knight guilty of a capital crime—an excessive and unjust punishment for an honorable member of the gentry. The abbot's actions not only violate the spirit of English law stipulated in *Bracton*, but also the letter of Church law laid out in Canon 18 of the Fourth Lateran Council which prohibited clerics from presiding over capital cases or from shedding blood.[13]

12 Christopher Hill, *The World Turned Upside Down: Radical Ideas During the English Revolution* (Harmondsworth: Penguin, 1975), 43–56 qtd. in Peter Stallybrass, "'Drunk with the Cup of Liberty': Robin Hood, the Carnivalesque, and the Rhetoric of Violence in Early Modern England," in *The Violence of Representation: Literature and the History of Violence*, ed. Nancy Armstrong and Leonard Tennenhouse (London: Routledge, 1989), 45–76 at 57.

13 Canons of the Fourth Lateran Council: "§18. Clerics to Dissociate from Shedding Blood: No cleric may decree or pronounce a sentence involving the shedding of blood, or carry out a punishment involving the same, or be present when such punishment is carried out. If anyone, however, under cover of this statute, dares to inflict injury on churches or ecclesiastical persons, let him be restrained by ecclesiastical censure. A cleric may not write or dictate letters which require punishments involving the shedding of blood, in

The abbot and his cellar master are in cahoots, confident that they will succeed because "The justice of Englonde / The abbot there dyde holde. / The hye-justyce and many mo / Had take in to theyrhonde / Holy all the knyghtes det, / To put that knyght to wronge" (*Gest* 371–6). Richard pleads with the Sheriff of Nottingham for justice and gets none. Eventually, Richard tricks them into thinking he does not have the money and takes satisfaction in paying his debt, to their chagrin (*Gest* 437–496). When Robin captures fifty-two monks, including the high cellarer who participates in trying to fleece Sir Richard, Robin asks about their errand, and the cellarer reveals that he was going to London for a great meeting "to maners in this londe, / Too reken with our reves,/That have done mochwronge" (*Gest* 1014–1016). This highlights the pervasive corruption among the civil servants—the bailiffs—who are meant to uphold the king's justice honorably, and who, ironically, will be dealt with by members of the Church who are equally corrupt.[14]

Even though he maintains his loyalty to the king, Robin acts against the king's legal agents, like the Sheriff of Nottingham. In the third fitte, the Sheriff of Nottingham, impressed with Little John's archery abilities, offers him a job, that he takes for a year while vowing to be the worst servant *ever* (*Gest* 613–616). John sets about despoiling the Sheriff's pantry and his household, abusing the discourteous butler, and eating the Sheriff out of house and home (*Gest* 633–652). Just as the Sheriff colludes with the Abbot and the corrupt chief justice to despoil good knights like Sir Richard, so Robin and his men rob him. Little John entices the Sheriff into the woods to hunt a "green hart" (*Gest* 737–752), that is really Robin Hood. After feeding the Sheriff from his own stores on his own silver plate, Robin says he will spare the Sheriff's life. Robin invites the Sheriff to join them, saying he will teach him to be an outlaw within the year (*Gest* 793–796). The Sheriff protests that the exilic life of an outlaw is too hard: "'This is harder order,' sayde the sherief, / 'Than any ankir or frere; / For all the golde in mery Englonde / I wolde nat longe dwell her'" (*Gest* 789–792). He says he would rather Robin cut off his head than stay

the courts of princes this responsibility should be entrusted to laymen and not to clerics. Moreover no cleric may be put in command of mercenaries or crossbowmen or suchlike men of blood; nor may a subdeacon, deacon or priest practice the art of surgery, which involves cauterizing and making incisions; nor may anyone confer a rite of blessing or consecration on a purgation by ordeal of boiling or cold water or of the red-hot iron, saving nevertheless the previously promulgated prohibitions regarding single combats and duels." https://pages.uoregon.edu/dluebke/Witches442/FourthLateran1215.html. Accessed Feb. 21, 2024.

14 W.R. Jones, "Keeping the Peace: English Society, Local Government and the Commissions of 1341–44," *The American Journal of Legal History*, 18.4 (Oct. 1974): 307–20 at 307.

another night, and he would forgive Robin for it (*Gest* 799–800), foreshadowing his eventual execution at Robin's hands. Despite depicting moments of idyllic freedom in the forest, the *Gest* presents a realistic picture of the hardships of outlawry: living in discomfort exposed to the elements, and in dread of enemies and the fatal consequences of the legal system.[15]

The *Gest*-poet contrasts the fealty of Robin with the dishonor of the Sheriff who has no intention of honoring the various oaths he swears. For instance, the Sheriff swears that he will never plot to harm Robin or his men, and that he will always help Robin's men if they are in need (*Gest* 805–812). However, the Sheriff violates this oath, arranging an archery tournament and luring Robin out to the competition with the possibility of winning a silver and gold arrow. Robin suspects this might be a trap and takes precautions (*Gest* 1156–1160). Robin wins, but as he prepares to return to the Greenwood with his prize, the Sheriff's men call for his arrest, violating the Sheriff's earlier oath: "Wo worth the, treason!" sayd Robyn, / "Full evyl thou art to knowe" (*Gest* 1183–1184). In the barrage of arrows that follows, Little John is wounded and Much carries him to Sir Richard's castle, where all the outlaws find refuge in repayment for their kindness and generosity toward the knight. Thwarted and angry, the Sheriff besieges Sir Richard's castle (*Gest* 1265–1272), calling him a traitor for sheltering "the kynges enemys / Agaynst the lawe and right" (*Gest* 1275–1276). But Robin is not the king's enemy, and while the King tells the Sheriff that *he* will deal with Robin and Sir Richard personally (*Gest* 1299–1300), the Sheriff disobeys. Here, the Sheriff decides that *he* is the law rather than the king. Angered that Robin walks the Greenwood freely, the Sheriff imprisons Sir Richard against the king's express orders—again acting against royal decree. The Sheriff's repeated disobedience highlights a bigger problem: the king apparently *allows* the Sheriff to undermine his authority without rebuking him. Thus, Robin directs his conflict at the Sheriff, not the king, maintaining a nostalgic (if unwarranted) view of royal power and responsibility.

The Sheriff, corrupt and forsworn, eventually faces justice at Robin's hands but it should be at the king's, or at least upon his order. Robin goes to Nottingham vowing revenge (*Gest* 1369–1372), confronts the Sheriff (*Gest* 1373–1378), asks after the king (*Gest* 1379–1380), and kills the Sheriff with an arrow (*Gest* 1385–1392). Robin acts in the king's name, executing the Sheriff publicly and beheading his corpse in the street for violating his oath to Robin: "Lye thou there, thou proudesherife, / Evyll mote thou cheve! / There myght no man to the truste / The whyles thou were a lyve" (*Gest* 1393–1396). Even though the

15 Jones, *Outlawry*, 38.

law, as interpreted in *Bracton*, allows the Sheriff to kill in the "administration of justice," the poet is clear that he violates the spirit of the law—possibly because, as far as we know, Robin has not been "lawfully found guilty" of anything (*Bracton* 2:340.24–25). Historically, *Bracton* indicts officials who act "out of malice or from pleasure in the shedding of blood" (*Bracton* 2:340.25), so while the Sheriff lawfully pursues Robin in the *Gest*, his evil purpose condemns him. Also in line with *Bracton*, Robin acts justly in executing him. However, the absence of royal justice troubles the Sheriff's execution. In a way, even though Robin acts on behalf of the king, it really is not his place. Thus, the nostalgic enactment of outlaw justice criticizes the king's indifference to the corruption of his officials and the *need* for an outlaw to act in his stead.

After killing the Sheriff, Robin then frees Sir Richard, telling him to run into the Greenwood until he can secure for them the king's pardon. The need to flee royal justice was sometimes the by-product of the King's pardon: "Paradoxically, the prerogative which enabled the king to show excessive leniency to the guilty tended to perpetuate an extraordinarily harsh method of treating the innocent, the involuntary slayers, those involved in fatal accidents or who slew in defense of life, honour, or property."[16] These offenders needed the king's pardon but were not always aware of how to secure it, or, because it was a matter of grace, whether they needed it or whether it would actually be conceded.[17] As Naomi Hurnard explains, "Those who had contributed in some way to a death yet qualified for pardon were likely to flee and might never apply for it, so being outlawed and suffering punishment in this form."[18] This legal system may explain Robin Hood's status as an outlaw, which none of the ballads explicitly reveal. However, it is possible that Robin's first crime is poaching—the *Gest* suggests as much when the king surveys all the deer on his land and vows to capture Robin at any cost. The king arrives in Nottingham to "take that gentyll knight/ And Robyn Hode, and yf he may" (*Gest* 1415–1416). Inquiring after Robin, he seizes Richard's lands when the corrupt locals "tolde hym the case" (*Gest* 1421). The king, ill-advised and capable of the same violence as Robin Hood, swears that he wants to see Robin and offers the lands of Sir Richard to anyone who brings him Richard's head. But an older knight warns the king that Robin will never allow a knight to be treated in such a manner (*Gest* 1433–1456). While the king does have the authority to order Richard's death and demand his head, his intemperate response borders on

16 Naomi Hurnard, *The King's Pardon for Homicide before AD 1307* (Oxford: Clarendon Press, 1969), viii.

17 Hurnard, *The King's Pardon*, viii.

18 Hurnard, *The King's Pardon*, viii.

petty vengeance. Here the exiled outlaw, facing the possibility of execution, still manages to uphold the *spirit* of the law, if not the *letter* of it. The poet evokes a sense of nostalgia for a fictional time when an intemperate king could be swayed into righteousness by the actions of one person, even one exiled from the legal community.

However, the poet's nostalgia has its limits. The king recognizes the corruption of his own officials, but he takes no responsibility for the state of government affairs. Dressed as an abbot, the king enters the forest with his "monks," and they meet Robin, who proceeds to try and relieve him of his wealth, thinking the king to be a corrupt churchman who has "chyrches and rentes both/ And gold full greteplenté" (*Gest* 1509–10). The king honestly tells Robin how much he is carrying, and Robin splits the forty pounds, giving half to his men and returning the other half to the "abbot" (*Gest* 1513–1531). When the disguised king presents the royal seal, "Robyn coud his courteysy, / And set hym on his kne. / 'I love no man in all the worlde / So well as I do my kynge; / Welcome is my lordesseale'" (*Gest* 1539–43). Robin's response to the royal seal in the *Gest* is the most important sign of his feelings toward king and law. Meetings between unrecognized kings and their subjects are a frequent trope in English ballads, owing their popularity to a "persistent illusion that the king, as the beneficent fount of justice, would right the people's wrongs if only he knew of them."[19]

The *Gest* implies a certain proximity of Sherwood to the king: the Sheriff reports to him directly, and the king is certainly mobile since he picks up and moves to Nottingham to wait six months for Robin's capture. Christine Chism points out that the "localization of law enforcement also strengthened the connections between these officials and the central authority they represented, thereby making the king much more aware of how his representatives were exercising his authority, and giving representatives improved prospects at the royal court, in parliament, and within judicial courts."[20] Of course, this would mean that the king is aware of the corruption among his administrators, despite Robin's unwavering loyalty. Even in his exiled state, Robin Hood functions as an agent of law; the ballads highlight the failings of the royal system that allows such corruption to flourish, criticizing the king who allows it or does not do enough to discover it and quash it.

---

19 Richard Helgerson, *Forms of Nationhood: The Elizabethan Writing of England* (Chicago: University of Chicago Press, 1992), 232.

20 Christine Chism, "Robin Hood: Thinking Globally, Acting Locally in the Fifteenth-Century Ballads," in *The Letter of the Law: Legal Practice and Literary Production in Medieval England*, ed. Emily Steiner and Candace Barrington (Cornell: Cornell University Press, 2002), 12–39 at 13.

Despite the apparent inequity in the system and the king's indifference to its failings, Robin's fealty to the king remains constant. To honor the "abbot" for his service to the king and his honesty, Robin prepares a feast (of the king's deer) and calls in all his men, who kneel before him (*Gest* 1549–1558). The king marvels to himself at the loyalty Robin Hood engenders (*Gest* 1559–1564)—a sign of Robin's honor and charisma but also an indictment of the king as an administrator. He judges Robin by the loyalty he inspires and the quality of his men while *his* own officials are foresworn, craven, greedy, and duplicitous. Robin's loyalty to the king does the king credit because of Robin's quality. Robin presents the king with a feast of fine aristocratic food, and then they hold an archery tournament; the penalty for losing is the forfeiture of all their gear and a "buffet" to the head (*Gest* 1569–1608). Robin wins consistently, but when he does lose, he will only accept the "buffet" from the "abbot" (*Gest* 1609–1620). At first the king refuses, but Robin insists, and the king clatters him on the head (*Gest* 1621–1630). The strength of the blow gives the king away. Robin recognizes his lord only then and pays him due deference: "Robyn beheld our comlykynge/ Wystly in the face, / So dyde Syr Rycharde at the Le, / And kneled downe in that place" (*Gest* 1637–40). The "wylde outlawes" (*Gest* 1641) also kneel before the king, who pardons them all on the condition that they come back with him to court in his service (*Gest* 1645–1658). In this idealistic moment, the exiled community of outlaws reintegrates into the fold because of their honor and loyalty to the legal structures embodied by the king and the king grants them pardons for simply obeying him.

However, the *Gest* proves that the king is willing to use the tactics of the outlaw for his own purposes, both in his treatment of Sir Richard and in his final escapade with Robin and his men. The king seals their deal and the pardons he grants them by buying cloth from Robin, clothing himself and his men in Robin's livery of Lincoln Green, and leading them all to Nottingham "outlawes as they were" (*Gest* 1692). The townspeople flee, fearing their king slain by the horde of outlaws and fearing that Robin means to kill them all—much to the amusement of the king, who laughs at their panic (*Gest* 1705–1720). The "outlaws" eat and drink, and the king fully reinstates Sir Richard. King Edward seeks out Robin, not the other way around; he plays a part, seeing himself as one with the people, mixing with the townsfolk, taking outlaws into his court, and ignoring their criminal deeds "for the sake of public approval and a sense of economic and social unity with the guildsmen."[21] The poem creates a nos-

21 Alexander L. Kaufman, "Nietzsche's Herd and the Individual: The Construction of Alterity in *A Lytell Geste of Robyn Hode*," in *Robin Hood in the Greenwood Stood: Alterity and Context in the English Outlaw Tradition*, ed. Stephen Knight (Turnhout: Brepols, 2011), 31–46 at 44.

talgic tableau of the king among loyal and faithful men, reveling in the brief freedom afforded him by the outlaw's exilic experience away from the corruption and injustice of his own court. As Barbara Hanawalt suggests, it is fitting for Robin Hood to be on equal footing with the king, but the ballads "stop short of a world turned upside down."[22] The *Gest* is infused with the desire to right injustices, but only those that threaten the stability of the existing order; it does not seek to replace that order with something new and more egalitarian.

Overall, the *Gest* creates a nostalgic picture of outlaw life—a fantasy of freedom and plenty in which the good guy always wins, and the king rewards his service and loyalty. Robin enters the king's service for fifteenth months, where he spends all his money on other knights and squires to establish a reputation for largesse that is not reciprocated by the king. This is another failure of this court, for courtiers—which Robin has now become—rely on the generosity and gifts of their sovereign.[23] In failing to repay Robin's generosity to everyone else, the king forces Robin—however unintentionally—back into exile. Broke and nostalgic for his past glory as "the best archere / That was in mery Englonde" (1747–8), he then retreats to the forest. When he leaves, he subverts the king's will by not returning after the allotted seven days, and so "For all drede of Edwarde our kynge, / Agayne wolde he not goo" (1799–1800). This implies that Robin's only outstanding crime is leaving the king's service without authorization. Robin may fear the king's anger, or perhaps his love; either way, he does not want to be called into service again, a request he obviously could not deny. Robin struggles to maintain his loyalty to the king, partly because of the king's neglect once he is at court, the same kind of neglect that leads to corruption and dissatisfaction within the ranks. He roams the Greenwood as an exile who finds freedom in his outlawry, who wishes to retain that freedom, and who, in that freedom, better serves the interests of the king by continuing to enforce the justice of forest law. In the end, Robin chooses voluntary exile to regain the freedom he knew as an outlaw, facing possible execution in the process for violating the king's will, which, despite the veneer of nostalgic idealism makes the exercise of law arbitrary and potentially unjust.

Guy of Gisborne also engages directly and extensively with the corruption of local officials through a particularly graphic scene of single combat to the

22 Barbara Hanawalt, "Ballads and Bandits: Fourteenth-Century Outlaws and the Robin Hood Poems," *Robin Hood: Anthology of Scholarship and Criticism*, ed. Stephen Knight (Cambridge: D.S. Brewer, 1999), 263–284 at 271.

23 Marie de France engages in similar criticism in her twelfth century *lai Lanval*, where King Arthur's neglect drives a loyal knight out of court and into the arms of a faery woman.

death in self-defense, as well as post-mortem decapitation and mutilation.[24] The ballad itself is relatively short at 234 lines (58 stanzas), so the body count (five total) and the scenes of mortal combat, mutilation, and homicide when Little John shoots the Sheriff of Nottingham in the back with an arrow, stand out. *Guy of Gisborne* begins with Robin relating a dream to Little John, who tells him not to fret because dreams are fleeting and should not be taken seriously. However, Robin decides that he must find the "two wight yeoman" (*Guy of Gisborne* 7) who assault him in his dream, taking his bow. He tells his men to prepare themselves and takes a reluctant John along with him. When they encounter a "wight yeoman" (*Guy of Gisborne* 25) leaning against a tree, wearing a dagger that "Had beene many a mans bane" (*Guy of Gisborne* 28) and a horse hide, complete with head, tail, and mane, John says Robin should stand aside and let him take on this stranger. Robin refuses, amazed that John would suggest that he sit out a fight. Swearing that if it would not break his bow, he would clatter John in the head, Robin and John part ways. When John arrives in Barnesdale, he finds two of his compatriots slain in a forest glade and Will Scarlett fleeing fast, pursued by the Sheriff of Nottingham and his men (*Guy of Gisborne* 45–54). John takes aim at the Sheriff, but his bow breaks and his arrow hits one William Trent, who better deserved "To hange upon a gallowe / Then for to lye in the greenwoode, / There slaine with an arrowe" (*Guy of Gisborne* 72–74). The Sheriff's men capture John and bind him to a tree. The Sheriff pronounces a sentence then and there, indicating that there will be no trial or court proceeding: "'Thou shalt be drawen by dale and downe,' quoth the sheriffe, / 'And hanged hye on a hill'" (*Guy of Gisborne* 79–80). The frequent references to hanging emphasize the very real threat of execution exiled outlaws face if captured by authorities who seem to have little interest in justice. This short ballad idealizes the outlaws who thwart the legal apparatus levied against them, creating a nostalgic episode where right triumphs over might.

Meanwhile, Robin and the stranger greet one another, and Guy of Gisborne (who has not yet been named) pretends to be another forester seeking Robin

---

24 The sole copy of *Guy of Gisborne* survives in the mid-seventeenth-century folio manuscript acquired by Thomas Percy, BL MS Add. 27879. Percy edited and published the poem as part of his collection, *Reliques of Ancient English Poetry*, 3 vols. (London: J. Dodsley, 1765). However, critics typically date the tale itself to either the late-fourteenth or the early-fifteenth centuries. See: Stephen Knight and Thomas Ohlgren, *Robin Hood and Other Outlaw Tales* (Kalamazoo, MI: Medieval Institute Publications, 2000), 169; and Richard Firth Green, "Violence in the Early Robin Hood Poems," in *'A Great Effusion of Blood'?: Interpreting Medieval Violence*, ed. Oren Falk, Daniel Thiery, and Mark Douglas Meyerson (Toronto: University of Toronto Press, 2004), 268–86 at 268. All references to *Guy of Gisborne* are from Knight and Ohlgren's edition. Line numbers are given in parentheses.

Hood: "'I seeke an outlaw,' quoth Sir Guye, / 'Men call him Robin Hood; / I had rather meet with him upon a day, / Then forty pound of golde'" (*Guy of Gisborne* 99–102). Robin does not reveal himself. The two agree to a series of three contests, beginning with an archery competition that Robin quickly wins. Guy asks Robin's name, but Robin initially refuses, asking Guy's instead. He replies: "'I dwell by dale and downe,' ... / 'And I have done many a curst turne; / And he that calles me by my right name / Calles me Guye of good Gysborne'" (*Guy of Gisborne* 135–138). Guy *admits* that he is a dastardly fellow who has done "many a curst turne;" he is a hired killer and Robin is his quarry, so Robin's life is definitely at stake. Robin then identifies himself and their jovial contest devolves into a two-hour hand-to-hand combat with knives. Stumbling on a tree root, Guy wounds Robin in his left side, but Robin calls upon the Virgin Mary, who gives him strength.[25] Leaping up, he slays the bounty hunter with a backhanded stroke and treats his corpse maliciously, decapitating him and then impaling his severed head upon the end of a bow like a hunting trophy. Next, Robin mutilates Guy's face, rendering it completely unrecognizable: "Robin pulled forth an Irish kniffe, / And nicked Sir Guy in the face, / That hee was never on a woman borne / Cold tell who Sir Guye was" (*Guy of Gisborne* 167–170). The vicious nature of the kill-or-be-killed combat undermines the nostalgic tenor of the outlaw life with the harsh reality of lethal justice. According to Renée Ward, this slaying scene is one of the most explicitly violent moments in the Robin Hood tradition.[26] But while this episode may seem exceptionally brutal and cruel, Robin acts in self-defense, as defined in *Bracton*, making it legitimate homicide rather than murder. Robin dons the horsehide to disguise himself as Guy, hoping the Sheriff will think the mutilated head is Robin's own so he can get close to John and save him from the hangman's noose. As Stuart Kane remarks, this disguise "allows him to cross the borders between man and animal, and outlaw and agent of authority."[27]

25 For more on the importance of Robin's devotion to the Virgin, especially to his position within social structures of the late Middle Ages, see: Larissa Tracy, "'For Our dere Ladyes sake': Bringing the Outlaw in from the Forest—Robin Hood, Marian, and Normative National Identity," *EIRC* 38 (Summer & Winter 2012): 35–65 at 38–43.

26 Renée Ward, "'Thou shalt have the better cloathe': Reading Second Skins in *Robin Hood and Guy of Gisborne*," in *Flaying in the Premodern World: Practice and Representation*, ed. Larissa Tracy (Cambridge: D.S. Brewer, 2017), 349–365 at 351. The severed head is a prominent and multivalent motif in pre-modern literature and culture. See: *Heads Will Roll: Decapitation in the Medieval and Early Modern Imagination*, ed. Larissa Tracy and Jeff Massey (Leiden: Brill, 2012).

27 Stuart Kane, "Horseplay: Robin Hood, Guy of Gisborne, and the Neg(oti)ation of the Bestial," in *Robin Hood in Popular Culture: Violence, Transgression, and Justice*, ed. Thomas Hahn (Cambridge: D.S. Brewer, 2000), 101–110.

Robin slays Guy in an act of self-defense—kill or be killed—a fair fight that he almost loses but in which he acts with the authority of justice. The bounty hunter's horsehide cloak allows him to complete the ruse and free Little John, but it is a means to an end rather than a gory celebration of violence.

The disfigurement serves a strategic purpose: convincing the Sheriff that the head belongs to Robin and that *he* is Guy, returning with *his* trophy to claim his fee. The subterfuge works, and the Sheriff asks "Guy" what he would like as payment. Robin responds that, having slain the master, he wants to kill the servant—Little John (*Guy of Gisborne* 199–202). The Sheriff thinks him mad for refusing a "knight's fee" (*Guy of Gisborne* 204) but grants his wish, happy to pass off the execution of official justice to a paid mercenary. Here the Sheriff's laxity in applying justice not only reveals his own corruption and indifference to the law, but it facilitates his own execution. Little John recognizes Robin's voice and knows that this is his rescue. Robin frees John with the same Irish knife he used to disfigure Guy's face and hands him Guy's bow (*Guy of Gisborne* 219–222). The Sheriff and all his men attempt to flee, but as he runs towards his house in Nottingham, "Litle John, with an arrow broade, / Did cleave his heart in twin" (*Guy of Gisborne* 233–234). In a reciprocal moment of justice, John executes the Sheriff just as the Sheriff planned to execute him. By shooting him in the back with an arrow (using Guy's bow), John actually doles out swifter justice than the drawing and hanging the Sheriff intended for him. While John kills an agent of the law, he also acts out of self-preservation, not simply out of malice. As Ward points out, this scene connects clearly to contemporary contexts and to the social and political upheavals of the late medieval period that upset the hierarchy of the feudal system.[28] Ward writes, "Thus, Robin's treatment of Guy, specifically his violence towards the bounty hunter's body, is a rejection of all that he and his second skin represent; it is an attempt to eradicate the new social order. Additionally, Robin's transferal of the hide to himself renders him an alternate source of justice, one which reinforces class boundaries and reinscribes the social hegemony of the very system that excludes him through the practice of outlawry."[29] The tale ends there but implies that Robin and his men restore order to the Greenwood having dealt with the corrupt officials of the town, and return to their place of exile.

Many of the values in the Robin Hood ballads echo earlier legal traditions in which the punishment fit the crime. As Hurnard notes, pre-Conquest legislation "had tackled the problem of differing degrees of liability and shown

28 Ward, "'Thou shalt have the better cloathe'," 350.

29 Ward, "'Thou shalt have the better cloathe'," 350.

itself sensitive to the finest distinctions."[30] Later medieval nostalgia for this era in texts like the Middle English *Havelok the Dane* (*c.*1295–1310) envisions a time when laws were kept, brutality was rarely necessary, and good men could live free of tyranny. According to Robert Rouse, this "[h]arks back to a utopian age of the universal application of law, a far cry from the reality of the legal segregation of the clerical and secular courts."[31] Outlaw narratives, especially those set in the pre-Conquest period, often function as reminders of England's judicial traditions and the supposed justice of earlier reigns before the Norman and, later, Angevin lines were in place. However, the reality of post-Conquest law in England was far more complicated. The laws of William I (*c.*1028–1087; r. 1066–1087) enacted as part of his conquest in 1066 "separated lay and ecclesiastical justice in conformity with continental practice and substituted mutilation for the death penalty."[32] Hurnard argues that it is far from certain that he did so, contending that if William "ever did issue such a decree the risk of undergoing its penalties must have been a powerful incentive to seek mitigation."[33] The law of exile in eleventh-century Normandy was rooted in both the Frankish and Scandinavian past,[34] but the majority of those banishment cases were "temporary situations which provided time and space for offended and offending parties to cool off and reconsider their positions."[35] There was the possibility of return, which precluded the need for familial vengeance and frequently led to reconciliation.[36] Capital punishment was often a last resort, and the ultimate power to levy a sentence of execution rested with the king who frequently granted mercy instead. William Rufus (*c.*1056–1100; r. 1087–1100) showed leniency to thieves, but his brother and successor Henry I (*c.*1068–1135; r. 1100–1135) did not shrink from inflicting capital punishment in addition to other forms of punishment.[37] However, Henry I's paramount aim was "the maintenance of good law and good order," and he relied on these

---

30 Hurnard, *The King's Pardon*, xiii.

31 Robert Allen Rouse, "English Identity and the Law in *Havelok the Dane, horn Childe and Maiden Rimnild* and *Beues of Hamtoun*," in *Cultural Encounters in the Romance of Medieval England*, ed. Corinne Saunders (Cambridge: D.S. Brewer, 2005), 69–84 at 74.

32 Doris M. Stenton, *English Justice between the Norman Conquest and the Great Charter 1066–1215* (Philadelphia: American Philosophical Society, 1964), 6.

33 Hurnard, *The King's Pardon*, 5 and 6.

34 Laura Napran, Introduction, *Exile in the Middle Ages*, ed. Laura Napran and Elisabeth Van Houts (Turnhout: Brepols, 2004), 4.

35 Napran, Introduction, 4.

36 Napran, Introduction, 4.

37 Hurnard, *The King's Pardon*, 6. See also: J.G. Bellamy, *The Criminal Trial in Later Medieval England: Felony Before the Courts from Edward I to the Sixteenth Century* (Toronto: University of Toronto Press, 1998), 70.

discretionary powers to avoid undue rigidity by following the traditional policy of the Saxon and Danish kings who preceded him.[38] Thus, the policy of "coupling mercy with sterner measures for the repression of crime was a conscious one," even though it was often abused for monetary gain or for recruiting soldiers into the king's forces.[39] The fifteenth-century Robin Hood narratives implicitly weigh and measure the exile of the outlaw hero and the constant threat of execution or other fatal justice against this historical template of secular English justice.

There was some continuity between pre- and post-Conquest judicial systems regarding execution and exile;[40] however, with the Conquest came new legal and social structures, new administrators, a new language, and new literature. Execution became far more common for heinous crimes like murder and treason, supplanting exile in many cases as the ultimate punishment.[41] For later medieval kings, criminal justice existed primarily to preserve the throne above all else, even financial profit.[42] According to John Bellamy, "the greatest crime, treason, was to be rooted out by every means at their disposal, the suspects convicted without fail, and then punished in a manner whose brutality was quite out of keeping with other English punishments."[43] Other felonies were viewed much more dispassionately as long as they did not incite a dangerous feud that directly affected the nobility or the monarchy.[44] Contemporary concerns inspire nostalgia in the early-fourteenth century, when the English King Edward II was overthrown and murdered (1327), the French Knights Templar were rounded up and subjected to torture (1307), and their leaders executed as heretics (1314). The progression of the fourteenth century also saw plague (1348), the pursuit of Edward III's claims to the French throne in the first campaigns of the Hundred Years War (1337–1453), the Papal Schism (1378–1417), Richard II's kingship contested by unfaithful barons (1388), and popular uprising (1381). Edward III's relatively stable reign gave way to dynastic uncertainty under his grandson Richard II. Against this backdrop, rhymes of Robin Hood began to appear, first in *Piers Plowman* (1377) and possibly in Geoffrey Chaucer's description of the Yeoman in the *General Prologue* to

38 Hurnard, *The King's Pardon*, 13.
39 Hurnard, *The King's Pardon*, 13.
40 Hurnard, *The King's Pardon*, xiv.
41 See: *Medieval and Early Modern Murder: Legal, Literary and Historical Contexts*, ed. Larissa Tracy (Woodbridge: Boydell Press, 2018) and *Treason: Medieval and Early Modern Adultery, Betrayal and Shame*, ed. Larissa Tracy (Leiden: Brill, 2019).
42 Bellamy, *The Criminal Trial*, 9.
43 Bellamy, *The Criminal Trial*, 9.
44 Bellamy, *The Criminal Trial*, 9.

the *Canterbury Tales*: "clad in cote and hood of grene. / A sheef of pecokarwes, bright and kene, / Under his belt he bar ful thriftily / (Wel koude he dresse his takelyemanly; / His arwesdrouped noght with fetheres lowe), / And in his hand he baar a mighty bowe" (1.103–108).[45]

Chaucer's satirical portrayal of the heavily-armed Yeoman, who travels in service of the Knight, and *The Tale of Gamelyn* (*c*.1350), which only survives in manuscripts of the *Canterbury Tales*,[46] represent the next stage in the development of these exile and outlaw legends after the thirteenth-century Latin *Gesta Herewardi*, which records the exploits of the legendary (and possibly historical) Hereward the Wake. The Yeoman may be emulating the figure who, by the 1380s, had become a popular outlaw hero in folktale and song, resisting corrupt authorities and representing the concerns of the rising middle class. Knight notes clear references to the name "Robin Hood" as early as the thirteenth century.[47] Thus, Chaucer's Yeoman may gesture to this evolving tradition and its popularity which takes its fullest form in the fifteenth-century Robin Hood ballads. The *Gest* and *Guy of Gisborne* evoke an earlier time—before the conflicts among the barons, before the Papal Schism challenged the faith of European Catholics, before the plague ravaged the population, before English patience with the king's martial attempts to claim the French throne were exhausted—a time when the king's justice prevailed, wielded by the devout and faithful outlaw.

Set in the time when Edward III was flexing his ambitions on the Continent and delegating the administration of law and order to lesser officials, the *Gest* and *Guy of Gisborne* center the outlaw as the vehicle for reasserting the king's rightful authority, complicating this nostalgic logic. In the king's absence—or in direct contravention of his orders—the outlaw acts lawfully against the supposed agents of the law. The king occupied the central place in nostalgic

45 Geoffrey Chaucer, *General Prologue, Canterbury Tales*, in *The Riverside Chaucer*, 3rd ed., gen. ed. Larry D. Benson (Boston: Houghton Mifflin, 1987). Fragment and line numbers are given in parentheses.

46 Despite its presence in manuscripts of the *Canterbury Tales*, and Skeat's inclusion of it as an appendix to his *Complete Works of Geoffrey Chaucer* (1884), Gamelyn's story is no longer regarded as the work of Chaucer but a text that he included in his papers to rewrite (Knight and Ohlgren, *Robin Hood*, 184). See also: John Scattergood, "*The Tale of Gamelyn*: The Noble Robber as Provincial Hero," in *Readings in Medieval English Romance*, ed. Carol M. Meale (Cambridge: D.S. Brewer, 1994), 159–94 at 160.

47 Stephen Knight, "Alterity, Parody, Habitus: The Formation of the Early Literary Tradition of Robin Hood," in *Robin Hood in the Greenwood Stood: Alterity and Context in the English Outlaw Tradition*, ed. Stephen Knight (Turnhout: Brepols, 2011), 1–30 at 3–4.

articulations of the medieval English nation.[48] Such fantasies, however, were no match for the realities of administration, which necessitated that the king exert power through easily corrupted intermediaries. When justice rests solely with the king, there is always room for corruption among those below him. According to W.R. Jones, "so long as the crown continued to depend on the community of local notables to provide the cadre of local government, it was obliged to make accommodations with individual venality and corruption."[49] It is against those accommodations that Robin Hood acts, instituting justice where the king cannot. The outlaw needs to weed out the corrupted officials who subvert the justice system for their own ends.

However, these narratives also tacitly criticize the king who is so engaged elsewhere that he allows such corruption to fester under his rule. As Thomas Hahn writes,

> scholars must devise tools to grapple with the oppositions built into these outlaw stories which are at once traditional and conservative, yet about resistance and rebellion; many versions celebrate the outlaw's anarchic instincts or his commitment to absolute justice, yet many end by revealing his unwavering support for "true" authority in the person of the king, the most powerful symbol of old values and national identity.[50]

In his fight against localized corruption, Robin taps into contemporary criticisms of local authority and re-inscribes the values of justice and loyalty that were understood to be at the core of English identity.[51] Indeed, Richard Helgerson writes that, more than a dream of justice, "these stories represent a dream of commonality, of common interests and common humanity, between the ruler and the ruled," denaturalizing class difference and claiming the king as one of the common people, or even, potentially, one of the band of outlaws.[52] Rather than advocating for a complete overthrow of royal structures

48 Geraldine Heng, "The Romance of England: *Richard Coer de Lyon*, Saracens, Jews, and the Politics of Race and Nation," in *The Postcolonial Middle Ages*, ed. Jeffrey Jerome Cohen (New York: Palgrave, 2000), 135–71 at 139.

49 Jones, "Keeping the Peace," 318.

50 Thomas Hahn, "Playing with Transgression: Robin Hood and Popular Culture," in *Robin Hood and Popular Culture*, ed. Thomas Hahn (Cambridge: D.S. Brewer, 2000), 1–11 at 9.

51 According to Rouse, there was a popular post-Conquest view of the pre-Conquest period as a Golden Age of law and order, a Golden Age envisaged as being specifically English, and "explicitly linked to the rule of a rightful king who rules within the bounds of the law of the realm" ("English Identity and the Law," 77).

52 Helgerson, *Forms of Nationhood*, 232.

and authorities, the ballads are more concerned with "the righting of wrong done and the downfall of those who control the law by bribery and the abuse of office; and the triumph of justice whose forces are, by an irony of fate, represented by those who are outside the law."[53] The ballads convey a sense of longing for a time, largely fictional, when individuals could set things right, the power of good could prevail, and the bad guy got what was coming to him, even if that meant a nasty but lawful and just execution.

The violence of the Robin Hood ballads, especially the *Gest* and *Guy of Gisborne*, often troubles modern critics who view what they see as brutality as unfitting for a good, heroic, outlaw who earns the respect of his king. Maurice Keen laments that the Robin Hood of the ballads is a "a full-blooded medieval brigand, who, even if his conduct is redeemed by a courtly generosity to the poor and deserving, is a brigand nevertheless and can be called by no other name. He is a desperate man, and he has recourse to desperate and violent remedies," essentially reveling in the blood of his enemies—an "outmoded pleasure, but to the middle ages it appeared natural and almost justifiable."[54] Keen rejects the romantic nostalgia of the ballads, admonishing audiences that "[i]t will not do to forget this, for if one does one will forget what an outlaw really was."[55] However, in the *Gest*, the poet's nostalgia for a time of justice and good governance survives in Robin Hood's defense of the king and his knights who represent a stable, more just vision of Edward III's England that rebukes the turmoil of Richard II's England and the subsequent Wars of the Roses. The ballad has moments of violence that may seem excessively or unnecessarily brutal, but Robin acts exactly as the king vows to, doing so in the King's name. Taken in the context of *Bracton*, Robin's pursuit of justice is entirely legitimate precisely because he does it for the love of justice, even though he is not a legal administrator. He executes the Sheriff swiftly, pronouncing his judgment and sentence in public and leaving his body in the street as a very visible reminder of the consequences of treason. That the king pardons him reinforces Robin's actions. Where he appears in the medieval Robin Hood narratives, the king is

53 Maurice Keen, "Robin Hood—Peasant or Gentleman," *Past & Present* 19 (April 1961): 7–15 at 7. Stephen Knight argues that Robin "opposes false authority," clarifying his own "organic and communal values against those of feudal authority, and … escapes the world of royal power." Stephen Knight, "Robin Hood versus King Arthur," in *In Strange Countries: Middle English Literature and its Afterlife*, ed. David Matthews (Manchester: Manchester University Press, 2011), 9–24 at 10. However, Robin Hood never fully "escapes the world of royal power," especially in the *Gest* where the king indulges in the outlaw life by temporarily joining Robin on his escapades.

54 Maurice Keen, *The Outlaws of Medieval Legend* (London: Routledge, 1961, rev. ed. 2000), 3.

55 Keen, *The Outlaws*, 3.

the last arbiter of justice, and Robin works to further *his* cause, even at the risk of his own execution. When the king's justice is absent, Robin takes the role of executioner upon himself.

Though Robin Hood and his band of Merry Men live in exile as outlaws, their rule in the Greenwood is a foil to the misrule of the courtly world, where administrators can be bought and loyalty is a commodity that dissipates when funding runs out, and where execution is a political tool rather than a legitimate exercise of law. In contrast, the world of the outlaws—the forest realm of the exile that becomes home—highlights the shortcomings of the ordinary world beyond its boundaries.[56] Robin Hood creates a new community in exile based on nostalgic claims of justice, law, and religious devotion, and the lines between exile and home blur. But he does it through the legal apparatus of revenge, executing his enemies within the accepted boundaries of social practice. Robin uses questionable methods to fulfill his vengeance, methods that potentially taint the justice of his actions, but ultimately the executions allow for Robin's restoration. In Edward Said's words, "Exile is never the state of being satisfied, placid or secure."[57] It is "life led outside habitual order. It is nomadic, decentered, contrapuntal; but no sooner does one get accustomed to it than its unsettling force erupts anew."[58] For Robin, this means remaining an outlaw, but one who operates within the wider community of loyal subjects to the king. In the literary context, the king's proximity and willingness to deal directly with outlaws like Robin Hood reflects nostalgic, wishful thinking on the part of the poet or audience who felt that justice, like royal scrutiny of local officials, was increasingly unattainable. These narratives may have struck a chord with English audiences who could find in them a reflection of either their desires, their situation, or their dissatisfaction, especially during the turmoil of the lingering campaigns of the Hundred Years War or, later, the civil unrest of the Wars of the Roses. Here the outlaw operates as a force for justice as allowed by law, despite his status as a legal exile, and he challenges those who would use execution as a tool for their own illegal ends. The problem is not the violence itself, but rather its illegitimacy. Thus, medieval exile and outlaw narratives reject the instability of exile by not only returning or resettling, but also by shaping the reclaimed home into a reflection of justice and nostalgia.

56 Douglas Gray, "The Robin Hood Poems," in *Robin Hood: An Anthology of Scholarship and Criticism*, ed. Stephen Knight (Cambridge: D.S. Brewer, 1999), 36.

57 Edward W. Said, "Reflections on Exile," in *Reflections on Exile and Other Essays* (Cambridge, MA: Harvard University Press, 2000), 186.

58 Said, "Reflections on Exile," 186.

CHAPTER 10

Non-human Execution, Objectification, and the Rise of Bodily Punishment in Late Medieval Flanders

Mireille J. Pardon

In fifteenth-century Flemish cities, the financial accounts of the bailiff, or *schout* as he was called in Bruges, recorded the money taken in and given out during the everyday functioning of the judicial system. These financial reports, usually called bailiff accounts (*comptes des baillis, baljuwsrekening*), reveal the darker aspects of everyday life in a fifteenth-century city, from gambling and slanderous gossip to homicide and highway robbery. In medieval Flanders, many accusations and legal disputes were resolved through a process called bailiff composition.[1] Composition payments were financial agreements negotiated between the bailiff and the accused that could take place at any point in the judicial process and prevented that process from moving forward. A composition payment was attractive to the accused because it removed the need for a legal trial that might result in a harsher penalty. Bailiff accounts recorded crimes resolved through composition payments as well as payments made to the town's executioner for carrying out corporal or capital sentences. Archival sources of urban justice, including bailiff accounts from the Low Countries and Northern France, show a transition away from financial penalties, such as bailiff compositions, and towards bodily punishment at the end of the Middle Ages.[2] Because spectacular judicial rituals showcased the power of the prince and

1 Guy Dupont, "Le temps des compositions. Pratiques judiciaires à Bruges et à Gand du XIVe au XVIe siècle (Partie 1)," in *Préférant miséricorde à rigueur de justice: Pratiques de la grâce (XIIIe–XVIIe siècles)*, ed. Bernard Dauven and Xavier Rousseaux (Louvain: Presses universitaires de Louvain, 2012), 53–95; David Nicholas, "Crime and Punishment in Fourteenth-Century Ghent (first part)," *Revue belge de philologie et d'histoire* 48.2 (1970): 289334.

2 Xavier Rousseaux, "Taxer ou chatier? L'émergence du pénal: enquête sur la justice nivelloise (1400–1650)" (Louvain: Université catholique de Louvain, 1990); Robert Muchembled, *Le temps des supplices: de l'obéissance sous les rois absolus, XVe–XVIIIe siècle* (Paris: A. Colin, 1992); Bruce Lenman and Geoffrey Parker, "The State, the Community, and the Criminal Law in Early Modern Europe," in *Crime and the Law: The Social History of Crime in Western Europe since 1500*, ed. Geoffrey Parker, V.A.C. Gatrell, and Bruce Lenman (London: London Europa Publications Limited, 1980), 1–48; David de La Croix, Xavier Rousseaux, and Jean-Pierre Urbain, "To Fine or to Punish in the Late Middle Ages," *Applied Economics* 28 (1996): 1213–24.

 | DOI:10.1163/9789004742598_012

his monopoly on violence, scholars often attribute this shift to state-building.[3] In addition to giving quantitative information about the frequency of different types of punishments, bailiff accounts include qualitative descriptions of crime and criminals. When the bailiff accepted a composition, he justified it by emphasizing the social connections and positive reputation of the accused. However, for those sentenced to execution, crime had the power to objectify the perpetrator and strip them of their identity in the community by placing them in the same category as non-human offenders. Though the majority of executions were performed on living criminals, fifteenth-century bailiff accounts from Bruges and the Liberty of Bruges (*Brugse Vrije, Franc de Bruges*) record the executions of dead bodies, falsely made goods, and domesticated animals. Instead of the personification of animal offenders or the animalization of human offenders, all executed subjects were objectified and reduced to a physical piece of the execution ritual. A change in mentalities accompanied the rise of spectacular justice: as corporal and capital punishments replaced financial penalties at the end of the Middle Ages in the Low Countries, the law increasingly cast those it condemned as inhuman and intrinsically irredeemable. Through objectification, execution encouraged the idea that "criminal" was an immutable category. For those condemned to death, their crime was an essential part of their identity, rendering them not only inhuman, but transforming them into an object whose only suitable role was violent purgation by the state.

When examining records of judicial practice in Flemish towns, one often looks through the eyes of the bailiff, the chief law enforcement officer of the town. Bailiffs played an important role in Flemish urban justice beginning in the twelfth century.[4] They represented the Count of Flanders in local legal processes and could pursue *ex officio* prosecutions as well as accept composition payments.[5] When the Duke of Burgundy inherited the County of Flanders in

3 Xavier Rousseaux, "L'histoire du crime et de la justice criminelle dans l'espace du Benelux," in *Crimes, pouvoirs et sociétés (1400–1800): anciens Pays-Bas et Principauté de Liège*, ed. Marie-Sylvie Dupont-Bouchat and Xavier Rousseaux (Kortrijk-Heule: U.G.A., 2001), 21–82; Pieter Spierenburg, *The Spectacle of Suffering: Executions and the Evolution of Repression from a Preindustrial Metropolis to the European Experience* (Cambridge: Cambridge University Press, 1984), 54–56, 200–207; Aude Musin, *Sociabilité urbaine et criminalisation étatique: La justice namuroise face à la violence de 1360 à 1555* (Turnhout: Brepols, 2017), 121–168.

4 Louis M. de Gryse, "Some Observations on the Origins of the Flemish Bailiff (Bailli): The Reign of Philip of Alsace," *Viator* 7 (1976): 243–294; Par H. Nowé, *Les baillis comtaux de Flandre, des origines à la fin du XIVe siècle* (Brussels: Hayez, 1928); David Nicholas, *Medieval Flanders* (New York: Routledge, 1992), 87–89.

5 Jan Van Rompaey, "Het compositierecht in Vlaanderen van de veertiende tot de achttiende eeuw," *Legal History Review* 29.1 (1961): 43–79; Nicholas, *Medieval Flanders*, 237–241.

1384, the bailiff became a ducal officer and submitted his financial reports several times a year to the Burgundian Chamber of Accounts in Lille.[6] Because the administrative language of the Burgundian Netherlands was French, the bureaucracy that connected urban administration to the central government through the Chamber of Accounts was conducted in French. However, the mother tongue of those who appear in such records of quotidian crime and punishment in Flemish cities would have been Dutch. The account books that bailiffs submitted have survived from many jurisdictions in the Burgundian Netherlands and are now housed in the National Archives of Belgium (*Algemeen Rjiksarchief, Archives générales du Royaume*) in Brussels, including those from fifteenth-century Bruges and the Liberty of Bruges, an outlying castellany. Despite the centralizing ambitions of the Burgundian Dukes, fifteenth-century justice in the Low Countries was still a patch-work system of overlapping jurisdictions with many available options for conflict resolution.[7] Therefore, bailiff accounts do not provide a full picture of the judicial system. If the accused could not successfully negotiate a composition payment with the bailiff, he might face a trial before the urban court of alderman who could sentence him to a fine, penitential pilgrimage, banishment or exile, corporal punishment, or execution. In addition to the urban courts of aldermen, there were also feudal and ecclesiastical courts, as well as private peace agreements, called *verzoening*.[8] Bailiff accounts only record two types of justice, composition payments and payments made to the executioner. As such, they show two opposing poles of the judicial system: the negotiated financial settlement that spared the accused the indignity of a trial and the public, bodily punishment by the executioner of the condemned.

There is a stark contrast in the language used to describe a criminal receiving corporal or capital punishment and one who was eligible for a monetary composition. When a bailiff accepted a composition payment, he took an exculpatory tone that emphasized the humanity of the offender and their standing in the community. In 1473 in Bruges, Katherine Misch was arrested by the *schout*

6 Robert Stein, "Burgundian Bureaucracy as a Model for the Low Countries? The Chambres des Comptes and the Creation of an Administrative Unity," in *Powerbrokers in the Late Middle Ages: The Burgundian Low Countries in a European Context* (Turnhout: Brepols, 2001), 3–25 at 7–10.

7 Jelle Haemers and Wouter Ryckbosch, "A Targeted Public: Public Services in Fifteenth-century Ghent and Bruges," *Urban History* 37.2 (2010): 203–25; Jos Monballyu, *Six Centuries of Criminal Law: History of Criminal Law in the Southern Netherlands and Belgium* (1400–2000) (Leiden: Brill, 2014), 50–60.

8 Ellen E. Kittell, "Travelling for Atonement: Civilly Imposed Pilgrimages in Medieval Flanders," *Canadian Journal for Netherlandic Studies* 31.2 (2010): 21–37.

after the dean of the fullers accused her of stealing cloth that she had been tasked with cleaning.[9] However, the *schout* decided to accept a composition payment from Katherine and let her go free because she returned the cloth, those she had stolen from were "contentez de leurs lainnes" [made content by their cloth], and no one else complained about her. The *schout* also notes that "autrement elle avoit esté à toujours de bonnes et honorables vie" [otherwise she had always lived a good and honorable life] and that she had the support of local notables, as he received "la prière de bonne gens" [the prayer of good men] on her behalf. Not all those who made composition payments were quite as conscientious as Katherine in terms of helping their victims recoup their losses. In the same bailiff account that records the story of Katherine, Guillaume Heindricx Neyts made a composition payment after buying and selling farm animals that he knew had been stolen. Though the farm animals never made it back to their original owners, the bailiff accepted a composition payment "veu que il estoit autrement de bonne fame et renommé" [in view that he [Guillaume] was otherwise of good reputation].[10] In describing a crime

9 Archives générales du Royaume [hereafter AGR], Chambre des comptes (CC), 13780, f. 32v. "De Katherine Misch, laquelle se avoit mesusée quant elle rapporta à l'ostel des drappiers les lainnes qu'elle avoit eue d'eulx pour les nectoyer et tendre selon les coustumes et manieres, de retenir devers elle furtivement par plusieurs fois aucunes quantitez de lainnes à grand dommaige et interestz desdit drapiers, pour lequel mesfait à la poursuite et accusacion du doyen des foullons et autres ausquelz lesdit lainnes par elle ainsi retenues appartenoient lesdit escoutette calenga et arresta ladite Katherine et pour ce que ledit escoutette entendi après que lesdit parties estoient contentez de leurs lainnes et que nulle partie se plainde d'elle et que autrement elle avoit esté à toujours de bonnes et honorables vie, ce consideré ledit escoutette à la prière de bonne gens l'a laissé composer" [From Katherine Misch who behaved improperly when she returned cloth to the house of the drapers that she had had from them in order to clean and stretch the fabric, as is customary. Upon returning it, she furtively took some quantity of cloth many times, causing great damage to the aforementioned drapers. For this crime, at the pursuit and accusation of the dean of the fullers and others to whom the aforementioned cloth that she had kept had previously belonged, the *schout* arrested Katherine and because the *scout* understood afterwards that the parties were content with their cloth and no one was complaining of her and otherwise she had always been of good and honorable life, considering this and at the prayer of good men, the *schout* let her make a composition payment]. All translations and transcriptions are my own.

10 AGR, CC, 13780, f. 36v–37r. "De Guillaume Heindricx Neyts lequel fu calengé par ledit escoutette de ce qu'il se avoit par plusieurs fois mesusé comme il confessoit, premiers qu'il avoit mené au marche de Bruges trois mouttons lesquelz il vendi, combien que il savoit bien lesdits mouttons estre emblez par ung nommé Jehan Christiaens, item le temps pendant qu'il fu banny du pays de Flandres, il print furtivement en la paroisse de Coolkercke quatre gelines lesquelles il tira et emporta avec lui, item il avoit achetté autres deux mouttons lesquelz il savoit estre emblez par ung nommé Hannin de Costre … et veu

eligible for composition, the bailiff weighed the deviant act committed by the accused against their positive identity in the community. The offender may have committed a crime, but their good reputation made them look sympathetic, likely to be reaccepted by their peers despite their offense.

Composition was possible for more serious crimes as well, including homicide.[11] In the same bailiff account that records the payments made by Katherine Misch and Guillaume Heindricx Neyts, as well as all other payments made between March 1, 1473, and March 1, 1474, the bailiff accepted four composition payments for homicide.[12] As with Katherine and Guillaume, the bailiff emphasized the positive reputation and social connections of the perpetrators. After a cobbler named Pieter was arrested because "il avoit navré en la ville de l'Escluse ung nommé Guillaume Banckaert natif de Yseghem si greifment que mort ensui" [he had injured in the town of Écluse a man named Guillaume Banckaert, a native of Yseghem, so grievously that death ensued], the bailiff agreed to accept a composition payment from Pieter because "il estoit ung povre joisne compaignon, sievant les querres et autrement de bonne fame et renommé" [he was a poor young man, who followed the rules and was otherwise of good reputation]. In addition, the bailiff adds that "le fait advenu de chaut sang et que satiffaction estoit faicte à partie" [the act occurred in hot blood and satisfaction was made to the opposing party].[13] Under the right cir-

aussi que autrement il estoit de bonne fame et renommé, ledit escoutette l'a composé" [From Guillaume Heindricx Neyts, who was arrested by the *scout* because he had, many times, behaved badly, as he confessed. First that he brought three lambs to the market in Bruges that he had bought knowing that the aforementioned lambs had been taken by one named Jehan Christaens. During the time when he was banished from Flanders, he furtively took in the parish of Koolkerke four hens which he brought away with him. He had also bought two other lambs which he knew had been taken by one named Hannin de Costre ... seeing that he was otherwise of good reputation, the *schout* accepted a composition from him].

11 Flemish law distinguishes between murder, which involved some element of betrayal or deception, and homicide. See: Philips Wielant, *Corte instructie in materie criminele*, ed. Jos Monballyu (Brussel: Paleis der academiën, 1995), Capital 87. While all convicted murderers faced execution, homicide could be resolved through composition if peace was made with the family of the victim and if the homicide was "necessary," as defined as in defense of one's self, one's goods, one's honor, or one's friends. See: Wielant, *Corte instructie in materie criminele*, Capital 68 and Capital 76. Given the rates at which homicide was composed [**see Table 3**], many slayings met these requirements.

12 AGR, CC, 13780, f. 22r–22v.

13 AGR, CC, 13780, f. 22r. "De Pieter Piusselinc savetier lequel fu calengé et mis en prison par ledit escoutette de ce qu'il estoit accusé que passé ung an ou plus il avoit navré en la ville de l'Escluse ung nommé Guillaume Banckaert natif de Yseghem si griefment que mort ensui, et veu et consideré qu'il estoit ung povre joisne compaignon, sievant les querres et autrement de bonne fame et renommé, le fait advenu de chaut sang et que satiffaction

cumstances, even the act of killing did not define the perpetrator. If a killer successfully made peace with the victim's family, they had the chance of being restored to the community through bailiff composition.[14] In some cases, like that of Pieter the cobbler, this restoration took a literal form as the accused was arrested and temporarily excluded from their community by being placed in prison to await their sentence. In other cases, the accused merely faced local rumors of guilt and the composition payment prevented any legal action from being taken against them. The bailiff did not, of course, only accept composition payments out of compassion for the accused. He had a financial incentive because composition payments made up part of his salary. It is likely that bailiffs approached people with little or no evidence against them in hopes of pressuring them into a payment under the empty threat of prosecution.[15] Whatever the reason, the bailiff had to justify the decision to accept a composition payment in his financial accounts and present the perpetrator as a socially-connected offender who was not a danger to the community, despite committing a crime. Though the specific act may have been criminal, the perpetrator was not corrupted by some inherent deviancy.

Whenever a corporal or capital punishment was carried out by the executioner, the bailiff had to pay him for "avoir fait la justice" [having done justice] as well as for some of the required materials.[16] In this part of bailiff accounts, a grand public spectacle is reduced to a mundane list of everyday objects: ropes and gloves, straw and wood, and, in the rare case of a conviction for

estoit faicte à partie ledit escoutette l'a laissé composer" [From Pieter Prusselinc, cobbler, who was arrested and put in prison by the *schout* because he was accused a year or more ago that he had injured in the town of Écluse one named Guillaume Banckaert, a native of Yseghem, so grievously that death ensued, and seeing that he was a poor young man, following the rules and otherwise of good reputation, the act coming from hot blood and that satisfaction was made with the opposing party, the aforementioned *scout* accepted a composition payment].

14 Making peace with the family's victim was required to make a composition payment for homicide. The language "satisfaction made to the (opposing) party" (*satisfacion fait à partie*) or "peace to the party" (*paix à partie*) appears in all compositions for homicide during this period while a reference to the injured party being "content" only appears sporadically for other crimes.

15 Van Rompaey, "Het compositierecht in Vlaanderen," 57; Nicholas, "Crime and Punishment," 301.

16 Similar records exist for France. See: William Chester Jordan, "Expenses Related to Corporal Punishment in France," in *Prowess, Piety, and Public Order in Medieval Society: Studies in Honor of Richard W. Kaeuper*, ed. Craig Nakashian and Daniel Franke (Leiden: Brill, 2017), 286–300; Leslie B. MacGregor, "Criminalising Animals in Medieval France: Insights from Records of Executions," *Open Library of Humanities* 5(1).15 (2019): 1–20.

counterfeiting, a very large pot.[17] Though boiling alive was the punishment for making counterfeit currency, most executions in late medieval Bruges and the Liberty of Bruges were less gruesome. The most common form of execution was hanging, but homicide, highway robbery, and arson were punishable by decapitation and sodomy by burning.[18] When women were sentenced to death for crimes that normally stipulated decapitation, they were buried alive or burned.[19] Regardless of the method of execution, the bailiff records how a series of officials came into contact with the condemned and received a payment: the executioner who interrogated him through the application of torture, the lawyer who argued his case, the priest who took his last confession, the driver who transported him, and finally, the executioner once again for the deed itself, for "avoir fait la justice" [having done justice] on the condemned.[20] The way the accounts divide the event into its parts makes it easy to forget the real division it describes: the physical division of a human body and the public, ceremonial division of the condemned from their community—both an execution and an exile.

While descriptions of composition payments list mitigating circumstances and emphasize the positive identity of the accused in the community, those condemned to death are described in terms of what they did instead of who they were. In some cases, they are not even listed by their proper name, but as *ung truant* [a truant, or vagabond].[21] In the examples of composition pay-

17 AGR, CC, 13776, f. 94r–94v. "pour avoir fait la justice de Denys le Clerc, lequel fu bouly pour ce qu'il avoit fait fausse monnoye … pour fair repayer le cauderon où il fu boult" [For having done justice on Danys le Clerc, who was boiled because he had made false currency … for having paid for the cauldron where he was boiled]. Executions for counterfeiting currency were rare. There was only one in Bruges 1450–1500 and none in the Liberty of Bruges during that period.

18 This typology of punishments is based on my observations of Flemish bailiff accounts. The variable methods of execution for different crimes were regional in the Middle Ages. See: Paul Friedland, *Seeing Justice Done: The Age of Spectacular Capital Punishment in France* (Oxford: Oxford University Press, 2012), 57–60.

19 A full typology is harder to establish for women, as they were executed less often than men during this period. The trend of executing women in ways that destroyed or concealed the body has also been observed in medieval France. See: Claude Gauvard, *Condamner à mort au Moyen Âge: pratiques de la peine capitale en France, XIII*e*–XV*e *siècle* (Paris: Presses Universitaires de France, 2018), 49.

20 In Flanders, the executioner was responsible for interrogating accused criminals as well as performing executions and corporal punishments. In other regions, interrogation by torture was the responsibility of other officials. See: Spierenburg, *The Spectacle of Suffering*, 27.

21 AGR, CC, 13710. f. 148r. "den zelven betaelt van tween truwanten ghenangelt te hebbene elc eene oore an eene stake ter causen van rudicheden bi hemlieden ghedaen" [The same

ments described earlier, Katherine and Pieter stole cloth and killed a man, respectively, but the bailiff does not describe them as a thief and a murderer. In records of execution, substantive nouns appear because the condemned is defined by their deviant act. Criminal labels such as *mordreur* [murderer], *desrobeur de chemin* [highway robber], *desrobeur de mer* [pirate], *feuillart* [brigand], *bouteur de feu* [arsonist], *coupeur des bourses* [cut-purse], and *sodomien* [sodomite] all appear in records of payments made to the executioner but never in records of composition payments. When a court deemed a crime serious enough to warrant public punishment upon the body of the accused, the sentence had the power to transform a person into a criminal. The legal descriptions objectified the condemned while a public official physically transformed their body through corporal punishment. By implying that crime was essential to the identity of the condemned, corporal and capital punishment stripped the offender of their human identity within the community and cast them as an irredeemable object ill-suited for rehabilitation. They were no longer a person who committed a crime, but a criminal.

While the purpose of a composition payment was to restore the offender to the community and reconcile feuding parties, executions and corporal punishments were designed to Other the condemned. Physical punishments were always performed in public and, in cases of execution, were proceeded by a procession to the site of execution with the accused dressed as a penitent.[22] Scholars have noted the religious dimension to these proceedings as the condemned had the opportunity to confess his crimes and thus die a "good death" through eleventh-hour repentance.[23] However, despite the opportunity for final confession, execution was ultimately a ritual of exclusion that permanently exiled the convicted criminal from earth. In late medieval Flanders, the standard method of execution was hanging; the body of the accused was left to decompose on the gallows. In 1472 Bruges, the *schout* took pity on the

man was paid for two truants who each had an ear pierced with a stake because of the rudeness done by the truants]. While most fifteenth-century Flemish bailiff accounts are in French, some accounts were in Dutch (1483–1485 and 1488) because of the Flemish revolt.

22 Bert Verwerft, "De beul in het Markizaat van Antwerpen tijdens de Bourgondische en Habsburgse periode (1405–1550)" (PhD Dissertation, University of Ghent, 2007), 108–112.

23 Mitchell Merback, *The Thief, the Cross and the Wheel: Pain and the Spectacle of Punishment in Medieval and Renaissance Europe* (Chicago: University of Chicago Press, 1999), 126–157; Achim Timmerman, "A Very Real Re-Enactment of the Passion: Sacred Landscape and Capital Punishment in Sixteenth-Century Swabia," in *Paysage sacré: Le paysage comme exégèse dans l'Europe de la première modernité*, ed. Denis Ribouillault and Michel Weemans (Florence: Olschki, 2011), 349–60.

friends of Pierre Quaret, hanged for theft, allowing them to take away his body in exchange for a payment. Yet, even when the body was released to the friends and family of the deceased, it could only be buried *en terre profane* [in profane ground].[24] Though dead, the perpetrator's body was exiled from the community by being denied a Christian burial in consecrated ground. For the most heinous of crimes, the executed body of the condemned was displayed on a wheel, lifted high on an upright pole.[25] Even in cases where the method of execution obliterated or concealed the dead body, such as burning or burying alive, a well-placed sign continued to humiliate the condemned. In the *Oudburg* of Ghent, a castellany made up of the rural areas surrounding the city, a woman named Katerine was executed for arson by live burial in 1470 and authorities placed a sign above her buried corpse. The bailiff recorded that her two sons complained of their *grand desplaisir* [great displeasure] at having to "journelement passer et repasser" [daily pass by again and again] the site of their mother's execution.[26] In exchange for a payment, the bailiff removed the sign. In cases of corporal punishment for lesser crimes, the executioner permanently marked the body of the accused by clipping the ears of cut-purses or vagabonds, branding forgers, and cutting off a hand of those who struck an authority figure.[27]

The process of objectifying the accused not only involved criminal labels and public ceremonies of exclusion, but also placing the executed person into a category that included corpses, falsely-made goods, and domesticated

---

24 AGR, CC, 13780, 12r–12v. "aucuns amis dudit Pierre vinrent devers icellui escoutette et lui requirent grace et congié de la pouvoir faire mettre jus de la justice et enterer en terre profane" [Some friends of aforementioned Pierre came to the *schout* and asked him for mercy and permission to be able to take it [the body] down from the scaffold and bury it in profane ground].

25 Bodies were displayed on a wheel for murder, highway robbery, and arson (though not in all instances of these crimes).

26 AGR, CC 14159, 8r. "laquelle Katerine à cause qu'elle eust esté soupechonnée et attainte coulpable de bouté fu, avoit esté mis et fait morir en une fosse et sur ledit fosse mis ung estacque auquel pendu ung pot en enseigne de bouté fu, lesquelz enfans commenoient journelement passer et repasser en alant de leur demeure devers Gand en leurs besoignes et affaires emprès ladit justice ce qui estoit à leur grant desplaisir, blasphème, et retardement de leurs mariages" [Katerine, because she had been under suspicion and shown to be guilty of setting a fire, had been killed in a pit, and on aforementioned pit, a stake was placed on which a sign of arson hung, that the aforementioned children had to pass by every day when going to their dwellings in Ghent, their tasks, and their business near the aforementioned place of justice, which was to their great displeasure, outrage, and the delay of their marriages].

27 As previously mentioned, this typology of punishments is composed from my observations of Flemish bailiff accounts.

animals. In fifteenth-century Bruges and the Liberty of Bruges, the executioner regularly "did justice on" things other than living, human criminals.

TABLE 10.1 Rates of the execution of things other than living human criminals, 1400–1500

	Total executions	Not a living human	% of executions
Bruges	412	64	15.5%
The Liberty of Bruges	153	45	29.4%

In the context of the judicial ritual, as described in bailiff accounts, it did not matter if the execution was performed on a living criminal or not. The legal ritual objectified the perpetrator by performing the same execution whether the object of the judicial act was a corpse, inanimate object, animal, or a living criminal. Thus, when an inhabitant of Bruges in the fifteenth century imagined a public execution, they may not have pictured a living or even human criminal climbing the platform.

TABLE 10.2 Non-human execution in Bruges and the Liberty of Bruges by type, 1400–1500

	Number of executions
Suicides	91
Inanimate objects	16
Animals	2
Total	109

The majority of the executions that involved human corpses in fifteenth-century Bruges were those of suicide victims. In the Liberty of Bruges from 1450–1460, in fact, the "execution" of suicide victims made up a little over half of all public executions.[28] This "execution" included the same trappings as the execution of a living criminal.[29] The bailiff paid the executioner for per-

28 During this decade, nine suicide victims (four women and five men) were executed posthumously. Eight living criminals were executed during the same period.

29 Hannes Lowagie, "'Bij desperatien': zelfmoord in het graafschap Vlaanderen tijdens de Bourgondische periode (1384–1500)," *Jaarboek voor Middeleeuwse Geschiedenis* 11 (2008):

forming the task, as well as paying a driver to transport the body to the site of execution. Drivers were paid the same amount for transporting a suicide victim, posthumously condemned for the crime of self-murder, as they were for a living prisoner condemned to death. The "execution" itself consisted of placing the dead body on an *estaque fourque* [a forked stake] where it would remain exposed to the elements.[30] The language used to describe the act of execution mirrors that used for a living criminal. In 1469 Bruges, the *schout* made a payment "audit pendeur pour avoir fait la justice de Marguerite, femme de Jehan de Witte naveur, laquelle fut pendue à une estaque pour ce qu'elle s'avoit despirée" [to the aforementioned hangman for having done justice on Marguerite, wife of Jehan de Witte, sailor, who was suspended on a stake for having committed suicide].[31] Directly below this entry, the *schout* also recorded a payment "audit pendeur pour avoir fait la justice de Pieter Lievins, lequel fu coppé la teste pour ce qu'il avoit tué ung nommé Maertin de Aertrycke" [to the aforementioned hangman for having done justice on Pieter Lievins, who had his head cut off because he had killed a man named Maertin de Aertrycke].[32] Consistently throughout the fifteenth century, the language of payments made to the executioner of Bruges does not distinguish between the living and the dead upon whom he "did justice."

Though the majority of these non-living-human executions were for suicide, falsely-made goods were burned by the executioner in a public ritual that also resembled the execution of a living human. In 1482 Bruges, the *schout* paid the executioner for "avoir fait la justice de deux tonneaulx de composte, lequlez furent ars sur le pond de Saint Jehan comme faulses" [having done justice on two barrels of compost which were burned on St. John's bridge as false things].[33] One page earlier in that same account book, the executioner also received a payment for "avoit fait la justice" [having done justice] on six women "lesquelz furent ars du pechie de zodomie" [who were burned for

97–137; Karl Andriessen and Karolina Krysinska, "Public Disgrace and Financial Gain: Punishment of Suicide in Mechelen 1366–1795," *Suicidology Online* 6.2 (2015): 56–60; Alexander Murray, *Suicide in the Middle Ages: The Violent Against Themselves* (Oxford: Oxford University Press, 1998), 120–148.

30 Friends or family of the victim had success paying the bailiff in exchange for the body of their loved one. These payments appear in the money collected section of bailiff accounts alongside bailiff composition payments. The bailiff often noted that it was unclear whether or not that death was actually the result of suicide and not an accident, and that is why he released the body.

31 AGR, CC, 13779, f. 35v.

32 AGR, CC, 13779, f. 35v.

33 AGR, CC, 13781, f. 48r.

the sin of sodomy].[34] In the bailiff accounts, there is no distinction between burning those convicted of sodomy and burning goods deemed "false."[35] It is unclear what exactly made an object "false," though in other descriptions of object execution, the goods are described as being "falsely made," suggesting that a merchant was attempting to swindle his customers with a substandard or impure product.[36] Over the course of the fifteenth century, there were sixteen instances of object executions in Bruges including ginger, cinnamon, figs, saltpeter, herring, cloth, and even beaver fur.[37] In all cases, the falsely-made goods were dispatched by burning. The bailiff made payments for wood, straw, and other materials necessary for making the fire in addition to the payment made for "doing justice," which amounted to the same price as for burning a human criminal.

While the majority of non-human executions involved falsely-made objects and suicide victims, the executioner also punished animals for their crimes. In 1495, the bailiff of the Liberty of Bruges paid the executioner to bury two pigs alive that had killed a child.[38] While this case is the only instance of an animal being executed for homicide in fifteenth-century Bruges or the Liberty of Bruges, animals involved in bestiality cases were burned alongside the human offenders. For example, in 1461 in the Liberty of Bruges, the executioner burned two men and three cows at the stake after the two men confessed to

34 AGR, CC, 13781, f. 47v. "À Charles vande Eede, pendeur, pour avoir fait la justice de Amphenie femme de Josse van Halle, josne femme de Jehan Betins, Hester de Witte, Lysbet vande Muelne, Katheline Croicx, et Katherine Ysenbaert, lesquelz furent ars du pechie de zodomie." [To Charles vande Eede, hangman, for having done justice on Amphenie, the wife of Josse van Halle, the young wife of Jehan Betins, Hester de Witte, Lysbet vande Muelne, Katheline Croicx, et Katherin Ysenbaert, who were burned for the sin of sodomy]. For more on the prosecution of female sodomy in medieval Flanders, see: J. Roelans, "Visible Women: Female Sodomy in the Late Medieval and Early Modern Southern Netherlands (1400–1550)," *BMGN—Low Countries Historical Review* 130.3 (2015): 3–24.

35 Sodomy in the Middle Ages referred to a range of non-procreative sexual behaviors, including masturbation, not merely male same-sex intercourse. For a legal description of sodomy as a crime in Flanders specifically, see: Wielant, *Corte instructie in materie criminele*, Capital 96.

36 For example, in 1442 Bruges, a cask of ginger was found to be falsely made: AGR, CC, 13774, f. 10v. "Au pendeur pour avoir fait la justice d'un tonneel de gingembre, liquel fu trouvé que c'estoit fause d'euvre" [To the hangman for having done justice on a barrel of ginger which was found to have been falsely made].

37 The case of beaver fur appears in 1445 Bruges. AGR, CC, 13775, f. 4r. "pour avoir fait la justice de certaines fourures de bevers, lesquelles furent ars sur le pont Saint Jehan" [For having done justice on certain beaver furs, which were burned on the bridge of Saint Jehan].

38 AGR, CC, 13710, f. 212r. "Audit Maistre Jaques, payé d'avoir fait justice et enfouy deux pourcheaulx, lesquelz avoient tué ung enfant" [To the aforementioned Master Jaques, paid for having done justice and buried two sows who had killed a child].

engaging in sexual acts with the cows.[39] Cases of animal execution are not limited in fifteenth-century Flanders and appear in archival records of capital punishment across continental Europe, beginning in the second half of the thirteenth century.[40] Medieval judicial proceedings involving animals fall into three main types: ecclesiastical trials for collective groups of wild animals often pests such as bugs or rats, executions for domestic animals who kill a human being, and cases of bestiality in which animals are punished alongside the offending humans.

Though animal executions are well attested, their frequency is hard to assess and likely varied in different regions.[41] Edward Payson Evans's *The Criminal Prosecution and Capital Punishment of Animals* (1906) remains the main voice of authority for a comprehensive list of such events, both the ecclesiastical trials and the secular executions. However, Evans relies heavily on secondary and tertiary sources, leading Leslie MacGregor and others to question the validity of some of the trials he documented.[42] MacGregor also suggests, based on her own work on financial records of executions in France, that Evans's list is incomplete and there are animal trials buried in archival records that have yet to be studied in detail.[43] Because of this need for further archival research, Michel Pastoureau described the state of scholarship on medieval animal trials as "une historiographie décevante" [a disappointing historiography] in 2004.[44] In fifteenth-century Flanders, in addition to the two pigs executed in 1495, there were at least two other examples of pigs being executed for killing a

39 AGR, CC, 13706, f. 30r. "Audit Jehan Blondeel, boureel, pour avoir examiné deux joosnes hommes et en après brulé à ung estaque avec trois vaches" [To the aforementioned Jehan Blondeel, executioner, for having examined two young men and afterwards burned them at the stake with three cows].

40 The first medieval animal execution occurred in 1266 in Fontenay-aux-Roses, after a pig killed a child, Edward Payson Evans, *The Criminal Prosecution and Capital Punishment of Animals: The Lost History of Europe's Animal Trials*, (London: William Heinemann, 1906), 140.

41 Animal executions are well-documented in continental Europe but do not appear in medieval England. J.J. Finkelstein identified the areas of highest concentration as southern and eastern France as well as neighboring areas in Switzerland, Italy, and Germany, J.J. Finkelstein, "The Ox That Gored," *Transactions of the American Philosophical Society* 71. 2 (1981): 1–89 at 67.

42 MacGregor, "Criminalising Animals in Medieval France: Insights from Records of Executions," 2; Anila Srivastava, "'Mean, dangerous, and uncontrollable beasts': Mediaeval Animal Trials," *Mosaic: An Interdisciplinary Critical Journal* 40.1 (2007): 127–43 at 130; Friedland, *Seeing Justice Done*, 9.

43 MacGregor, "Criminalising Animals in Medieval France," 3.

44 Pastoureau, *Une histoire symbolique du Moyen Âge occidental*, 32, 36.

child: in Brussels in 1462 and in Ypres in 1459.[45] None of these appear in Evan's list of trials and they are also missing from counts of animal executions in the Low Countries.[46] Like the punishment of dead bodies or inanimate objects, the execution of animals in late-medieval Bruges, though rare, was part of the ordinary functioning of the judicial system. While not as common as the other types of non-human execution in Flanders, the execution of domesticated animals illuminates how people thought about an executed subject in the fifteenth-century cities.

Despite a challenging source base with yet unexploited opportunities for original archival research, the execution of animals in the Middle Ages has provided fertile ground for exploring the practical function of punishment and the boundary between man and beast. Evans and other early researchers saw animal trials as evidence that medieval justice was primitive, but modern scholarship has progressed past such dismissals of medieval animal trials as uncivilized and irrational.[47] Some scholars take anthropological approaches by exploring the social value that such judicial proceedings had for the community. For Nicholas Humphrey, courts of law held animals responsible for their actions in order "to domesticate chaos, to impose order on the world of accidents," and help people make sense of painful events.[48] Similarly, Paul Friedland saw the execution of animals, as well as effigies and dead bodies, as "a means of overcoming the fact of the crime and healing from the wound inflicted by it."[49] The community invested time, money, and an attention to

45 F. Vanhemelryck, *De criminaliteit in de ammanie van Brussel van de late middleleeuwen tot het einde van het Ancien régime (1404–1789)* (Brussels: Paleis der Academiën, 1981), 339; Diegerick, "Mélanges pour servir à l'histoire des moeurs, des usages, des faits, des hommes, de la littérature et des arts de la ville d'Ypres et de l'ancienne West-Flandre," 380–81.

46 Evans, *The Criminal Prosecution and Capital Punishment of Animals: The Lost History of Europe's Animal Trials*; Fuchs, *De hond aan de galg*, 5–7; Janssen, "Dieren als dader?", 44.

47 Evans saw animal trials as showing the "rude instinct of revenge" (*The Criminal Prosecution*, 184). Similar explanations, such as "mental confusions" and "intellectual fog of the age," seen in Frazer, *Folk-Lore of the Old Testament*, 3:445, or how "the savage, in his rage, obliterates all distinctions between man and beast" in Hyde, "The Prosecution and Punishment of Animals and Lifeless Things in the Middle Ages and Modern Times", 722.

48 Nicholas Humphrey, *The Mind Made Flesh: Essays from the Frontiers of Psychology and Evolution* (Oxford: Oxford University Press, 2002), 251. Humphrey also wrote this in his forward to the 1987 edition of Evans's *The Criminal Prosecution and Capital Punishment of Animals*.

49 Friedland, *Seeing Justice Done*, 107. Similar ideas also appear in Paul Schiff Berman, "Rats, Pigs, and Statues on Trial: The Creation of Cultural Narratives in the Prosecution of Animals and Inanimate Objects," *New York University Law Review* 69 (1994): 288–326 at 323.

formal procedure when executing animals because of its cathartic effect for the public, comparable to the effect of a human execution.

Scholars interested in medieval mentalities have used animal trials to investigate medieval ideas about humanity's relationship to the animal kingdom and the boundary between them. By subjecting animals to human justice, medieval courts expressed their control over the natural world, reasserting the hierarchy of man over beast that an animal had disrupted by killing a person.[50] For some, this was aimed at deterrence: if even a pig could be subjected to the letter of the law, what hope did a human criminal have of escaping justice?[51] According to Esther Cohen, learned ideas of human justice having dominion over the earth combined with popular anthropomorphism to produce the phenomenon of animal trials.[52] In this view, the practice of applying human judicial procedures to animals and sentencing them to public punishment suggests the personification of criminal creatures. This personification meant that medieval judicial procedures assigned legal and moral responsibility to animals for their actions and smudged the line between man and beast.[53] For Joyce Salisbury and Susan Crane, animal trials fit into a larger narrative about the complex relationship between animals and humans in medieval society, as seen in beast fables, bestiaries, religious texts, and other sources.[54] Salisbury places the appearance of animal trials in the thirteenth century on a larger trajectory that she sees in the development of animal-human relations, from being two discrete categories in the early Middle Ages towards more blurred boundaries by the late Middle Ages. Though Salisbury and others offer convincing evidence of anthropomorphized animals in medieval thought and practice, the specific example of animal execution does not fit well into this

50 Finkelstein, "The Ox That Gored," 70; Patrick J.J. Phillips, *Medieval Animal Trials: Justice for All* (Lewiston, N.Y.: Edwin Mellen Press, 2013).

51 Jody Enders, "Homicidal Pigs and the Antisemitic Imagination," *Exemplaria* 14.1 (2002): 201–38 at 220–221. For an argument against non-human execution as deterrence, see: Paul Friedland, "Beyond Deterrence: Cadavers, Effigies, Animals and the Logic of Executions in Premodern France," *Historical Reflections/Réflexions Historiques* 29.2 (2003): 295–317.

52 Esther Cohen, *The Crossroads of Justice: Law and Culture in Late Medieval France* (Leiden: Brill, 1993), 100–133; Esther Cohen "Law, Folklore and Animal Lore," *Past & Present* 110 (1986): 6–37; Joyce E. Salisbury, *The Beast Within: Animals in the Middle Ages* (New York: Routledge, 1994), 108–115.

53 Though this theory has found skilled defenders in modern scholarship with Esther Cohen and Joyce Salisbury, the idea that animal trials show the legal personification of animals appears as early as Osenbruggen, *Studien zur deutschen und schweizerischen Rechtsgeschichte*.

54 Salisbury, *The Beast Within*; Susan Crane, *Animal Encounters: Contacts and Concepts in Medieval Britain* (Philadelphia: University of Pennsylvania Press, 2013).

model. Animals may have faced execution, but they were not treated like humans in secular courts, nor assigned human characteristics of rationality and moral responsibility for their actions.

For most cases involving animals in fifteenth-century Bruges, the animals were treated as property. People were regularly fined for damage that their animals did to the land or to the property of others and, especially in the Liberty of Bruges, the theft of farm animals seems to have been common. Even in cases where an animal killed a human, most did not face execution. In 1470 in Bruges, a mare was confiscated from its owner and sold by the bailiff because it had run over a child who died as a result.[55] Over the course of the fifteenth century, the *schout* of Bruges confiscated horses that killed someone on at least four separate occasions, each time selling the horse and retaining the profit.[56] Comparing the four cases of confiscation to the single case of animal execution in the Liberty of Bruges in the fifteenth century, the execution a homicidal animal seems to have been the exception, not the norm.[57]

The confiscation of dangerous beasts conformed to contemporary legal prescriptions. For late-medieval Flanders, the most relevant juridical text is Filips Wielant's *Corte instructie in materie criminele* (1510). Wielant advises the law to confiscate and then sell for profit animals who kill, and only advocates for animal execution in cases of bestiality in which they are to be burned alongside the human offenders.[58] Similar assertions appear in earlier customary law, such as the *Coustumes et stilles de Bourgoigne* (*c.*1270–1360), which recommends that local lords confiscate and then sell an ox or horse that has killed someone. While one ought not "do justice" on oxen and horses that kill, the *Coustumes* specifies that "if other beasts or Jews do it, they should be hanged by their hind feet," leaving the door open for animal executions while

55 AGR, CC, 13779, 42v. "receu à cause de la vendicion d'un jument, à quoy ledit escoutette avoit mis main comme confiscqué à monditseigneur pour ce que ladit jument avoit couru sur ung petit enfant et ledit enfant tellement blessié qu'il brief après en morut" [Money received from selling a mare, which the *scout* had confiscated on behalf of the lord because the aforementioned mare had run over a small child and injured the child so much that he died a short time after].

56 There are at least three similar cases, one in Bruges in 1476 (AGR, CC, 13781, f. 2v) and two in 1482 (AGR, CC, 13781, f. 33r and f. 37v).

57 It is likely that the type of animal was significant. Evans and many others since have noted that the majority of animals executed for homicide were pigs. For why pigs may have been treated differently than other animals, see: Karl Steel, *How to Make a Human: Animals and Violence in the Middle Ages* (Columbus: Ohio State University Press, 2011), 183–4.

58 Wielant, *Corte instructie in materie criminele*. Capital 145 for confiscation, Capital 96 for bestiality.

dehumanizing Jewish criminals.[59] Additional endorsements of animal execution in the Middle Ages are hard to find. In thirteenth-century France, a time and place where animal trials are reliably attested, Philippe de Beaumanoir's *Coutumes de Beauvaisis* calls the practice "senseless because dumb beasts have no understanding of what is good and what is evil."[60] Thomas Aquinas made similar arguments about the rationality of animals to forbid the practice of giving benedictions and maledictions to animals, thus condemning ecclesiastical proceedings against collections of insects and other pests.[61]

Forty-five years after Wielant's legal treatise, another Flemish jurist, Joos de Damhouder stated that "a beast is punishable, if it commits the crime through natural malice, and not through the instigation of others."[62] Explicit descriptions of animal culpability are rare in medieval legal writing, but do appear in that of Guy Pape, a fifteenth-century French jurist who approved of trials and punishments for "brutish animals."[63] For Damhouder and Pape there was at least some degree of malicious intent on the part of animals, a departure from most earlier writings which denied the rationality of animals.[64] Paul Friedland argues that the change over time is a result of jurists seeking a way to reconcile a long-standing customary practice with contemporary legal principles.[65] Though Damhouder and Pape give little in the way of explanation, in sixteenth-century France, Pierre Ayrault considered animal execution a method of deterrence, both for human and animal criminals.[66]

Though some animals were certainly executed after killing a human, such as the aforementioned pigs buried alive in 1495, there is little evidence that these animals faced all parts of the judicial process. Scholars convinced of the

---

59 "Coustumes et stilles de Bourgoigne," in *Essai sur l'histoire du droit français au Moyen Age*, ed. Charles Giraud (Paris: Videcoq, 1842), 2:302. "Lon dit et tient selon droit et la coustume de Bourgoingne que se un beuf ou un cheuau fait un ou pluseurs homicides il nan doiuent poinct morir, ne lon nen doit faire justice, feur quilz doiuent estre pris par le seigneur, en qui justice ilz ont fait le delit, ou par ses gens, et lui sont confisquez et doiuent estre vendus et exploictiez au prouffit du dit seigneur, mes se autres bestes ou juyf le font, ilz doiuent estre pendus par les piez derreniers."

60 Friedland, *Seeing Justice Done*, 113.

61 Thomas Aquinas, *Summa theologica,* second part of the second part, quaestio 76.

62 de Damhouder, *Praxis rerum criminalium*, 539.

63 Pape, *Decisiones parlamenti delphinatus*. Quaestio 238.

64 On the (ir)rationality of animals, see: Crane, *Animal encounters*, 48–68; Salisbury, *The Beast Within*, 26–29, 111–113.

65 Friedland, *Seeing Justice Done*, 116.

66 This is also stated explicitly in some sixteenth-century trial records. In 1595 Leiden, a dog was hanged for killing a child, as an example for "others, especially other bad dogs" (Van Bruaene, "Revolting Beasts," 35).

legal personification of criminal animals often emphasize how "animals were treated to the full code of secular law, just like human defendants."[67] However, others, such as Jacob J. Finkelstein and Karl von Amira before him, emphasize that the main difference between the ecclesiastical trials against swarms of pests and secular courts sentencing homicidal animals to death was that the latter was merely a summary execution, since animals were not granted a trial or any other aspects of human justice besides capital punishment.[68] Though archival sources detail ecclesiastical procedures against bugs and rats, the records surviving from secular courts are records of execution. In some cases, original sources that describe payments made to an executioner have grown into tales of a full trial in secondary and tertiary sources. One of the most well-known cases of animal execution is the so-called Sow of Falaise, a pig who was executed for killing a child in 1386 and was apparently dressed in the clothes of a man to appear before the court. As Paul Friedland has shown, the story of a formal trial against the pig and the details about his clothing were later inventions.[69] The original medieval source resembled those seen for animals executed in Flanders: a series of payments made to the executioner for killing a dangerous animal. Similarly, there is little evidence that animals were interrogated under torture before receiving execution.[70] Certainly, in the case of Flanders, bailiffs made payments to the executioner for interrogating human suspects as well as payments to priests for taking confessions, but when the two pigs were executed in the Liberty of Bruges in 1495, only a payment for the execution appears. Though some suggest that there are lessons to be learned from medieval law in terms of extending legal protections to non-human sentient creatures, there is no compelling evidence that the medieval justice system treated animals like humans, only that executioners

67 Allie Terry-Fritsch, "Animal Trials, Humiliation Rituals, and the Sensuous Suffering of Criminal Offenders in Late Medieval and Early Modern Europe," in *Visualizing Sensuous Suffering and Affective Pain in Early Modern Europe and the Spanish Americas*, ed. Heather Graham and Lauren G. Kilroy-Ewbank (Leiden: Brill, 2017), 53–81 at 58; "All the trials were conducted with the same serious concern for legal points as trials of humans" (Salisbury, *The Beast Within*, 111).

68 Finkelstein, "The Ox That Gored," 64 and 69; Karl von Amira, *Thierstrafen und Thierprocesse* (Innsbruck: Wagnerischen Universitäts-Buchhandlung, 1891), 550; Thomas A. Fudgé, *Medieval Religion and Its Anxieties: History and Mystery in the Other Middle Ages* (New York: Palgrave Macmillan, 2016), 24.

69 Friedland, *Seeing Justice Done*, 3–9.

70 Enders, "Homicidal Pigs," 213. Though Enders notes a lack of concrete evidence for torture, she also cites arguments that torture did sometimes occur and entertains the possibility.

carried out lethal punishments upon them.[71] In addition, although animals in fifteenth-century Flanders could be executed for physical harm they inflicted on a human, an entire host of other, softer resolution options for homicide remained closed to them: private peace settlements, monetary compositions, and banishment. In Sven Gins's analysis of the execution of a sow for homicide in 1457 in Savigny-sur-Étang, he makes a similar observation, concluding that the many reconciliatory options of Burgundian customary law that spared human offenders the gallows during this period were closed to the porcine defendant. For Gins, subjecting animals to a select few human judicial procedures blurred boundaries in a way that ultimately celebrated human distinctiveness, "reifying the so-called human/nonhuman divide" to the detriment of the animal offender.[72]

Another problem with the theory of personification is that the majority of human-perpetrated killings, even those that reached the attention of the bailiff, did not result in execution in fifteenth-century Flanders. As seen in the table below, many more human killers were successfully able to negotiate a composition payment after having made peace with the family of the victim than were sentenced to death.

TABLE 10.3 The number of composition payments made for a killing compared to the number of executions, 1450–1500

	Composition payments	**Executions**
Bruges	86	33
Liberty of Bruges	105	12

This table ignores group activity, counting multiple individuals making a group composition together for a single crime or a sentence of execution given to multiple people for a single crime as one event. For more on the prosecution of human killers in fifteenth-century Flanders, see: Mireille J. Pardon, "Necessary Killing: Crime, Honour, and Masculinity in Late Medieval Bruges and Ghent," in *Patriarchy, Honour, and Violence: Masculinities in Premodern Europe*, ed. Jacqueline Murray (Toronto: Centre for Reformation and Renaissance Studies, 2022), 71–91.

71 Some find inspiration for modern animal rights in medieval animal trials, see: Jen Girgen, "The Historical and Contemporary Prosecution and Punishment of Animals," *Animal Law* 9 (2003): 97–133; Katie Sykes, "Human Drama, Animal Trials: What the Medieval Animal Trials Can Teach Us About Justice for Animals," *Animal Law Review* 17.2 (2011): 273–311; Bruce Holsinger, "Of Pigs and Parchment: Medieval Studies and the Coming of the Animal," *PMLA* 124.2 (2009): 616–23 at 618.

72 Sven Gins, "Casting Justice Before Swine: Late Mediaeval Pig Trials as Instances of Human Exceptionalism," *Sophia* (2023): 27. E-pub ahead of print release.

However, bailiff accounts do not provide a full picture of the judicial system. Those who received a temporary or permanent banishment, made a private peace settlement, received a letter of remission that repealed their death sentence, or simply were acquitted of the crime are not included here. Thus, the chances of being executed for killing are actually even lower than they appear when compared to composition payments.

For both animal and human killers, execution was ordered only in exceptional circumstances for particularly heinous crimes. Building on previous scholarship that suggests trials humanized animal offenders, recent scholarship argues that executions transformed both the human and animal killer, putting them in an "in between place" by dehumanizing one while endowing the other with human characteristics, such as rationality and moral responsibility.[73] In the words of Claude Gauvard, writing on execution in medieval France, the criminal was "bestialized at the same time that the beast was humanized."[74] However, this reading of non-human execution does not account for the executions of dead bodies and inanimate objects and overestimates the degree to which animals sentenced to execution were treated like humans by the judicial system. In the context of fifteenth-century Flanders, given the prevalence of executions of dead bodies and commercial goods, the execution ritual did not merely bestialize the offender, but objectified him, animal or human. The animal offender was not personified because all the elements of medieval justice that emphasized the humanity of the condemned—their potential for composition payments, their last confession to a priest, even their interrogation by the executioner—were denied to them.

Nor was the human offender particularly bestialized in ordinary execution procedures. An exception is the so-called "Jewish execution," where a Jewish criminal would sometimes be suspended between two dogs. This form of execution appears in German sources from the late thirteenth to early seventeenth centuries in several variations: the dogs are either living or dead and the condemned are either hanged normally or suspended upside down.[75] In 1434 Basel, two Jews condemned for theft "were urged repeatedly to turn Christian, so as not to die like beasts" and a sudden convert faced decapitation while the other was suspended between two dogs.[76] Similarly, a fifteenth-century chronicler in the city of Dortmund recorded that "the three dogs were hanging

73 Terry-Fritsch, "Animal Trials," 55. Enders, "Homicidal Pigs," 204.

74 Gauvard, *Condamner à mort au Moyen Âge*, 262.

75 Rudolf Glanz, "The 'Jewish Execution' in Medieval Germany," *Jewish Social Studies* 5.1 (1943): 3–26.

76 Glanz, "The 'Jewish Execution' in Medieval Germany," 4.

together on the gallows" in reference to a Jewish criminal executed between two dogs.[77] The rhetoric employed with this kind of execution symbolically equated the Jewish criminal with a dog by treating them the same way at the gallows.[78]

In most cases of execution, though, humans were not treated like animals, nor animals like humans. For particularly odious crimes, both animal and human offenders lost their identity in society (property for animals and person for humans). The executioner performed justice on an irredeemable criminal, a thing now bereft of former ties, ownership, or sociability, violently removing *it* from the community. Instead of animals being seen as human in exceptional circumstances, execution objectified both human and animal killers, transforming them for the audience before physically transforming them through judicial violence. Domesticated pigs, barrels of herring, live criminals, and self-drowned bodies were all objects of justice, a routine but spectacular act performed by the urban executioner and paid for by the bailiff.

Financial penalties still dwarfed bodily punishments in fifteenth-century Flanders, but the role of the executioner was increasing. Capital punishment, as well as public, shame-based punishments, were on the rise. The most rigorous demonstration of this phenomenon from a quantitative perspective is Xavier Rousseaux's work in Nivelles, where he tracked with statistical precision the evolution from a "medieval, urban-based, tax-oriented system" to a "modern, state-based, punishment-focused system" during the fifteenth and sixteenth centuries.[79] Similar studies of individual cities in the Low Countries and France have come to the same conclusion, as rates of fines, bailiff compositions, penitential pilgrimages, and banishments fell and an elaborate system of corporal punishments took their place.[80] The conventional explanation for this evolution, enunciated emphatically by Pieter Spierenburg's

77 Norbert Schnitzler, "Anti-Semitism, Image desecration, and the Problem of 'Jewish execution'," in *History and Images*, 357–78 at 375.

78 Cohen, *The Crossroads of Justice*, 92–93. For an exploration of dog symbolism in relation to Jews beyond simply bestialization, see: Schnitzler, "Anti-Semitism," 374–376.

79 Rousseaux, "Taxer ou chatier? L'émergence du pénal: enquête sur la justice nivelloise (1400–1650);" de La Croix, Rousseaux, and Urbain, "To Fine or to Punish in the Late Middle Ages."

80 Hannelore Van Hamme, "Stedelijk particularisme versus vorstelijke centralisatie en hun impact op de bestraffing van criminaliteit in het vijftiende-eeuwse Gent (ca. 1419–ca. 1480)," *Handelingen der Maatschappij voor Geschiedenis en Oudheidkunde te Gent* LV (2001): 707–26; J. van Herwaarden, *Opgelegde bedevaarten: een studie over de praktijk van opleggen van bedevaarten (met name in de stedelijke rechtspraak) in de Nederlanden gedurende de late middeleeuwen (ca. 1300–ca. 1550)* (Assen: Van Gorcum, 1978); Muchembled, *Le temps des supplices: de l'obéissance sous les rois absolus, XVe–XVIIIe siècle*; Dirk

The Spectacle of Suffering, attributes this transition to the need of nascent states to assert control, seeing "the display of physical punishment as a manifestation of authority."[81] Whether it is Spierenburg's "spectacle of suffering," Richard van Dülmen's "theater of horror," or even Michel Foucault's "spectacle of the scaffold," scholars see the judicial ritual as theatrically reinforcing the power of the prince by publicly punishing the body of the condemned.[82] Thus, the evolution from financial to physical punishment was intimately tied to the rise of state power and developed of a centralized judicial bureaucracy. Yet such an explanation views the rise of bodily punishment, a public ritual in which the entire community participated, only from the point of view of ruling powers. Despite an emphasis on state power, Foucault notes that in public executions "the main character was the people, whose real and immediate presence was required for the performance."[83] Such performances of judicial violence not only exhibited the power of the state, they also transformed the accused before their community. The executioner exiled the condemned from the community, not just through their death and denial of a Christian burial, but also by stripping them of their identity within the community and dehumanizing them by performing the same justice on them as they performed on inanimate objects, dead bodies, and sometimes animals.

The growing role of the executioner in the Flemish penal system at the end of the Middle Ages shows more than rising state power. As people received bodily punishments for a wider range of offences, fewer people qualified for a reconciliation that emphasized their humanity and social connections within their community. The shift towards spectacular punishment changed how people thought about criminals: the convict became irredeemable as their crime became an essential part of their identity. In other words, they were a murderer instead of someone who once killed a man. The executed subject was not merely dehumanized or bestialized, but also objectified by a judicial ritual that treated them the same way it treated corpses, pigs, or barrels of spices. Whether the subject of the procedure was animal, human, or an inanimate object, an execution violently removed a dangerous object from the community before an assembled crowd. Certainly, when Katherine's sons entreated the city bailiff to remove the sign of their mother's execution in 1473, they did

Arend Berents, *Misdaad in de Middeleeuwen: een onderzoek naar de criminaliteit in het laat-middeleeuwse Utrecht* (Haarlem: Gottmer, 1976).

81 Spierenburg, *The Spectacle of Suffering*.

82 van Dülmen, *Theatre of Horror*; Michel Foucault, *Discipline and Punish: The Birth of the Prison* (New York: Vintage Books, 1995), 32.

83 Foucault, *Discipline and Punish*, 57.

not view their mother as an object. But the procedure that she had undergone encouraged objectification by placing her into a mental category that included non-humans. Instead of humanized animals or bestialized humans, evidence from Flanders suggests that execution transformed humans and animals into something else entirely. Instead of believing in the human rationality of the murderous pigs of 1495 Bruges, the assembled crowd viewed them as inherently monstrous and irredeemable—not dissimilar to how they viewed the many homicidal humans dispatched by the same executioner during his many years of service.

CHAPTER 11

No Face behind the Mask: Hangmen in Medieval and Early Modern English Culture

Ben Parsons

Representations of hangings and beheadings in early modern popular literature can often seem as ritualized as the spectacles they describe. On occasion, however, they will slip free of their formulas in striking ways. A case in point is *Groanes from Newgate* [**see Figure 11.1**], written in September 1663 by an author who identifies himself only as a "Person of quality."[1] In essence, *Groanes* is a parody of the broadside elegies that proliferated during the English Civil War (1642–1651) and remained popular as an offshoot of printed news-discourse after the Restoration (1660).[2] It takes care to emulate the established conventions of the form: like more sincere accounts of the deaths of Archbishop James Ussher or the earls of Huntingdon and Essex, it is surrounded by a funereal black border and emphasizes the nobility of its subject, with a frontispiece depicting a somber (though obviously fabricated) coat of arms.[3] Yet at the same time, *Groanes* is also a specimen of the form it is burlesquing, since it deals with the death of a verifiable, even notable public figure. As the subtitle goes on to explain, it concerns "Edvvard Dun, Esq: The Cities Common Hangman, who Dyed Naturally in his bed, the 11th. of September, 1663." The text then proceeds to bemoan Dun's death in high classical style, assuming the voice of the "New-gate Muse" to mourn the loss of the "dextrous *art*" with which "he would pull out a *Traytor*'s heart." The real root of the tragedy, however, is not the fact of Dun's passing, but that it did not take place on the

1 *Groanes from Newgate* (London: Edward Crowch, 1663), Wing G2055.

2 See: James D. Garrison, "Elegy," in *Oxford Handbook of British Poetry, 1660–1800*, ed. Jack Lynch (Oxford: Oxford University Press, 2016), 528–46.

3 John Quarles, *An Elegie on the most reverend and learned James Vsher L. Archbishop of Armagh* (London: John Stafford, 1656), Wing Q126; J.B, *A mournfull elegie, in pious and perpetuall memory of the most honourable, Robert, Earle of Essex and Evve, Viscount Hereford* (London: Thomas Banks, 1646), Wing M2986A. Further examples of the genre and its characteristic format include Thomas Howard, *An elegie vpon the death of Thomas, Earle of Strafford* (London: s.n., 1641), Wing H1528; Alexander Spicer, *An elegie on the much lamented death of the Right Honorable Sir Arthur Chichester Knight* (London: Robert Bird, 1643), STC 23100; S.H., *Funerall Elegies, Or the Sad Muses in Sables* (London: Thomas Wilson, 1655), Wing H117.

 | DOI:10.1163/9789004742598_013

scaffold; paradoxically, it is a gallows lament for an execution that did not, in fact, occur. As the "Muse" declares in the course of pouring out her "grief": "It was (oh *Death!*) an unjust thing/Thou should'st deny him his own *swing*." The text concludes by neatly and concisely pulling together its threads of parody, eulogy, mock-classicism, and dark comedy; in place of the traditional FINIS, its final word is FUNIS [rope].

Groanes is an eccentric text, and like all eccentric texts is interesting in several respects. It has value at a straightforward documentary level, providing a firm date for Dun's death and confirming some details of his career, even if it reduces the man himself to a bloodthirsty caricature.[4] In terms of cultural history, it is similarly suggestive, showing that the topical elegy had attained enough cohesion as a genre to be open to parody. Muted political tension also runs through the piece. While it sets itself up as broadly comic, with an epigraph quoting Cato's advice "inter pone tuis interdum gaudia curis" [introduce sometimes levity into your cares], it evokes a particularly contentious event from recent history.[5] Its frontispiece refers explicitly to the ritual "executions" of the corpses of Oliver Cromwell, Henry Ireton, and John Bradshaw at Tyburn in 1661, actions which even Pepys privately confessed "do trouble me"; obviously implicating Dun in the affair, the arms it assigns to him show a triangular gibbet with the names of the three dead regicides inscribed beneath.[6] But what is perhaps most striking about the *Groanes* is the level of playfulness and inventiveness it shows in its treatment of the hangman. It seems to view his trade above all as a collection of images to be exploited for imaginative and creative ends. By envisioning the gibbet and noose as Dun's device, and making "the noble *Hemp* ... the Ax, the Block, the Knife" act as his "mourners," the text plays with the apparatus of execution; it treats execution above all as raw material for its satirical fantasy, a set of elements to be reassembled into a burlesque of heraldry and official ceremony. In short, the author sees

4 Evidence suggests that Dun approached his role with an apolitical professionalism bordering on embarrassment, rather than the gloating sadism implied by the *Groanes*. His appearance in popular satires from the 1650s shows that he took office during the Commonwealth and continued to perform it after the Restoration of Charles II in 1660; more tellingly, his will, which is appended to a later edition of *Groanes*, makes no mention of his status as hangman, describing him instead as "Citizen and Comb-maker." See: William Chappell and J. Woodfall Ebsworth, eds., *Roxburghe Ballads*, 9 vols. (Hertford: Stephen Austin and Sons, 1869–1901), 7.658–60; *The Last Will and Testament of Squire Dun* (London: George Horton, n.d.), Wing L528A.

5 *Disticha Catonio*, 3.6, *Minor Latin Poems*, ed. J. Wight Duff and Arnold M. Duff (London: William Heinemann, 1934), 610.

6 Samuel Pepys, *Diary*, ed. Robert Latham and William Matthews, 10 vols. (London: HarperCollins, 2000), 1.309.

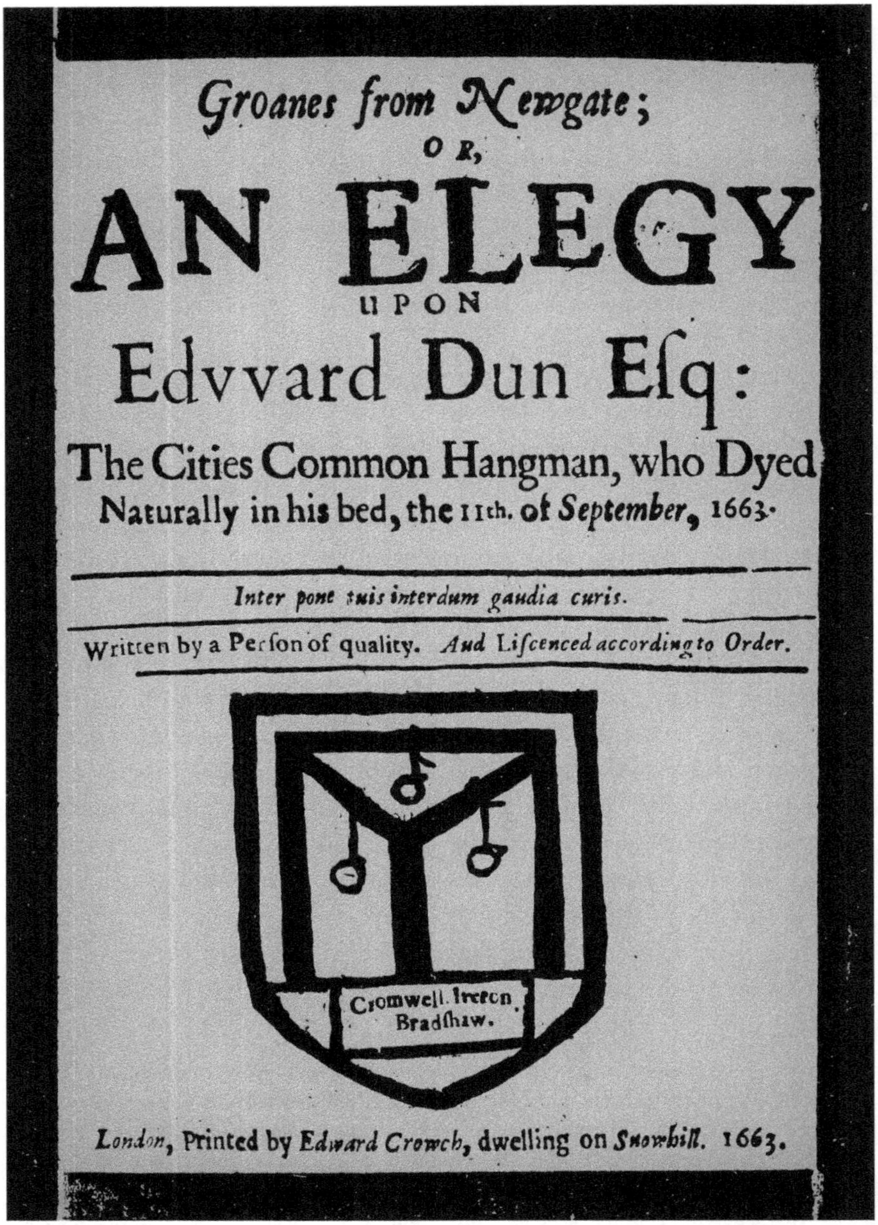

Groanes from Newgate;
OR,
AN ELEGY
UPON
Edvvard Dun Esq:
The Cities Common Hangman, who Dyed Naturally in his bed, the 11th. of September, 1663.

Inter pone tuis interdum gaudia curis.

Written by a Person of quality. And Liscenced according to Order.

London, Printed by Edward Crowch, dwelling on Snowhill. 1663.

FIGURE 11.1 Frontispiece of *Groanes from Newgate, or, An elegy upon Edvvard Dun, Esq.* (1663), with Dun's supposed coat of arms

Dun's profession as a fertile seam of meaning from which he can make literary capital.

The meanings *Groanes* finds in Dun's profession go far beyond those its author creates; it also calls on numerous pre-existing tropes and resonances. Its mocking treatment of Dun as a nobleman, for instance, looks back to a long-running joke associated with his office. The allusion is to a curious stunt at the College of Heralds in 1616, when Ralph Brooke duped Sir William Segar into conferring arms on Gregory Brandon, common hangman from *c.*1611, apparently to prove Segar's laxity in awarding such honors; from that point, London's hangmen were flippantly referred to as "squire" or "esquire" by custom.[7] The central jibe of the text, that Dun died "*untimely* in his *bed*" rather than sampling his own wares, provides a further example. It rests on the longstanding cliché of the hangman dying on his own gallows, one which surfaces with suspicious regularity in the popular criminal biographies of the *Newgate Calendar* and Old Bailey proceedings.[8] Indeed, Dun himself had already become a stock figure in satires and polemics in the decades before *Groanes* appeared: he interrogates the Parliamentarian Arthur Haselrig in one anonymous dialogue, and is ironically honored as a "worthy patriot" in the third part of Samuel Butler's *Hudibras* (1678).[9] Overall, *Groanes* treats Dun less as a man and more as a cultural resource. Although it records the fact and date of his death, it evokes him not as a concrete historical individual, but a nucleus around which various symbols and narratives have cohered. His status as the "Cities Common Hangman" has turned him into a pool of ready-made meanings that the text and texts like it can exploit for comedic and political ends.

---

7 Anthony Wagner, *Heralds of England: A History of the Office and College of Arms* (London: H.M. Stationery Office, 1967), 219, 389.

8 The hangmen Pascha Rose (d. 1686), John Price (d. 1718), and William Marvell (d. 1719?) are all reputed to have died in this manner, although the last-named was more likely transported or "Whipt a Mile" at his own request. See: *True Account of the Behaviour and Confession of the Criminals, Condemned on Saturday the 22nd of May* (London: E. Mallet, 1686), 3; *Complete Newgate Calendar*, ed. John L. Rayner and G.T. Crook, 5 vols. (London: Navarre Society, 1926), 2.265–70; *Proceedings on the King's Commission of the Peace … on Wednesday, Thursday, Friday being the 14th, 15th, and 16th, of this Instant October* (London: J. Philips, 1719), 1–2, 7; Alfred F. Robbins, "The Common Hangman," *Notes and Queries* 10.8.8 (1907): 353–54.

9 *The Hang-mans lamenration* [sic] (London: Thomas Vere and William Gilbertson, 1660), Wing H650; Samuel Butler, *Hudibras*, 3.2.1534–36, ed. John Wilders (Oxford: Clarendon Press, 1967), 180. "Squire Dun" appears either as a speaker or character in some sixteen further ballads and texts of popular protest printed between 1655 and 1663. The earliest date from the Commonwealth, i.e. *The merry bell-man's out-cryes* (London: s.n., 1655), 4 (Wing C64); *Fortvnes lottery* (London: Thomas Vere, 1657), 3 (Wing P3365A).

Dun's absorption into popular discourse raises a number of questions. Some are immediate and obvious: what meanings and resonances were located in his office, what larger attitudes can be identified within them, and what implications do they carry for capital punishment as a practice? However, when taking a longer view, a range of further and perhaps more provocative concerns appear. The fact is that the *Groanes*' treatment of its subject represents a relatively new development in English popular culture. Its readiness to insert Dun into its elaborate parodies and mine him for comedic ends stands in marked contrast to the depiction of executioners in previous centuries. Dun's predecessors cross into discourse only in more limited ways, and seem to hold fewer resonances for authors and audiences; overall, medieval sources show much less interest in executioners, despite their comparable fascination with execution itself. There is, in effect, a clear moment at which these functionaries developed the values attached to them by *Groanes*, and in which they crystallize as objects of attention and literary invention. What is more, this transition is not merely cosmetic: it can be read as a Foucauldian "rupture" or "discontinuity," pinpointing shifts in the mechanics of power and the "certain rules" by which they operate, especially as they move from monarchic to bourgeois forms.[10]

Of course, Dun was not the only early modern headsman who attracted allusion and impersonation. Despite the deep impression he left on print culture, he merely embodies a general fascination with axemen in the period. One figure of comparable significance is the Jacobean hangman "Maister Derrick," who is intermittently evoked as a curative against "Papists" or "Cheating theeues" in moral literature from *c.*1606, and whose infamy caused his name to become a synonym for a crane or hoist.[11] But it was Dun's immediate successor, Jack Ketch, who had the strongest pull on the popular imagination. John or Jack Ketch remained in the position of common hangman until his death in 1686, albeit with the occasional hiatus spent in the debtors' prison at Marshalsea.[12] It is hard to overstate Ketch's presence in seventeenth-century popular discourse. His name became a generic term for executioner while he was still in office, and continued to be a major point of reference well into

10 Michel Foucault, *The Archaeology of Knowledge*, trans. A.M. Sheridan Smith (London: Routledge, 2002), 4, 138.

11 Richard West, *The court of conscience or Dick Whippers sessions* (London: George Eld, 1607), sig. D1v (STC 25263); *The shamefull downefall of the Popes kingdome* (London: s.n., 1606), fol. 1 (STC 11620.5); Robert Hendrickson, *Dictionary of Eponyms* (New York: Dorset Press, 1972), 90.

12 Geoffrey Abbott, *Lords of the Scaffold: A History of the Executioner* (London: St. Martin's Press, 1991), 48–49.

the nineteenth century and beyond, not least of all in the Punch and Judy puppet-shows staged at Georgian and Victorian fairgrounds.[13] During his own lifetime, he featured pervasively in pamphlet and ballad literature, becoming so firmly absorbed into fiction that few concrete facts about him can be verified; even the correct form of his name is uncertain.[14]

What is particularly remarkable about Ketch's literary career is the high level of versatility he is accorded. In trial proceedings he appears simply as an officer of the court; in ballads on the Rye House Plot (1683) and Monmouth Rebellion (1685) he is the nemesis of "Traytours;" in burlesque almanacs he features in surreal and nonsensical "prognostications;" in moral literature he is an "Eye Witness" to the power of heartfelt penance; in literary disputes he serves as a jocular threat against plagiarists.[15] His dramatic functions in these texts are as variable as their genres: at times he is a mouthpiece for criticism, and at others an object of ridicule in his own right, especially during his spells at Marshalsea "amongst Bankrupts and Tatterdemallions;" in some texts he appears as a character and in others as a speaking persona, most pointedly in the so-called *Apologie of John Ketch* (1683), where he is made to repent the botched execution of Lord William Russell and "the hard usage he is said to have had in the Severing of his Head from his Body."[16] His flexibility as a signifier reached its highest pitch in the "print crisis" around the Popish Plot (1678–81), when he

13 V.A.C. Gatrell, *The Hanging Tree: Execution and the English People 1770–1868* (Oxford: Oxford University Press, 1994), 109–59; Ryan Howard, *Punch and Judy in 19th Century America* (Jefferson, NC: McFarland, 2013), 20–22. For an early example of his name taking on a generalized meaning, predating the OED's earliest sources, see *A Pleasant Discourse Between the Old and New Jack Catch* (London: D.M., 1685), Wing P2546, an imagined dialogue between "Old Catch" and "New Catch" (or OC and NC), apparently on the occasion of "the Latters being Whip'd from Rosemary-Lane to the Hermitage … for Scandalous Words."

14 Tim Wales, "Ketch [Catch], Jack [John] (d.1686)," *Oxford Dictionary of National Biography*, ed. Colin Matthew and Brian Harrison, 60 vols. (Oxford: Oxford University Press, 2004), 31.443–46.

15 *A true narrative of the proceedings at the Sessions-house in the Old-Bayly; from Friday the 14th of this instant January, to Munday the 17th* (London: D.M., 1676), 4 (Wing T2815A); *Sir Thomas Armstrong's Last Farewell* (London: J. Dean, 1684), fol. 1 (Wing S3891A); *The Loyal Man's Letany* (London: George Croom, 1685), fol. 1 (Wing L3353); *Poor Robin, a Prognostication* (London: Company of Stationers, 1683) sig. C4 (Wing A2202); Stephen Trigg, *Most Strange and Terrible Astrological Predictions* (London: J. Harefinch, 1684), 3 (Wing T2275); *A Protestant Letter to the Lords in the Tower* (London: s.n., 1680), fol. 1 (Wing B120); *The Character of Wit's Squint-Eyed Maid* (London: W. Davis, 1681), 2 (Wing C2031).

16 *A Dialogue between Jack Ketch and his Journey-man* (London: J. Dean, 1683), Wing D1314; *The Man of Destiny's Hard Fortune* (London: T.M., 1679), 5 (Wing K355); *The Apologie of John Ketch, Esq.* (London: John Brown, 1683), fol. 1 (Wing K354).

proved equally useful for supporters and critics of the anti-Catholic conspiracy theorist Titus Oates.[17] Nevertheless, although Ketch loomed large over his period as the archetypal headsman, his status is only an extreme manifestation of a general principle. Ketch merely underscores the plenitude of meanings the early modern executioner could carry.

In preceding centuries, by contrast, a different situation presents itself. The first English executioner to have crossed into popular discourse appears to have been "Bull the hangman," who attained some macabre celebrity in the final decades of the Elizabethan period (1558–1603). Much like Ketch and Dun after him, he appears both by allusion and direct reference across a range of genres, from recusant martyrologies and homiletic treatises to texts of a more facetious slant, such as *Tarlton's Jests* (*c.*1590) and Robert Greene's coney-catching pamphlets; he even retained sufficient renown after his death to be recalled as "an ex'ellent hangman" in the 1630s.[18] Before Bull's tenure on the scaffold, however, little literary use was made of the hangman. It is in fact difficult to find written traces of any kind describing earlier officials. Even in the early Tudor period they grow indistinct, and references to them become more elusive. Their presence tends only to be recorded by happenstance, usually when they run afoul of the law themselves or show some deviation from conventional practice. Hence we know the name of "Cratwell," the "conninge butcher in quarteringe of men" who put to death the nun and visionary Elizabeth Barton in 1534, since he himself received the same treatment some four years later: Charles Wriothsley notes that Cratwell was taken to Clerkenwell to be "hanged on a payre of gallowes, newe made" after being found guilty of "robbinge a bouth in Bartlemewe fayre," while Edward Hall adds that his death was witnessed by "aboue twentie thousand people as I my self iudged."[19] In 1559, Henry Machyn provides a snapshot of a slightly later figure, omitting his name but recording

17 Harold M. Weber, *Paper Bullets: Print and Kingship under Charles II* (Lexington, KY: University Press of Kentucky, 1996), 164. Among the texts that use Ketch to attack "plotters who Act for old Nick and the Pope" are *Treason rewarded at Tiburn* (London: F. Coles, et al., 1678), Wing T2080 and *A Nest of Plots Discovered* (London: General Assembly of Hawkers, 1679), Wing N469; conversely, Ketch is used against Oates in *Thompson Tell-Lyes* (London: G. Parker, 1682), Wing T1019A, and John Zeale, *Narrative of the Phanatical Plot* (London: John Zeale, 1683), Wing Z10.

18 *The Life and Death of Mr. Edmund Geninges Priest* (Saint-Omer: Charles Boscard, 1614), 92 (STC 11728); Thomas Adams, *The Happines of the Church* (London: G.P., 1618), 361 (STC 120); *Tarltons Iests* (London: Iohn Budge, 1613), sig. C3 (STC 23683.3); Robert Greene, *The Second Part of Conny-Catching* (London: Iohn Wolfe, 1591), sig. D2v (STC 12281); John Taylor, *Bull, Beare, and Horse* (London: M. Parsons, 1638), sig. A5v (STC 23739).

19 Charles Wriothesley, *A Chronicle of England During the Reigns of the Tudors: From AD 1485 To 1559*, ed. William Douglas Hamilton, 2 vols. (London: Camden Society, 1871–77), 1.85;

another of his distinguishing features: he refers to the death at "Tyborne" of "the hangman with the stump-lege for stheft, wyche he had hangyd mony and man and quartered mony."[20] Likewise, we have a few broad hints about the figure commissioned to kill Anne Boleyn in May 1536. According to Sir William Kyngston, Constable of the Tower, he had been brought over from France for the occasion: in a letter to Thomas Cromwell, Kyngston reports that "the executur of Cales" [i.e. Calais] had arrived to "handle that matter."[21] A second, contemporary letter to Lord Lisle from John Husee makes clear why the event was outsourced to a French headsman. Husee informs his master that "the Queen suffered with sword this day within the Tower" rather than the more customary but less efficient English axe.[22] But even these cases are merely glimpses standing out against a general paucity of information.

The medieval period presents a dramatically different case from even the early sixteenth century. Moving into the fifteenth and fourteenth centuries, the fog thickens even further, and the disappearance of the figures is almost total. While sporadic references do occur, even the most tantalizing lines of inquiry end up revealing little, and in some cases fail to hold up to sustained scrutiny. Onomastic sources provide a few traces, but these are by and large isolated and scattershot, and it is usually unclear how directly they refer to agents of justice. Assize records preserve a few suggestive surnames, such as "Godwin Hongmonesone" in 1278, "Walter Hangeman" in 1305, and "John Hangeman" in 1327, which may denote their owners' occupations, or may be nicknames or even patronyms; similarly, a deed of 1337 refers to a "Hengeman Lane" in Leicester, which may or may not be the location of a provincial gallows or its operators' lodgings.[23] More problematic still are the sources cited by the *Middle English Dictionary* [hereafter MED]. The dictionary finds the earliest reference to the office of "public hangman, executioner, or torturer" in Edward III's wardrobe accounts from the second half of the 1340s.[24] It is doubtful, however, that

---

Edward Hall, *Chronicle Containing the History of England*, ed. Henry Ellis (London: J. Johnson, 1809), 826.

20 Henry Machyn, *The Diary of Henry Machyn, Citizen and Merchant-Taylor of London*, ed. John Gough Nichols (London: Camden Society, 1848), 109.

21 James Gairdner, ed., *Letters and Papers, Foreign and Domestic, Henry VIII, January–June 1536* (London: H.M. Stationery Office, 1887), 374.

22 *Letters and Papers*, 385.

23 H.C. Maxwell Lyte, ed., *Calendar of Patent Rolls, Edward I: 1272–1281* (London: H.M. Stationery Office, 1901), 294; Bertil Thuresson, *Middle English Occupational Terms* (Lund: Gleerup, 1950), 146; Barrie Cox, *Place-Names of Leicestershire* (Nottingham: English Place-Name Society, 1998), 40.

24 "hang-man," n. 1. (a), MED.

this document has any real connection to capital punishment, let alone to the administration of torture. The relevant sections detail two acquisitions of costume fabric for a group described as Edward's "hengmannis," whose members are named as "Ricardo de Yatesley, Fyge, et Ricardo Merser" in the first instance and "Johanni Fige, Ricardo Vergous, et Ricardo Vynegere" in the second.[25] Promising though the record seems, it is unlikely to refer to executioners. These names are more likely those of the "henchmen," a company of boys in the royal household who served as pages on ceremonial occasions; "hengestmanni" or "henxmen" continue to feature regularly in royal accounts up to the reign of Elizabeth I, when the office was abolished.[26] Moreover, the fact that the figures all have playful culinary nicknames (i.e., Fig, Verjuice, Vinegar), and were later succeeded by the similarly dubbed "Mustard" and "Garlic," hardly seems compatible with the grim office the *MED* assigns them; nor does the fact that Richard Vynegere continued to receive royal favor later in life, reappearing in the 1360s as a king's sergeant with property in Ireland.[27] Again, most clues and signals prove to be mere tricks of the light; medieval English executioners are almost untraceable, having failed to attract the same level of attention as their early modern successors. Even medieval witnesses are often confused over their existence: Robert Bartlett quotes Thomas of Chobham's claim that England had no official hangmen in the early thirteenth century, an observation that, while demonstrably untrue, underlines their obscurity.[28]

As might be expected, scholarship often treats this lack of information as a barrier to inquiry, a frustrating oversight that impedes knowledge of early capital punishment. The silence of the historical record gives rise to an extraordinary outburst in Alfred Marks' scathing history of Tyburn, which inveighs against the hypocrisy and "public ingratitude" that has effaced all memory of the early hangmen, lamenting that "we seek in vain monuments to the executive officer, without whose aid law and order would have been mere empty names."[29] Popular histories, likewise, prefer to begin on the firm ground of the

25 Nicholas Harris Nicolas, "Observations on the Institution of the Most Noble Order of the Garter … illustrated by the Accounts of the Great Wardrobe of King Edward the Third," *Archaeologia* 31 (1846): 1–163 at 85, 94.

26 See: J.A.H. Murray, "Henchman," *Notes and Queries* 9.1 (1898): 154. The Latin version is used, for instance, in a treason-trial from September 1522, where it refers to a boy in Henry VIII's household: National Archives, Kew, KB 9/492/2.

27 W. Mark Ormrod, *Edward III* (New Haven: Yale University Press, 2011), 319–20; H.C. Maxwell Lyte, ed., *Calendar of the Fine Rolls Preserved in the Public Record Office: Edward III 1327–1377* (London: H.M. Stationery Office, 1923), 272.

28 Robert Bartlett, *The Hanged Man: A Story of Miracle, Memory, and Colonialism in the Middle Ages* (Princeton: Princeton University Press, 2004), 44.

29 Alfred Marks, *Tyburn Tree: Its History and Annals* (London: Brown, Langham, and Company, 1908), 44.

documented figures, often with a prefatory nod to earlier functionaries "lost in the mists."[30] However, while their frustrations are well grounded, these protests overlook the most interesting questions here—why exactly medieval headsmen prove so fugitive in the records, and why they failed to draw the sustained commentary and portrayal associated with later figures, let alone the dense aggregation of meanings surrounding Ketch and "Squire Dun."

On the face of it, there is little obvious reason for this invisibility. After all, in a practical and literal sense, executioners were defined by their conspicuousness. Despite the persistent stereotype of the axeman cowled in a dark hood, English headsmen are likely to have worn the same eye-catching, brightly colored costume that marks their continental peers in manuscript illuminations and other visual sources [**see Figure 11.2**].[31] But more importantly, the scaffold itself is a highly visible presence in the culture of the period. It proves an especially important touchstone in the same sorts of popular genres that later paid such lavish attention to Ketch. There are numerous examples of macabre slang from the Middle Ages, much of it fetishizing the same aspects of capital punishment that feature in later patois.[32] A great deal of this vocabulary focuses on Tyburn specifically. Hence, John Lydgate (*c.*1370–*c.*1451) describes inveterate criminals as "Tyburne coloppys" [Tyburn morsels], a term also found in *Cocke Lorelles Boat* (1518).[33] Likewise, the morality play *Hick Scorner* (*c.*1513) has its vice-characters describe their dissolute lives as honoring "saint Tyburn of Kent" or making "to Tyburn a pilgrimage," while their counterparts in *Youth* (*c.*1514) are destined "to preach at Tyburn."[34]

Other terms single out the paraphernalia of execution or its rituals. Thomas Hoccleve (*c.*1367–1426) refers to decadent fashions as walking the "hempen lane," while John Skelton (*c.*1460–1529) similarly warns against being "cawte in an hempen snare."[35] Along the same lines, William Langland (*c.*1325–*c.*1390)

---

30 Brian J. Bailey, *Hangmen of England: from Ketch to Pierrepoint, 300 Years of Execution* (London: W.H. Allen, 1989), 1; James Bland, *The Common Hangman: English and Scottish Hangmen Before the Abolition of Public Executions* (London: Henry, 1984).

31 See: Hannele Klemettilä, *Epitomes of Evil: Representation of Executioners in Northern France and the Low Countries in the Late Middle Ages* (Turnhout: Brepols, 2006), 117–18.

32 See further: Andrew McCall, *The Medieval Underworld* (London: Hamish Hamilton, 1979), 176.

33 John Lydgate, *The Assembly of Gods*, 697–98, ed. Oscar Lovell Triggs (Chicago: University of Chicago Press, 1895), 22; *Cocke Lorelles bote* (London: Wynkyn de Worde, 1518), sig. C1 (STC 5456).

34 *Hick Scorner*, 264, 941, and *Youth*, 255, *Two Tudor Interludes*, ed. Ian Lancashire (Manchester: Manchester University Press, 1980), 181, 233, 119.

35 Thomas Hoccleve, *Regiment of Princes*, 454, ed. Charles R. Blyth (Kalamazoo, MI: Medieval Institute Publications, 1999), 52; John Skelton, "Agenst Garnesche," 163, *Complete English Poems*, ed. John Scattergood (Harmondsworth: Penguin, 1983), 133.

FIGURE 11.2 Sir Hugh Spencer (Hugh Le Despenser) fastened to a ladder and disembowled alive while a crowd of spectators gathers around a fire below the ladders. Taken from BnF MS Fr. 2643, fol. 11r

makes an early allusion to Psalm 15.5 as a "neck verse" by which an offender might plead benefit of clergy through proving his literacy: he calls it "a murye verset / That hath take fro Tybourne twenty stronge theves."[36] This lexis is not

36 William Langland, *Piers Plowman: B-text*, 12.188–89, ed. A.V.C. Schmidt (London: Dutton, 1978), 142.

radically different from later cant in its choice of details; it looks forward to the "Peddelars Frenche" outlined by Thomas Harman (fl.1547–1567), the idioms quoted by Christopher Marlowe (1564–1593), Thomas Nashe (1567–*c.*1601), and Thomas Dekker (*c.*1572–1632), or the ironic praise of "this worthy noble herbe" "Gallowgrasse" or "Neckeweede" given by the physician William Bullein (*c.*1515–1576).[37] In effect, the medieval popular imagination both anticipates and parallels early modern culture in its willingness to engage with the gibbet, and in the relish and inventiveness with which it does so. However, for all this enthusiasm for the trappings of execution, the director of the "tomlyng cast" or granter of "the blysse of euerlastyng galowis" remains curiously absent, giving rise to no fanciful metaphors of his own.[38] As a consequence, there seems to be more at work in the anonymity of hangmen than a mere lapse in the records. Medieval indifference to executioners is neither accidental nor confined to one or two isolated texts; it forms a larger pattern across the culture of the period.

The omission of the hangman is even more pronounced in full-fledged portrayals of beheadings and hangings. As the work of Rosemary Woolf, Robert Mills, Jody Enders and above all Caroline Walker Bynum emphasizes, scenes of execution proved intensely resonant at all cultural levels in the English Middle Ages, exerting a powerful magnetism across spiritual, moral, and aesthetic discourses.[39] Executions resonated with the public in part because theatricality, spectacle, and codification were woven into their social praxis, as Michel Foucault and Esther Cohen have discussed in their comments on capital punishment as a "complex of governmental messages."[40] Yet when the scaffold makes its way from spectacle to text, the executioner tends to be left out of this revisualization, or features only in a perfunctory or impersonal way. An important case in point is Geoffrey Chaucer's *Canterbury Tales*. Chaucer's relationship with the law could hardly have been closer. As scholarship has recognized

37 Edward Viles and F.J. Funivall, *Rogues and Vagabonds of Shakespeare's Youth* (London: Chatto and Windus, 1907), 84; William Bulleyn, "Booke of Compounds," *The Babees Book*, ed. Frederick J. Furnivall, EETS o.s. 32 (London: Kegan Paul, 1869); Eric Partridge, *Routledge Dictionary of Historical Slang*, 6th ed. (London: Routledge, 2003), 2489.

38 *Hye Way to the Spyttell Hous* (London: Robert Copland, 1536), sig. B3v (STC 5732); Dame Juliana Berners, *The Boke of Saint Albans*, English Experience 151 (Amsterdam: Da Capo, 1969), sig. F5v.

39 Rosemary Woolf, *The English Religious Lyric in the Middle Ages* (Oxford: Clarendon Press, 1968); Robert Mills, *Visions of Excess: Pain, Pleasure and the Penal Imaginary* (Cambridge: University of Cambridge Press, 2000); Jody Enders, *The Medieval Theater of Cruelty: Rhetoric, Memory, Violence* (Ithaca: Cornell University Press, 1999); Caroline Walker Bynum, *Fragmentation and Redemption* (New York: Zone Books, 1994), 13.

40 Michel Foucault, *Discipline and Punish*, trans. Alan Sheridan (London: Penguin, 1991), 202; Esther Cohen, *Crossroads of Justice* (Leiden: Brill, 1993), 156.

since the work of Joseph Allen Hornsby, legislation and jurisprudence are major preoccupations in Chaucer's work; his life records also make clear his intimate involvement in the structures and processes of the law.[41] In fact, these professional activities brought Chaucer into uncomfortable proximity with the death penalty on occasion, especially during the Merciless Parliament of 1388; in his ill-fated colleague Thomas Usk, Chaucer had at least one close associate who would die on the scaffold.[42] Accordingly, it is not difficult to find references to execution scattered through the *Tales*. In the *Knight's Tale*, "stranglyng and hangyng by the throte" are among the dark powers claimed by Saturne (1.2458), and the same outcome is nearly forced on the text's protagonists (1.1743–47). In the *Merchant's Tale*, the mismatched husband and wife call on the noose and *poena cullei* [penalty of the sack] to vouchsafe their honesty, swearing "elles be I hanged by the hals" (4.2379) and "put me in a sake / And in the nexte ryuer do me drenche" (4.2199–200).[43] If Neil Cartlidge is correct about the likely course of the fragmentary *Cook's Tale*, then it may also have been heading towards a climactic scene on the scaffold.[44]

A recurrent feature across these allusions is Chaucer's readiness to draw emotive significance from the gibbet; he does not hesitate to approach the gallows as a potent source of pathos. One of the most instructive examples occurs in the forensic context of the *Man of Law's Tale*, during Custance's trial for murder:

> Have ye nat seyn somtyme a pale face,
> Among a prees, of hym that hath be lad
> Toward his deeth, wher as hym gat no grace,
> And swich a colour in his face hath had
> Men myghte knowe his face that was bistad

41 Joseph Allan Hornsby, *Chaucer and the Law* (Norman, OK: Pilgrim Books, 1988); Martin M. Crow and Clair C. Olson, *Chaucer Life-Records* (London: Oxford University Press, 1966).

42 For a recent overview of Usk's career, downfall and links to Chaucer, see: Marion Turner, "Usk, Thomas," *Encyclopedia of Medieval Literature in Britain*, gen. ed. Siân Echard and Robert Rouse, 4 vols. (Chichester: Wiley-Blackwell, 2017), 4.1846–49.

43 All citations of the *Canterbury Tales* are from Geoffrey Chaucer, *Riverside Chaucer*, gen. ed. Larry D. Benson, 3rd ed. (Oxford: Oxford University Press, 2008). Fragment and line numbers are given in parentheses. See further: Larissa Tracy, "'Mordre wol out': Murder and Justice in Chaucer," *Medieval and Early Modern Murder: Legal, Literary and Historical Contexts*, ed. Larissa Tracy (Woodbridge: Boydell Press, 2018), 115–36.

44 Neil Cartlidge, "Wayward Sons and Failing Fathers: Chaucer's Moralistic Paternalism—And a Possible Source for the Cook's Tale," *Chaucer Review* 47 (2012): 134–60.

> Amonges alle the faces in that route?
> So stant Custance, and looketh hire aboute. (2.644–51)

This stanza was clearly designed to be a self-contained, heightened, and confrontational moment, intended to wring maximum impact from the scene it pictures. With its marshalling of formal devices such as apostrophe and erotema, both of which seek the imaginative participation of the reader, it recalls the tradition of passion meditation, attempting to stimulate the mental and emotional faculties by means of graphic language and imagery. Such is its vividness, in fact, that it is singled out by Larry Benson as a point at which Chaucer's contemporary experiences seem to break into his fiction.[45] Yet for all its calculated immediacy and affectiveness, the executioner has no role to play in the passage. It picks out the procession to the scaffold, the deportment of the victim, and the "prees" or "route" of observers, all of which are used to excite the required sensation of pity; the enactor of the death sentence himself apparently has nothing to add to this accumulation of effects, and is accordingly excluded.[46] The passage can be compared to the mass execution at the end of the *Prioress's Tale*, another emotionally charged moment in a text that explicitly cultivates pathos and uses execution for rhetorical ends. The text presents the deaths of the Jews, who are dragged "with wilde hors" to be "heng ... by the lawe," as an obvious counterpoint to the murder of the martyred "clergeon," sharpening the emphatic injustice of the boy's death (7.633–36, 679–81). Once again, however, the hangman is conspicuous only by his absence; the figure does not carry any impact that the text can latch on to when awakening the audience's pity.

This inhibition is not confined to Chaucer, or to the intellectual circles he occupied. Even at a more obviously popular level, the same pattern holds true. A pertinent example is a ballad on the deaths of the so-called "traytours of Scotlond" William Wallace and Simon Fraser, who were hanged, drawn, and quartered in 1305 and 1306 respectively.[47] The form of execution the two men suffered was still a relative novelty in the early fourteenth century, despite its later ubiquity; the historical record indicates that it was specially selected by

45 Benson, "Introduction," *Riverside Chaucer*, xx.

46 For a discussion of exile and execution in *The Man of Law's Tale*, see in this volume: Gila Aloni, "A Re-examination of Constance's Exile—Geoffrey Chaucer's *Man of Law's Tale* and Constance's Return Home", 141–58.

47 "Lystneth, lordynges/ Execution of Sir Simon Fraser," *The Complete Harley 2253 Manuscript*, ed. Susanna Greer Fein, 2 vols. (Kalamazoo, MI: Medieval Institute Publications, 2014), 2.98–109. The lyric is catalogued 1889 in the New Index of Middle English Verse [hereafter NIMEV].

Edward I to make the strongest possible show of authority over two men he regarded with special opprobrium.[48] The king's desire to create a formidable spectacle seems to have been successful, at least judging from the number of chronicles and other contemporary sources that deal with the deaths.[49] The ballad itself also reflects the theater implicit in their sentences: it does not merely record the mutilations of Wallace and Fraser but memorializes them as continuous, ongoing moments. Although its gloating triumphalism reaches for a different affect than Chaucer's Man of Law or Prioress, it similarly tries to restage the executions in the imagination of the reader. It works systematically through the injuries to the two men's bodies, directing attention to each in turn, and adding copious circumstantial detail. In its account, Wallace is "todrawe, seththe he was anhonge, / Al quic biheueded, ys boweles ybrend," before his "heued to Londone Brugge wes send" and his "quarters sende to is oune contre" (18–20, 26). Fraser likewise is drawn "with feteres ant with gyves" from the Tower to Cheapside bearing "a gerland on ys heued," before receiving the same treatment as his predecessor once "he com to galewes": "he was yopened, is boweles ybrend" (177–180, 185–187). As a whole, the poem functions much like the body-parts on display in London and Scotland: it also seeks a "myrour to be," its visual intensity designed to ensure "that monie myhten se / Ant drede" (27–29). But, as in Chaucer's work, even this program of intensive detail does not extend to the headsmen who dismembered the two rebels. Indeed, the poem's insistent use of the passive voice succeeds in effacing their presence almost totally, keeping the focus trained on the victims and their broken anatomies, rather than on the agencies performing the mutilation. Once again, the text attaches no significance to the men who directed the rope and axe, and cannot find a place for them in the crowing, lurid atmosphere it generates.

Even when Middle English texts do take notice of executioners, the differences between their approaches and the early modern cult of the hangman are immediately noticeable. Headsmen appear occasionally in genres such as the hagiography and passion drama, where their presence can scarcely be ignored. Nevertheless, they still tend to become visible only under certain conditions, and in ways that either deny them consequence or resist drawing parallels with their real-life counterparts. Two texts typical in these respects are the *vita* of

48 J.G. Bellamy, *The Law of Treason in England in the Later Middle Ages* (Cambridge: Cambridge University Press, 1970), 30; Fiona Watson, *Under the Hammer: Edward I and Scotland, 1286–1307* (East Linton: Tuckwell, 1998), 213.

49 Roy J. Goldstein, *The Matter of Scotland: Historical Narrative in Medieval Scotland* (Lincoln, NA: University of Nebraska Press, 1993), 215; Joseph Stevenson, *Documents Illustrative of Sir William Wallace* (Glasgow: Maitland Club, 1841).

Alban from *The South English Legendary* (c.1285) and the *Crucifixion* (c.1477) from the York Corpus Christi cycle. Both award some prominence to the performers of capital punishment. The *Legendary* features a reluctant executioner who refuses to carry out the sentence against Alban and promptly joins him on the block, thereby securing his own redemption "so þat in oure Louerdes name boþe ymartered were;" the *Crucifixion* offers probably the most sustained treatment of execution in Middle English from the perspective of the enactor, giving only 24 of its 300 lines to Jesus, and the rest to the four Roman soldiers who will "boldely do this dede" with their "hammeres and nayles large and lange."[50] But even these instances consider the executioner in a tightly circumscribed way. The headsman in the Alban story only receives attention because he ceases to be a headsman, once "his swerd þat he bar an honde fram him wel uer caste" (75); he also remains conspicuously nameless despite dying for his newfound faith.[51] Likewise, the York play does not treat the soldiers as executioners specifically, despite the activity in which they are engaged. Rather, the play paints them in a different light altogether. The emphatically practical and logistical vocabulary they use, with its references to construction problems, types of nail, "cordis," "booryngis," and the best ways to fix Christ to the cross, identifies them as craftsmen above all, much like the urban audience for whom and by whom the play was staged; the play even suggests that they are intended to represent fallen humanity as a whole, forcing "an awareness of direct involvement in the responsibility for Christ's sacrifice" on the spectators.[52] In other words, they are not characterized or defined as executioners, let alone equated with the contemporary functionaries; this status rapidly falls by the wayside as they are made to support a larger set of meanings. The play, therefore, despite giving center stage to the men that carry out the "dome that this doote schall dye" (5), does not locate particular significance in the office of headsman. Its executioners only become significant by being redrawn, and having their actual occupation overridden with newer, broader resonances.

The absence of information about medieval English hangmen, therefore, is not merely an unfortunate or accidental break in the records. Rather, it arises from a deep-seated blind spot in the culture of the period. The silence

50 Charlotte D'Evelyn and Anna J. Mill, eds., *South English Legendary*, EETS o.s. 87, 3 vols (London: Oxford University Press, 1956–9), 1.240–1; "Play 35: Crucifixio Christi," *York Corpus Christi Plays*, ed. Clifford Davidson (Kalamazoo, MI: Medieval Institute Publications, 2011), 293.

51 Alban's penitent *carnifex* is similarly anonymous in the *Legendary*'s probable source, Bede's *Historia Ecclesiastica*, 1.7: Bede, *Ecclesiastical History of the English Nation*, ed. J.E, King, 2 vols. (Cambridge, MA: Harvard University Press, 1976–79), 1.40.

52 Christine Richardson and Jackie Johnson, *Medieval Drama* (London: MacMillan, 1991), 73.

of historiography is matched by a similar reticence in literary discourse, which time and again fails to find any value in depicting executioners, even when playing with the gibbet or exploiting its emotional pull. The presence of this aporia is interesting, especially when set against the popular fixation on hangmen found in later centuries. To some extent, there may be greater continuity between the two eras than meets the eye: one could view the unspeakable medieval hangmen, on the one hand, and the profusion of language around the seventeenth-century figures, on the other, as two sides of the same coin. Both seem to mark an equal sense of distaste around the office, albeit one that still recognizes its fundamental necessity and utility. The silence of the medieval sources can be seen as an English equivalent of the impulse that placed executioners in the nebulous class of *advenae* [outsiders] in northern European states. Much as French and Dutch *bourreaux* were obliged to live on the outskirts of the settlements they served, and to wear distinctive badges and clothing, so the English executioner is pushed beyond the peripheries of written discourse itself.[53] Of course, as in the case of his continental peers, this marginal status does not constitute a full-fledged rejection of the executioner, since it situates him at the limits of acceptability rather than outside them; in fact, placing the hangman on the fringes of language also shields him from critique. The refusal to name or depict the headsman, in other words, can be seen as a simultaneous expression of disgust and grudging acceptance.

Although they follow a different tack, early modern portrayals of the hangman rest on much the same ambivalence. A common thread running through them is the idea that executioners are both part of the legal apparatus and outside it, both agents of order and its disruptors. Ketch is the supreme example, an organ of justice who shows a vexed proximity to illegality; this perhaps explains why writers and graphic artists took pains to paint him as a bloodthirsty sadist, and eagerly pounced on his periodic spells in gaol [**see Figure 11.3**]. But, as usual, Ketch merely represents a wider tendency in its most emphatic form. The same dualism also appears in the euphemism "finisher of the law," popularized by Motteux in his 1694 translation of Rabelais, a term which makes the hangman the fulfilment of justice while placing him on its outer edges.[54] *Groanes from Newgate* also casts Dun as a figure of similar

53 Michael Goodich, *Other Middle Ages: Witnesses at the Margins of Medieval Society* (Philadelphia: University of Pennsylvania Press, 1998), 4; Ruth Mellinkoff, *Outcasts: Signs of Otherness in Northern European Art of the Late Middle Ages*, 2 vols. (Berkeley: University of California Press, 1993), 1.54.

54 Francois Rabelais, *Works*, trans. Thomas Urquhart and Peter Motteux, 2 vols. (London: Bohn, 1851), 2.395. A similar blending of meaning is perceptible in other European languages. In Middle High German the office was sometimes termed "Nachrichter" (after

FIGURE 11.3 "Jack Ketch Arrested" (1770s), engraving by an unknown artist
© NATIONAL PORTRAIT GALLERY, LONDON. USED WITH PERMISSION

ambiguity, not just in its expectation that Dun should have died by "his own *swing*," but in its emphasis on the fundamental incompatibility of his trade with Christianity. In one of its most arresting conceits, it shows him treating the gallows like "the *Altars* of the *Heathen Gods*," offering "Men for Sacrifice" in "plenty." The abiding sense is, as Addison succinctly states, that "the hangman is generally a worse malefactor, than the criminal that suffers by his hand"; by enacting justice he is thought to violate it, straying close to criminality and pagan barbarism by carrying out the spectacular butchery judicial authority demands.[55]

These contradictory views clearly rest on the same muted revulsion found in medieval sources, albeit couched in different terms. Again, they seem founded on a generalized unease over the performance of execution; indeed, their very overdetermination of the hangman points to indecision over his exact social value, and a refusal to commit to one assessment or another. To some extent, this irresolution is only to be expected, since it is a natural by-product of public execution and its objectives. As Foucault explains, popular resistance was not merely an intermittent or aberrant threat to the scaffold, but integral to its processes. In his account, the entire point of public execution was to invite "the vengeance of the people" to align itself with "the vengeance of the sovereign," effectively making the crowd the final arbiters of guilt, "the witnesses, the guarantors, of the punishment;" but this process always carried with it an attendant risk of dissent, since "the people, drawn to the spectacle intended to terrorize it, could express its rejection of the punitive power."[56] Indeed, for Foucault, it is the unpredictability and volatility of execution that drove the movement from spectacular "atrocity" to the more tightly controlled disciplinary regimes of the post-Enlightenment period: as he writes, "the development of capitalist society" called for the suppression of "punishments that were spectacular in their manifestations and haphazard in their application" in favor of penalties less concerned with "expenditure and excess."[57] Peter Burke reaches much the same conclusion, noting that "official rituals had to coexist with popular rituals" during execution, with the result that "the crowd did not necessarily

judge), in Middle Dutch "scharprechter" (blade judge), and in French "l'exécuteur de la haute justice" (the enactor of high justice). See: Margarethe Ruff, *Zauberpraktiken als Lebenshilfe* (Frankfurt: Campus Verlag, 2003), 92, 182; Nicoline van der Sijs, *Chronologisch woordenboek* (Amsterdam: Veen, 2002), 642; Joseph-Nicolas Guyot, *Répertoire universel et raisonné de jurisprudence*, 64 vols. (Paris: Chez Pancoucke, 1776–83), 24.51–55.

55 *Whig-Examiner*, September 14, 1710, 1.

56 Foucault, *Discipline and Punish*, 58–59.

57 Foucault, *Discipline and Punish*, 58–59, 87.

interpret proceedings in the same way as the authorities."[58] Again, the grim theater of the gibbet actively invites a dual response, because the potential for resistance and acceptance alike is woven into its fabric.

Yet while this ambivalence is shared by the cultures of both periods, it does not behave in the same way across them; it is subject to some important transitions that help to explain the shifting conception of the hangman. In particular, what changes between the two cultures is the point upon which their more critical strands are focused. In medieval sources, these hostile and interrogative tendencies have relative freedom, and at times gain a surprisingly sharp edge. For instance, in the *Prioress's Tale* it is possible for Chaucer to implicate the "provost" and to raise troubling questions about his summary brutality, as Richard Rex and others have shown.[59] It is similarly possible for an anonymous quatrain from 1381 to connect overuse of "þe ax" and "þe stool" directly with "kyng Rycharde" himself.[60] The York *Crucifixion* goes further still, implicating all humanity in the death of Christ. In all of these cases, resistance and incrimination are relatively uncontained, and can be freely turned against a variety of agencies and authorities, no matter how wide-ranging or subversive they might become in the process. Without a clearly defined actor to draw their focus, the dismissive currents of public execution flow in a range of directions; given the tendency to cast beheading or hanging as "the personal power of the sovereign" in action, they can even be directed at the monarch himself.[61]

In the seventeenth-century texts, on the other hand, disquiet is trained exclusively on the person of the hangman. The hangman effectively becomes a lightning rod for any challenge execution might inspire, rather than the magistrates, legislators, or monarchs whose verdicts he enacts. *Groanes from Newgate* again encapsulates this process. It awards Dun sole responsibility for the desecration of Cromwell, Ireton, and Bradshaw's remains, depicting him as a nightmarish figure "*knuckle deep* in *blood*;" at the same time, however, it assures the reader that his victims were legitimate targets for such treatment, having "murther'd their own *King*." Many of the pamphlets dealing with Ketch work in the same way, especially those that make him apologize for the deaths of Lord Russell, the Duke of Monmouth, or the victims of Titus Oates's fantasies. Nor are these sentiments confined to print; from time to time the

---

58 Peter Burke, *Popular Culture in Early Modern Europe* (New York: Harper, 1978), 279.

59 Richard Rex, "Wild Horses, Justice, and Charity in the Prioress's Tale," *Papers on Language and Literature* 22 (1986): 339–51; Larissa Tracy, *Torture and Brutality in Medieval Literature* (Cambridge: D.S. Brewer, 2015), 176–87.

60 Rossell Hope Robbins, ed., *Historical Poems of the XIV and XV Centuries* (New York: Columbia University Press, 1959), 54. The lyric is numbered 3306 in NIMEV.

61 Foucault, *Discipline and Punish*, 80.

historical record also shows them being put into practice. At Edinburgh in 1736, the execution of the smuggler Andrew Wilson mushroomed into a full-blown riot after his hangman was pelted with stones and almost "tore to Pieces by the Mob;" in 1649, the headsman Richard Brandon was threatened with drowning by a Thames boatman for his presumed involvement in the execution of Charles I.[62] As soon as the hangman became visible as a distinct personality, in other words, he became an object of culpability and blame.

At final count, therefore, the movement from the faceless medieval hangman to the cult of "bloody Ketch" proves to be a form of scapegoating: the axeman's loss of anonymity diverts critical energies away from the legal institutions he serves, and directs them towards his name and person instead.[63] The question that remains, of course, is why this disavowal should have occurred at the point in time it did. It is unlikely to reflect a new hesitance over violence or bloodshed in the name of the law: the period saw, if anything, greater reliance on spectacular punishment in English legislation, culminating in the Waltham Black Act of 1723 and the "Bloody Code" it brought into force. There is also little evidence of any major sea change in seventeenth-century legal thought beyond "a piecemeal, tinkering, and minimally effectual reform," even despite the upheavals of the Civil War, Commonwealth, and Restoration.[64] Returning to Foucault, however, the new status of the hangman might be seen as the start of a gradual movement towards a rationalized, bourgeoise conception of punishment, one which saw the "excess" of the scaffold as a "bad economy of power" bringing into play a "confused and inadequate multiplicity of authorities."[65] It can hardly be a coincidence that the cult of the hangman reached its highest pitch in the 1680s, when the country moved towards the "Glorious Revolution" and the English middle classes cemented their power. The new prominence of the hangman is one of the first tentative steps away from punishment towards discipline as Foucault conceives the two terms: as bourgeois culture started to impose its economizing sensibilities on the law, while still depending on older "ceremonies by which power is manifested," the hangman became a means of channeling the subversive, uncontrollable energies intrinsic to execution, and of steering them away from the actual sites of

62 *Authentick Extract of the Proceedings in the Trial of Capt. John Porteous* (London: John Baskett, 1737), 34; Sollom Emlyn, ed., *Complete Collection of State-Trials and Proceedings upon High-Treason*, 6 vols. (London: J. Walthoe et al, 1730), 2.385.

63 *News from the North* (London: John Dean, 1683), 2 (Wing N1011).

64 Barbara Shapiro, "Law Reform in Seventeenth Century England," *American Journal of Legal History* 19 (1975): 280–312 at 306 and 312. See further: John Walliss, *The Bloody Code in England and Wales, 1760–1830* (Basingstoke: Palgrave Macmillan, 2018).

65 Foucault, *Discipline and Punish*, 79–80, 87.

authority.[66] He ceases to be a mere appendage of legal procedure and becomes a sort of shield to absorb tensions that might otherwise implicate the magistracy and judiciary. Ultimately, despite the irreverence of a text like *Groanes from Newgate*, the emergence of the hangman as a conspicuous figure shows popular discourse responding to the changes Foucault outlines. It reflects the appearance of a new type of power, one that is increasingly squeamish about the carnivalesque potential of public execution and seeks to insulate itself from its unruly and inefficient displays.

66 Foucault, *Discipline and Punish*, 23, 10.

CHAPTER 12

Portraits of a Poisoner: Interpreting the End of the Marquise de Brinvilliers

Susan Small

On the evening of July 17, 1676, Charles Le Brun, first painter to King Louis XIV, was among the thousands of people who watched as the notorious poisoner, Marie-Madeleine Dreux d'Aubray, Marquise de Brinvilliers, was trundled in a cart through the streets of Paris to the Place de Grève, where she was decapitated and her body burnt to ashes. It is said that Le Brun was so haunted by the expression on the Marquise's face that not until the following day did he feel able to sketch the famous *Portrait de la marquise de Brinvilliers* [**Figure 12.1**] that is now housed in the Cabinet des dessins of the Musée du Louvre. On the far right of the portrait is the faint sketch of a man said to be Edme Pirot, her confessor who provided a written record of her execution.[1] Pirot records Le Brun's presence in the crowd that evening and offers insight into the circumstances surrounding the creation of the portrait. His 150-page memoir, *La marquise de Brinvilliers: récit de ses derniers moments (Manuscrit du P. Pirot, son confesseur)* [*The Marquise de Brinvilliers: An account of her final moments (Manuscript of Father Pirot, her confessor)*], acts as a verbal counterpart to Le Brun's visual representation of the Marquise as she was taken to her death.[2]

The Marquise's execution, which generated Pirot's narrative and Le Brun's portrait, also triggered the infamous Affair of the Poisons that shook the foundations of the court of Louis XIV. She was convicted of murder for poisoning her father and two brothers, and the attempted murder of her sister. Information released at the Marquise de Brinvilliers' trial led to the discovery of an underground network of fortune-tellers supplying potions and poisons

1 Charles Le Brun, *Portrait de la marquise de Brinvilliers*, 1676, Musée du Louvre, Cabinet des dessins, Fonds des dessins et miniatures, INV 27668, Recto: . The portrait, which measures 00.308m high × 00.246m wide (approximately 12.1 in. high × 9.7 in. wide), was drawn in black chalk with sanguine and white highlights on double-sided brown paper.

2 Edme Pirot, *La Marquise de Brinvilliers, Récit de ses derniers moments (Manuscrit du P. Pirot, son confesseur). Notes et documents sur sa vie et son procès par G. Roullier*, 2 vols. (Paris, Alphonse Lemerre, 1883). The Bibliothèque nationale de France holds a bound copy of the original manuscript dated "24 mai 1894": https://gallica.bnf.fr/ark:/12148/btv1b90095336/f3.image. All quotations are from the Roullier edition; volume and page number appear in parentheses. All translations, unless otherwise indicated, are my own.

 | DOI:10.1163/9789004742598_014

FIGURE 12.1 Charles Le Brun, Ecole française, *Portrait de la marquise de Brinvilliers*, INV 27668, Recto, Fonds des dessins et miniatures, Petit format © LOUVRE. HTTP://ARTS-GRAPHIQUES.LOUVRE.FR/DETAIL/OEUVRES/0/213507-PORTRAIT-DE-LA-MARQUISE-DE-BRINVILLIERS-MAX

to members of the aristocracy, including the king's mistress, Madame de Montespan. In the three years following the trial, hundreds of people were arrested and dozens executed, condemned to hard labor, or sent into exile. In the hysterical climate surrounding the Marquise de Brinvilliers' torture, trial, and execution and the sensational events that followed, rumors and retellings abounded. In his preface to Pirot's manuscript, which was not published until more than two centuries later, the editor, G. Rouiller, presents the publication as a corrective to the numerous and, he says, highly inaccurate accounts of what happened during those few days in July 1676. Pirot's account of the Marquise de Brinvilliers' final days and Le Brun's famous portrait of her at that time each portray her differently. So, what are audiences to believe? In addition to the conflicting accounts, there are missing sketches, a lost original, contradictory timelines, questions of artistic intention, more rumors, and hearsay. Sorting through the evidence to discover what really happened in those final few days—even moments—before her execution enables us to reconstruct the visual and narrative landscape in which the most sensational criminal trial in seventeenth-century French history took place and to understand its role in the Affair of the Poisons that followed.

Despite the claim by popular biographer Hugh Stokes that the many historical documents relating to the trial and execution "allow the last days of Madame de Brinvilliers to be reconstructed with remarkable accuracy," the documentation relating to the creation of her portrait is rife with contradiction and misinformation.[3] Contemporary accounts conflict on several elements, including when Le Brun sketched his famous portrait; the existence of a supposedly-lost second sketch; a painting attributed to Le Brun of the Marquise's severed head; and allegations that the painter exploited the sensationalism of the execution to further his own artistic ends. Pirot's discussion of Le Brun's portrait of the Marquise provides valuable insight into how the foremost painter of the day witnessed the event and elucidates the controversial circumstances surrounding the image's creation but it has problems of its own. His narrative occasionally reads like a description of the famous portrait: "Je montay après elle & je me mis comme j'estois auparavant auprès d'elle, mon bonnet en teste, tenant le crucifix en ma main gauche pour luy faire regarder …" [I climbed in after her and sat, as I had before, next to her, my hat on my head, holding the crucifix in my left hand so that she would look at it …] (2:63); however, the analogy between the visual and verbal interpretations can be deceptive. The composition of Le Brun's sketch does correspond closely to Pirot's description, but

3 Hugh Stokes, *Madame de Brinvilliers and her times 1630–1676* (London: John Lane, 1912), vii.

Pirot never saw the portrait and had to rely on hearsay to determine whether the figures were an accurate representation of the "she" and "I" in his narrative: "Je ne sçay si cela luy ressemble; on m'a dit qu'ouy, & pour faire connoistre que c'est une femme que l'on mène au supplice, il a mis auprès d'elle un homme en bonnet quarré sans s'arrester à la ressemblance qu'on dit qu'il n'a point du tout avec moy" [I don't know if it looks like her; I've heard that it does, and that in order to portray that this is a woman who is being taken to her execution, he put next to her a man in a square hat without worrying about whether it looked like me, which people say it doesn't at all] (2:7–8). In other words, the accuracy of the iconic portrait of the seventeenth century's most famous criminal could not be verified by the man who was both literally and figuratively closest to her in the moments before her execution. Instead, a portrait measuring no more than 10″ × 12″, sketched by a man who saw the Marquise for only a few minutes as the cart carrying her and her confessor passed through a jeering crowd, gained a notoriety that the 150-page handwritten account by that confessor, the man who spent her final days with her, never achieved. Le Brun's portrait of the Marquise de Brinvilliers passed into the prestigious *Cabinet du roi* [*King's Cabinet*] collection after his death in 1690 and was copied by such notable artists as Antoine Coypel (1661–1722) and Jean Restout (1692–1768), along with countless others.[4] In the process, it symbolized the collective memory of the

4 "Atelier de Le Brun; entré dans le Cabinet du Roi en 1690; paraphe de J. Prioult (L. 2953); marque du Louvre (L. 1886a). Dernière provenance: Cabinet du Roi. Mode d'acquisition: Saisie royale. Année d'acquisition: 1690" [Atelier Le Brun: entered into the Cabinet du Roi in 1690; initialed by J. Prioult (L. 2953); stamp of the Louvre (L 1886a). Last provenence: Cabinet du Roi. Method of acquisition: Saisie royale: 1690]: http://arts-graphiques.louvre.fr/detail/oeuvres/0/213507-Portrait-de-la-marquise-de-Brinvilliers. The entry for the Coypel painting in the 1926 visitor's guide to the Musée Carnavalet, which notes that the artist viewed the Marquise from the Notre-Dame Bridge, implies that this was an original portrait and not a copy of Le Brun's: [Salle 47] "Vitrine centrale: la marquise de Brinvilliers, dessin d'Antoine Coypel (ancienne collection Funck-Brentano). Ce dessin offre l'intérêt de montrer comment apparut à Mme de Sévigné, la célèbre empoisonneuse, quand elle la vit, d'une maison du pont Notre-Dame, conduite dans un tombereau à la place de Grève (lettre du 17 juillet 1696 [sic])." Guide du visiteur / Le Musée Carnavalet (Paris, Editions et publications contemporaines, 1926), n.p.: https://gallica.bnf.fr/ark:/12148/bpt6k62247798/texteBrut. [Room 47] Central glass case: the Marquise de Brinvilliers, drawing by Antoine Coypel (former Funck-Brentano collection). This drawing offers the advantage of showing how the famous poisoner appeared to Mme de Sévigné, when she saw her from a house on the Notre-Dame bridge as she was carried in a cart to the place de Grève (letter of July 17, 1696)]. Restout's portrait in the Musée Carnavalet, on the other hand, is clearly a copy of Le Brun's. The art historian, Louis-Antoine Prat, remarks that "… par rapport au croquis de Le Brun, Restout à éliminé la figure de l'assistant à droite, et amoindri la puissance de l'expression. … On notera d'autre part que le motif est inversé par rapport à l'original" [in relation to Le Brun's sketch, Restout eliminated the figure of the assistant on the right, and lessened the power of the expression. … It will

execution while copies of Pirot's manuscript languished in academic and religious libraries for more than two hundred years.[5] Moreover, despite the publication of a printed copy of the manuscript in 1883, it has never been widely read, and public interest in the execution narrative has been fueled primarily by selective and often sensationalized versions of Pirot's original account.

The issues arising from this scattershot record are perhaps most evident in the rumors that the famous sketch now in the Louvre is not the only portrait of the Marquise drawn by Le Brun that day, or in the days following her execution. It was also rumored that Le Brun did not sketch the Marquise as she passed but, according to Pirot: "qu'il en conçut l'idée qu'il eut présente tout le soir & la nuit suivante, & que le lendemain il en tira un craïon avec ses couleurs" [that he conceived the idea of it that was on his mind all that evening and the following night, and that the following day he made a sketch of it with his chalks] (2:7). Pirot himself, whose description of the original portrait corresponds so closely to the famous sketch, indicates that he heard a rumor about another portrait that Le Brun wanted to sketch. Claiming that there was something of the tiger in the face of the Marquise, Le Brun supposedly wanted to draw the head of a tiger next to hers to show the similarity between the two: "Il [Le Brun] prétend même, dit-on, que ce visage tient du tigre & *il le veut faire voir* en tirant auprès de luy une teste de tigre & montrant le rapport qui se trouvera entre les deux" [People say that he [Le Brun] claims that this face has something of the head of a tiger about it & he wants to show this by drawing next to it a tiger's head & showing the relation that is to be found between the two] (2:8). Pirot admits that he does not have the imagination himself to see the resemblance but adds that he was so surprised at her manner that he could see the painter making such a comparison. He notes that it would be consistent with Le Brun's

---

also be noted that the motif is inverted in relation to the original]. Louis-Antoine Prat, *Le dessin français au XVIIIe siècle* (Paris: Louvre Éditions, 2017), 92. See also: https://www.parismuseescollections.paris.fr/fr/musee-carnavalet/oeuvres/la-marquise-de-brinvilliers.

5 In her analysis of the Brinvilliers affair from the perspective of the famous contemporary letter-writer, Madame de Sévigné, Ellen R. Welch argues that it was, for Madame de Sévigné, this collective memory, and not the judgment of the courts, that would ultimately determine the historical importance of the execution: "In Sévigné's letters on the Brinvilliers affair, we see the flip side of the theatrical dimension of the spectacular destruction of the criminal body that figures its witnesses as an audience—*un public*—who will respond emotionally, pass judgement, and eventually engage in discussion about the event. By validating and circulating such an alternative, popular viewpoint on the trial and its violent conclusion, Sévigné implied that Brinvilliers's final judgement was not to be found in the royal law courts but rather in this public domain of collective memory." Ellen R. Welch, "State Truths, Private Letters, and Images of Public Opinion in the Ancien Régime: Sévigné on Trials," *French Studies* 67.2 (April 2013): 170–183 at 183.

famous theory and practice of physiognomy, the art of comparing human and animal faces.

Such a comparison is a filter; it refocuses the viewer's attention through the narrowed lens of the artistic eye, taking it away from the portrait's main subject and directing it toward only those features that are relevant to the comparison. To draw the face of a tiger next to that of the Marquise with the express intention of showing the resemblance between the two obscures or suppresses any other mode of interpretation. For the second time in as many pages, Pirot implicitly rejects the notion that Le Brun's portrayal is an accurate representation of the woman he has come to know so well. Arguably, Le Brun's task as a physiognomist painter is to make the movement inherent in such representation "legible," painting thereby becoming "un art essentiellement narratif" [an essentially narrative art].[6] From this perspective, the ambivalence and uncertainty characterizing Pirot's written record of the portrait are easily superseded in the visual medium by a highly affective representation imposing the artist's interpretation of his subject and his own singular vision of the event. Indeed, in the eighteenth century, the renowned Swiss philosopher and physiognomist, Johann Caspar Lavater, categorized Le Brun's sketch of the Marquise as an exercise in physiognomy rather than a faithful rendition, noting in his *L'art de connaitre les hommes par la physionomie* (1775–1778) that "[l]e grand observateur des passions, Lebrun, se plaça sur son passage *pour* saisir et retracer les traits de sa physionomie à ses derniers instans" [the great observer of passions, Lebrun, placed himself along her route *in order to* capture and retrace the features of her physiognomy during her final moments] (My emphasis).[7] Quite apart from the fact that Le Brun's portrait does not represent the Marquise "during her final moments" but, rather, at a single moment on her journey towards the scaffold, it is, as a simple exercise in technique, a model rather than a representation.

6 "la peinture est alors consideree comme un art essentiellement narratif." See: Jean-Jacques Courtine's book review of Jennifer Montagu's *The Expression of Passions* (New Haven: Yale University Press, 1994) in *The French Review* 70.4 (March 1997): 625–6 at 626.

7 Johann Caspar Lavater, *L'art de connaitre les hommes par la physionomie*, ed. Moreau (de la Sarthe) (Paris: Depelefol, 1835), 1:381. This artistic intention is also noted in the nineteenth century by the *homme de lettres*, Armand Fouquier, who writes that, "C'est à ce moment, et au milieu de cette multitude, que la vit Lebrun, le peintre du roi; elle avait alors les sourcils froncés, le visage plissé, les yeux allumés, quelque chose du tigre. Le grand peintre regarde cette femme avec une grande curiosité d'artiste. …" [It is at this moment, and in the midst of this multitude, that Lebrun, the King's painter, saw her; her brows were then furrowed, her face wrinkled, her eyes ablaze; she had something of the tiger about her. The great painter looks at this woman with a great artistic curiosity,,,]. A. Fouquier, *Causes célèbres de tous les peuples* (Paris: H. Lebrun, 1861), 4:36.

Among the inventory of Le Brun's works in the Louvre are several studies of the eyes and eyebrows of the tiger, attesting to his artistic interest in the physical facial features of the animal.[8] A note appended to his sketches of tiger, lynx, and cat eyes in an exhibition of the curator Louis-Jean-Marie Morel d'Arleux's *Dissertation Sur Un Traité De Charles Le Brun, Concernant Le Rapport De La Physionomie Humaine Avec Celle Des Animaux* (1806) proposes, as Lavater did more generally, that "[t]his series of eyes is probably a comparative exercise in 'ferocity'."[9] Moreover, in his commentary on another of the artist's paintings, *Le martyre de saint Etienne*, Le Brun's student and biographer, Claude Nivelon, describes the "yeux de tigres féroces et bestiales" [ferocious and bestial tigers' eyes] of the saint's attackers.[10] Therefore, Le Brun's interest in the eyes and eyebrows of the tiger has been documented, but nowhere in the inventories of his works of art is there a sketch of a tiger's head, nor is there a record of one being copied or reproduced. That the painter should have wanted to do a comparative study of the head of the Marquise and that of a tiger is completely in line with both his previous animal sketches and his theory and practice of physiognomy. That he actually did, however, is an open question.

The history of the portrait of the Marquise de Brinvilliers now in the Louvre is well documented, but for more than one hundred and fifty years following her execution there was no further record of what could be called the "tiger portrait." Then, suddenly, and explosively, in perhaps the most famous and most influential retelling of the execution narrative, Alexandre Dumas' *La Marquise de Brinvilliers* (1839–40), the rumor reappeared, now transformed into reality. Dumas claims to have based his own version of the story on an unpublished copy of Pirot's manuscript to which he was given access by the

8 Lydia Beauvais, *Charles Le Brun, 1619–1690*, Musée du Louvre, Département des arts graphiques (Paris: Réunion des Musées Nationaux, 2000), 2:644, 2281 Inventaire 28242, album 11, fol. 64. The images are also reproduced in *Johann Caspar Lavater, L'art de connaitre les hommes par la physionomie*, ed. Moreau (de la Sarthe) (Paris, Depelefol, 1835), 9:167.

9 L.-J.-M. Morel d'Arleux, *Dissertation Sur Un Traité De Charles Le Brun, Concernant Le Rapport De La Physionomie Humaine Avec Celle Des Animaux; Ouvrage Enrichi De La Gravure Des Dessins Tracés Pour La Demonstration De Ce Système* (L.P. Dubray, 1806): https://www.royalacademy.org.uk/art-artists/book/dissertation-sur-un-traite-de-charles-le-brun-concernant-le-rapport-de-la. "Les Maîtres des arts graphiques," Exhibition on Line: Archive (Part II), "Le Brun's System on Physiognomy," L.-J.-M. Morel d'Arleux (after Charles Lebrun), Plate 35, "Tiger Eyes, Lynx Eyes, Cat Eyes": http://www.maitres-des-arts-graphiques.com/-EXBArchive.Physiognomie2.html.

10 Claude Nivelon, *Vie de Charles Le Brun et description détaillée de ses ouvrages* (Geneva, Droz, 2004), 151.

philologist and literary historian Paulin Paris.[11] However, whereas Pirot merely mentions a rumor that Le Brun wanted to portray the resemblance between the head of the Marquise and that of a tiger "en tirant *auprès de luy* une teste de tigre" [by drawing next to it the head of a tiger], Dumas writes that Le Brun not only drew the head of a tiger but also, in fact, made two drawings: "le beau dessin du Louvre *et en regard de ce dessin* une tête de tigre" [the fine drawing in the Louvre *and next to this drawing* the head of a tiger] (my emphasis). This description also suggests that the iconic drawing now held in the Louvre—the portrait that Dumas refers to as "le beau dessin du Louvre"—was not replaced at some point by a portrait in which the head of the Marquise was next to that of a tiger, but rather simply exhibited next to a separate drawing of the head of a tiger.

Published in 1846, some six years after Dumas' account, a British article on physiognomy by Francis Jacox provides some confirmation that the rumored tiger drawing actually existed and was being exhibited at the Louvre around the time Dumas wrote his piece. Jacox, citing Dumas as his source, writes, "The Marchioness of Brinvilliers, murderess wholesale and retail, is said to have had the very look of a tiger-cat, in moments of excitement if not of stealthy repose. Lebrun made the sketch of her now in the Louvre, placing near it *another sketch* of a tiger, to show that the principal features were the same" (my emphasis).[12]

Even Jacox's corroboration of Dumas's seemingly irrefutable evidence of an extant tiger sketch does not, however, entirely stem the flow of misinformation

11 "À compter de ce moment, grâce à la relation manuscrite qu'a laissée M. Pirot, et que notre savant ami Paulin Paris a bien voulu mettre à notre disposition, nous pourrons suivre presque pas à pas Madame de Brinvilliers jusque au-delà du supplice. Cette relation était entièrement inédite, et, quoiqu'on la trouve citée dans Gayot de Pitaval et dans Richer, ils n'en ont fait aucun usage" [From that moment on, thanks to the account left by M. Pirot, and which our learned friend, Paulin Paris, kindly put at our disposal, we can follow Madame de Brinvilliers almost step by step up to and beyond her execution. This account was entirely unpublished, and, although one can find it cited in Gayot de Pitaval and in Richer, they didn't make any use of it]. Alexandre Dumas, *Les Crimes célèbres* (Paris: Presses Pocket, 1948), 91 n. 24. Although Dumas states that the manuscript he consulted had never been published, the Bibliothèque nationale de France holds an eighteenth-century leatherbound copy of Pirot's manuscript with a publication date of 1701–1800: "Edme Pirot, *Relation de la mort de la Brinvilliers*, par M. PIROT, docteur de Sorbonne, Manuscrit, Papier [Manuscript, Paper].—XVIIIe siècle, 177 feuillets [18th century, 177 folios].—275 × 177 mm.—Reliure maroquin rouge, aux armes du roi [Moroccan red binding, under the royal coat of arms], Bibliothèque nationale de France. Département des manuscrits. Français 10982." http://archivesetmanuscrits.bnf.fr/ark:/12148/cc424304. A digitized version of the manuscript is available at https://gallica.bnf.fr/ark:/12148/btv1b90095336.

12 Francis Jacox, "Brutish Affinities of the Human Face Divine: Recreations in Comparative Physiognomy," *The New Monthly Magazine and Humorist*, 132 (Jan. 1864): 36–52, at 39.

regarding the composition of the portrait of the Marquise. An anonymous online translation of Dumas's text translates the original French "fit le beau dessin qui est au Louvre, *et en regard de ce dessin une tête de tigre* " as "made the fine drawing which is now in the Louvre, *giving to the figure the head of a tiger*" (my emphasis), implying that there is a single drawing exhibited in the Louvre and that in that drawing the head of the Marquise had been replaced by that of a tiger.[13] Although this is clearly a mistranslation of Dumas' original text rather than a report of a third, as yet undiscovered, sketch, *Marquise Brinvillier* (sic), a large-print, paperback English translation of the book, repeats the error, highlighting the issues surrounding the dissemination of misinformation regarding the portrait.

An article on poisons published in France by the physician Charles Flandin in 1846, the same year as Jacox was writing in England, confirms Dumas' and Jacox's claim that a portrait of the Marquise was in the Louvre at that time, but he seems to suggest that there was a single drawing on display: "Le tableau est au Louvre. À côté de la tête de la Brinvilliers, l'artiste de génie a placé une tête de tigre" [The portrait is in the Louvre. Beside the head of la Brinvilliers, the brilliant artist placed the head of a tiger].[14] Fourteen years later, historian Jules Michelet writes in his influential article, "La décadence morale du XVIIe siècle" ["The Moral Decadence of the 17th Century"], that Le Brun had made a single drawing, placing the head of the tiger next to that of the Marquise: "II prétend que ce visage tient du tigre, et *il a fait une tête de tigre à côté*." [He claims that this face has something of the tiger about it, and he drew the head of a tiger beside it] (my emphasis).[15] Michelet's article not only supports the contention that there was a single drawing; however, it also adds

13 Alexandre Dumas, "The Marquise de Brinvilliers," *Celebrated Crimes*, Vol. 8 (New York: P.F. Collier & Son, 1910), n.p.: https://www.gutenberg.org/files/2756/2756-8.txt; Alexandre Dumas, *Marquise Brinvillier* (sic) (2019), 59.

14 Charles Flandin, "Les poisons chez les Anciens," *Revue scientifique et industrielle* sous la direction du Dr. Quesneville 27.11, Deuxième série (Paris: Louis Colas, 1846): 5–71 at 63 n.1. Also in Charles Flandin, *Traité des poisons, ou toxicologie appliquée a la médecine légale, à la physiologie et à la thérapeutique* (Paris: Mallet-Bachelier, 1853), 3:122 n.1. Only one year later, the French anatomist, Dr. Galet, noted that there had been something of the tiger in the much-feared Cardinal Richelieu (1585–1642) as well: "Chez Richelieu, il y a du tigre dans l'ensemble de la physionomie, et dans chaque trait, si sèchement arrêté, une volonté de fer" [In Richelieu, there is something of the tiger in his physiognomy as a whole, and in each feature, so clearly defined, a will of iron]. *Le corps de l'homme, ou L'anatomie et la physiologie humaines mises à la portée de toutes les classes de la société* … 3 (Paris: Didier, Libra, Ire-Éditeur, 1854), n.p.: https://gallica.bnf.fr/ark:/12148/bpt6k63476l2g/texteBrut.

15 Jules Michelet, "La décadence morale du XVIIe siècle," *Revue des deux mondes* 26 (April 1860): 538–61 at 555.

another twist to the complex history of the elusive tiger portrait. Writing that Le Brun was inspired by the horror of the crowd around him to sketch the Marquise and a tiger, he then notes that that drawing no longer existed. When the frenzy died down, writes Michelet, Le Brun made a second drawing, and it was that drawing which resided in the Louvre at the time he was writing: "Il la suivit d'abord dans ce dessin, inspiré de l'horreur publique; je crois qu'il n'existe plus aujourd'hui. Plus calme, il fit ensuite le beau dessin du Louvre …" [He at first followed it in this drawing, inspired by the public horror; I believe that it no longer exists today. When he was calmer, he then made the fine drawing in the Louvre ….].[16]

A year later in 1861, Armand Fouquier followed Michelet, saying that Le Brun had made a single sketch with the head of a tiger next to that of the Marquise: "avait même placé une tête de tigre *dans son dessin*, en regard de celle de Mme de Brinvilliers" [had even placed a tiger's head *in his drawing,* next to that of Mme de Brinvilliers], adding like Michelet, that the tiger drawing no longer existed: "Mais ce n'est pas, assurément, le dessin dont parle Pirot qui est venu jusqu'à nous. L'admirable dessin du Louvre ne représente qu'une tête fort pathétique, les yeux levés au ciel, avec une espérance pleine de crainte" [But it is certainly not the drawing that Pirot talks about that has come down to us. The admirable drawing in the Louvre only represents a deeply poignant head, the eyes raised to the heavens, with a hope full of fear].[17]

Curator Frédéric Reiset's inventory of works on display on the second and third floors of the Louvre in 1869 echoes Fouquier's description of the portrait. Reiset writes, "Portrait de la marquise de Brinvilliers, fait d'après nature, en 1676, au moment où elle allait subir son jugement. Ses traits altérés portent les traces de la torture. D'une de ses mains elle tient un petit crucifix. Un prêtre, dont la figure est légèrement indiquée à droite, met un cierge dans son autre main" [Portrait of the Marquise de Brinvilliers, drawn from nature, in 1676, at the moment when she was going to undergo her sentence. The altered features bear the traces of the torture. In one of her hands she is holding a small crucifix. A priest, whose figure is lightly indicated on the right, is putting a candle

16 Michelet, "Décadence morale," 555. In his own book on the Affair of the Poisons, historian Frantz Funck-Brentano discredits Michelet's article, writing that "Michelet a consacré à la marquise de Brinvilliers une étude dans la *Revue des Deux Mondes*. C'est un récit très inexact et rempli de lacunes. Le petit roman d'Alexandre Dumas lui est préférable, au point de vue historique" [Michelet wrote a study of the Marquise de Brinvilliers in the *Revue des Deux Mondes*. It is a very inexact story, full of gaps. The little novel by Alexandre Dumas is preferable, from a historical point of view]. Frantz Funck-Brentano, *Le drame des poisons* (Paris: Hachette, 1909), 2.

17 Armand Fouquier, *Causes célèbres de tous les peuples* (Paris, H. Lebrun, 1861), 4:36.

in her other hand].[18] Two years later, in his *Musée féminin. Galerie des grandes criminelles. La Marquise de Brinvilliers* (1871), Narcisse Blanpain echoed both Michelet and Fouquier, writing that Le Brun drew the face of a tiger next to that of the Marquise, but that the drawing no longer existed: "… en regard du dessin de Madame de Brinvilliers, il plaça même une tête de tigre pour mieux faire ressortir la ressemblance des principaux traits. Toutefois, ce n'est pas ce tableau qui est venu jusqu'à nous. L'admirable dessin dont nous avons fait tirer une copie au Louvre ne représente qu'une tête fort pathéthique. …" [… next to the drawing of Madame de Brinvilliers, he even placed a tiger head in order to better bring out the resemblance between the two. However, it is not this painting that came down to us. The admirable drawing of which we had a copy drawn at the Louvre represents only a very poignant head].[19]

Thus, the consensus in France was that Le Brun's tiger portrait, as a single sketch or as a sketch of the head of the Marquise and that of a tiger side by side, no longer existed. Abroad, however, reports of its continued existence persisted. Three years after Blanpain's 1871 statement that the portrait in the Louvre represented the Marquise alone, a letter to the editor in an 1874 issue of a British journal reads,

> I was reflecting on that marvellous portrait of MARIA MARGARET, Marchioness of Brinvilliers, in the Louvre of Paris. … When the wretched woman ascended the scaffold, the crowd it appears began to hoot and cry out against her. It was at that moment that the peculiar savageness of expression of her otherwise beautiful features caught the eye of LE BRUN, reminding him of the glare of the tigress. And after the Marchioness's death the idea so haunted him that he could never rest until he had transferred it to canvas. There was the unhappy Marchioness with all the lines of fury visibly expressed in her features, and there, by her side, was a tiger, so that the spectator might see for himself how far the savageness corresponded. One cannot conceive that LE BRUN, with his fine artistic skill, and I should also hope generous sentiments, though the two by no means necessarily go together, could have felt any pleasure in so exhibiting

18 Frédéric Reiset, *Notice des dessins, cartons, pastels miniatures et émaux exposés dans les salles du 1er et au 2e étage au Musée imperial du Louvre*, Deuxième partie (Paris, Charles de Mourgues Frères, 1869), No. 853: 60–61.

19 Narcisse Blanpain, *Musée féminin. Galerie des grandes criminelles. La Marquise de Brinvilliers* (Paris: Dentu, 1871), 454: https://gallica.bnf.fr/ark:/12148/bpt6k63706658/f474.item.

> the poor fallen woman thus to the gaze of the world merely to show his skill.[20]

Arguably, the letter-writer must have seen the tiger portrait in the Louvre more than fourteen years earlier, prior to Michelet's 1860 article claiming that it was no longer there, but even if that is true, the vividness of the description and the striking analogy the letter-writer later makes between the ferocity of the Marquise and that of the defendant in a current criminal case attest to a continuing fascination with the image of a woman with "the glare of a tigress" being hunted down and killed. Indeed, despite the numerous mid-nineteenth-century claims by influential French intellectuals that the tiger portrait no longer existed, the image of the Marquise as a tiger had already become part of a rich and diverse international mystique surrounding her trial and execution.

For example, Sir Arthur Conan Doyle's "The Leather Funnel" (1902), is a disturbing tale of the supernatural based on the trial and torture of the Marquise de Brinvilliers; it ends with the following lines: "'She was a cruel tigress,' said Dacre, as he turned away. 'I think it is evident that like other tigresses her teeth were both strong and sharp.'"[21] Less chilling but perhaps even more surprising is the American George Alfred Townsend's 1865 biography of Abraham Lincoln's assassin, John Wilkes Booth, which includes the following description of Booth's co-conspirator, Mary Surratt (1823–1865) executed for her part in the assassination:

> Yet, sometimes, across Mrs. Surratt's face a stealthiness creeps—a sort of furtive, feline flashing of the eye, like that of one which means to leap sideways. At these times her face seems to grow hard and colorless, as if

20 *The Trial at Bar of Sir Roger C.D. Tichborne, Bart.*, in the Court of Queen's Bench at Westminster, Before Lord Chief Justice Cockburn, Mr. Justice Mellor, & Mr. Justice Lush, for Perjury (Commencing Wednesday, April 23, 1873, and Ending Saturday, February 28, 1874), 403. https://play.google.com/books/reader?id=SREPAQAAMAAJ&pg=GBS.PA403.

21 Sir Arhur Conan Doyle, "The Leather Funnel," *McClure's Magazine* (1902). One critic writes, "The [teeth] marks on the funnel are not textual evidence, but material evidence created by the victim's body in her death throes. Dacre characterizes them as predatory, demonstrating the same man-killing power that made her punishment appropriate, and offering the narrator the most tangible evidence that her crimes were in proportion to her penalty." James Krasner, "Torture, Literature, and History in Arthur Conan Doyle's 'The Leather Funnel,'" *Linguæ & Rivista di lingue e culture moderne* 2 (2018): 11–22, at 20.

> that tiger expression which Pradier caught upon the face of Brinvilliers and fastened into a masque, had been repeated here.[22]

Townsend does not name his source, and there is no record of a masque of the Marquise de Brinvilliers among the eighty-five works of the sculptor Jean-Jacques (aka James) Pradier (1790–1852) listed in the inventory of the French Ministry of Culture.[23] Pradier's *Tête de femme implorant* (n.d.), "Sujet représenté: portrait (femme, tête, prière)" [*Head of a woman imploring* (n.d), "Subject represented: portrait (woman, head, prayer)"] certainly evokes the portrait on display in the Louvre during Pradier's lifetime, though it resembles more a wounded animal than Townsend's figurative image of a predatory one, and is not identified in the inventory as a representation of the Marquise.[24]

Portraying the face of the Marquise as a masque was not, however, unknown in French artistic circles at the time, although "masque" was used there as well in a figurative rather than a literal sense. In his seminal *Charles Le Brun et les arts sous Louis XIV* (1899), noted art historian Henry Jouin refers to the Marquise's face in the portrait at the Louvre as a masque, but rather than the "furtive, feline" tiger masque described by Townsend, he describes a face ravaged by despair. Indeed, assured of the iconic status of this image of the Marquise, Jouin writes, "Le masque terrible de la Brinvilliers n'a plus besoin qu'on le décrive. Il est au Louvre" [The terrible masque of la Brinvilliers no longer needs to be described. It is in the Louvre].[25] Jouin's assurance that this "terrible masque" no longer required description may have been somewhat premature, however, for in *Les grands procès de l'histoire* (1923), the historian and criminal defense lawyer Henri Robert, goes to great lengths detailing the monstrous masque of a violent tiger that covered the face of the notorious poisoner whose portrait was then hanging in the Louvre: "… [Le Brun] ait cru voir le mufle fumant du tigre en furie dans le masque convulsé de colère de la

22 George Alfred Townsend, *The life, crime, and capture of John Wilkes Booth, with a full sketch of the conspiracy of which he was the leader, and the pursuit, trial and execution of his accomplices* (New York: Dick & Fitzgerald, 1865), Letter 8: The Trial, 141.

23 French Ministry of Culture, "La plateforme ouverte du patrimoine: Jean-ĵacques Pradier": https://www.pop.culture.gouv.fr/search/list?mainSearch=%22Jean-%C4%B5acques%20pradier%22.

24 French Ministry of Culture, "La plateforme ouverte du patrimoine: Tête de femme implorant": https://www.pop.culture.gouv.fr/notice/joconde/M0341003811.

25 Henry Jouin, *Charles Le Brun et les arts sous Louis XIV* (Paris: Imprimerie nationale,1899), 1:306. For a description of this portrait, see also: Frédéric Reiset, *Notice des dessins, cartons, pastels miniatures et émaux exposés dans les salles du 1er et au 2e étage au Musée imperial du Louvre*, Deuxième partie (Paris, Charles de Mourgues Frères, 1869), No. 853:60–61.

Brinvilliers qui couvrait, à ce moment, le visage de la Brinvilliers " [... [Le Brun] believed he could see the fuming muzzle of the raging tiger in the convulsed mask of anger that, at that moment, covered the Brinvilliers woman's face].[26]

The mid- to late-nineteenth-century resurgence of interest in the image of the condemned Marquise as a tiger, may be attributed to the *zeitgeist* that embraced the contemporary image of the condemned Maximilien Robespierre (1758–1794) as a tiger:

> the tiger-cat reputation that Robespierre acquired on his death is more useful for comprehending an aspect of the nineteenth century's political imaginary, and the subterranean role that physiognomic portraiture has played in shaping subsequent historiography, than in allowing us to understand what Robespierre was really like or really all about. For many of those throughout the nineteenth century who contemplated the French Revolution, this was a fitting end for a tyrannical and bestial monster, pointing a moral, adorning a tale, and exemplifying a physiognominal precept.[27]

In the same way, the portrayal of the Marquise de Brinvilliers as a tiger is less a representation of the Marquise herself than an example of Le Brun's theory of physiognomy and the reflection of a public demand for accountability.

In his manuscript account, Pirot fails to confirm that Le Brun's portrait—or portraits—of the Marquise de Brinvilliers offer a true likeness of the woman he knew so well; like the images of Robespierre as a tiger, they offer a useful window onto the culture of the time, but do not illustrate what she "was really like or really all about." The descriptions of the tiger portrait of the Marquise, suggest that this woman with the teeth of a tiger must, like Robespierre, "have been a terrible malefactor indeed if her crimes are in proportion to her penalty."[28] Yet Pirot finally explains that the portraits do not tell the true story, and that if Le Brun had passed by and drawn her moments later, " il luy aurait fait un visage aussi reposé qu'il luy en a fait un hagard & effaré" [he would have given her a face that was as serene as the one he did give her was haggard and afraid] (2:58). In other words, Le Brun's portrait captures a single moment in

---

26 Henri Robert, *Le Procès de la Marquise de Brinvilliers*, Les Écrivains Contemporains. Série Historique 88 (Paris, Payot, mai 1963), 32. Also in Henri Robert, "La marquise de Brinvilliers," *Les grands procès de l'Histoire*, Vol. 2 (Paris, Payot, 1924).

27 Colin Jones, "French Crossings: III. The Smile of the Tiger," *Trans R Hist Soc* (2012), 22: 3–35.

28 Conan Doyle, "The Leather Funnel."

the Marquise's journey towards her death; it is not inaccurate but neither does it represent her state of mind in the final moments before her execution. But there is one last twist to this story.

The 1909 Hachette edition of archivist and historian Frantz Funck-Brentano's (1862–1947) *Le Drame des poisons* contains images, not only of the iconic "*Portrait de la marquise de Brinvilliers et du Père Pirot* (Dessin de Charles Lebrun)" [*Portrait of the Marquise de Brinvilliers and Father Pirot* (Drawing by Charles Lebrun)] but also of a painting called "*La tête de la marquise de Brinvilliers décapitée* (Tableau de Charles Lebrun)" [*The Head of the Decapitated Marquise de Brinvilliers* (Painting by Charles Lebrun)].[29] The black-and-white image shows the head of a woman who appears to be asleep, lying on a fine cloth with a sword and a crown resting against the left side of her face [**Figure 12.2**]. The caption reads: "Tête de la Marquise de Brinvilliers décapitée. *D'après* le tableau de Charles Lebrun" [*From* the painting by Charles Lebrun] (My italics). The authenticity of the painting, already somewhat attenuated by the addition of "D'après," is further eroded by the fact that Funck-Brentano, who quotes Pirot two pages earlier as saying that the executioner cut off the Marquise's hair before her execution and threw her head in the fire afterwards, pictures her in this painting with a full head of dark hair and a face untouched by flames.[30] However, an April 29, 1921 sales catalogue of the art comprising Funck-Brentano's private collection, lists not only Antoine Coypel's *La Marquise de Brinvilliers allant au supplice* but also: "No. 182: LEBRUN (Attribué à CH.), *Tête de la Marquise de Brinvilliers décapitée.* Peinture. Voir F. FUNCK-BRENTANO: *Le Drame des Poisons*" [LEBRUN, (Attributed to CH.), *Head of the Decapitated Marquise de Brinvilliers.* Painting. See F. FUNCK-BRENTANO: *Le drame des Poisons*].[31]

---

29 Frantz Funck-Brentano, "Portrait de la marquise de Brinvilliers et du Père Pirot (Dessin de Charles Lebrun), Frontispiece," and "La tête de la marquise de Brinvilliers décapitée (Tableau de Charles Lebrun)," in *Le drame des poisons* (Paris, Hachette, 1909), 91.

30 "... il lui coupa les cheveux par derrière et aux deux côtés" [... he cut off her hair at the back and on both sides], (Funck-Brentano, 88). Pirot adds that, after also cutting off her head, the executioner "prit le corps habillé comme il estoit pour le descendre en bas et le mettre sur le bucher avec la teste encore toute bandée" [picked up the body dressed as it was in order to take it down and put it on the fire with the head still completely blindfolded] (2:173).

31 The catalogue notes that this painting by Coypel is reproduced in *Le drame des poisons*, but the frontispiece is listed in the Table des gravures as "Portrait de la marquise de Brinvilliers (Dessin de Charles Lebrun)" in the 1909 edition of the book, and as "La Marquise de Brinvilliers allant au supplice" under the frontispiece image itself, attributed to Coypel but only said to be "D'après le dessin original de Ch. Lebrun, conservé au Musée

In his *Biographie universelle* (1854), Louis Gabriel Michaud explains that after she was executed, the Marquise de Brinvilliers' severed head was displayed in the museum at Versailles.[32] Some years earlier, however, a certain Dr. Leroy, a phrenologist who went to the museum to examine the skull, concluded that it was actually the skull of a younger woman, later identified as Angélique-Nicole Carlier Tiquet, who, like the Marquise, was tortured and executed in 1689 for plotting to kill her husband.[33] Perhaps, the tiger woman had finally been laid to rest.

The iconic portrait of the Marquise de Brinvilliers now in the Louvre [**see Figure 12.1**] is problematic because it is at odds with both the various written accounts of the days leading up to her execution and her representation in other images, now lost. Pirot's largely inaccessible manuscript account and the labyrinthine legal documents relating to her trial and execution have been superseded by the story told in sensationalist novels and on dubious websites. Unlike the alleged tiger portrait, which portrayed the Marquise as a powerful woman, the portrait in the Louvre has enshrined her in the public eye as a pathetic, downtrodden creature. Those who do read the manuscript account, however, will find that this image does not represent the Marquise de Brinvilliers as Edme Pirot knew her, and of whom he would have painted a very different picture: "Enfin si je la peignais fidèlement comme je la connais encore, j'en ferais une tête dont tous les gens raisonnables & religieux seraient

---

du Louvre." *Catalogue des tableaux anciens & modernes, par ou attribués à: Bastien-Lepage, Bovin, Chintreuil, Corot, Courbet, David, Decamps, Deveria, Dupré, Fabritius, Géricault, Lebrun, Pillement, Poelemburg, Ravier, Troyon, etc., aquarelles, gouaches, dessins, gravures, sculptures, ayant composé la collection de Monsieur F. Funck-Brentano* dont la vente aura lieu à Paris, Hôtel Drouot, salle n°1, le vendredi 29 avril 1921 à deux heures. Catalogue de vente https://bibliotheque-numerique.inha.fr/viewer/50039/?offset=1#page=28&viewer=picture&o=search&n=0&q=Brinvilliers.

32 "On montre sa tête au muséum de Versailles la régularité remarquable des os semble attester qu'elle fut en effet douée d'une grande beauté. …" Louis Gabriel Michaud, *Biographie universelle ancienne et moderne: ou histoire, par ordre alphabétique, de la vie publique et privée de tous les hommes qui se sont fait remarquer par leurs écrits, leurs actions, leurs talents, leurs vertus ou leurs crimes* (Paris: Mme C. Desplaces, 1854), 548.

33 Émile Debout, *Esquisse de la phrénologie et de ses applications exposées aux gens du monde par le docteur Debout* (Paris: H. Lebrun, 1843), Ch. 4, n.p.: https://gallica.bnf.fr/ark:/12148/bpt6k6305344p/texteBrut. See also: Régis Olry, "Encore une histoire de crâne," https://oraprdnt.uqtr.uquebec.ca/pls/public/gscw031?owa_no_site=1313&owa_no_fiche=215, Augustin Cabanès, "Le prétendu crâne de la Brinvilliers," *Les indiscétions de l'histoire* (Geneva, Farnot, 1977), 1:193, and Alain Baraton, *Vice et Versailles: Crimes, trahisons, et autres empoisonnements au palais du Roi-Soleil* (Paris: Grasset & Fasquelle, 2011), Ch. 9.

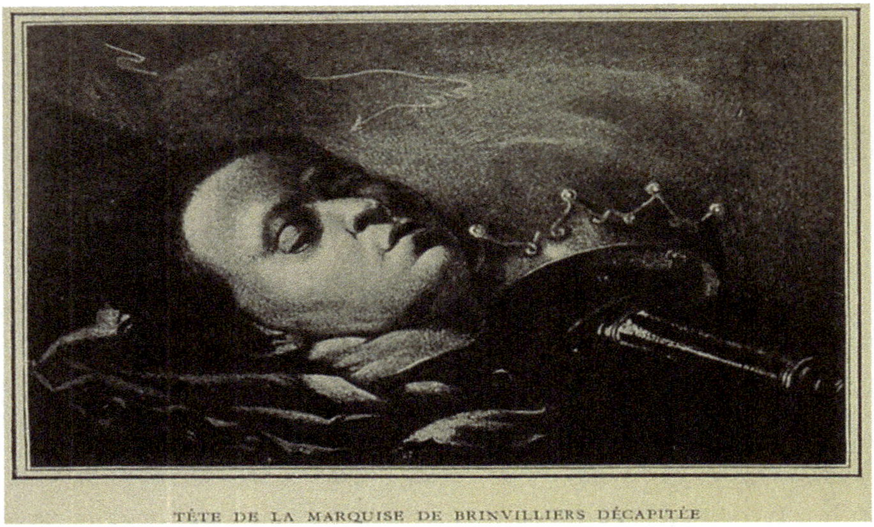

FIGURE 12.2 "The severed head of the marquise de Brinvilliers from the painting by Charles Lebrun" from the 1909 Hachette edition of *Le drame des poisons* by archivist and historian Frantz Funck-Brentano (1862–1947)

autant édifiés que surpris" [In fact, if I faithfully painted her as I know her still, I would give her a head by which all reasonable and religious people would be as edified as they would be surprised] (1:58).

Select Bibliography

Primary Sources

Alighieri, Dante. *La commedia secondo l'antica volgata.* Edited by Giorgio Petrocchi. Milan: Mondadori, 1966–67.

Alighieri, Dante. *The Divine Comedy of Dante Alighieri: Inferno.* Translated by Allen Mandelbaum. New York: Bantam, 1980.

Alighieri, Dante. *The Divine Comedy of Dante Alighieri: Paradiso.* Translated by Allen Mandelbaum. New York: Bantam, 1984.

Alighieri, Dante. *The Divine Comedy of Dante Alighieri: Purgatorio.* Translated by Allen Mandelbaum. New York: Bantam, 1982.

Annales capituli Cracoviensis. In *Annales Cracovienses priores cum kalendario.* Edited by Zofia Kozłowska-Budkowa, 19–105. Monumenta Poloniae Historica, Nova series 5. Warsaw: PWN, 1978.

Annales capituli Posnanensis. In *Annales Poloniae Maioris.* Edited by Brygida Kürbis, 21–78. Monumenta Poloniae Historica, Nova series 6. Warsaw: PWN, 1962.

Annales Polonorum vel Trascae dicti. Edited by August Bielowski, 826–61. Monumenta Poloniae Historica 2. Lviv: Akademia Umiejętności, 1872.

Annales Silesiaci compilati. Edited by Mieczysław Błażowski, 657–79. Monumenta Poloniae Historica 3. Lviv: Akademia Umiejętności, 1878.

Annales suecici medii aevi. Edited by Göte Paulsson. Lund: Gleerup, 1974.

Annales S. Crucis. Edited by Anna Rutkowska-Płachcińska, Monumenta Poloniae Historica, Nova series 12. Warsaw: Polska Akademia Umiejętności, 1996.

Biskupa sögur, vol. 3: Árna saga biskups; Lárentíus saga biskups; Söguþáttur Jóns Halldórssonar biskups; Biskupa ættir. Íslenzk fornrit 17. Edited by Guðrún Ása Grímsdóttir. Reykjavík: Hið íslenzka fornritafélag, 2008.

Boccaccio. *Famous Women.* Translated by Virginia Brown. Cambridge, MA: Harvard University Press, 2001.

Boethius. *Consolation of Philosophy.* Translated by S.J. Tester, Loeb Classical Library 74. Cambridge: Harvard University Press, 1973.

Chaucer, Geoffrey. *The Man of Law's Tale.* In *The Riverside Chaucer.* 3rd ed. Edited by Larry D. Benson, 89–104. Boston: Houghton Mifflin, 1987.

Christine de Pizan. *Debate of the Romance of the Rose.* Edited and translated by David F. Hult. Chicago and London: The University of Chicago Press, 2010.

Christine de Pizan. *La Cité des Dames.* Edited by Thérèse Moreau and Éric Hicks. Paris: Stock, 2000.

Christine de Pizan. *The Book of the City of Ladies.* Translated by Earl Jeffrey Richards. New York: Persea, 1982, 1988.

Chronica principum Poloniae. Edited by Zygmunt Węclewski, 423–578. Monumenta Poloniae Historica 3. Lviv: Polska Akademia Umiejętności, 1878.

Cronica 1202–1377. Edited by Wojciech Kętrzyński. In idem "O rocznikach polskich." *Rozprawy Wydziału Historyczno-Filozoficznego Akademii Umiejętności w Krakowie*. Series II 9 (1896): 164–354 [Edition of *Cronica* in Annex I, pp. 348–53].

Diplomatarium Norvegicum. Vols. I–XXIII. Edited by C.C.A. Lange et al. Christiania/Oslo: Norsk historisk kjeldeskrift-institutt/Riksarkivet, 1847–2011.

Diplomatarium Suecanum. Vols. I–XI. Edited by J.G. Liljegren et al. Stockholm: KVHAA/Riksarkivet, 1829–.

Erikskrönikan enligt Cod. Holm. D2 jämte avvikande läsarter ur andra handskrifter. Samlingar utgivna av Svenska fornskriftsällskapet. Serie 1, Svenska skrifter, nr. 68. Edited by Rolf Pipping. Uppsala: Svenska fornskriftsällskapet, 1963.

Gallus Anonymus. *Gesta principum Polonorum. The Deeds of the Princes of the Poles*. Edited, translated, and annotated by Paul W. Knoll and Frank Schaer. Central European medieval texts 3. Budapest: Central European University Press, 2003.

Gautier de Coinci. *Les Miracles de Nostre Dame*. Edited by V.F. Koenig. 4 vols. Geneva: Droz, 1955–70.

Herman de Laon. *De miraculis sanctae Mariae Laudunensis*. Edited by Alain Saint-Denis. Paris: CNRS éditions, 2008.

Ioannis Dlugossii Annales seu cronicae Incliti Regni Poloniae. Edited by Jan Dąbrowski, Zofia Kozłowska-Budkowa, Stanisław Gawęda, Krzysztof Baczkowski, et al. 11 vols. in 12 bks. Warsaw: PWN, 1964–2003.

Jacobus de Voragine. *Legenda aurea: vulgo historia lombardica dicta*. by Johann Georg Theodor Graesse. 3rd ed. Breslau: Koebner 1890, 1st ed. 1845 Repr. Osnabrück: O. Zeller, 1969.

Jean Miélot. *Miracles de Nostre Dame collected by Jean Miélot, secretary to Philip the Good, duke of Burgundy, Reproduced in facsimile from Douce manuscript 374 in the Bodleian Library for John Malcolm of Poltalloch with text, introduction and annotated analysis by George F. Warner, M.A.* Edited by George F. Warner. Westminster: Nichols and Sons, 1885.

Joannis de Czarnkow Chronicon Polonorum. Edited by Jan Szlachtowski, 601–756. Monumenta Poloniae Historica 2. Lviv: Akademia Umiejętności, 1872.

La Cantilène de Sainte Eulalie. Edited by Brigitte L.M. Bauer and Jonathan Slocum. The University of Texas at Austin Linguistics Research Center, 2020: https://lrc.la.utexas.edu/eieol/ofrol/40.

La Vie des pères, "Belle-Mère." Brussels, Bibliothèque Royale de Belgique. MS 9229–30.

La Vie des pères. Edited by Félix Lecoy. 3 vols. Paris: Société des anciens textes français, 1987–1999.

La Vie des pères, "Belle-Mère." Paris, Bibliothèque de l'Arsenal. MS 5204.

La Vie des pères, "Belle-Mère." The Hague, Koninklijke Bibliotheek. MS 71 A 24.

Les Miracles de Nostre Dame par personnages. Edited by Gaston Paris and Ulysse Robert. 8 vols. Paris: Firmin Didot pour la Société des anciens textes français, 1876–93.

'Liber fundationis Claustri Sancte Marie Virginis in Heinrichow' czyli Księga Henrykowska. Edited by Roman Grodecki. 2nd ed. Wrocław: Muzeum Archidiecezjalne, 1991.

Lites ac res gestae inter Polonos Ordinemque Cruciferorum. Edited by Ignacy Zakrzewski and Jadwiga Karwasińska. 2 vols. Poznań: Biblioteka Kórnicka, 1890–1935.

Olaus Petri. *En swensk cröneka*. Edited by Jöran Sahlgren. Uppsala: Sveriges kristliga studentrörelses förl., 1917.

Philippe de Beaumanoir. *The* Coutumes de Beauvaisis *of Philippe de Beaumanoir*. Edited and translated by F.R.P. Akehurst. Philadelphia: University of Pennsylvania Press, 1992.

Rocznik Krasińskich. Edited by August Bielowski, 127–34. Monumenta Poloniae Historica 3. Lviv: Akademia Umiejętności, 1878.

Rocznik kujawski. Edited by August Bielowski, 204–12. Monumenta Poloniae Historica 3. Lviv: Akademia Umiejętności, 1878.

Schlesisches Urkundenbuch V: 1282–1290. Edited by Winfried Irgang. Cologne: Böhlau, 1993.

St. Augustine. *Confessions*, vol. 2. Translated by William Watts. Cambridge, MA: Harvard University Press, 1912.

St. Augustine. *On the Freedom of the Will*. Translated by Carroll Mason Sparrow. Charlottesville: University of Virginia, 1947.

The Chronicle of Duke Erik: A Verse Epic from Medieval Sweden. Translated by Erik Carlquist and Peter C. Hogg. Lund: Nordic Academic Press, 2012.

The Danish Medieval Laws: The Laws of Scania, Zealand and Jutland. Edited by Ditlev Tamm and Helle Vogt. Abingdon: Routledge, 2016.

Ustawa urządzenia żup Krakowskich soli wydana przez Kazimierza Wielkiego roku 1368. Edited by Zygmunt Antoni Helcel, 217–224. Starodawne Prawa Polskiego Pomniki 1. Warsaw: Księgarnia Sennewalda, 1856.

Vincent de Beauvais. *Le Speculum Historiale de Vincent de Beauvais*. Edited by M. Tarayre. Paris: Champion, 1999.

Vita sanctae Hedwigis ducissae Silesiae. Edited by Aleksander Semkowicz, 501–655. Monumenta Poloniae Historica 4. Lviv: Akademia Umiejętności, 1885.

Zwód zupełny Statutów Kazimierza Wielkiego. Edited by Zygmunt Antoni Helcel, 44–206. Starodawne Prawa Polskiego Pomniki 1. Warsaw: Księgarnia Sennewalda, 1856.

Secondary Sources

Aloni, Gila. "Geoffrey Chaucer's 'Lyne Oriental': Mediterranean and Oriental Languages in the *Treatise on the Astrolabe.*" *Mediterranean Historical Review* 16 (2002): 69–77.

Aloni, Gila. "M(ons)ters in laws: Maternal Models in the Man of Law's Tale." *Médiévales* [44]: 1–10.

Åqvist, Gösta. *Kungen och rätten. Studier till uppkomsten och den tidigare utvecklingen av kungens lagstiftningsmakt och domsrätt under medeltiden.* Lund: Institutet för rättshistorisk forskning, 1989.

Arias Guillén, Fernando. *The Triumph of an Accursed Lineage: Kingship in Castile from Alfonso X to Alfonso XI (1252–1350).* Abingdon: Routledge, 2021.

Ariès, Philippe. *The Hour of Our Death.* Harmondsworth: Peregrine, 1981.

Ariès, Philippe *Western Attitudes Towards Death from the Middle Ages to the Present.* Baltimore: Johns Hopkins, 1974.

Ashe, Laura. "'Exile-and-return' and English Law: The Anglo-Saxon Inheritance of Insular Romance." *Literature Compass* 3 (2006), 300–17.

Atkinson, Clarissa W. *The Oldest Vocation: Christian Motherhood in the Middle Ages.* Ithaca, NY: Cornell University Press, 1991.

Bagge, Sverre. *From Viking Stronghold to Christian Kingdom: State Formation in Norway, c. 900–1350.* Copenhagen: Museum Tusculanum Press, 2010.

Banaszkiewicz, Jacek. "Król i łaźnia, Bóg i łaźnia (Gall Anonim o Bolesławie Chrobrym; 'Provest' vremennych let' o stworzeniu Pierwszego Człowieka)." In *Wyobraźnia średniowieczna.* Edited by Teresa Michałowska, 205–22. Warsaw: Wydawnictwo Instytutu Badań Literackich, 1996.

Bardach, Juliusz. *Historia państwa i prawa Polski. Do połowy XV wieku.* Warsaw: PWN, 1965.

Bartlett, Robert. *Trial by Fire and Water: The Medieval Judicial Ordeal.* Oxford: Clarendon, 1986.

Bellamy, John. *Crime and Public Order in England in the Later Middle Ages.* London: Routledge, 1973.

Bergqvist, Kim. "Debating the Limitations of Kingship in Fourteenth-Century Sweden: Political Language and Norms in Romance and Chronicle." In *The* Eufemiavisor *and Courtly Culture: Time, Texts and Cultural Transfer*, edited by Olle Ferm et al., 67–85. Stockholm: KVHAA, 2015.

Bergqvist, Kim. "Kings and Nobles on the Fringes of Christendom: A Comparative Perspective on Monarchy and Aristocracy in the European Middle Ages." In *The Routledge History of Monarchy*, edited by Elena Woodacre et al., 622–635. Abingdon: Routledge, 2019.

Bergqvist, Kim. "Osämja och fiendskap mellan kungar och stormän: Lojalitetskonflikter och politiska värden i Norge och Sverige, c. 1250–1370." *Collegium Medievale* 32.2 (2019): 171–191.

Block, Edward A. "Originality, Controlling Purpose, and Craftsmanship: Chaucer's *Man of Law's Tale.*" PMLA 68 (1953): 572–616.

Blom, Grethe Authén. *Norge i union på 1300-tallet.* 2 vols. Trondheim: Tapir, 1992.

Borowski, Stanisław. *Ściganie przestępstw z urzędu w średniowiecznem prawie polskiem*, Warsaw: Uniwersytet Warszawski, 1933.

Bothwell, J.S. *Falling from Grace: Reversal of Fortune and the English Nobility, 1075–1455.* Manchester: Manchester University Press, 2008.

Brilioth, Yngve. *Svenska kyrkans historia, vol. 2: Den senare medeltiden, 1274–1521.* Stockholm: Svenska kyrkans diakonistyrelses bokförlag, 1941.

Bryan, W.F., and Germaine Dempster, eds. *Sources and Analogues of Chaucer's Canterbury Tales.* New York: Humanities, 1941.

Burkert, Walter. *Homo necans. The Anthropology of Ancient Greek Sacrificial Ritual and Myth.* Berkeley: University of California Press, 1986.

Cantarella, Eva. *I supplizi capital in Grecia e a Roma.* Milan: Rizzoli, 1991.

Cetwiński, Marek. "Porwanie Henryka Grubego. Próba interpretacji." In *Genealogia—władza i społeczeństwo w Polsce średniowiecznej*, edited by Andrzej Radzimiński, 276–89. Toruń: Wydawnictwo Uniwersytetu Mikołaja Kopernika, 1999.

Cetwiński, Marek. "Przestępcy i sprawiedliwość w 'Księdze Henrykowskiej.'" In *Kultura prawna w Europie Środkowej*, edited by Antoni Barciak, 300–7. Katowice: Instytut Górnośląski, 2006.

Claassen, Jo-Marie. *Displaced Persons: The Literature of Exile from Cicero to Boethius.* Madison: University of Wisconsin Press, 1999.

Claussen, M.A. "'Peregrinatio' and 'Peregrini' in Augustine's 'City of God.'" *Traditio* 46 (1993): 33–75.

Clément, François. "Variations andalouses sur le corps du délit. corps puni, corps humilié dans l'Occident musulman medieval." In *Corps outragés, corps ravagés de l'Antiquité au Moyen Âge*, edited by Lydie Bodiou, Véronique Mehl, and Myriam Soria, 503–22. Turnhout: Brepols, 2011.

Crouch, David. "Chivalry and Courtliness: Colliding Constructs." In *Soldiers, Nobles and Gentlemen: Essays in Honour of Maurice Keen*, edited by Peter Coss and Christopher Tyerman, 32–48. Woodbridge: Boydell Press, 2009.

Curry, Walter Clyde. *Chaucer and the Medieval Sciences.* New York: Barnes & Noble, 1960.

Dalewski, Zbigniew. "Pokuta Bolesława Chrobrego." In *Księga. Teksty o świecie średniowiecznym ofiarowane Hannie Zaremskiej*, edited by Halina Manikowska, 73–101. Warsaw: Instytut Historii Polskiej Akademii Nauk, 2018.

Daniel, Norman. *The Arabs and Medieval Europe.* London: Longman, 1979.

De Wilde, P.M. "Between Life and Death: The Journey into the Other World." In *The Naked Text: Chaucer's Legend of Good Women*, edited by Sheila Delany, 175–87. Berkeley: University of California Press, 1994.

De Wilde, P.M. "Womanliness in The *Man of Law's Tale.*" *Chaucer Review* 9 (1974): 63–72.

Dharmaraj, Glory. "Multicultural Subjectivity in Reading Chaucer's *Man of Law's Tale.*" *Medieval Feminist Newsletter* 16 (1993): 4–8.

Dinshaw, Carolyn. *Chaucer's Sexual Poetics.* Madison: University of Wisconsin Press, 1989.

Du châtiment dans la cité. Supplices corporels et peine de mort dans le monde antique. Table ronde de Rome, 9–11 novembre 1982. Rome: École Française de Rome, 1984.

DuBruck, E. and B. Gusick, eds. *Death and Dying in the Middle Ages.* New York: Peter Lang, 1999.

Edwards, A.S.G. "Critical Approaches to The *Man of Law's Tale.*" In *Chaucer's Religious Tales*, edited by David Benson and Elizabeth Robertson, 85–94. Cambridge: D.S. Brewer, 1990.

Ellis, Roger. *Patterns of Religious Narrative in the* Canterbury Tales. Totowa, NJ: Barnes & Noble, 1986.

Ferm, Olle. "Transformations sociales et émergence de nouvelles élites dans le royaume de Suède, 1220–1350." In *Les élites nordiques et l'Europe occidentale (XIIe–XVe siècle)*, edited by Tuomas M.S. Lehtonen and Élisabeth Mornet, 53–65. Paris: Publications de la Sorbonne, 2007.

Field, Rosalind. "The King over the Water: Exile-and-Return Revisited." In *Cultural Encounters in the Romance of Medieval England*, edited by Corinne Saunders, 41–53. Cambridge: D.S. Brewer, 2005.

Firnhaber-Baker, Justine. "Introduction: Medieval Revolt in Context." In *The Routledge History Handbook of Medieval Revolt*, edited by Justine Firnhaber-Baker with Dirk Schoenaers, 1–15. Abingdon and New York: Routledge, 2017.

Foronda, François. "El miedo al rey. Fuentes y primeras reflexiones acerca de una emoción aristocrática en la Castilla del siglo XIV." *e-Spania* 4 (2007), http://e-spania.revues.org/2273. Accessed 5 June 2022.

Foronda, François. *El espanto y el miedo: golpismo, emociones políticas y constitucionalismo en la Edad Media.* Madrid: Dykinson, 2013.

Foucault, Michel. *Discipline and Punish: The Birth of the Prison.* Harmondsworth: Penguin, 1977.

Fouracre, Paul. "Why Were So Many Bishops Killed in Merovingian Francia?" In *Bischofsmord im Mittelalter*, edited by Natalie Fryde and Dirk Reitz, 13–35. Berlin: Vandenhoeck & Ruprecht, 2003.

Furnivall, F.J., Edmund Brock, and W.A. Clouston, eds. *Originals and Analogues of Some of Chaucer's "Canterbury Tales."* London: Trubner, 1887.

Gawlas, Sławomir. "Kazimierz Wielki—jaki był?" In *Świat średniowiecza. Studia ofiarowane Profesorowi Henrykowi Samsonowiczowi*, edited by Agnieszka Bartoszewicz et al., 761–87. Warsaw: Wydawnictwa Uniwersytetu Warszawskiego, 2010.

Gawlas, Sławomir. *O kształt zjednoczonego królestwa: Niemieckie władztwo terytorialne a geneza społeczno-ustrojowej odrębności Polski*. Warsaw: DiG, 2000.

Gąsiorowski, Antoni. "'Districtus' w Wielkopolsce początków XIV wieku." *Roczniki Historyczne* 32 (1966): 173–93.

Gilkær, Hans Torben. *The Political Ideas of St. Birgitta and Her Spanish Confessor, Alfonso Pecha: Liber Celestis Imperatoris ad Reges: A Mirror of Princes*. Translated by Michael Cain. Odense: Odense University Press, 1993.

Gillingham, John. "French Chivalry in Twelfth-Century Britain?" *Historian* 122 (2014): 6–10.

Gillingham, John. *The English in the Twelfth Century: Imperialism, National Identity, and Political Values*. Woodbridge: Boydell Press, 2000.

Gołdyn, Paweł. "Ukamienowanie i rozszarpanie w polskiej wczesnośredniowiecznej praktyce karnej." *Czasopismo Prawno-Historyczne* 58.2 (2006): 127–33.

Górecki, Piotr. "Violence and the Social Order in a Medieval Society: The Evidence From the Henryków Region, ca.1150–ca.1300." In *'The man of many devices, who wandered full many ways': Festschrift in Honour of János M. Bak*, edited by Balazs Nagy and Marcell Sebők, 91–104. Budapest: Central European University Press, 1999.

Górecki, Piotr. *The Text and the World: The 'Henryków Book', Its Authors, and Their Region, 1160–1310*. New York: Oxford University Press, 2015.

Grajewski, Henryk. *Kara śmierci w prawie polskim do połowy XIV wieku*. Warsaw: Wydawnictwo Prawnicze, 1956.

Grebe, Sabine. "Why Did Ovid Associate His Exile with a Living Death?," *The Classical World* 103:4 (2010): 491–509.

Guillén, Claudio. "On the Literature of Exile and Counter-Exile." *Books Abroad*, 50.2 (1976): 271–280.

Haki Antonsson. "*Árna saga biskups* as Literature and History." *Journal of English and Germanic Philology* 116.3 (2017): 261–85.

Hamre, Lars. "Oprørsret." *Kulturhistoriskt lexikon för nordisk medeltid* (1967), vol. 12: cols. 629–631.

Hanak, Walter K. *The Nature and the Image of Princely Power in Kievan Rus', 980–1054: A Study of Sources*. Leiden: Brill, 2014.

Handelsman, Marceli. "Die Strafe im polnisch-schlesischen Rechte im XII u. XIII Jahrhundert." *Zeitschrift für vergleichende Rechtswissenschaft* 18 (1905): 209–65.

Handelsman, Marceli. *Kara w najdawniejszym prawie polskim*. Warsaw: Wende i S-ka, 1908.

Hansen, Elaine Tuttle. *Chaucer and the Fiction of Gender*. Berkeley: University of California Press, 1992.

Harrison, Dick. "Murder and Execution within the Political Sphere in Fifteenth-Century Scandinavia." *Scandia* 63.2 (1997): 259–79.

Heck, Roman. "Akcenty społeczne i moralizatorskie w 'Kronice książąt polskich.'" In *'Cultus et cognitio'. Studia z dziejów średniowiecznej kultury*, edited by Stefan K. Kuczyński, 181–92. Warsaw: PWN, 1976.

Helle, Knut. "Audun Hugleiksson 'Hestakorn'." *Norsk biografisk leksikon*. Available at https://nbl.snl.no/Audun_Hugleiksson_"Hestakorn. Accessed 7 June 2022.

Helle, Knut. "Towards Nationally Organised Systems of Government." In *The Cambridge History of Scandinavia*. Vol. 1, *Prehistory to 1520*, edited by Knut Helle, 345–52. Cambridge: Cambridge University Press, 2003.

Helle, Knut. *Konge og gode menn i norsk riksstyring ca. 1150–1319*. Bergen: Universitetsforlaget, 1972.

Hendrix, Laurel L. "'Pennannce profytable': The Currency of Custance in Chaucer's *Man of Law's Tale*." *Exemplaria* 6 (1994): 141–66.

Hirsh, John C. "Reopening *The Prioress's Tale*." *Chaucer Review* 10.1 (1975): 30–45.

Hjärne, Erland. *Fornsvenska lagstadganden*. Vols. 1–3. Uppsala: Almqvist & Wiksell, 1951.

Imsen, Steinar. "Dronningmagt i Norge." In *Dronningemagt i Middelalderen: Festskrift till Anders Bøgh*, edited by Kasper H. Andersen and Jeppe Büchert Netterstrøm, 241–73. Aarhus: Aarhus Universitetsforlag, 2018.

Jankofsky, Klaus P. "Public Executions in England in the Late Middle Ages: The Indignity and Dignity of Death." *OMEGA—Journal of Death and Dying* 10.1 (1980): 43–57.

Jordan, William Chester. *From England to France: Felony and Exile in the High Middle Ages*. Princeton: Princeton University Press, 2015.

Jurek, Tomasz. "Lubiąskie epitafium księcia Henryka głogowskiego. Nowo odkryty zabytek poezji łacińskiej z początków XIV wieku." *Roczniki Historyczne* 71 (2005): 185–99.

Jurek, Tomasz, and Michał Rzepiela. *Dziedzic Królestwa Polskiego: Książę głogowski Henryk (1272–1309)*. Poznań: Wydawnictwo Poznańskiego Towarzystwa Przyjaciół Nauk, 1993.

Källström, Hanna. "Holmger Knutsson—en långlivad lokal helgonkult i Uppland." *Fornvännen: Journal of Swedish Antiquarian Research* 107.3 (2012): 179–88.

Keiser, George R. "The Spiritual Heroism of Chaucer's Custance." In *Chaucer's Religious Tales*, edited by David Benson and Elizabeth Robertson, 121–36. Cambridge: D.S. Brewer, 1990.

Kolve, V.A. "The Rudderless Ship and the Sea." *Imagery of Narrative: The First Five Canterbury Tales*. 297–358. Stanford, CA: Stanford University Press, 1984.

Kotecki, Radosław. "'Aeternum Dei servitium ad sanctum locum'. Pokuta zabójców Pięciu Braci Męczenników w relacji Brunona z Kwerfurtu." *Kwartalnik Historyczny* 121.1 (2014): 41–71.

Labuda, Gerard. "Zapiska o zaburzeniach chłopskich w dobrach klasztoru przemęckiego w roku 1309." *Roczniki Historyczne* 20 (1952): 121–38.

Lange, Christian. *Justice, Punishment and Medieval Muslim Imagination*. New York: Cambridge University Press, 2008.

Lavezzo, Kathy. "Beyond Rome: Mapping Gender and Justice in *The Man of Law's Tale*." *Studies in the Age of Chaucer* 24 (2002): 149–80.

Line, Philip. *Kingship and State Formation in Sweden, 1130–1290*. Leiden: Brill, 2007.

Lovén, Christian and Herman Bengtsson. "De heliga hertigarna Erik och Valdemar." *Historisk tidskrift* 131.2 (2011): 227–49.

Lynch, L. Kathryn. "Storytelling, Exchange, and Constancy: East and West in Chaucer's *Man of Law's Tale*." *Chaucer Review* 33 (1999): 409–22.

Mann, Jill. *Feminist Readings: Chaucer*. New York: Harvester Wheatsheaf, 1991.

Marafioti, Nicole and Jay Paul Gates, eds. *Capital and Corporal Punishment in Anglo-Saxon England*. Woodbridge: Boydell Press, 2014.

Martin, Céline. "Ervig and Capital Penalties: The Way of Exile." In *Framing Power in Visigothic Society: Discourses, Devices, and Artifacts*, edited by Eleonora Dell' Elicine and Céline Martin. 133–158. Amsterdam: Amsterdam University Press, 2020.

Mattison, Alyxandra. "The Execution and Burial of Criminals in Early Medieval England: An Examination of Changes in Judicial Punishment Across the Norman Conquest, c. 850–1150." PhD Dissertation, University of Sheffield, 2016.

Mazzotta, Giuseppe. "Dante and the Virtues of Exile." In *Exile in Literature*, edited by María-Inés Lagos-Pope, 49–71. Cranbury, NJ: Associated University Presses, 1988.

McInnes, Iain A. "'A somewhat too cruel vengeance was taken for the blood of the slain': Royal Punishment of Rebels, Traitors, and Political Enemies in Medieval Scotland, c. 1100–c. 1250." In *Treason: Medieval and Early Modern Adultery, Betrayal, and Shame*, edited by Larissa Tracy. 119–46. Leiden: Brill, 2019.

Merback, Mitchell B. *The Thief, the Cross, and the Wheel: Pain and the Spectacle of Punishment in Medieval and Renaissance Europe*. London: Reaktion, 1999.

Metlitzki, Dorothee. *The Matter of Araby in Medieval England*. New Haven, CT: Yale University Press, 1977.

Meyer, Poul. "Dødsstraf." In *Kulturhistoriskt lexikon för nordisk medeltid* (1980), vol. 3: cols. 455–59.

Michalski, Maciej. *Kobiety i świętość w żywotach trzynastowiecznych księżnych*. Poznań: Wydawnictwo Poznańskie, 2004.

Mills, Robert. *Suspended Animation: Pain, Pleasure, and Punishment in Medieval Culture*. London: Reaktion Books Ltd., 2005.

Miłosz, Czeslaw. "Notes on Exile." *Books Abroad* 50.2 (1976): 281–284.

Moxó, Salvador de. "De la nobleza vieja a la nobleza nueva. La transformación nobiliaria castellana en la Baja Edad Media." *Cuadernos de Historia* 3 (1969): 1–209.

Mrozowicz, Wojciech. "Pieśń o wójcie krakowskim Albercie—przekaz historyczny w poetyckim sztafażu." *Annales Universitatis Paedagogicae Cracoviensis. Studia Historica* 13 (2013): 32–42.

Munro, Dana Carleton. "The Western Attitude toward Islam during the Period of the Crusades." *Speculum* 6.3 (1931): 329–43.

Murata, Sachiko, and William C. Chittick. *The Vision of Islam*. New York: Paragon House, 1994.

Napran, Laura and Elisabeth van Houts, eds. *Exile in the Middle Ages: Selected Proceedings from the International Medieval Congress, University of Leeds, 8–11 July 2002*. Turnhout: Brepols, 2004.

Nastalska-Wiśnicka, Joanna. *'Rex martyr'. Studium źródłoznawcze nad legendą hagiograficzną św. Wacława (x–xiv w.)*. Lublin: Werset, 2010.

Niebrzydowski, Sue. "Monstrous (M)othering: The Representation of the Sowdaness in Chaucer's *Man of Law's Tale*." In *Consuming Narratives: Gender and Monstrous Appetite in the Middle Ages and Renaissance*, edited by Liz Herbert McAvoy and Teresa Walters, 196–207. Cardiff: University of Wales Press, 2002.

Nordberg, Michael. *I kung Magnus tid. Norden under Magnus Eriksson, 1317–1374*. Stockholm: Norstedts, 1995.

Pac, Grzegorz. *Kobiety w dynastii Piastów. Rola społeczna piastowskich żon i córek do połowy xii wieku—studium porównawcze*. Toruń: Wydawnictwo Naukowe Uniwersytetu Mikołaja Kopernika, 2013.

Patterson, Lee. *Chaucer and the Subject of History*. Madison: University of Wisconsin Press, 1991.

Pauk, Marcin R. "'Washing Hands in a Sinner's Blood': Ducal Power, Law and Religious Zeal in the Process of Central European Christianization—Preliminary Remarks." In *Leben zwischen und mit den Kulturen: Studien zu Recht, Bildung und Herrschaft in Mitteleuropa*, edited by Renata Skowrońska-Kamińska and Helmut Flachenecker, 23–34. Würzburg, Toruń: Wydawnictwo Naukowe Uniwersytetu Mikołaja Kopernika, 2015.

Pease, Arthur Stanley. "Notes on Stoning among the Greeks and Romans," *Transactions and Proceedings of the American Philological Association* 38 (1907): 5–18.

Peters, Edward. *Torture*. Philadelphia: University of Pennsylvania Press, 1985.

Pigg, Daniel F. "Refiguring Martyrdom: Chaucer's Prioress and Her Tale." *Chaucer Review* 29 (1994): 67–73.

Pipping, Rolf. *Kommentar till Erikskrönikan*. Helsinki: Svenska litteratursällskapet i Finland, 1926.

Randa, Laura E. *Society's Final Solution: A History and Discussion of the Death Penalty*. Lanham, MD: University Press of America, 1997.

Raybin, David. "Custance and History: Woman as Outsider in Chaucer's *Man of Law's Tale*." *Studies in the Age of Chaucer* 12 (1990): 65–84.

Ricciardelli, Fabrizio. *The Politics of Exclusion in Early Renaissance Florence*. Turnhout: Brepols, 2007.

Rose, Christian M. "The Jewish Mother-in-Law: Synagoga and *The Man of Law's Tale*." In *Chaucer and the Jews*, edited by Sheila Delany, 3–23. New York: Routledge, 2002.

Royer, Katherine. "Reading the Execution Ritual in Late Medieval England." *Historical Reflections / Réflexions Historiques* 29.2 (2003): 319–39.

Russell, J.C. "The Canonization of Opposition to the King in Angevin England." In *Haskins Anniversary Essays in Mediaeval History*, edited by C.H. Taylor and J.L. La Monte, 279–90. Boston, MA: Houghton Mifflin, 1929.

Russell, P.E. *The English Intervention in Spain and Portugal in the Time of Edward III and Richard II*. Oxford: Clarendon, 1955.

Said, Edward. *Orientalism*. New York: Random House, 1978.

Said, Edward. *Reflections on Exile and Other Essays*. Cambridge, MA: Harvard University Press, 2000.

Schibanoff, Susan. "Worlds Apart: Orientalism, Antifeminism, and Heresy in Chaucer's *Man of Law's Tale*." *Exemplaria* 8.1 (1996): 59–96.

Schildgen, Brenda Deen. *Pagans, Tartars, Moslems, and Jews in Chaucer's "Canterbury Tales."* Gainesville: University Press of Florida, 2001.

Schück, Herman. "Sweden under the Dynasty of the Folkungs." In *The Cambridge History of Scandinavia*. Vol. 1, *Prehistory to 1520*, edited by Knut Helle, 392–410. Cambridge: Cambridge University Press, 2003.

Serrano Ruano, Delfina. "Stoning as Punishment of Illegal Sexual Relations (*Zina*) in the Heart of the Maliki School: Doctrine, Legal Practice and Individual Attitudes in the Face of the Crime", *'Al-Qantara*, 26.2 (2005), 449–73.

Skeie, Tore. *Alv Erlingsson. Ffortellingen om en adelsmanns undergang*. Oslo: Spartacus, 2009.

Southern, R.W. *Western Views of Islam in the Middle Ages*. Cambridge, MA: Harvard University Press, 1962.

Stark Zitter, Emmy. "Anti-Semitism in Chaucer's *Prioress's Tale*." *Chaucer Review* 25 (1991): 277–84.

Svanberg, Jan. *Furstebilder från Folkungatid*. 2nd ed. Skara: Västergötlands museum, 2012.

Tolan, John V. *Saracens: Islam in the Medieval European Imagination*. New York: Columbia University Press, 2002.

Tracy, Larissa, and Jeff Massey, eds. *Heads Will Roll: Decapitation in the Medieval and Early Modern Imagination*. Leiden: Brill, 2012.

Tracy, Larissa, ed. *Flaying in the Premodern World: Practice and Representation*. Cambridge: D.S. Brewer, 2017.

Tracy, Larissa, ed. *Treason: Medieval and Early Modern Adultery, Betrayal and Shame*. Leiden: Brill, 2019.

Tracy, Larissa. "'For Our dere Ladyes sake': Bringing the Outlaw in from the Forest—Robin Hood, Marian, and Normative National Identity." *Explorations in Renaissance Culture* (*EIRC*) 38 (Summer & Winter 2012): 35–66.

Tracy, Larissa. "'Mordre wol out': Murder and Justice in Chaucer." In *Medieval and Early Modern Murder: Legal, Literary and Historical Contexts*, edited by Larissa Tracy, 115–36. Woodbridge: Boydell Press, 2018.

Tracy, Larissa. "Knight of God or the Goddess?: Rethinking Religious Syncretism in 'Sir Gawain and the Green Knight,'" *Arthuriana* Vol. 17.3 (2007): 31–55.

Tracy, Larissa. "Peace Weaving and Gold Giving: Anglo-Saxon Queenship in *Havelok the Dane*." In *Remembering the Present: Generative Uses of England's Pre-Conquest Past*, edited by Brian O'Camb and Jay Paul Gates, 168–194. Leiden: Brill, 2019.

Tracy, Larissa. *Torture and Brutality in Medieval Literature: Negotiations of National Identity*. Cambridge: D.S. Brewer, 2012.

Valente, Claire. "Simon de Montfort, Earl of Leicester, and the Utility of Sanctity in Thirteenth-Century England." *Journal of Medieval History* 21.1 (1995): 27–49.

Vauchez, André. *Sainthood in the Later Middle Ages*. Translated by Jean Birrell. Cambridge: Cambridge University Press, 1997.

Vercamer, Grischa. "Das Bad des Königs—beschreibt Gallus Anonymus ein genuin piastisches/polnisches Ritual?" *Frühmittelalterliche Studien* 43, no. 1 (2009): 349–72.

Vogt, Helle. "The King's Power to Legislate in Twelfth and Thirteenth Century Denmark." In *Law and Power in the Middle Ages: Proceedings from the Fourth Carlsberg Academy Conference on Medieval Legal History*, edited by Per Andersen, Mia Münster-Swendsen and Helle Vogt, 5–14. 2nd ed. Copenhagen: DJØF Publishing, 2012.

Watkins, Carl. "Saints and Martyrs in Late Medieval Religious Culture." In *The Medieval World*, edited by Peter Linehan, Janet L. Nelson, and Marios Costambeys, 385–402. 2nd ed. London: Routledge, 2018.

Watts, John. *The Making of Polities: Europe, 1300–1500*. Cambridge: Cambridge University Press, 2009.

Westerhof, D. *Death and the Noble Body in Medieval England*. Cambridge: D.S. Brewer, 2008.

Wilson, Stephen. "The Myth of Motherhood: The Historical View of European Child-Rearing." *Social History* 9 (1984): 181–98.

Wiszewski, Przemysław. *'Domus Bolezlai': Values and Social Identity in Dynastic Traditions of Medieval Poland (c. 966–1138)*. Leiden: Brill, 2010.

Index